Praise for Eric Tyson's
Mutual Funds For Dummies®

"Eric Tyson gets it. *Mutual Funds For Dummies* cuts through the clutter that clouds personal finance for millions of Americans. This is a must-read for the savvy investor and novice alike."

> — **Gerry Dick, Indianapolis Economic Development Corp., and Host, *Indiana Business This Week*, WRTV/WFYI-TV, Indianapolis**

"I was clueless and intimidated by the terminology and information that I need to know about investing into mutual funds. This book has given me confidence as well as a sturdy foundation to begin investing."

> — **Clifford Record, Colt's Neck, New Jersey**

"You don't have to be a novice to like *Mutual Funds For Dummies*. . . . Author Eric Tyson clearly has a mastery of his subject. He knows mutual funds and he knows how to explain them in simple English. . . . It's hard to imagine a more accessible sourcebook."

> — ***Kiplinger's Personal Finance Magazine***

"*Mutual Funds For Dummies* . . . is an excellent source for not only the novice investor but also for someone looking to enhance their understanding of one of the fastest growing investment tools."

> — ***Northwest Arkansas Times***

"I handle my mother's money and my own family's, so it is very important that I make all the right moves and decisions. I didn't have any confidence until I studied Eric Tyson's books."

> — **Lisa Patten, Lake Junaluska, NC**

". . . Injects common sense into the dizzying world of mutual funds."

> — ***Oakland Tribune*, CA**

"I liked how easy the book is to read. I understand more now about mutual funds than I did before I read the book — it's excellent."

— Dennis Pipper, Lansing, MI

"A book that should help investors be smarter . . . readable, comprehensive. . . . Tyson's encyclopedic book is chockful of useful examples and advice for both new and experienced investors. . . ."

— *Christian Science Monitor*

"*Mutual Funds For Dummies* . . . brought me up to speed financially."

— Riccardo Heald, New York, NY

"Comprehensive, well-organized information in an easy-to-read format."

— Dianne L. Zimmerman, Rockville, MD

"*Mutual Funds For Dummies* gives good common sense advice about putting your financial house in order."

— John B. Fout, MBA

"I wish my finance teachers in college had been this interesting and informative."

— Lori Buono, reader

"Eric Tyson is far and away the best writer, most readable author, and most honest and intelligent voice in America today in the areas of personal finance and mutual fund investing."

— David Diaman, Enrolled Agent

"Never have I been as impressed with the advice and insight offered by a columnist, as I have been by Eric Tyson! Finally, there is someone in print cogently and lucidly speaking financial truth and common sense."

— Kenneth S. Imbriale, Staten Island, NY

"Accurate, easy-to-read, and humorous; 'teaches' the reader rather than preaching at the reader!"

— Victoria L. Simmons, High Point, NC

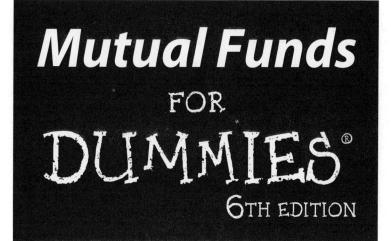

Mutual Funds

FOR

DUMMIES®

6TH EDITION

Pick up the latest edition of these other bestsellers, also by Eric Tyson, published by Wiley Publishing, Inc.

Investing For Dummies®

Personal Finance For Dummies®

Home Buying For Dummies®, with Ray Brown

House Selling For Dummies®, with Ray Brown

Mortgages For Dummies®, with Ray Brown

Taxes For Dummies®, with David J. Silverman and Margaret Atkins Munro

Mutual Funds FOR DUMMIES®

6TH EDITION

by Eric Tyson, MBA

Author of *Personal Finance For Dummies* and *Investing For Dummies*

WILEY

Wiley Publishing, Inc.

Mutual Funds For Dummies®, 6th Edition

Published by
Wiley Publishing, Inc.
111 River St.
Hoboken, NJ 07030-5774
www.wiley.com

Published by Wiley Publishing, Inc., Indianapolis, Indiana

Published simultaneously in Canada

For general information on our other products and services, please contact our Customer Care Department within the U.S. at 877-762-2974, outside the U.S. at 317-572-3993, or fax 317-572-4002.

For technical support, please visit www.wiley.com/techsupport.

Wiley also publishes its books in a variety of electronic formats. Some content that appears in print may not be available in electronic books.

Library of Congress Control Number: 2010929313

ISBN: 978-0-470-62321-3

Manufactured in the United States of America

10 9 8 7 6 5 4 3 2

WILEY

About the Author

Eric Tyson, MBA, is a bestselling author and syndicated columnist. Through his counseling, writing, and teaching, he teaches people to manage their personal finances better and successfully direct their own investments.

He has been involved in the investing markets in many capacities for the past two decades. Eric first invested in mutual funds back in the mid-1970s, when he opened a mutual fund account at Fidelity. With the assistance of Dr. Martin Zweig, a now-famous investment market analyst and frequent guest on PBS's *Wall Street Week,* Eric won his high school's science fair for a project on what influences the stock market!

Since that time, Eric has (among other things) worked as a management consultant to Fortune 500 financial service firms and earned his bachelor's degree in economics at Yale and an MBA at the Stanford Graduate School of Business. Despite these handicaps to clear thinking, he had the good sense to start his own company, which took an innovative approach to teaching people of all economic means about investing and money.

An accomplished freelance personal finance writer, Eric is the author of the national bestsellers *Personal Finance For Dummies* and *Investing For Dummies* and coauthor of *Home Buying For Dummies* and *Taxes For Dummies* and was an award-winning columnist for the *San Francisco Examiner.* His work has been featured and quoted in dozens of national and local publications, including *Newsweek, The Wall Street Journal, Forbes, Kiplinger's Personal Finance Magazine,* the *Los Angeles Times,* and *Bottom Line/Personal,* and on NBC's *Today Show,* ABC, CNBC, PBS's *Nightly Business Report,* CNN, CBS national radio, Bloomberg Business Radio, and Business Radio Network. He's also been a featured speaker at a White House conference on retirement planning.

Despite his "wealth" of financial knowledge, Eric is one of the rest of us. He maintains a large inventory of bumble-bee colored computer books on his desk for those frequent times when his computer makes the (decreasing amount of) hair on his head fall out.

Eric's Web site is www.erictyson.com.

Dedication

To my wife, Judy; my family — especially my parents, Charles and Paulina; my friends; and to my counseling clients and students of my courses for teaching me how to teach them about managing their finances.

Author's Acknowledgments

Many people contribute to the birth of a book, and this book is no exception. First, I owe a deep debt of gratitude to James Collins, who inspired me when I was a young and impressionable business school student. Jim encouraged me to try to improve some small part of the business world by being an entrepreneur and focusing solely on what customers needed rather than on what made the quickest buck.

The technical reviewer for this edition of the book was Mercer Bullard. He helped to improve each and every chapter, and I am thankful for that.

Thanks to all the good people in the media and other fields who have taken the time to critique and praise my previous writing so that others may know that it exists and is worth reading. And to those too lazy to open the book just because of its bright yellow color and title, I say, "Don't judge a book by its cover!"

And a final and heartfelt thanks to all the people on the front lines and behind the scenes at Wiley who helped to make this book and my others a success. A big round of applause, please, for Kelly Ewing as project editor and as outstanding copy editor. Special thanks to Mike Baker. Thanks also to the Composition, Graphics, Proofreading, and Indexing staff for their great efforts in producing this book.

P.S. Thanks to you, dear reader, for buying my books.

Publisher's Acknowledgments

We're proud of this book; please send us your comments at http://dummies.custhelp.com.
For other comments, please contact our Customer Care Department within the U.S. at 877-762-2974,
outside the U.S. at 317-572-3993, or fax 317-572-4002.

Some of the people who helped bring this book to market include the following:

Acquisitions, Editorial, and
Media Development

Project Editor: Kelly Ewing *(Previous Edition:*
Chad R. Sievers, Mike Baker)

Senior Acquisitions Editor: Mike Baker

Assistant Editor: Erin Calligan Mooney

Senior Editorial Assistant: David Lutton

General Reviewer: Mercer Bullard

Senior Editorial Manager: Jennifer Ehrlich

Editorial Supervisor and Reprint Editor:
Carmen Krikorian

Editorial Assistant: Jennette ElNaggar

Cover Photo: © Gaertner/Alamy

Cartoons: Rich Tennant
(www.the5thwave.com)

Composition Services

Project Coordinator: Katherine Crocker

Layout and Graphics: Carl Byers

Proofreaders: John Greenough, Toni Settle

Indexer: Sharon Shock

Publishing and Editorial for Consumer Dummies

Diane Graves Steele, Vice President and Publisher, Consumer Dummies

Kristin Ferguson-Wagstaffe, Product Development Director, Consumer Dummies

Ensley Eikenburg, Associate Publisher, Travel

Kelly Regan, Editorial Director, Travel

Publishing for Technology Dummies

Andy Cummings, Vice President and Publisher, Dummies Technology/General User

Composition Services

Debbie Stailey, Director of Composition Services

Contents at a Glance

Table of Contents

Introduction

Whether you're a regular reader of investing books or this is your first, *Mutual Funds For Dummies,* 6th Edition, which is completely revised and updated, provides practical and profitable techniques of mutual fund investing that you can put to work now and for many years to come.

Mutual funds aren't literally for dummies — in fact, they're a wise investment choice for people from all walks of life. Mutual funds are investment companies that combine your money with that from many other people to create a large pool of assets that can be invested in stocks, bonds, or other securities. Because your assets are part of a much larger whole, the best mutual funds enable you to invest in securities that give you low-cost access to leading professional money managers.

With the best money managers investing your nest egg in top-flight investments that match your financial goals, you can spend your time doing the activities in life that you enjoy and are best at. Mutual funds should improve your investment returns as well as your social life!

I practice what I preach. All my investments that I've devoted to securities (stocks and bonds) are invested through funds. Why? For the simple reason that I'm confident the best fund managers that I recommend in this book can do a superior job (higher returns, less cost) than I could by researching and selecting individual stocks and bonds on my own.

I've enjoyed successfully investing in mutual funds for more than 25 years. As a financial counselor, writer, and lecturer, I've helped investors make informed investing decisions with mutual funds as part of comprehensive personal financial management. So I know the questions and challenges that you face when you invest in funds. I wrote this book to answer, in plain English, your fund-investing questions.

What's New in This Edition

Life and the investment world change. Although the essence of what makes mutual funds worthy of your investment dollars hasn't changed since the last edition of this book was published several years ago, the fund industry has certainly seen new developments. In this newly updated sixth edition, here are the major issues:

- ✔ Coverage of the 2008–09 global stock market panic and how funds and fund investors fared and what can be learned from that experience

- ✔ Alternatives to mutual funds — growth of exchange-traded funds, shake-out in hedge funds, researching your own stocks and bonds and creating your own fund, private money managers, closed-end funds, and so on

- ✔ Increasing numbers of specialized funds, such as those investing in gold, real estate, market-neutral funds, and so on

- ✔ Opportunities and pitfalls investing in funds online with expanded and updated coverage of Web sites and software

- ✔ New tax laws and their impact on smart fund-investing strategies

- ✔ Updates to the funds and resources that I recommend

How This Book Is Different

Many investment books confuse folks. They present you with some newfangled system that you never figure out how to use without the help of mathematicians and a Nobel laureate as your personal tutors. Books that bewilder more than enlighten may be intentional because the author may have another agenda: to get you to turn your money over to him to manage or to sell you his pricey newsletter(s). Writers with an agenda may imply — and sometimes say — that you really can't invest well, at least not without what they're selling.

Going another route, too many investment books glorify rather than advise. They place on a pedestal the elite few who, during decidedly brief periods in the history of the world and financial markets, managed to beat the market averages by a few percentage points or so per year. Many of these books (and their publishers) suggest that reading them shows you the strategies that led Superstar Money Manager of the Moment to the superlative performance that the book glorifies. "He did it his way; now you can, too," trumpets the marketing material. Not so. Reading a book about what made Kobe Bryant a phenomenal basketball player or Shakespeare a great playwright won't help you shoot a basket or versify like these famous folks. By the same token, you can't discover from a book the way to become the next Wall Street investment wizard.

Mutual Funds For Dummies, 6th Edition, helps you avoid fund-investing pitfalls and maximizes your chances for success. When you want to buy or sell a mutual fund, your decision needs to fit your overall financial objectives and individual situation. Fund investors make many mistakes in this regard. For example, they invest in funds that don't fit their tax situation.

This book also covers pesky issues completely ignored by other mutual fund books. For novice fund investors, simply finding and completing the correct application in the blizzard of forms that fund companies offer can be a challenge. And if you invest in mutual funds outside of tax-sheltered retirement accounts, you're greeted by the inevitable headache from figuring out how to report distributions at tax time. This book puts you on the right path in order to avoid these problems.

The truth is, investing isn't all that difficult — and funds are the great equalizer. There's absolutely no reason, except perhaps a lack of time and effort on your part, why you can't successfully invest in mutual funds. In fact, if you understand some basic concepts and find out how to avoid major mistakes that occur for some fairly obvious reasons, you can be even more successful than most so-called investment professionals.

Foolish Assumptions

Whenever an author sits down to write a book, he has to make some assumptions about his audience, and I've made a few that may apply to you:

- ✔ You're looking for sensible investments.

- ✔ You've done some research (or perhaps thought about doing some) on mutual funds and found the thousands of fund choices to be a bit daunting.

- ✔ Your investment portfolio contains or has contained mutual funds, and you're looking for up-to-date information on how changes in the economy and financial markets can affect the decisions you make.

If one or more of these descriptions rings true, you're in the right place. Mutual funds are a huge business, and they can be confusing. Today, thousands of mutual funds account for more than $11 *trillion* under management. Although the basic principle behind mutual funds sounds simple enough — pooled money from many individuals that's invested in stocks, bonds, or other securities — you have to understand the different types of investments, such as stocks and bonds, and the way they work.

Unfortunately, you have too many individual funds from which to choose — hundreds of mutual fund companies, brokerage firms, insurers, banks, and so on are selling thousands of funds. Even experienced investors suffer from information overload. Lucky for you, I present short lists of great funds that meet different needs.

And because no investment, not even one of the better mutual funds, is free of flaws and shortcomings, I explain how to avoid the worst funds — and the numerous mediocre ones — that clutter the investment landscape. I also help you understand when investing in funds may not be appropriate for you and what your best options may be.

How This Book Is Organized

The sections that follow contain a preview, of sorts, of the various sections in this book and what they cover.

Part 1: Mutual Funds: Sharing Risks and Rewards

Part I defines and demystifies what mutual funds are and discusses what they're good for. Before you're even ready to start investing in funds, your personal finances need to be in order, so I give you some financial house-cleaning tips. You can also discover the importance of fitting mutual funds to your financial goals. Part I also covers how to pick great funds, how to avoid loser funds, where and how to purchase funds, and how to read all those pesky reports that fund companies tend to produce.

Part 11: Evaluating Alternatives to Funds

Mutual funds are hardly the only game in town for those folks seeking someone to manage their money. In recent years, exchange-traded funds and hedge funds, for example, have been pitched to many investors. Other investors believe that they can be their own best stock and bond pickers. This part discusses all the fund-investing alternatives and more to help you select which option(s) are best for your situation.

Part 111: Separating the Best from the Rest

This part explains what makes a fund and fund company worth investing in. You see how to read and understand common fund documents. I also explain the best venues and avenues for buying funds and help you think through whether to enlist the services of an adviser.

Part IV: Crafting Your Fund Portfolio

This part shows you how to build a portfolio that includes mutual funds to accomplish your specific financial goals. You start off by exploring the basic strategies of portfolio construction. Then for each of the major fund types — money market, bond, and stock — you get specific fund recommendations. I also discuss specialty funds. A chapter of sample fund portfolios based on real-life scenarios brings together the important concepts in this section. Last but not least, I cover how to complete the often-pesky paperwork funds demand of you.

Part V: Keeping Current and Informed

After you have a good fund portfolio up and running, you shouldn't have to devote much time to maintaining it. This part covers what you do need to do, including chapters on how to evaluate your funds' performance and deal with the tax issues that come up on your investments. I also offer some tips on how to minimize aggravations when you deal with fund companies and discount brokers.

If you're still not satisfied, you can find out about the scores of individuals, companies, and publications that rank and predict financial market gyrations. I warn you about the bad ones and the dangers of blindly following gurus, and I reveal which, if any, of them really are gurus. You also discover how to use the best mutual fund information sources, how to tell the difference between good and bad newsletters, and where to turn for more information. You may want to know how to use your computer to track and even invest in mutual funds online — so this part tells you how to do that, too.

Part VI: The Part of Tens

Broaden your thinking with these chapters that offer ten or more ideas about important fund issues and concepts. I discuss common fund-investing mistakes made by investors, ease some fund-investing fears that you may have, and cover issues to consider before hiring an adviser. In the appendix, you find the contact information for all the top-notch funds I recommend.

Icons Used in This Book

Throughout this book, you can find friendly and useful icons that enhance your reading pleasure and flag special types of information. So, when you meet one of these margin-hugging doodads, consider the following:

This icon points out something that can save you time, headaches, money, or all of the above!

The warning icon helps steer you away from mistakes and boo-boos that others have made when investing in mutual funds.

Something around here could really cost you big bucks (maybe even an arm and a leg!) if you don't devote your attention to these icons.

This icon denotes Eric's favorite mutual funds.

Eminently skippable stuff here, but if you don't read it, you may not seem as astute at the next cocktail party when mutual fund trivia games begin. Neat but nonessential stuff — read at your leisure.

Eric's told me as much as he can, but he thinks that I may need or want to check it out more on my own before I make a move.

This icon designates something important that I want you to *make sure* you don't forget when you're making your own fund-investing decisions!

Where to Go from Here

You don't need to read this book cover to cover. But if you're a beginner or you want to fully immerse yourself in the world of fund investing, go for it! However, you may have some specific questions today, and you'll want some other information tomorrow. No problem there, either. *Mutual Funds For Dummies,* 6th Edition, is well organized and easier to use than other fund investing books. Use the Table of Contents or the Index to speed your way toward what you need to know and get on with your life.

Part I

Mutual Funds: Sharing Risks and Rewards

The 5th Wave   By Rich Tennant

That's the Harrisons. Never have I seen an investment portfolio start so strong and go south so quickly.

In this part . . .

This part gives you an excellent grounding in the fundamentals of mutual fund investing. You also find out how to fit mutual funds neatly with the rest of your finances, and you get an inside look at how and when to invest in the best mutual funds.

Chapter 1

Making More Money, Taking Less Risk

*I*n my years of work as a financial adviser and a columnist answering many readers' questions, I've seen the same, avoidable mistakes being made over and over. Often, these investing mistakes occurred for one simple reason: a lack of investment understanding. People didn't know what their investing options were and why particular options were inferior or superior to others.

By reading this book, you can prevent yourself from making investment mistakes. And you can take advantage of an excellent investment vehicle: mutual funds — the best of which offer you diversification, which reduces your risks, and low-cost access to highly diversified portfolios and professional money managers, who can boost your returns with less risk. And mutual funds can fit nicely in the context of your overall financial plans and goals. This chapter gives you an investment overview so that you can see how mutual funds fit into the overall investment world.

Introducing Mutual Funds

If you already understand stocks and bonds, their risks and potential returns, and the benefits of diversification, terrific. You can skip this chapter. Most people, however, don't really comprehend investment basics, which is one of the major reasons why people make investment mistakes in the first place.

After you understand the specific types of securities (stocks, bonds, and so on) that funds can invest in, you've mastered one of the important building blocks to understanding mutual funds. A *mutual fund* is a vehicle that holds other investments: When you invest in a mutual fund, you're contributing to a big pool of money that a mutual fund manager uses to buy other investments, such as stocks, bonds, and/or other assets that meet the fund's investment objectives.

Differences in investment objectives are how mutual funds broadly categorize themselves, like the way an automaker labels a car a *sedan* or a *sport utility vehicle.* This label helps you, the buyer, have a general picture of the product even before you see the specifics. On the dealer's lot, the salesmen take for granted that you know what *sedan* and *sport utility vehicle* mean. But what if the salesman asks you whether you want a Pegasus or a Stegosaurus? If you don't know what those names mean, how can you decide?

Mutual fund terms, such as *municipal bond fund* or *small-cap stock fund,* are thrown around casually. Fact is, thanks to our spending-oriented culture, the average American knows car models better than types of mutual funds! In this chapter (and in Chapter 2), I explain the investment and mutual fund terms and concepts that many writers assume you already know (or perhaps that they don't understand well enough themselves to explain to you). But don't take the plunge into mutual funds until you determine your overall financial needs and goals.

Making Sense of Investments

Your eyes can perceive dozens of different colors, and hundreds, if not thousands, of shades in between. In fact, you can see so many colors that you can easily forget what you discovered back in your early school days — that all colors are based on some combination of the three primary colors: red, blue, and yellow. Well, believe it or not, the world of investments is even simpler than that. The seemingly infinite number of investments out there is based on just two primary kinds of investments: lending investments and ownership investments.

Lending investments: Interest on your money

Lending is a type of investment in which the lender charges the borrower a fee (generally known as *interest*) until the original loan (typically known as the *principal*) gets paid back. Familiar lending investments include bank certificates of deposit (CDs), United States (U.S.) Treasury bills, and bonds issued by corporations, such as Coca-Cola. In each case, you're lending your money to an organization — the bank, the federal government, or a company — that pays you an agreed-upon rate of interest. You're also promised that your principal (the original amount that you loaned) will be returned to you in full on a specific date.

The best thing that can happen with a lending investment is that you're paid all the interest in addition to your original investment, as promised. Although getting your original investment back with the promised interest won't make you rich, this result isn't bad, given that the investment landscape is littered with the carcasses of failed investments that return you nothing — including lunch money loans that you never see repaid!

Lending investments have several drawbacks:

- ✔ **You may not get everything you were promised.** Under extenuating circumstances, promises get broken. When a company goes bankrupt (remember Bear Stearns, Enron, Lehman, WorldCom, and so on), for example, you can lose all or part of your original investment (from purchased bonds).

- ✔ **You get what you were promised, but because of the ravages of inflation, your money is simply worth less than you expected it to be worth.** Your money has less purchasing power than you thought it would. Suppose that you put $5,000 into an 18-year lending investment that yielded 4 percent. You planned to use it in 18 years to pay for one year of college. Although a year of college cost $5,000 when you invested the money, college costs rose 8 percent a year; so in 18 years when you needed the money, one year of college cost nearly $20,000. But your investment, yielding just 4 percent, would only be worth around $10,100 — nearly 50 percent short of the cost of college because the cost of college rose faster than did the value of your investment.

- ✔ **You don't share in the success of the organization to which you lend your money.** If the company doubles or triples in size and profits, the growth is good for the company and its owners. As a bondholder (lender), you're sure to get your interest and principal back, but you don't reap any of the rewards. If Bill Gates had approached you many years ago for money to help make computer software, would you rather have loaned him the money or *owned* a piece of the company, Microsoft?

Ownership investments: More potential profit (and risk)

You're an *owner* when you purchase an asset, whether a building or part of a multinational corporation, that has the ability to generate earnings or profits. Real estate and stock are common ownership investments.

Ownership investments can generate profits in two ways:

- ✔ **Through the investment's own cash flow/income:** For example, as the owner of a duplex you receive rental income from tenants. If you own stock in a corporation, many companies elect to pay out a portion of their annual profits (in the form of a *dividend*).

- ✔ **Through *appreciation* in the value of the investment:** When you own a piece of real estate in an economically vibrant area or you own stock in a growing company, your investment should increase in value over time. If and when you sell the investment, the difference between what you sold it for and what you paid for it is your (pre-tax) *profit.* (The IRS, of course, will eventually expect its share of your investment profits.) This potential for appreciation is the big advantage of being an owner versus a lender.

On the downside, ownership investments may come with extra responsibilities. If the furnace goes out or the plumbing springs a leak, you, as the property owner, are the one who must fix and pay for it while your tenant gets to kick back in his recliner watching football games and guzzling beer. And you're the one who must pay for insurance to protect yourself against risks, such as fire damage or accidents that occur on your property.

Moreover, where the potential for appreciation exists, the potential for *depreciation* also exists. Ownership investments can decline in value as we most recently saw in the late 2000s. Real estate markets can slump, stock markets can plummet, and individual companies can go belly up. For this reason, ownership investments tend to be riskier than lending investments.

Surveying the Major Investment Options

When you understand that fundamentally only two kinds of investments — ownership and lending— exist, you can more easily understand how a specific investment works . . . and whether it's an attractive choice to help you achieve your specific goals.

Which investment vehicle you choose for a specific goal depends on where you're going, how fast you want to get there, and what risks you're willing to take. Here's an inventory of investment vehicles to choose from, along with my thoughts on which vehicle would be a good choice for your situation.

Savings and money market accounts

You can find savings and money market accounts at banks; money market funds are available through mutual fund companies. All are lending investments based on short-term loans and are about the safest in terms of risk to your investment among the various lending investments around. Relative to the typical long-term returns on growth-oriented investments, such as stocks, the interest rate (also known as the *yield*) paid on savings and money market accounts is low but doesn't fluctuate as much over time. (The interest rate on savings and money market accounts generally fluctuates as the level of overall market interest rates changes.)

Bank savings accounts are backed by an independent agency of the federal government through Federal Deposit Insurance Corporation (FDIC) insurance. If the bank goes broke, you still get your money back (up to $250,000 per depositor, per insured bank). Money market funds, however, aren't insured.

Should you prefer a bank account because your investment (principal) is insured? No. Savings accounts and money market funds have essentially equivalent safety, but money market funds tend to offer higher yields. Chapter 11 provides more background on money market funds.

Bonds

Bonds are the most common lending investment traded on securities markets. Bond funds also account for about 20 percent of all mutual fund assets. When issued, a bond includes a specified *maturity date* — the date when your principal is repaid. Also specified when a bond is issued is the interest rate, which is typically *fixed* (meaning it doesn't change over time).

Bonds, therefore, can fluctuate in value with changes in interest rates. If, for example, you're holding a bond issued at 5 percent and the market level of interest rates increase to 7 percent for newly issued similar bonds, your bond will decrease in value. Why would anyone want to buy your bond at the price that you paid if it yields just 5 percent and she can get a similar bond yielding 7 percent somewhere else? (See Chapter 12 for more information.)

Bonds differ from each other in the following ways:

✔ **The type of institution to which you're lending your money:** Institutions include state and local governments (municipal bonds), the federal government (treasuries), mortgage holders (Government National Mortgage Association, or GNMA), and corporations (corporate bonds). Foreign governments or corporations can also issue bonds. The taxability of the interest paid by a bond is tied to the type of entity issuing the bond. Corporate, mortgage, and foreign government bond interest is fully taxable. Interest on government bonds issued by U.S. entities is usually free of state and/or federal income tax.

✔ **The credit quality of the borrower to whom you lend your money:** The probability that a borrower will pay you the interest and return your entire principal on schedule varies from institution to institution. Bonds issued by less-creditworthy institutions tend to pay higher yields to compensate investors for the greater risk that the loan will not be fully repaid.

✔ **The length of maturity of the bond:** Short-term bonds mature in a few years, intermediate bonds in around 5 to 10 years, and long-term bonds within 30 years. Longer-term bonds generally pay higher yields, but their value is more sensitive to changes in interest rates.

Stocks

Stocks are the most common ownership investment traded on securities markets. They represent shares of ownership in a company. Companies that sell stock to the general public (called *publicly held* companies) include aircraft manufacturers, automobile manufacturers, banks, computer software producers, food manufacturers, hotels, Internet companies, mining companies, oil and gas firms, publishers, restaurant chains, supermarkets, wholesalers, and many types of other (legal) businesses!

When you hold stock in a company, you share in the company's profits in the form of annual dividends (although some companies don't pay dividends) as well as an increase (you hope) in the stock price if the company grows and makes increasing profits. That's what happens when all is going well. The downside is that if the company's business declines, your stock can plummet or even go to $0 per share.

Besides occupying different industries, companies also vary in size. In the financial press, you often hear companies referred to by their *market capitalization,* which is the total value of their outstanding stock. This is what the stock market and the investors who participate in it think a company is worth.

You can choose from two very different ways to invest in bonds and stocks. You can purchase individual securities, or you can invest in a portfolio of securities through a mutual fund. I discuss stock mutual funds in Chapter 13 and individual securities (and other alternatives to mutual funds) in Part II.

Overseas investments

Overseas investment is a potentially misleading category. The types of overseas investment options, such as stocks and bonds and real estate, aren't fundamentally different from your domestic options. However, overseas investments are often categorized separately because they come with their own set of risks and rewards.

Here are some good reasons to invest overseas:

✔ **Diversification:** International securities markets don't move in lock step with U.S. markets, so adding foreign investments to a domestic portfolio offers you a smoother ride over the long term.

✔ **Growth potential:** When you confine your investing to U.S. securities, you're literally missing a world of opportunities. The majority of investment opportunities are overseas. If you look at the total value of all stocks and bonds outstanding worldwide, the value of U.S. securities is now in the minority. The U.S. isn't the world — numerous overseas economies are growing faster.

Some people hesitate to invest in overseas securities because they feel that doing so hurts the U.S. economy and contributes to a loss of U.S. jobs. Fair enough. But I have two counterarguments:

✔ If you don't profit from the growth of economies and companies overseas, someone else will. If money is to be made there, Americans may as well make some of it.

✔ The U.S. already participates in a global economy — making a distinction between U.S. companies and foreign companies is no longer appropriate. Many companies headquartered in the U.S. also have overseas operations. Some U.S. firms derive a large portion of their revenue and profits from their international divisions. Conversely, many firms based overseas also have operations in the U.S. Increasing numbers of companies are worldwide operations.

Dividends and stock price appreciation recognize no national boundaries! You aren't unpatriotic if you invest globally. Profits from a foreign company are distributed to all stockholders, no matter where they live.

Real estate

Perhaps the most fundamental of ownership investments, real estate has made many people wealthy. Not only does real estate produce consistently good rates of return (averaging around 8 to 10 percent per year) over long investment periods, but you can also purchase it with borrowed money. This leverage helps enhance your rate of return when real estate prices are rising.

As with other ownership investments, the value of real estate depends on the health and performance of the economy, as well as on the specifics of the property that you own:

- ✔ If the local economy grows and more jobs are being produced at higher wages, real estate should do well.

- ✔ If companies in the community are laying off people, and excess housing is sitting vacant because of previous overbuilding, rents and property values are likely to fall.

 For investors who have time, patience, and capital, real estate can make sense as part of an investment portfolio — check out *Real Estate Investing For Dummies* (Wiley), which I coauthored. If you don't want the headaches that come with purchasing and maintaining a property, you can buy mutual funds that invest in real estate properties and related companies (see Chapter 14).

Gold, silver, and the like

Whenever bad things happen, especially inflation, credit crises, and international conflicts, some investors seek out gold, silver, and other precious metals. Over the short term, these commodities may produce hefty returns, but their long-term record is more problematic. See Chapter 14 for all the details and how you might diversify your portfolio using specialty funds investing in this sector.

Annuities

Annuities are investment products with some tax and insurance twists. They behave like savings accounts, except that they should give you slightly higher yields, and insurance companies back them. As with other types of retirement accounts, the money that you put into an annuity compounds without taxation until withdrawal. However, unlike most other types of retirement accounts — 401(k)s, SEP-IRAs, and Keoghs — an annuity gives you no upfront tax deductions for your contributions.

Annuities also charge relatively high fees. That's why it makes sense to consider contributing to an annuity *after* you fully fund the tax-deductible retirement accounts that are available to you. The best annuities available today are distributed by *no-load* (commission-free) mutual fund companies. For more information about the best annuities and situations for which annuities may be appropriate, be sure to read Chapter 15.

Life insurance

Some insurance agents love to sell cash-value life insurance. That's because these policies that combine life insurance protection with an account that has a cash value — usually known as *universal, whole,* or *variable life* policies — generate big commissions for the agents who sell them.

Cash-value life insurance isn't a good investment vehicle. First, you should be saving and investing through tax-deductible retirement savings plans, such as 401(k)s, IRAs, and Keoghs. Contributions to a cash-value life insurance plan provide you *no* upfront tax benefit. Second, you can earn better investment returns through efficiently managed mutual funds that you invest in outside of a life policy.

The only reason to consider cash-value life insurance is that the proceeds paid to your beneficiaries can be free of estate taxes. Especially in light of recent years' tax law changes, you need to have a substantial estate at your death to benefit from this feature. Through the use of bypass trusts, married couples can pass along double these amounts. And, by giving away money to your heirs while you're still alive, you can protect even more of your nest egg from the federal estate taxes. (Term life insurance is best for the vast majority of people. Please consult the latest edition of my book, *Personal Finance For Dummies,* 6th Edition (Wiley), which has all sorts of good stuff on insurance and other important personal finance issues.)

Don't fall prey to life insurance agents and their sales pitches. You shouldn't use life insurance as an investment, especially if you haven't exhausted your ability to contribute to retirement accounts. (Even if you've exhausted contributing to retirement accounts, you can do better than cash-value life insurance by choosing tax-friendly mutual funds and/or variable annuities that use mutual funds; see Chapters 11 through 15 for the details.)

Limited partnerships

Avoid limited partnerships (LPs) sold directly through brokers and financial planners. They are inferior investment vehicles. That's not to say that no one has ever made money on them, but LPs are so burdened with high sales commissions and investment-depleting management fees that you can do better with other vehicles.

LPs invest in real estate and a variety of businesses. They pitch that you can get in on the ground floor of a new investment opportunity and make big money. Usually, they also tell you that while your investment is growing at 20 percent or more per year, you'll get handsome dividends of 8 percent or so per year. It sounds too good to be true because it is.

Many of the yields on LPs have turned out to be bogus. In some cases, partnerships propped up their yields by paying back investors' *principal* (original investment), without telling them, of course. The other hook with LPs is tax benefits. What few loopholes that did exist in the tax code for LPs have largely been closed. The other problems with LPs overwhelm any small tax advantage, anyway.

The investment salesperson who sells LPs stands to earn a commission of up to 10 percent or more. That means that only 90 cents (or less) per dollar that you put into an LP actually gets invested. Each year, LPs typically siphon off 2 percent or more of your money for management and other expenses. Efficient, no-load mutual funds, in contrast, put 100 percent of your capital to work (thanks to no commissions) and charge 1 percent per year or less in operating fees.

Most LPs have little or no incentive to control costs. In fact, they may have a conflict of interest that leads them to charge more to enrich the managing partners. And, unlike mutual funds, in LPs you can't vote with your feet. If the partnership is poorly run and expensive, you're stuck. That's why LPs are called *illiquid* — you can't withdraw your money until the partnership is liquidated, typically seven to ten years after you buy in. (If you want to sell out to a third party in the interim, you have to sell at a huge discount. Don't bother unless you're totally desperate for cash.)

The only thing limited about an LP is its ability to make you money. If you want to make investments that earn you healthy returns, stick with stocks (using mutual funds), real estate, or your own business.

Reviewing Important Investing Concepts

If you reviewed the beginning of this chapter, you have the fundamental building blocks of the investing world. Of course, as the title of this book suggests, I focus on a convenient and efficient way to put it all together — mutual funds. But before doing that, this section reviews some key investing concepts that you continually come across as an investor.

Getting a return: Why you invest

An investment's *return* measures how much the investment has grown (or shrunk, as the case may be). Return figures are usually quoted as a rate or percentage that measures how much the investment's value has changed over a specified period of time. So if an investment has a five-year annualized return of 8 percent, then every year for the past five years that investment, on average, has gotten 8 percent bigger than it was the year before.

So what kind of returns can you expect from different kinds of investments? I say "can" because we're looking at history, and history is a record of the past. Using history to predict the future, especially the near future, is dangerous. History won't exactly repeat itself, not even in the same fashion and not necessarily when you expect it to.

Over the past century, ownership investments like stocks and real estate returned around 8 to 10 percent per year, handily beating lending investments such as bonds (around 5 percent) and savings accounts (roughly 4 percent) in the investment performance race. Inflation averaged around 3 percent per year, so savings account and bond returns barely kept up with increases in the cost of living. Factoring in the taxes that you must pay on your investment earnings, the returns on lending investments actually didn't keep up with these increases. (For comparisons of various mutual funds' returns, please see Chapter 17.)

Measuring risks: Investment volatility

Obviously, if you read the previous section, you know you should put all your money in stocks and real estate, right? The returns sure look great. So what's the catch?

The greater an investment's potential return, the greater (generally) is its risk, particularly in the short term. But the main drawback to ownership investments is *volatility* (the size of the fluctuations in the value of an investment). Last century, for example, stocks declined by more than 10 percent in a year approximately once every five years. Drops in stock prices of more than 20 percent occurred about once every ten years (see Figure 1-1). Thus, in order to earn those generous long-term stock market returns of about 10 percent per year, you had to tolerate volatility and be able to hold onto the investment for a number of years to wait out sharp, short-term declines. That's why you absolutely should *not* put all your money in the stock market.

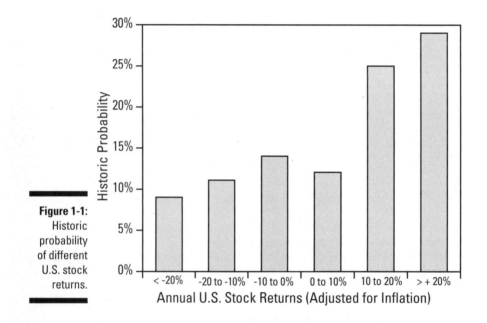

Figure 1-1: Historic probability of different U.S. stock returns.

In Figure 1-2, you see bonds that have had fewer years in which they've provided rates of return that were as tremendously negative or positive as stocks. Bonds are less volatile, but, as I discuss in the preceding section, on average you earn a lower rate of return.

Some types of bonds have higher yields than others, but nothing is free, either. A bond generally pays you a higher rate of interest as compared with other bonds when it has

   ✔ **Lower credit quality,** which compensates for the higher risk of default and the higher likelihood that you'll lose your investment.

   ✔ **Longer-term maturity,** which compensates for the risk that you'll be unhappy with the bond's interest rate if interest rates move up.

✔ **Callability,** which retains an organization's or company's right to buy back (pay off) the issued bonds before the bonds mature.

Companies like to be able to pay off early if they've found a cheaper way to borrow the money. Early payback is a risk to bondholders because they may get their investment money returned to them when interest rates have dropped.

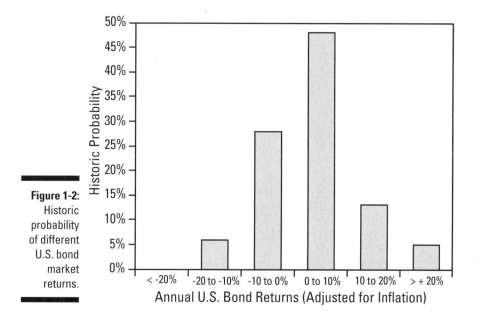

Figure 1-2: Historic probability of different U.S. bond market returns.

Diversifying: A smart way to reduce risk

Diversification is one of the most powerful investment concepts. It requires you to place your money in different investments with returns that aren't completely correlated. Now for the plain-English translation: With your money in different places, when one of your investments is down in value, the odds are good that at least one other is up.

To decrease the odds that all your investments will get clobbered at the same time, put your money in different types or classes of investments. The different kinds of investments include money market funds, bonds, stocks, real estate, and precious metals. You can further diversify your investments by investing in international, as well as domestic markets.

You should also diversify within a given class of investments. For example, with stocks, diversify by investing in different types of stocks that perform well under various economic conditions. For this reason, mutual funds, which are diversified portfolios of securities, are highly useful investment vehicles. You buy into the mutual fund, which in turn pools your money with that of many others to invest in a vast array of stocks or bonds.

You can look at the benefits of diversification in two ways:

- Diversification reduces the volatility in the value of your whole portfolio. In other words, when you diversify, you can achieve the same rate of return that a single investment can provide, but with reduced fluctuations in value.

- Diversification allows you to obtain a higher rate of return for a given level of risk.

Chapter 2

Mutual Funds: Pros and Cons

· ·

· ·

I'm not sure where the *mutual* in mutual funds comes from; perhaps it's so named because the best funds allow many people of differing economic means to mutually invest their money for

- ✔ Easy diversification
- ✔ Access to professional money managers
- ✔ Low investment management costs

No matter where the word came from, mutual funds, like any other investment, have their strengths and weaknesses that you need to know about before you invest your money. This chapter discusses the advantages and disadvantages of mutual funds.

Getting a Grip on Mutual Funds

A *mutual fund* is a collection of investment money pooled from many investors to be invested for a specific objective. When you invest in a mutual fund, you buy shares and become a *shareholder* of the fund. The fund manager and his team of assistants determine which specific securities (for example, stocks or bonds) they should invest the shareholders' money in, in order to accomplish the objectives of the fund and keep shareholders happy.

A misconception some investors hold regarding mutual funds is that they invest in stocks and, therefore, are too risky. They don't, and they're not. By using mutual funds, you can invest in a whole array of securities, ranging from money market funds, bonds, stocks, and even real estate.

All mutual funds aren't created equal. Some funds, such as money market funds, carry virtually zero risk that your investment will decline in value. Bond funds that invest in shorter-term bonds don't generally budge by more than several percentage points per year. And you may be surprised to find out in Chapter 13 that some conservative stock funds aren't that risky if you can plan on holding them for a decade or more.

Because good mutual funds take most of the hassle out of figuring out which securities to invest in, they're among the best investment vehicles ever created:

- ✔ Mutual funds allow you to *diversify* your investments — that is, invest in many different industries and companies instead of in just one or two. By spreading the risk over a number of different securities representing many different industries and companies, mutual funds lessen your portfolio's instability and the chances of a large loss.

- ✔ Mutual funds enable you to give your money to the best money management firms and managers in the country.

- ✔ Mutual funds are the ultimate couch potato investment! However, unlike staying home and watching television or playing video games, investing in mutual funds can pay you big rewards.

What's really cool about mutual funds is that when you understand them, you realize that they can help you meet many different financial goals. Maybe you're building up an emergency savings stash of three to six months' living expenses (a prudent idea, by the way). Perhaps you're saving for a home purchase, retirement, or future educational costs. You may know what you need the money for, but you may not know how to protect the money you have and make it grow.

Don't feel bad if you haven't figured out a long-term financial plan or don't have a goal in mind for the money you're saving. Many people don't have their finances organized, which is why I write books like this one! I talk more specifically in Chapter 3 about the kinds of goals mutual funds can help you accomplish.

Financial intermediaries

A mutual fund is a type of financial intermediary. (Now that's a mouthful!) Why should you care? Because if you understand what a financial intermediary is and how mutual funds stack up to other financial intermediaries, you'll better understand when funds are appropriate for your investments and when they probably aren't. A *financial intermediary* is nothing more than an organization that takes money from people who want to invest and then directs the money to those who need investment *capital* (another term for money).

Suppose that you want to borrow money to invest in your own business. You go to a bank that examines your financial records and agrees to loan you $20,000 at 8 percent interest for five years. The money that the banker is lending you has to come from somewhere, right? Well, the banker got that money from a bunch of people who deposited money with the bank at, say, 2 percent interest. Therefore, the banker acts as a financial intermediary, or middleman — one who receives money from depositors and lends it to borrowers who can use it productively.

Insurance companies do similar things with money. They sell investments, such as annuities (see Chapter 1) and then turn around and lend the money — by investing in bonds, for example — to businesses that need to borrow. (Remember, a *bond* is nothing more than a company's promise to repay borrowed money over a specified period of time at a specified interest rate.)

The best mutual funds are often the best financial intermediaries for you to invest through because they skim off less (that is, they charge lower management fees) to manage your money and allow you more choice and control over how you invest your money.

Open-end versus closed-end funds

Open end and closed end are general terms that refer to whether a mutual fund company issues an unlimited or a set amount of shares in a particular fund:

- ✔ **Open-end funds:** *Open end* simply means that the fund issues as many (or as few) shares as investors demand. Open-end funds theoretically have no limit to the number of investors or the amount of money that they hold. You buy and sell shares in such a fund from the fund company.

- ✔ **Closed-end funds:** *Closed-end* funds are those where the mutual fund companies decide upfront, before they take on any investors, exactly how many shares they'll issue. After they issue these shares, the only way you can purchase shares (or more shares) is to buy them from an existing investor through a broker. This process happens with buying and selling stock, too.

The vast majority of funds in the marketplace are open-end funds, and they're also the funds that I focus on in this book because the better open-end funds are superior to their closed-end counterparts.

Open-end funds are usually preferable to closed-end funds for the following reasons:

✔ **Management talent:** The better open-end funds attract more investors over time. Therefore, they can afford to pay the necessary money to hire leading managers. I'm not saying that closed-end funds don't have good managers, too, but generally, open-end funds attract better talent.

✔ **Expenses:** Because they can attract more investors, and therefore more money to manage, the better open-end funds charge lower annual operating expenses. Closed-end funds tend to be much smaller and, therefore, more costly to operate. Remember, operating expenses are deducted out of shareholder returns before a fund pays its investors their returns; therefore, relatively higher annual expenses depress the returns for closed-end funds.

Brokers who receive a hefty commission generally handle the initial sale of a closed-end fund. Brokers' commissions usually siphon anywhere from 5 to 8 percent out of your investment dollars, which they generally don't disclose to you. (Even if you wait until after the initial offering to buy closed-end fund shares on the stock exchange, you still pay a brokerage commission, although it is generally a lot less than the initial sale commission.) You can avoid these high commissions by purchasing a *no-load* (commission-free), open-end mutual fund. (See "Funds save you money and time," later in this chapter, for details on no-load funds.)

✔ **Fee-free selling:** With an open-end fund, the value of a share (known as the *net asset value*) always equals 100 percent of what the fund's investments (less liabilities) are currently worth. And you don't have the cost and troubles of selling your shares to another investor as you do with a closed-end fund. Because closed-end funds trade like securities on the stock exchange and because you must sell your shares to someone who wants to buy, closed-end funds sometimes sell at a discount. Even though the securities in a closed-end fund may be worth, say, $20 per share, the fund may sell at only $19 per share if sellers outnumber buyers.

You could buy shares in a closed-end fund at a discount and hold on to them in hopes that the discount disappears or — even better — turns into a *premium* (which means that the share price of the fund exceeds the value of the investments it holds). You should *never* pay a premium to buy a closed-end fund, and you shouldn't generally buy one without getting at least a 5 percent discount (to make up for its deficiencies, versus its open-ended peers, especially higher expenses).

Sorry to complicate things, but I need to make one clarification. Open-end funds can, and sometimes do, decide at a later date to "close" their funds to new investors. This doesn't make it a closed-end fund, however, because investors with existing shares can generally buy more shares from the fund company. Instead, the fund becomes an open-end fund that's closed to new investors!

Opting for Mutual Funds

To understand why funds are so sensible is to understand how and why funds can work for you. Keep reading in this section to discover their many benefits. (Funds also have their drawbacks — I cover them in the section, "Addressing the Drawbacks," later in this chapter.) In Part II of this book, I compare mutual funds to other investing alternatives so you can clearly understand when funds are and aren't your best choice.

Fund managers' expertise

Mutual funds are investment companies that pool your money with the money of hundreds, thousands, or even millions of other investors. The company hires a portfolio manager and a team of researchers whose full-time job is to analyze and purchase investments that best meet the fund's stated objectives.

Typically, fund managers are Chartered Financial Analysts (CFAs) and/or graduates of the top business and finance schools in the country, where they study the principles of portfolio management and securities valuation and selection. In addition to their educational training, the best fund managers typically have a decade or more of experience in analyzing and selecting investments.

A mutual fund management team does more research and due diligence than you could ever have the energy or expertise to do in what little free time you have. Investing in mutual funds can help your friendships, and maybe even your love life, because you'll have more free time and energy!

Consider the following activities that an investor should do before investing in stocks and bonds:

- ✔ **Analyze company financial statements:** Companies whose securities trade in the financial markets are required to issue reports every three months detailing their revenue, expenses, profits and losses, and assets and liabilities. Unless you're a numbers geek, own a financial calculator, and enjoy dissecting tedious corporate financial statements, this first task alone is reason enough to invest through a mutual fund and leave the driving to the mutual fund management team.

- ✔ **Talk with the muckety-mucks:** Most fund managers log thousands of frequent-flier miles and hundreds of hours talking to the folks running the companies they're invested in or are thinking about investing in. Because of the huge amount of money they manage, large fund companies even get visits from company executives, who fly in to grovel at the fund managers' feet. Now, do you have the correct type of china and all the place settings that etiquette demands of people who host such high-level folks?!

✔ **Analyze company and competitor strategies:** Corporate managers have an irritating tendency to talk up what a great job they're doing. Some companies may look as if they're making the right moves, but what if their products are soon to lag behind the competition's? The best fund managers and their researchers take a skeptical view of what a company's execs say — they read the fine print and check under the rugs. They also keep on top of what competitors are doing. Sometimes they discover investment ideas better than their original ones this way.

✔ **Talk with company customers, suppliers, competitors, and industry consultants:** Another way the mutual fund managers find out whether a company's public relations story is full of holes instead of reality is by speaking with the company's customers, suppliers, competitors, and other industry experts. These people often have more balanced viewpoints and can be a great deal more open about the negatives. These folks are harder to find but can provide valuable information.

✔ **Attend trade shows and review industry literature:** It's truly amazing how specialized the world's becoming. Do you really want to subscribe to business newsletters that track the latest happenings with ball bearing or catalytic converter technology? They'll put you to sleep in a couple of pages. Unlike popular mass-market publications, they'll also charge you an arm and a leg to subscribe.

Are you, as the investor, going to do all these tasks and do them well? Nothing personal, but I doubt that you will. Even in the unlikely event that you could perform investment research as well as the best fund managers, don't you value your time? A good mutual fund management team happily performs all the required research for you, does it well, and does it for a fraction of what it costs you to do it haphazardly on your own.

Funds save you money and time

Chances are the last thing you want to do with your free time is research where to invest your savings. If you're like many busy people, you've kept your money in a bank just to avoid the hassles. Or maybe you turned your money over to some smooth-talking broker who sold you a high-commission investment that you still don't understand but are convinced will make you rich.

Mutual funds are a cheaper, more communal way to get the investing job done. A mutual fund spreads out the cost of extensive — and expensive — research over thousands of investors. How does a mutual fund save you time and money? Let me count the ways:

A (brief) history of mutual funds

Mutual funds date back to the 1800s, when English and Scottish investment trusts sold shares to investors. Funds arrived in the United States in 1924. They were growing in assets until the late 1920s, when the Great Depression derailed the financial markets and the economy. Stock prices plunged and so did mutual funds that held stocks.

As was common in the stock market at that time, mutual funds were *leveraging* their investments — leveraging is a fancy way of saying that they put up only, for example, 25 cents on the dollar for investments they actually owned. The other 75 cents was borrowed. That's why, when the stock market plunged in 1929, some investors and fund shareholders got clobbered. They were losing money on their investments *and* on all the borrowed money. But, like the rest of the country, mutual funds, although bruised, pulled through this economic calamity.

The Securities Act of 1933 and the Investment Company Act of 1940 established ground rules and oversight of the fund industry by the Securities and Exchange Commission (SEC). Among other benefits, this landmark federal legislation required funds to register and have those materials be reviewed by the SEC *before* issuing or selling any fund shares to the public. Funds were required to disclose cost, risk, and other information in a uniform format through a legal document called a *prospectus* (see Chapter 8).

During the 1940s, '50s, and '60s, funds grew at a fairly high and constant rate. From less than $1 billion in assets in 1940, fund assets grew to more than $50 billion by the late '60s — more than a fiftyfold increase. Before the early '70s, funds focused largely on investing in stocks. Since then, however, money market mutual funds and bond mutual funds have mushroomed. They now account for about 50 percent of all mutual fund assets.

Today, thousands of mutual funds manage about $11 trillion.

✔ **Mutual funds can produce a much better rate of return over the long haul than a dreary, boring bank or insurance company account.** You can purchase by writing a check or calling a toll-free number. What does it cost to hire such high-powered talent to do all the dreadful research and analysis? A mere pittance if you pick the right funds. In fact, when you invest your money in an efficiently managed mutual fund, the cost should be less than it would be to trade individual securities on your own.

✔ **Mutual funds manage money efficiently through effective use of technology.** Innovations in information-management tools enable funds to monitor and manage billions of dollars from millions of investors at a very low cost. In general, moving around $5 billion in securities doesn't cost them much more than moving $500 million. Larger investments just mean a few more zeros in the computer data banks.

The most efficiently managed mutual funds cost less than 1 percent per year in expenses. (Bond funds and money market funds cost much less — good ones charge just 0.5 percent per year or less.) Some of the larger and more established funds, including index funds (see Chapter 10), charge annual expenses of less than 0.2 percent per year.

✔ **Many mutual funds don't charge a commission (load) to purchase or redeem shares.** Commission-free funds are called *no-load funds*. Such opportunities used to be rare. Fidelity and Vanguard, the two largest distributors of no-load funds today, exacted sales charges as high as 8.5 percent during the early 1970s. Even today, some mutual funds known as *load funds* charge you a commission for buying or selling shares in their funds. (See Chapter 7 for the complete story on fund fees.)

Fund diversification minimizes your risk

Diversification is a big attraction for many investors who choose mutual funds. Here's an example of why, which should also explain what diversification is all about: Suppose you heard that Phenomenal Pharmaceuticals developed a drug that stops cancer cells in their tracks. You run to the phone, call your broker, and invest all your savings in shares of Phenomenal stock. Years later, the Food and Drug Administration (FDA) denies the company approval for the drug, and the company goes belly up, taking your entire nest egg with it.

Your money would've been much safer in a mutual fund. A mutual fund may buy some shares of a promising, but risky, company like Phenomenal without exposing investors like you to financial ruin. A fund owns stocks or bonds from dozens of companies, diversifying against the risk of bad news from any single company or sector. So when Phenomenal goes belly up, the fund may barely feel a ripple.

Diversifying like that on your own would be difficult — and expensive — unless you have a few hundred thousand dollars and a great deal of time to invest. You'd need to invest money in at least 8 to 12 different companies in various industries to ensure that your portfolio could withstand a downturn in one or more of the investments.

Mutual funds typically invest in 25 to 100 securities, or more. Proper diversification increases the probability that the fund receives the highest possible return at the lowest possible risk, given the objectives of the fund.

I'm not suggesting that mutual funds escape without share-price declines during major market downturns. For example, during the early 2000s bear market, many mutual funds declined in value. But again, the investors who were most harmed were those who held individual stocks that, in the worst cases, ended up plummeting to zero as companies went bankrupt or those investors who loaded up on technology and Internet stocks that dropped 80 to 90 percent or more. The same fate befell investors who were overloaded with stock in financial firms like AIG, Bear Stearns, Lehman, and so on that plunged far more than the broad market averages in the late 2000s bear market.

Although most mutual funds are diversified, some aren't. For example, some stock funds, known as *sector funds,* invest exclusively in stocks of a single industry (for instance, healthcare). Others focus on a single country (such as India). I'm not a fan of such funds because of the lack of diversification and because such funds typically charge higher operating fees. It's also worth noting that investors who bought sector funds investing exclusively in Internet stocks got hammered in the technology stock crash of the early 2000s. Many of those funds dropped 80 percent or more, whereas broadly diversified funds fared far better. (The same thing happened in the late 2000s to investors in financial sector funds.) I talk more about narrowly focused stock funds in Chapter 13.

Funds undergo regulatory scrutiny

Before a fund can take in money from investors, the fund must go through a tedious review process by the Securities and Exchange Commission (SEC). After it offers shares, a mutual fund is required to publish in its prospectus (see Chapter 8) historical data on the fund's returns, its operating expenses and other fees, and its rate of trading (turnover) of the fund's investments.

But know that government regulators aren't perfect. Conceivably, a fund operator could try to slip through some bogus numbers, but I wouldn't lose sleep worrying about this, especially if you invest through the larger, reputable fund companies recommended in this book.

You choose your risk level

Choosing from a huge variety of mutual funds, you can select the funds that meet your financial goals and take on the kinds of risks that you're comfortable with. Funds to choose from include

  ✔ **Stock funds:** If you want your money to grow over a long period of time (and you can put up with some bad years thrown in with the good), select funds that invest more heavily in stocks. (Check out Chapter 13 for the complete story on stock funds.)

✔ **Bond funds:** If you need current income and don't want investments that fluctuate as widely in value as stocks do, consider bond funds (see Chapter 12).

✔ **Money market funds:** If you want to be sure that your invested principal doesn't drop in value because you may need to use your money in the short term, you can choose a money market fund (see Chapter 11).

Most investors choose a combination of these three types of funds to diversify and help meet different financial goals. I get into all that information in the chapters to come.

Fund risk of bankruptcy is nil

Mutual funds don't work like banks and insurance companies, hundreds of which have failed in recent decades. (The number going under spiked during the late 2000s recession.) Banks and insurers can fail because their *liabilities* (the money customers have given them to invest) can exceed their *assets* (the money they've invested or lent). When a big chunk of a bank's loans goes sour at the same time that its depositors want their money back, the bank fails. That happens because banks have less than 20 cents on deposit for every dollar that you and I place with them. Likewise, if an insurance company makes several poor investments or underestimates the number of claims that insurance policyholders will make, it too can fail.

Such failures can't happen with a mutual fund. The situation in which the investors' demand for withdrawals of their investment exceeds the value of a fund's assets simply can't occur because for every dollar of assets that a fund holds for its customers, that mutual fund has a dollar's worth of redeemable securities.

That's not to say that you can't lose money in a mutual fund. The share price of a mutual fund is tied to the value of its underlying securities: If the underlying securities, such as stocks, decrease in value, so, too, does the net asset value (share price) of the fund. If you sell your shares when their price is less than what you paid for them, you get back less cash than you originally put into the fund. But that's the worst that can happen; you can't lose all your investment in a mutual fund unless every single security owned by that fund simultaneously becomes worthless — an extraordinarily unlikely event.

You may be interested to know that the specific stocks and/or bonds that a mutual fund buys are held by a *custodian* — a separate organization or affiliate of the mutual fund company. The employment of a custodian ensures that the fund management company can't embezzle your funds (like hedge fund crook Bernie Madoff did) or use assets from a better-performing fund to subsidize a poor performer.

Funds save you from sales sharks

Stockbrokers (also known as financial consultants) and commission-based financial planners make more money by encouraging trading activity and by selling you investments that provide them with high commissions — limited partnerships and mutual funds with high-load fees, for example. Brokers and planners also get an occasional message from the top brass asking them to sell some newfangled investment product. All this creates inherent conflicts of interest that can prevent brokers from providing objective investment and financial advice and recommendations.

The better no-load (commission-free) fund companies discussed in this book generally don't push specific products. Their toll-free telephone lines are staffed with knowledgeable people who earn salaries, not commissions. Sure, they want you to invest with their company, but the size of their next paycheck doesn't depend on how much they persuade you to buy or trade.

You have convenient access to your money

What I find really terrific about dealing with the best mutual fund companies is that they're set up for people who don't like to waste time going to a local branch office and waiting in line. I don't know about you, but I enjoy waiting in lines, especially in places like a bank, about as much as I enjoy having my dentist fill a cavity.

With mutual funds, you can make your initial investment from the comfort of your living room by filling out and mailing a simple form and writing a check. (Computer lovers can open and fund accounts online as I discuss in Chapter 16.) Later, you can add to your investment by mailing in a check or by authorizing money transfers by phone or online from one mutual fund account to another.

Selling shares of your mutual fund for cash is usually easy. Generally, all you need to do is call the fund company's toll-free number or click your computer mouse at your investment firm's Web site 24/7. Some companies even have representatives available by phone 24 hours a day, 365 days a year. (Signature guarantees, although much less common, are still sometimes required by fund companies.)

Many mutual fund companies also allow you to wire money back and forth from your local bank account, allowing you to access your money almost as quickly through a money market fund as through your local bank. (As I discuss in Chapter 11, you probably need to keep a local bank checking account to write smaller checks and for immediate ATM access to cash.)

Don't fret about the crooks

Folks who grew up only dealing with local banks often worry about others having easy access to the money you've invested in mutual funds. Even if someone were able to convince a fund company through the toll-free phone line or on its Web site that he were you (say, by knowing your account number and Social Security number), the impostor, at worst, could only request a transaction to occur between accounts registered in your name. You'd find out about the shenanigans when the confirmation arrived in the mail, at which time you could call the mutual fund company and undo the whole mess. (Just by listening to a tape of the phone call, which the fund company records, or a record of the online transaction, the company could confirm that you didn't place the trade.)

No one can actually take money out of your account, either. Suppose that someone does know your personal and account information and calls a fund company to ask that a check be sent from a redemption on the account. Even in such a scenario, the check would be sent to the address on the account and be made payable to you.

The only way that someone can actually take money out of your account is with your authorization. And there's only one way to do that: by completing a full trading authorization or power-of-attorney form. I generally recommend that you not grant this authority to anyone. If you do, make sure that the investment firm makes checks payable only to you, not to the person requesting the money from the account.

When dealing with a money market fund, in particular, the ease of access is even greater. Most money market funds also offer check-writing privileges. These accounts often carry a restriction, however, that your bank checking account doesn't have: Money market checks must be greater than a specified minimum amount — typically $250.

If you like to conduct some transactions in person, some of the larger fund companies, such as Fidelity, and certain discount brokers, such as Charles Schwab and TD Ameritrade, have branch offices in convenient locations.

Addressing the Drawbacks

Although I'm a fan of the best mutual funds, I'm also well aware of their drawbacks, and you need to know them, too. After all, no investment vehicle is perfect, and you need to understand mutual fund negatives before you take the plunge.

Still, the mutual fund drawbacks that I'm concerned about are different from the ones that some critics like to harp on. Here's my take on which mutual fund drawbacks you shouldn't worry about — and which ones you should stop and think about a little more.

Don't worry about these . . .

If you've read some articles or heard some news stories about the downsides of mutual funds, you may have heard of some of the following concerns. However, you shouldn't let them trouble you:

- ✔ **The investment Goliath:** One of the concerns I still hear about is the one that, because the fund industry is growing, if stock fund investors head for the exits at the same time, they may get stuck or trampled at the door. You could make this argument about any group of investors including institutions. Little evidence suggests that most individual investors are prone to rash moves. Mutual funds have grown in importance simply because they're a superior alternative for a whole lot of people.

- ✔ **Doing business long distance:** Some people, particularly older folks who grew up doing all their saving through a local bank, feel uncomfortable doing business with a company that they can reach only via a toll-free number, the mail, or a Web site. But please recognize the enormous benefits of mutual funds *not* having branch offices all over the country. Branch offices cost a lot of money to operate, which is one of the reasons why bank account interest rates are so scrawny.

  If you feel better dropping your money off in person to an organization that has local branch offices, invest in mutual funds through one of the firms that I recommend in Chapter 9. Or do business with a fund company that's headquartered near your abode. (See the Appendix for the main addresses of the fund companies recommended in this book.)

- ✔ **Fund company scandals:** A number of funds (none that were recommended in the previous editions of this book) earned negative publicity due to their involvement in problematic trading practices. In the worst cases, some fund managers placed their own selfish agendas (or that of certain favored investors) ahead of their shareholders' best interests. Rightfully, these fund companies have been hammered for such behavior and forced to reimburse shareholders and pay penalties to the government. However, the amount of such damage and reimbursement has been less than 1 percent of the affected fund's assets, which pales in comparison to the ongoing drag of high expenses discussed in the next section. The parent company responsible for an individual fund should be an important consideration when deciding which funds to entrust with your money. Avoid fund companies that don't place their shareholders' interests first. (I definitely don't recommend those companies in this book.)

Worry about these (but not too much) . . .

No doubt you hear critics in the investment world state their case for why you should shun funds. Not surprisingly, the most vocal critics are those who compete with fund companies.

You can easily overcome the common criticisms raised about fund investing if you do your homework and buy the better available mutual funds, which I show you how to do in this book. Make sure that you consider and accommodate these factors before you invest in any mutual fund:

✔ **Volatility of your investment balance:** When you invest in mutual funds that hold stocks and/or bonds, the value of your funds fluctuates with the general fluctuations in those securities markets. These fluctuations don't happen if you invest in a bank certificate of deposit (CD) or a fixed insurance annuity that pays a set rate of interest yearly. With CDs or annuities, you get a statement every so often that shows steady — but slow — growth in your account value. You never get any great news, but you never get any bad news either (unless your insurer or bank fails, which could happen).

Over the long haul, if you invest in solid mutual funds — ones that are efficiently and competently managed — you should earn a better rate of return than you would with bank and insurance accounts. And if you invest in stock funds, you'll be more likely to keep well ahead of the double bite of inflation and taxes.

If you panic and rush to sell when the market value of your mutual fund shares drops (instead of holding on and possibly taking advantage of the buying opportunity), then maybe you're not cut out for funds. Stock fund investors who joined the panic taking place in late 2008 and early 2009 and sold got out at fire sale prices and missed out on an enormous rebound that took place beginning in early 2009. Take the time to read and internalize the investment lessons in this book, and you'll soon be an honors graduate from my Mutual Fund University!

✔ **Mystery (risky) investments:** Some mutual funds (not those that I recommend) have betrayed their investors' trust by taking unnecessary risks by investing in volatile financial instruments such as futures and options (also known as *derivatives*). Because these instruments are basically short-term bets on the direction of specific security prices (see Chapter 1), they're very risky when not properly used by a mutual fund. If a fund discloses in its prospectus that it uses derivatives, look to see whether the derivatives are used only for hedging purposes to reduce risk instead of as speculation on stock and bond price movements, which would increase risk.

✔ **Investments that cost an arm and a leg:** Not all mutual funds are created equal. Some charge extremely high annual operating expenses that put a real drag on returns. (Again, you won't find such funds on my recommended lists in this book.) I talk more about expense ratios and how to find great funds with low expenses in Chapter 7.

✔ **Taxable distributions:** The taxable distributions that funds produce can also be a negative. When fund managers sell a security at a profit, the fund must distribute that profit to shareholders in the fund (dividends are also passed through). For funds held outside tax-sheltered retirement accounts, these distributions are taxable. I fill you in on taxes and mutual funds in Chapter 10.

Some people — especially brokers and self-anointed gurus who advocate investing in individual securities — argue that taxes on mutual fund distributions are a problem big enough to justify the avoidance of mutual funds altogether, especially for higher-tax-bracket investors. They don't have to be. If you're concerned about the money you're investing outside of tax-sheltered retirement accounts, don't worry — I have a solution: See my recommended tax-friendly funds in Chapters 11 through 13.

Chapter 3

Funding Your Financial Plans

*I*n this chapter, I explain how to fit mutual funds into a thoughtful personal financial plan so the mutual funds you invest in and the other personal finance decisions you make help you achieve your goals.

One thing to remember before you dive in: Don't become obsessed with making, saving, and investing money that you neglect what money can't buy: your health, friends, family, and exploration of career options and hobbies.

The Story of Justine and Max

Justine and Max, both in their 20s, recently married and excited about planning their life together, heard about a free financial-planning seminar taking place at a local hotel. A financial planner taught the seminar. One of his points was, "If you want to retire by the age of 65, you need to save at least 12 percent of your income every year between now and retirement . . . the longer you wait to start saving, the more painful it'll be."

For the couple, the seminar was a wake-up call. On the drive home, they couldn't stop thinking and talking about their finances and their future. Justine and Max had big plans: They wanted to buy a home, to send the not-yet-born kiddies to college, and to retire by age 65. And so it was resolved: A serious investment program must begin right away. Tomorrow, they'd fill out two applications for mutual fund companies that the financial planner had distributed to them.

Within a week, they'd set up accounts in five different mutual funds at two firms. No more paltry-return bank savings accounts — the funds they chose had been returning 10 or more percent per year! Unlike most of their 20-something friends who didn't own funds or understand what funds were, they believed they were well on their way to realizing their dreams.

Although I have to admire Justine and Max's initiative (that's often the biggest hurdle to starting an investment program), I must point out the mistakes they made by investing in this fashion. The funds themselves weren't poor choices — in fact, the funds they selected were solid: Each had competent managers, good historic performance, and reasonable fees. Among the mistakes they made:

- ✔ **They completely neglected investing in their employers' retirement savings plans.** They missed out on making tax-deductible contributions. By investing in mutual funds outside of their employers' plans, they received no tax breaks.

- ✔ **They were steered into funds that didn't fit their goals.** They ended up with bond funds, which were okay funds as far as bond funds go. But bond funds are designed to produce current income, not growth. Justine and Max, looking to a retirement decades away, were trying to *save* and *grow* their money, not produce more current income.

- ✔ **To add tax insult to injury, the income generated by their bond funds was fully taxable because the funds were held outside of tax-sheltered retirement accounts.** The last thing Justine and Max needed was more taxable income, not because they were rolling in money — neither Justine nor Max had a high salary — but because, as a two-income couple, they already paid significant taxes.

- ✔ **They didn't adjust their spending habits to allow for their increased savings rate.** In their enthusiasm to get serious about their savings, they made this error — probably the biggest one of all. Justine and Max *thought* they were saving more — 12 percent of their income was going into the mutual funds versus the 5 percent they'd been saving in a bank account. However, as the months rolled by, their outstanding balances on credit cards grew. In fact, when they started to invest in mutual funds, Justine and Max had $1,000 of revolving debt on a credit card at a 14 percent interest rate. Six months later, this debt had grown to $2,000.

The extra money for investment had to come from somewhere — and in Justine and Max's case, some of it was coming from building up their credit card debt. But, because their investments were highly unlikely to return 14 percent per year, Justine and Max were actually losing money in the process.

I tell the story of Justine and Max to caution you against buying mutual funds in haste or out of fear before you have your own financial goals in mind.

Lining Up Your Ducks Before You Invest

The single biggest mistake that mutual fund investors make is investing in funds before they're prepared — both financially and emotionally. It's like trying to build the walls of a house without a proper foundation. You have to get your financial ship in shape — sailing out of port with leaks in the hull is sure to lead to an early, unpleasant end to your journey. And you have to figure out what you're trying to accomplish with your investing and what you're comfortable with.

Throughout this book, I emphasize that mutual funds are specialized tools for specific jobs. I don't want you to pick up a tool that you don't know how to use. This section covers the most important financial steps for you to take *before* you invest so you get the most from your mutual fund investments.

Pay off your consumer debts

Consumer debts include balances on credit cards and auto loans. If you carry these types of debts, *do not* invest in mutual funds until these consumer debts are paid off. I realize that investing money may make you feel like you're making progress; paying off debt, on the other hand, just feels like you're treading water. Shatter this illusion. Paying credit card interest at 14 or 18 percent while making an investment that generates only an 8 percent return isn't even treading water; it's sinking!

You won't be able to earn a consistently high enough rate of return in mutual funds to exceed the interest rate you're paying on consumer debt. Although some financial gurus claim that they can make you 15 to 20 percent per year, they can't — not year after year. Besides, in order to try and earn these high returns, you have to take great risk. If you have consumer debt and little savings, you're not in a position to take that much risk.

I go a step further on this issue: Not only should you delay any investing until your consumer debts are paid off, but also you should seriously consider tapping in to any existing savings (presuming you'd still have adequate emergency funds at your disposal) to pay off your debts.

Review your insurance coverage

Saving and investing is psychologically rewarding and makes many people feel more secure. But, ironically, even some good savers and investors are in precarious positions because they have major gaps in their insurance coverage. Consider the following questions:

- ✔ Do you have adequate life insurance to provide for your dependents if you die?
- ✔ Do you carry long-term disability insurance to replace your income in case a disability prevents you from working?
- ✔ Do you have comprehensive health insurance coverage to pay for major medical expenses?
- ✔ Have you purchased sufficient liability protection on your home and car to guard your assets against lawsuits?

Without adequate insurance coverage, a catastrophe could quickly wipe out your investments. The point of insurance is to eliminate the financial downside of such a disaster and protect your assets.

In reviewing your insurance, you may also discover unnecessary policies or ways to spend less on insurance, freeing up more money to invest in mutual funds. See the latest edition of my book, *Personal Finance For Dummies,* 6th Edition (Wiley), to discover the best ways to buy insurance and whip all of your finances into shape.

Figure out your financial goals

Mutual funds are goal-specific tools (see "Reaching Your Goals with Funds" later in this chapter), and humans are goal-driven animals, which is perhaps why the two make such a good match. Most people find that saving money is easier when they save with a purpose or goal in mind — even if their goal is as undefined as a "rainy day." Because mutual funds tend to be pretty specific in what they're designed to do, the more defined your goal, the more capable you are to make the most of your mutual fund money.

Granted, your goals and needs will change over time, so these determinations don't have to be carved in stone. But unless you have a general idea of what you're going to do with the savings down the road, you won't really be able to thoughtfully choose suitable mutual funds. Common financial goals include saving for retirement, a home purchase, an emergency reserve, and stuff like that. In the second half of this chapter, I talk more about the goals mutual funds can help you to accomplish.

Another benefit of pondering your goals is that you better understand how much risk you need to take to accomplish your goals. Seeing the amount you need to save to achieve your dreams may encourage you to invest in more growth-oriented funds. Conversely, if you find that your nest egg is substantial, given what your aspirations are, you may scale back on the riskiness of your fund investments.

Determine how much you're saving

Many folks don't know what their savings rate is. By *savings rate,* I mean, over a calendar year, how did your spending compare with your income? For example, if you earned $40,000 last year, and $38,000 of it got spent on taxes, food, clothing, rent, insurance, and other fun things, you saved $2,000. Your savings rate then would be 5 percent ($2,000 of savings divided by your income of $40,000).

If you already know that your rate is low, nonexistent, or negative, you can safely skip this step because you also already know that you need to save more. But figuring out your savings rate can be a real eye-opener.

Examine your spending and income

To save more, you must reduce your spending, increase your income, or both. This isn't rocket science, but it's easier said than done.

For most people, reducing spending is the more feasible option. But where do you begin? First, figure out where your money is going. You may have some general idea, but you need to have facts. Get out your checkbook and debit card records, credit card bills, and any other documentation of your spending history and tally up how much you spend on dining out, operating your car(s), paying your taxes, and everything else. When you have this information, you can begin to prioritize and make the necessary trade-offs to reduce your spending and increase your savings rate.

Earning more income may help you save more to invest if you can get a higher-paying job or increase the number of hours you're willing to work. Watch out, though: Many people's spending has a nasty habit of soaking up increases in income. If you're already working many hours, tightening the belt on your spending is better for your emotional and social well-being.

Maximize tax-deferred retirement account savings

Saving money is difficult for most people. Don't make a tough job impossible by forsaking the terrific tax benefits that come from investing through retirement savings accounts. Employer-based 401(k) and 403(b) retirement plans offer substantial tax benefits. Contributions into these plans are generally federal- and state-tax-deductible. And after the money is invested inside these plans, the growth on your contributions is tax-sheltered as well. Furthermore, some employers will match a portion of your contributions.

Some investors make the common mistake of neglecting to take advantage of retirement accounts in their enthusiasm to invest in nonretirement accounts. Doing so can cost you hundreds of thousands of dollars over the years. Fund companies are happy to encourage this financially detrimental behavior, too. They lure you into their funds without educating you about using your employer's retirement plan first because the more you invest through your employer's plan, the less you have available to separately invest in their funds.

Prioritizing your financial goals

Only you know what's really most important to you and how to prioritize your goals. And prioritize you must — because your desires outstrip your ability to save and accomplish your goals. Now that doesn't mean that you can't fulfill your dreams. With an average income, you can, with proper planning, achieve most of the financial goals identified throughout this chapter. But you do have to be realistic about how many balls you can juggle at any one time.

That may mean, for example, that you have to reduce your retirement plan contributions while you save for a down payment on a home. Or that you have to downscale the size of your dream house a bit if you really want Junior to attend a pricey, private college.

Again, you're the best person to decide what trade-offs to make. However, because of the tax breaks that come with retirement account contributions, retirement funding should always be near the top of your priority list. *Remember:* Making retirement account contributions reduces your tax bill, effectively giving you more dollars with which to accomplish your various goals.

And, as suggested by its name, your emergency reserve fund should always be a top priority, especially if your income is unstable and/or you have no family to fall back on. On the other hand, if you have a steady job and at least a few solvent family members, you can probably afford to build up this fund more slowly and in conjunction with other savings goals.

Determine your tax bracket

When you're investing in mutual funds outside of tax-sheltered retirement accounts, the profits and distributions that your funds produce are subject to taxation. So the type of fund that makes sense for you depends, at least partially, on your tax situation.

If you're in a high income tax bracket, give preference to mutual funds such as tax-free bond funds and stock funds with low levels of distributions (especially highly taxed short-term capital gains). In other words, focus more on stock funds that derive more of their expected returns from appreciation rather than from taxable distributions. If you're in a low bracket, avoid tax-free bond funds because you end up with a lower return than in taxable bond funds. (In Part IV of this book, I explain how to select the best fund types to fit your tax status.)

Assess the risk you're comfortable with

Think back over your investing career. You may not be a star money manager, but you've already made some investing decisions. For instance, leaving your excess money in a bank savings or checking account is a decision — it may indicate that you fear volatile investments.

How would you deal with an investment that dropped 10 to 50 percent in a year? Some of the more aggressive mutual funds that specialize in volatile securities like growth stocks, small company stocks, emerging market stocks, and long-term and low-quality bonds can quickly fall. If you can't stomach big waves in the financial markets, don't get in a small boat that you'll want to bail out of in a storm. Selling after a large drop is the equivalent of jumping in to the frothing sea at the peak of a pounding storm.

You can invest in the riskier types of securities by selecting well-diversified mutual funds that mix a dash of aggressive securities with a healthy helping of more stable investments. For example, you can purchase an international fund that invests the bulk of its money in companies of varying sizes in established economies and that has a small portion invested in riskier, emerging economies. That would be safer than investing the same chunk in a fund that invests solely in small companies that are just in emerging countries.

Review current investment holdings

Many people have a tendency to compartmentalize their investments: IRA money here, 401(k) there, brokerage account somewhere else. Part of making sound investment decisions is to examine how the pieces fit together to make up the whole. That's where jargon like *asset allocation* comes into play. *Asset allocation* simply means how your investments are divvied up among the major types of securities or funds, such as money market, bond, United States (U.S.) stock, international stock, and so on.

Another reason to review your current investments before you buy into new mutual funds is that some housecleaning may be in order. You may discover holdings that don't fit with your objectives or tax situation. Perhaps you'll decide to clear out some of the individual securities that you know you can't adequately follow and that clutter your life.

Consider other "investment" possibilities

Mutual funds are a fine way to invest your money but hardly the only way. You can also invest in real estate, invest in your own business or someone else's, or pay down mortgage debt more quickly. Again, what makes sense for you depends on your goals and personal preferences. If you dislike taking risks and detest volatile investments, paying down your mortgage may make better sense than investing in mutual funds.

Reaching Your Goals with Funds

Mutual funds can help you achieve various financial goals. The rest of this chapter gives an overview of some of these more common goals — saving for retirement, buying a home, paying for college costs, and so on — that you can tackle with the help of mutual funds. For each goal, I discuss what kinds of funds are best suited to it and point you to the part of the book that discusses that kind of fund in greater detail.

As you understand more about this process, notice that the *time horizon* of your goal — in other words, how much time you have between now and when you need the money — largely determines what kind of fund is appropriate:

> ✔ If you need to tap in to the money within two or three years or less, a money market or short-term bond fund may fit the bill.
>
> ✔ If your time horizon falls between three and seven years, you want to focus on bond funds.
>
> ✔ For long-term goals, seven or more years down the road, stock funds are probably your main ticket.

But time horizon isn't the only issue. Your tax bracket, for example, is another important consideration in mutual fund selection. (See Chapter 10 for more about taxes.) Other variables are goal specific, so take a closer look at the goals themselves. Throughout the rest of this chapter, I also give you plenty of non-mutual-fund-related tips on how to tackle these goals. *Remember:* Mutual funds are just part of the overall picture and a means to the end of achieving your goals.

The financial pillow — an emergency reserve

Before you save money toward goals, accumulate an amount of money equal to about three to six months of your household's living expenses. This fund isn't for keeping up on the latest consumer technology gadgets. It's for emergency purposes: for your living expenses when you're between jobs, for unexpected medical bills, for a last-minute plane ticket to visit an ailing relative. Basically, it's a fund to cushion your fall when life unexpectedly trips you up. Call it your pillow fund. You'll be amazed how much of a stress reducer a pillow fund is.

How much you save in this fund and how quickly you build it up depends on the stability of your income and the depth of your family support. If your job is steady and your folks are still there for you, then you can keep the size of this fund on the smaller side. On the other hand, if your income is erratic and you have no ties to benevolent family members, you may want to consider building up this fund to a year's worth of expenses.

The ideal savings vehicle for your emergency reserve fund is a money market fund. See Chapter 11 for an in-depth discussion of money market funds and a list of the best ones to choose from.

The golden egg — investing for retirement

Uncle Sam gives major tax breaks for retirement account contributions. This deal is one you can't afford to pass up. The mistake that many people at all income levels make with retirement accounts is not taking advantage of them and delaying the age at which they start to sock money away. The sooner you start to save, the less painful it is each year, because your contributions have more years to compound.

Each decade you delay approximately doubles the percentage of your earnings that you should save to meet your goals. For example, if saving 5 percent per year starting in your early 20s would get you to your retirement goal, waiting until your 30s may mean socking away 10 percent; waiting until your 40s, 20 percent; beyond that, the numbers get troubling.

Taking advantage of saving and investing in tax-deductible retirement accounts should be your number-one financial priority (unless you're still paying off high-interest consumer debt on credit cards or an auto loan).

Retirement accounts should be called tax-reduction accounts. If they were called that, people might be more excited about contributing to them. For many people, avoiding higher taxes is the motivating force that opens the account and starts the contributions. Suppose you're paying about 35 percent between federal and state income taxes on your last dollars of income (see Chapter 10 to determine your tax bracket). For most of the retirement accounts described in this chapter, for every $1,000 you contribute, you save yourself about $350 in taxes in the year that you make the contribution. You can invest this savings until it's taxed when withdrawn in retirement. Some employers will match a portion of your contributions to company-sponsored plans, such as 401(k) plans — getting you extra dollars for free.

On average, most people need about 70 to 80 percent of their annual preretirement income throughout retirement to maintain their standard of living. If you haven't recently thought about what your retirement goals are, looked into what you can expect from Social Security (okay, cease the giggling), or calculated how much you should be saving for retirement, now's the time to do it. My book, *Personal Finance For Dummies,* 6th Edition (Wiley), goes through all the necessary details and explains how to come up with more money to invest.

When you earn employment income (or receive alimony), you have the option of putting money away in a retirement account that compounds without taxation until you withdraw the money. With many retirement accounts, you can elect to use mutual funds as your retirement account investment option. And if you have retirement money in some other investment option, you may be able to transfer it into a mutual fund company (see Chapter 16).

If you have access to more than one type of retirement account, prioritize which accounts to use by what they give you in return. Your first contributions should be to employer-based plans that match your contributions. After that, contribute to any other employer or self-employed plans that allow tax-deductible contributions. If you've contributed the maximum possible to tax-deductible plans or don't have access to such plans, contribute to an IRA. The following sections include the major types of accounts and explain how to determine whether you're eligible for them.

401(k) plans

For-profit companies typically offer 401(k) plans, which typically allow you to save up to $16,500 per year (tax year 2010), $22,000 for those 50 and older. Your contributions to a 401(k) are excluded from your reported income and are free from federal and state income taxes but not from FICA (Social Security) taxes.

Absolutely don't miss out on contributing to your employer's 401(k) plan if your employer matches a portion of your contributions. Your company, for example, may match half of your first 6 percent of contributions (so you save a lot of taxes and get a bonus from the company). Check with your company's benefits department for your plan's details.

Smaller companies (those with fewer than 100 employees) can consider offering 401(k) plans, too. In the past, administering a 401(k) was prohibitively expensive for smaller companies. If your company is interested in this option, contact a mutual fund organization, such as T. Rowe Price, Vanguard, or Fidelity, or a discount brokerage house, such as Charles Schwab or TD Ameritrade.

403(b) plans

Many nonprofit organizations offer 403(b) plans to their employees. As with a 401(k), your contributions are federal- and state-tax-deductible. The 403(b) plans often are referred to as *tax-sheltered annuities,* the name for insurance-company investments that satisfy the requirements for 403(b) plans. *No-load* (commission-free) mutual funds can be used in 403(b) plans. Check which mutual fund companies your employer offers you to invest through — I hope you have access to the better ones covered in Chapter 9.

Employees of nonprofit organizations generally are allowed to contribute up to 20 percent or $16,500 of their salaries ($22,000 for those individuals 50 and older) — whichever is less. Employees who have 15 or more years of service may be allowed to contribute more. Ask your employee benefits department or the investment provider for the 403(b) plan (or your tax adviser) about eligibility requirements and details about your personal contribution limits.

If you work for a nonprofit or public-sector organization that doesn't offer this benefit, make a fuss and insist on it. Nonprofit organizations have no excuse not to offer a 403(b) plan to their employees. This type of plan includes virtually no out-of-pocket setup expenses or ongoing accounting fees like a 401(k) (see the preceding section). The only requirement is that the organization must deduct the appropriate contribution from employees' paychecks and send the money to the investment company that handles the 403(b) plan. (Some state and local governments offer plans that are quite similar to 403(b) plans and are known as Section 457 plans.)

Small business plans

If you're self-employed or a small business owner, you can establish your own retirement savings plans. Simplified employee pension individual retirement account (SEP-IRA) plans require little paperwork to set up. They allow you to sock away 20 percent of your self-employment income (business revenue minus expenses) up to a maximum of $49,000 per year. Each year, you decide the amount you want to contribute — you have no minimums. Your contributions to a SEP-IRA are deducted from your taxable income, saving you big-time on federal and state taxes. As with other retirement plans, your money compounds without taxation until withdrawal.

Keogh (profit sharing) plans are another retirement savings option for the self-employed. They can and should be established through the no-load fund providers recommended in this book. Keogh plans require a bit more paperwork to set up and administer than SEP-IRAs do. (I show you the differences in Chapter 16.) Keoghs now have the same contribution limits as SEP-IRAs — 20 percent of your self-employment income (revenue less your expenses), up to a maximum of $49,000 per year.

Keogh plans allow business owners to maximize the contributions to which they're entitled relative to employees in two ways:

- ✔ Keogh plans allow vesting schedules, which require employees to remain with the company a number of years before they earn the right to their retirement account balances. If an employee leaves prior to being fully vested, the unvested balance reverts to the remaining plan participants.

- ✔ Keogh plans allow for Social Security integration. Integration effectively enables high-income earners (usually the owners) to receive larger percentage contributions for their accounts than the less highly compensated employees. The logic behind this benefit is that Social Security taxes top out when you earn more than $106,800 (for tax year 2010). Social Security integration allows you to make up for this ceiling.

When establishing your Keogh plan at a mutual fund or discount brokerage, ask what features its plans allow — especially if you have employees and are interested in vesting schedules and Social Security integration.

Individual Retirement Accounts (IRAs)

Anyone with employment (or alimony) income can contribute to Individual Retirement Accounts (IRAs). You may contribute up to $5,000 each year ($6,000 if you're age 50 and older) or the amount of your employment or alimony income if it's less than these amounts in a year. If you're a nonworking spouse, you may be eligible to contribute into a spousal IRA.

Your contributions to an IRA might be tax deductible. For the tax year 2010, check out these eligibilities:

- ✔ If you're single and your adjusted gross income (AGI) is $56,000 or less for the year, you can deduct your IRA contribution.

- ✔ If you're married and file your taxes jointly, you're entitled to a full IRA deduction if your AGI is $89,000 per year or less.

If you make more than these amounts, you can take a full IRA deduction if you aren't an active participant in any retirement plan. To know for certain whether you're an active participant is to look at the W-2 form that your employer sends you early in the year to file with your tax returns. Little boxes indicate whether you're an active participant in a pension or deferred-compensation plan. If either box is checked, you're an active participant.

If you're a single-income earner with an AGI above $56,000 but below $66,000, or part of a couple with an AGI above $89,000 but below $109,000, you're eligible for a partial IRA deduction, even if you're an active participant. The size of the IRA deduction that you may claim depends on where you fall in the income range. For example, a single-income earner at $61,000 is entitled to half ($2,500) of the full IRA deduction (assuming they are under age 50) because his or her income falls halfway between $56,000 and $66,000. (***Note:*** These thresholds are for tax year 2010. They'll increase in the tax years ahead.)

If you yourself are not an active participant in a retirement, but your spouse is an active participant, then you may take a full IRA if your AGI is $167,000 or less. A partial is allowed in this case if your AGI is between $167,000 to $177,000.

If you can't deduct your contribution to a standard IRA account, consider making a nondeductible contribution to a newer type of IRA account called the *Roth IRA.* Single taxpayers with an AGI of $105,000 or less and joint filers with an AGI of $167,000 or less can contribute up to $5,000 per year to a Roth IRA ($6,000 for those individuals age 50 and older). Although the contribution isn't deductible, earnings inside the account are shielded from taxes, and unlike a standard IRA, qualified withdrawals from the account, including investment earnings, are free from income tax.

To make a qualified withdrawal from a Roth IRA, you must be at least 59½ and have held the account for at least five years. An exception to the age rule is made for first-time homebuyers, who are allowed to withdraw up to $10,000 toward the down payment on a principal residence.

The white picket fence — saving for a home

A place to call your own is certainly the most tangible element of the American dream. Not only does a home generally appreciate in value over the long term, but it also should keep you dry in a thunderstorm (assuming, of course, that you have a good roof!).

To get the best mortgage terms for a house, you should aim for making a down payment of 20 percent of the purchase price. (For a $250,000 home, that's $50,000.) So unless you have some other sources available (such as a loan from your parents), you have some saving up to do.

If you're looking to buy a home soon, then a money market fund is the best place to store your down payment money (see Chapter 11). If your target purchase date is in a few years, then consider a short-term bond fund (see Chapter 12). In the rare case that you start saving a decade or more in advance, you can choose a balanced mix of stocks and bonds.

The ivory tower — saving for college

A college education for the kiddies is certainly part of the American dream today — not surprising when you consider that a college degree has quickly replaced the high school diploma as the entrance bar to the U.S. job market. Unfortunately, the financial services industry has fully exploited the opportunity to deepen parental anxiety over educational expenses. Although mutual funds can help send your kids off to college, their specific role may be different from what you'd expect.

Saving in your own name

Few subject areas have more misinformation and bad advice than what is dished out on investing for your children's college expenses. Too many investment firms publish free guides that contain poor advice and scare tactics. Their basic premise is that, by the time your tyke reaches age 18 or so, college is going to cost more money than you could possibly imagine. Thus, you'd better start saving a lot of money as soon as possible. Otherwise, you'll have to look your 18-year-old in the eyes some day and say, "Sorry, we can't afford to send you to the college you have your heart set on."

Yes, college is expensive, and it's not getting cheaper. But what the financial services companies don't like to tell you is that you don't have to pay for all of it yourself. Thanks to financial aid, most people don't. By financial aid, I mean more than just grants and scholarships; I'm also talking about low-cost loans, which are by far and away the most common form of aid.

What's really sad about the scare tactics some investment companies use is that these tactics effectively encourage parents to establish investment accounts in their children's names. The drawbacks for doing so are twofold:

Tips on how to afford college

So, how are you going to be able to afford sending your children to Prestige U. or even Budget Community College? Gain financial aid and plug the gap between what college costs are and what you can afford with these tips:

✔ **Fund your retirement accounts first.** Self-centered as it may seem, you're really doing yourself and your kids a tremendous financial favor if you fully fund your retirement accounts before tucking away money for college. First, you save yourself taxes. As discussed in the section, "The golden egg — investing for retirement" earlier in this chapter, 401(k), 403(b), SEP-IRA, and Keogh plans give you an immediate tax deduction at the federal and state levels. And after the money is inside these retirement accounts, it compounds without taxation over the years.

Second, the more money you save and invest outside retirement accounts, the less financial aid (loans and grants) your child qualifies for. Strange as it may seem, the financial aid system ignores 100 percent of the money you invest *inside* retirement accounts.

✔ **Apply for financial aid.** College is expensive and, unless you're affluent, you and your child will need to borrow some money. Consider these educational loans as investments in your family. Much financial aid, including grants and loans, is available regardless of need, so don't make the mistake of not applying and researching.

The financial aid system examines your income, assets and liabilities, number of children in college, and stuff like that. Based on an analysis, the financial aid process may determine that you can afford

to spend, for example, $17,000 per year on college for your child. That doesn't mean that your child can only consider schools that cost up to that amount. In fact, if your son or daughter desires to go to a $48,000-per-year private school, loans and grants may be able to cover the difference between what the financial aid system says you can afford and what the college costs. If you don't apply for aid, you may never know what you and your child are missing out on.

✔ **Investigate all your options.** In addition to financial aid, you may be able to use other sources to help pay college expenses. If you're a homeowner, for example, you may be able to tap in to home equity. The kids' grandparents also may be financially able to help out. (It's better for the grandparents to hold the money themselves until it's needed.)

✔ **Teach your children the value of working, saving, and investing.** If you're one of the fortunate few who can pay for the full cost of college yourself, more power to you. But even if you can, you may not be doing as well by your children as you may like to believe. When children set goals and find how to work, save, and make wise investments, these values pay dividends for a lifetime. So does your spending time with your children instead of working so hard to try and save enough to pay for 100 percent of their college costs.

Encourage your children to share in the cost of their education. They can contribute in different ways, either upfront or by paying off some of the outstanding loans after they graduate. Either way, your children will appreciate their education more.

✔ **You limit the amount of financial aid for which your child is eligible.** The financial aid system heavily penalizes money held in your child's name by assuming that about 20 percent of the money in your child's name (for example, in custodial accounts) should be used annually toward college costs. By contrast, only 6 percent of the nonretirement money held in your name is considered available for college expenses annually.

✔ **You give your child free rein over your hard-earned investment.** When you place money in your child's name, he or she has a legal right to that money in most states at age 18 or 21. That means that your 18- or 21-year-old could spend the money on an around-the-world junket, a new sports car, or anything else his or her young mind can dream up. Because you have no way of knowing in advance how responsible your children will be when they reach ages 18 or 21, you're better off keeping money earmarked for their college educations out of their names.

If you can and want to pay for the full cost of your child's education, you have an income tax incentive to put money in your child's name. Under what's known as the *kiddie tax* system, income generated by investments held in your child's name is usually taxed at a lower rate than your own. But remember that by saving money in a child's name, you're reducing that child's chances for financial aid. That's why I say don't invest in your child's name unless you want to pay for your child's full college costs yourself.

You get the benefits of tax-deferred growth and professional investment management by mutual fund companies through 529 plans. You may derive some state tax perks as well using a 529 plan. Because the money in 529 plans is earmarked for college, however, investing in these plans may have some negative consequences on college financial aid.

Using mutual funds for college cost funding

To keep up with or stay ahead of college price increases (which are rising faster than overall inflation), you must invest for growth. At the same time, you have to keep an eye on your time horizon; kids grow up fast (see "Reaching Your Goals with Funds" earlier in the chapter.)

The younger your child is, the more years you have before you need to tap the money and, therefore, the greater the risk. A simple rule: Take a number between 30 (if you're aggressive) and 50 (if you're more conservative) and add that to your child's age. Got that number? That's the percentage you should put in bonds; the rest should go into stocks. Be sure to continually adjust the mix as your child gets older.

For a list of good stock and bond funds to invest in, see Chapters 11 and 12. Pay particular attention to *hybrid funds,* which invest in both stocks and bonds and may already reflect your desired mix. If you want to find out more about getting your finances in order and planning for college costs, read my book *Personal Finance For Dummies,* 6th Edition (Wiley).

Part II
Evaluating Alternatives to Funds

The 5th Wave   By Rich Tennant

"That's right, Martin's talking to someone right now about some sort of offshore investment."

In this part . . .

This part covers alternatives to mutual funds. Some folks consider picking their own stocks and bonds, whereas others want in on the new exchange-traded fund craze. High rollers may look longingly at hedge funds or other managed money alternatives. This part covers them all and more and explains the good and bad of each and when and how to use them.

Chapter 4

Selecting Your Own Stocks and Bonds

. . . .

In This Chapter

▶ Understanding the pros and cons of being your own investment manager

▶ Exploring how to pick your own stocks and bonds

. . . .

*I*nvesting in stocks and bonds via mutual funds is one of several ways to tap in to stocks and bonds. Some investors believe that they don't need mutual funds and that they should go and directly invest in their own stocks and bonds. However, doing so is often much riskier than relying on mutual funds. This chapter discusses why people choose their own stocks and bonds and what you need to do if you decide to do so.

Choosing Your Own Stocks and Bonds

According to numerous books, newsletters, Web sites, and articles, mutual funds are *not* the place to be. They're boring, conservative, and prone to mediocre returns. According to the pronouncements of these gurus, you can get rich quick by investing in these individual stocks.

Not only do these pundits say that investing in individual stocks provides Himalayan returns . . .

"How we beat the stock market — and how you can, too. 23.4 percent annual return." — subtitle of *The Beardstown Ladies' Common-Sense Investment Guide*

Novices can ". . . nearly double the S&P 500 posting returns in excess of 20 percent per year . . . you might be able to fish out greater than 30 percent per year on your own without assuming considerably greater risk." — David and Tom Gardner, *The Motley Fool Investment Guide*

"Forget bonds . . . real estate . . . build a portfolio entirely of stocks. Returns an annual average of 34 percent." — Matt Seto, 17 years old, *The Whiz Kid of Wall Street's Investment Guide*

"I have been able to obtain fantastic returns on so many stock market plays: 260,000 percent annualized one-hour returns; 10,680 percent annualized in two days and so many more . . . These trades are sort of like a magic trick. At first it seems 'stupendous' — otherworldly. But as you learn the trick, you say 'it's a piece of cake.'" — Wade Cook, *Stock Market Miracles*

. . . but they also say that anyone can do it with little effort . . .

"It's not an exaggeration to say that fifth graders can wallop the market after one month of analysis. You can too." — *The Motley Fool Investment Guide*

"An amateur who devotes a small amount of study to companies in an industry he or she knows something about can outperform 95 percent of the paid experts who manage mutual funds, plus have fun in doing it." — Peter Lynch, *Beating the Street*

Do the stock specialists' claims sound too good to be true? Well, they are.

Beware the claims of stock-picking gurus

It's easy to dismiss the outrageousness of the claims made by someone like Wade Cook in the previous section. Even if you don't know that Cook was for many years in trouble with securities regulators and the courts (and is now serving prison time), your common sense tells you that five- and six-digit returns are well outside the realm of reasonable expectations for stock performance.

But what about the more believable performance claims, in the range of 20 and 30 percent, that can so easily dupe an investor into thinking they're true — like the annualized return of 23.4 percent claimed by the Beardstown Ladies?

The Beardstown investment club's claim of 23.4 percent annualized returns made me suspicious. Stocks historically return just 10 percent per year, yet this club, in its book, was claiming to ". . . have been outperforming mutual funds and professional money managers 3 to 1." When the club was unwilling to document its performance claims, I assumed they were false.

Turns out its claims were indeed bogus. Shane Tritsch, a reporter for *Chicago* magazine, wrote a piece entitled "Bull Marketing" in which he exposed gross inaccuracies in how the Beardstown investment club calculated its stock market returns. Tritsch was tipped off to potential problems by a note that was added to the copyright page of the paperback edition of the Beardstown book that said that the club's 23.4 percent annualized returns were determined "by calculating the increase in their total club balance over time. Because this increase includes the dues that the members pay regularly, this return may be different from the return that might be calculated for a mutual fund...."

May be different? Indeed. Translated, the disclosure was saying that the 23-plus percent returns were being goosed by including new investment principal (regular dues' payments). Using documents from the investment club that were provided by a *Wall Street Journal* reporter, a senior research analyst named Jim Raker, from mutual fund publisher Morningstar, told me that he calculates that the investment club earned a return of a mere 9 percent per year — a far cry from the 23-plus percent returns claimed by the club.

Even worse, though, is that the Beardstown investment club *under*performed the market. For the period in question (from 1983 to 1992), while the Beardstown club actually earned just 9 percent per year, the Standard & Poor's 500 index — the widely followed index for the U.S. stock market — returned about 16 percent. In fact, if you'd invested in lower-risk bonds, you would've earned nearly 12 percent per year and still outperformed the stock picks of the Beardstown club!

Whenever an author, an investment newsletter, or an investment manager claims to have produced a particular rate of return, especially a market-beating return, I always ask for proof before I'm willing to put the claim in print myself. Otherwise, how do I know whether the claims are real or advertising hype?

As for Peter Lynch, who states in his book that an amateur stock picker can easily beat 95 percent of the pros, shame on him! Widely regarded as one of the best mutual fund managers in his day, Lynch knows more than anyone how much hard work goes into beating the market. In fact, during the years that Lynch piloted Fidelity's Magellan fund, he was known for his workaholic 70- and 80-hour workweeks. He stated publicly that the primary reason he retired early was to spend more time with his family. That leaves everyone else to question: He worked this hard to do something that he says amateurs can do with ease and that you, as an investor, don't really need his skills for?

The notion that most average people and noninvestment professionals can invest in individual stocks with minimal effort and beat the best full-time, experienced money managers is, how should I say, ludicrous and absurd. But it does seem to appeal to some people's egos — until the returns come in (or don't come in, as the case may be).

Stock picking with Jim Cramer

If you ever watch CNBC, you've likely come across Jim Cramer, a former hedge fund manager, who now hosts an investment show at the network and operates a Web site among other endeavors. If you've seen it, he yells and screams and jumps around while pounding on various sound-producing buttons.

Cramer rose to fame through his strongly opinionated buy-and-sell recommendations on regular CNBC stock market programming and his supposed extraordinary investment returns from his days running a hedge fund bearing his name. But there's a problem: Despite repeated requests from me, Cramer's former and current firms have been unable (and unwilling) to produce any independently audited tracking of Cramer's claimed returns.

Compounding this lack of any proof is a uniformly poor to mediocre track record of his stock picks and pans in recent years. Several independent tracking services have found that his stock market predictions have underperformed the broad market averages. (Please see the "Guru Watch" section of my Web site, www.erictyson.com, for the details on Cramer and other investing pundits.)

Also, I had no trouble finding numerous folks who shelled out $400 yearly for his online newsletter and were greatly disappointed. One reader said, "I got caught up in watching his nightly show and then I paid for his Action Alerts service. That service sends e-mail alerts every day telling you what to buy and sell. Well after nine months, I lost a lot of money, and his portfolio is currently showing a 1.3% gain for the year to date (ever notice he doesn't mention that on his shows!). I could've just purchased the S&P 500 and would be way ahead. His trading ideas do not work, and his recommendations to not use mechanical stop loss trades have resulted in huge losses in my portfolio."

Know the drawbacks of investing in individual securities

The stock-picking cheerleaders cite plenty of reasons and make hyped claims to get you to invest in individual stocks. But they're loath to mention the drawbacks of selecting and trading individual securities. You won't buy their books and newsletters or visit their Web sites if they can't promise you effortless riches, so you may not openly get the following information from the "stock-picking-is-easy" writers:

✔ **Stock picking takes significant research time and expense.** Before buying an individual security (stock or bond), you should know a great deal about the company you're investing in. Relevant questions that you need to answer include

- What products or services does the company sell?

- What are the company's prospects for future growth and profitability?

- How does the company's performance compare to its competitors' performances — both recently and over the long haul?

- Are technological or other changes in the works that might harm or improve its business?

- How much debt does the company have?

You need to do your homework on these questions, not only before you make your initial investment, but also on a continuing basis as long as you hold an investment. Gathering this information and accessing quality research on a company take time and money. And you have to conduct this legwork for every company that you consider investing in. That's how Lynch filled up his marathon workweeks as a fund manager.

Be honest with yourself. If you're really going to research and monitor your individual securities, the extra work ultimately will take time away from other pursuits. In worst-case situations, I've seen busy people spend almost as many hours on the weekend and in the evenings with their portfolios as they do with family and friends. If you can really afford the time for this type of hobby, more power to you. But remember, no one I know of has ever said on her deathbed, "I wish I had spent more time watching my investments." You only get one chance to live your life — once squandered, your time is gone forever.

✔ **Stock trading incurs higher transaction costs.** Even when you use a discount broker (described in Chapter 9), the commissions you pay to buy or sell securities are higher (as a percentage of the amount invested) than what a fund company pays. Note two exceptions to the rule that individual security purchases cost too much:

- You can purchase government bonds directly from the Federal Reserve without charge.

- Deep-discount brokers (see Chapter 9) can be quite cheap for wealthy investors making large purchases.

✔ **Individual stocks offer less likelihood of diversification.** Unless you have several hundred thousand dollars to invest in dozens of different securities, you probably can't afford to develop a diversified portfolio. For example, when investing in stocks, you should hold stock in companies belonging to different industries, in different companies within an industry, and so on. Not properly diversifying adds to the risk of losing your shirt.

✔ **Individual stocks bring more accounting and bookkeeping chores.**
When you invest in individual securities outside retirement accounts,
you must keep track of your purchase and dividend history (if you
reinvest them). Every time you sell a specific security, you must report
that transaction on your tax return.

Even if you pay someone else to complete your tax return, you still have
the hassle of keeping track of statements and receipts. (On the plus side,
however, *you* control selling decisions with individual securities; with
funds, managers who trade can lead to capital gains distributions for
you. As I discuss in Chapter 10, you can select mutual funds that are tax
friendly for your situation, including funds that are managed, so as to
minimize or even eliminate capital gains distributions.)

Understand the psychology of selecting stocks

Some folks just don't, won't, or can't enjoy having all their money tied up in
mutual funds. Some people say that funds are, well, kind of boring. It's true
that following the trials, tribulations, successes, and failures of a favorite
company can provide you plenty of excitement (sometimes more than you
want). A fund, on the other hand, is a little more abstract. You pour money
into it and don't have specific corporate dramas to follow.

Over the years, among investors who prefer to invest their portfolios in
individual securities, I've noticed some common characteristics:

✔ **The boaster:** You enjoy going to parties and telling of your successes in
the stock market. Although the thought has never (hopefully) crossed
your mind of sending copies of a brokerage statement to friends and
relatives, you've been known on more than a few occasions to offer
unsolicited stock tips and investment advice.

✔ **The controller:** You hate delegating jobs to others, especially important
ones, because no one does as good a job as you do. Investing much or
all of your money in mutual funds and leaving all the investment decisions
to the fund manager won't make you a happy camper. You may also
believe that you can sidestep a market slide and get back in before
prices skyrocket.

✔ **The free spirit:** You're the type who says, "I don't care if there are trillions
invested in mutual funds. I don't care if everyone's using word processors
rather than typewriters." You like to be just a little bit different and
independent.

How to Pick Your Own Stocks and Bonds

If you really want to invest in individual stocks and bonds, I suggest that you limit your purchase of individual securities to no more than 20 percent of the *total* money you've invested in stocks and bonds (including those you've invested in via mutual funds). Be realistic as to why you're investing in them. And before you plunk down too much money in stocks and bonds of your own choosing, remember the sage words of Jack Bogle, who's often called the mutual fund investor's best friend:

> "Attempting to build an investment program around a handful of individual securities is, for all but the most exceptional investors, a fool's errand . . . Specific stock bets should be made, if at all, in small portions, and more for the excitement of the game than for the profit."

Yes, Bogle was the founder and former CEO of a large mutual fund company, Vanguard. But, no, his comments aren't self-serving: Vanguard also operates a discount brokerage company that handles individual securities trades for customers who want to do them.

In the long haul, you're not going to earn higher returns than full-time professional money managers who invest in the securities of the same type and risk level that you are. As with hiring a contractor for home remodeling, you need to do your homework to find good fund managers. Even if you think that you can do as well as the best, remember that even superstar money managers like Peter Lynch have beaten the market averages by only a few percentage points per year.

In my experience, more than a few otherwise smart, fun-loving people choose to invest in individual securities because they think that they're smarter or luckier than the rest. If you're like most people, I can safely say that, in the long run, your individually selected stocks and bonds won't outperform those of a full-time investment professional.

I've noticed a distinct contrast between the sexes on this issue (which is backed up by research). Perhaps because of differences in how people are raised, testosterone levels, or whatever, men tend to have more of a problem taming their egos and admitting that they're better off turning the stock and bond selection over to a pro. Maybe this trait is genetically linked to not wanting to ask for directions!

Before you set out to compete in the investment world, get smarter and wiser. The latest edition of my book, *Investing For Dummies* (Wiley), explains how to analyze company financial statements and compare and select stocks and bonds as well as use the best investment research sources such as Value Line.

Also, don't overlook the opportunity to piggyback from all the research and knowledge of the best money managers. By using the lists of best funds recommended in this book, you can use those funds' reports to figure out what stocks and bonds some of the most talented money managers in the world are buying. (*Note:* The listing of a fund's portfolio still could be several months out of date because of the way funds issue their reports.)

Should you join an investment club?

Investment clubs are a little bit like having your own hands-on mutual fund. Each club member chips in some money. Then the group gets together for periodic meetings to discuss stocks and to make investment decisions. (Although investment clubs could, of course, select other investments, such as bonds, most clubs choose stocks.)

These groups can be valuable as an educational forum if you utilize good information sources. If the group members are somewhat clueless and the meetings are rambling, these groups can end up degenerating into the blind leading the blind.

Investment clubs may have social or hobby value (which are most clubs' major benefits), but they can hurt your checkbook more than they help:

✔ The members of investment clubs are part-time amateurs. You could end up making some poor decisions and losing money (or not making nearly as much as you would if you'd been in some good mutual funds).

✔ It's highly unlikely that everyone in the group is in the same tax situation. Thus, the club's investments may work for some members' tax situations but not for others'.

✔ Beware of stockbrokers (and others trolling for prospective clients) who've been known to participate in investment clubs and volunteer as leaders. Although their participation may be harmless, more often than not, these brokers have a hidden agenda to reel in new business clients.

Consider forming a financial reading club and discussion group rather than an investment club. You can get together and discuss financial periodicals, books, and investment strategies. This way, you can advance your level of financial knowledge, find out about new resources from others, and enjoy the fun, camaraderie, and other benefits that come from doing things in a group.

Better yet, join a bowling league or a softball team and leave the investing to fund managers!

Chapter 5

Exchange-Traded Funds and Other Fund Lookalikes

*T*he hallmarks of the investment and economic system are constant change, innovation, and choice. Index mutual funds, which track a particular market index (see Chapter 10) and the best of which feature low costs, have been around for decades.

Exchange-traded funds (ETFs) represent a twist on index funds — ETFs trade like stocks do and offer some potential advantages over funds. However, some cheerleaders pitching ETFs gloss over drawbacks to ETFs and fail to disclose their agenda in promoting ETFs.

Some other fund wannabes compete for your investment dollars too. This chapter offers the straight scoop on these alternatives.

Understanding Exchange-Traded Funds

For many years after their introduction in the 1970s, index mutual funds got little respect and money. Various pundits and those folks with a vested financial interest in protecting the status quo, such as firms charging high fees for money management, heaped criticism on index funds. (As I explain in Chapter 13, index funds replicate and track the performance of a particular market index, such as the Standard & Poor's 500 index of 500 large company U.S. stocks.) Critics argued that index funds would produce sub-par returns. Investors who've used index funds have been quite happy to experience their funds typically outperforming about 70 percent of the actively managed funds over extended time periods.

In recent years, increasing numbers of financial firms have developed *exchange-traded funds* (ETFs). Most ETFs are, essentially, index funds with one major difference: They trade like stocks on a stock exchange. The first ETF was created and traded on the American Stock Exchange in 1993 and was known as a Spider. (It tracked the Standard & Poor's 500 index.) Now hundreds of ETFs trade comprising about $700 billion — a large sum indeed — but that's less than 7 percent of the total invested in mutual funds.

Before you decide to invest in ETFs, take a moment to read this section. It explains the advantages and disadvantages of investing in ETFs and helps you wade through the many ETFs to find the best one for you.

Understanding ETF advantages

Like index funds, the promise of ETFs is low management fees. I say promise because when evaluating ETFs, you must remember that the companies creating and selling ETFs, which are mostly large Wall Street investment firms, are doing it to make a nice profit for their firm. Although the best index funds charge annual fees of less than 0.2 percent, the vast majority of ETFs actually charge fees much greater than that.

Take a look at Table 5-1 for an analysis that I recently conducted of ETF expense ratios.

Table 5-1	An Analysis of ETF Expense Ratios
Expense Ratio	*Percentage of ETFs*
0.60% and higher	47%
0.50% to 0.59%	14%
0.40% to 0.49%	12%
0.30% to 0.39%	7%
0.25% to 0.29%	7%
0.20% to 0.24%	6%
0.15% to 0.19%	2%
0.10% to 0.14%	4%
0.07% to 0.09%	1%

The vast majority of ETFs have expense ratios far higher than the best index funds. I compare the best index funds with the best ETFs (which do have low expense ratios) in the section, "Identifying the best ETFs," later in this chapter.

In addition to possible slightly lower expenses, the best ETFs have one possible additional advantage over traditional index funds: Because ETFs may not be forced to redeem shares to cash and recognize taxable gains (which can happen with an index fund), they may be tax friendlier for non-retirement account investors. (***Note:*** ETFs do have to sometimes sell and buy new holdings as adjustments are made to the underlying index that an ETF tracks.)

If you can't meet the minimum investment amounts for index funds (which are typically several thousand dollars), you face no minimums when buying an ETF. However, you must factor in the brokerage costs to buy and sell ETF shares through your favorite brokerage firm, and be sure that those fees don't greatly boost your costs. For example, if you pay a $10 transaction fee through an online broker to buy $1,000 worth of an ETF, $10 may not sound like a lot but it represents 1.0 percent of your investment and wipes out the supposed cost advantage of investing in an ETF. Because of the brokerage costs, ETFs aren't a good vehicle for investors who seek to make regular monthly investments.

Eyeing ETF drawbacks

Meanwhile, some of the drawbacks to ETFs include the following:

- **Three-day settlement waiting period:** A possible disadvantage with ETFs is that like stocks, you have a three-day settlement process when selling shares. So, for example, if you sell shares of an ETF on Monday, you won't have the proceeds to invest into a regular mutual fund until Thursday. (This delay wouldn't be a problem if you're going back into another ETF or buying a stock — because a purchase order placed on Monday wouldn't settle until Thursday.) If you're out of the market for several days, the market price can move significantly higher, wiping out any supposed savings from a low-expense ratio.

- **Potential fees for dividend and capital gain reinvestments:** With a traditional mutual fund you can without cost reinvest dividend and capital gains distributions into more shares of the fund. However, with an ETF, you may have to pay for this service, or it may not be available through the broker that you use.

- **Disproportionate amount of stocks:** One problem with a number of the indexes that ETFs track (and with some index funds) is that certain stocks make up a disproportionately large share of the index. For example, I don't care for the Standard & Poor's 500 index because each of the 500 stocks' composition in the index is driven by each stock's portion of total market value. Check out Table 5-2 that shows the composition of the index at the end of 1999. This list mostly represented a who's who of many overpriced technology stocks that subsequently got clobbered in the early 2000s bear market.

Table 5-2	The Companies of the Standard & Poor's 500 Index at the End of 1999		
Stock	*Rank in Index*	*Market Value*	*Percent of Index*
Microsoft Corp	1	604,078	4.92%
General Electric	2	507,734	4.14%
Cisco Systems	3	366,481	2.99%
Wal-Mart Stores	4	307,843	2.51%
Exxon Mobil	5	278,218	2.27%
Intel Corp	6	274,998	2.24%
Lucent Technologies	7	234,982	1.91%
IBM	8	194,447	1.58%
Citigroup Inc	9	187,734	1.53%
America Online	10	169,606	1.38%

✔ **Invested segments too narrow:** Many of the newer ETFs coming out invest in narrow segments, such as one specific industry or one foreign country. As with sector mutual funds (see Chapter 13), such funds undermine the diversification value of fund investing and tend to have relatively high fees. Morningstar, an investment research company, says, ". . . ETFs offer new opportunities to sap returns by racking up transaction costs and/or chasing short-term trends."

✔ **Excessive risks and costs with leverage:** In recent years, ETF issuers have come out with increasingly risky and costly ETFs. One particular class of ETFs I especially dislike are so-called *leveraged ETFs*. What these ETFs purport to do is magnify the move of a particular index — for example, the Standard & Poors 500 stock index — by double or triple. So, a double-leveraged S&P 500 ETF is supposed to increase by 10 percent for every 5 percent increase in the S&P 500 index. *Inverse leveraged ETFs* are supposed to move in the opposite direction of a given index. So, for example, a double-leveraged inverse S&P 500 ETF is supposed to increase by 10 percent for every 5 percent decrease in the S&P 500 index.

My investigations of whether the leveraged ETFs actually deliver on their objectives shows that they don't, not even close. For example, in the two-year period ending in early 2010, one double-inverse S&P 500 ETF (brought to my attention by a reader who owned and asked me about it) fell by 43 percent, a period during which it should have increased about 28 percent because the S&P 500 index actually fell by 14 percent.

Seeing the pros and cons of trading ETFs

One supposed advantage of trading ETFs is that, unlike the regular index mutual funds that I recommend in this book, you can trade (buy or sell) ETFs throughout the day when the stock market is open. When you buy or sell an index mutual fund, your transaction occurs at the closing price on the day that you place the trade (if the trade is placed before the market closes).

Sure, the flexibility sounds alluring, but consider a few drawbacks:

- ✔ **Timing your moves in and out of the stocks:** Being able to trade in and out of an ETF during the trading day isn't a necessity, nor is it even a good practice. In my experience of working with individual investors, most people find it both nerve-racking and futile to try to time their moves in and out of stocks with the inevitable fluctuations that take place during the trading day. In theory, traders want to believe that they can buy at relatively low prices and sell at relatively high prices, but that's far easier said than done.

- ✔ **Paying a brokerage commission every time you buy or sell shares:** With no-load index funds, you generally don't pay fees to buy and sell. But with ETFs, because you're actually placing a trade on a stock exchange, you pay a brokerage commission every time you trade. For example, if you buy an ETF with a seemingly low expense ratio of 0.1 percent and you pay $10 to trade the ETF through an online broker, that's equal to paying two years' worth of management fees if you invest $5,000 in the ETF!

- ✔ **Figuring out if the current price on an ETF is above or below the actual value of the securities it holds:** Because ETFs fluctuate in price based on supply and demand, when placing a trade during the trading day, you face the complication of trying to determine whether the current price on an ETF is above or below the actual value. With an index fund, you know that the price at which your trade was executed equals the exact market value of the securities it holds.

Because ETFs trade like stocks, you can use limit order and stop loss orders as well as sell them short or trade them on margin. I generally don't recommend these strategies for nonprofessional investors.

Identifying the best ETFs

For the vast majority of investors, you don't need to complicate your lives by investing in ETFs. Only use them if you're a more advanced investor who understands index funds and you have found a superior ETF to an index fund you're interested in.

Beware of "financial advisers" in love with ETFs

I began work as a financial adviser in 1990. I was just about the only practitioner at the time who worked solely on an hourly basis. Most of the fee-based advisers at that time managed their client's portfolios by using mutual funds. I was struck by the fact that many advisers didn't use or recommend low-cost index funds. In speaking with some of these advisers, I got the sense that they were somewhat threatened by index funds because the investing process was so simplified that clients might question the value in paying the adviser an ongoing fee of about 1 percent to manage their money among funds.

Interestingly, some advisers today boast that they use ETFs as the investment vehicle to manage their client's portfolio. Ironically, they crow about the low cost of ETFs. Why do some advisers now embrace and tout ETFs when they didn't advocate index funds? ETFs are complicated and new enough that advisers feel safer using them and not worry about having clients feel that they could do this on their own. Advisers who charge ongoing management fees while using ETFs aren't performing low-cost investment management. If the ETFs they're using average about 0.5 percent in annual fees, paying the adviser 1 percent per year on top of that to shift your money around among various ETFs triples your costs! See Chapter 24 for how to find a good adviser.

Be sure to check whether the ETF you're considering is selling at a premium or discount to its net asset value. (You can find this information on the ETF provider's Web site after the market's close each business day.) I strongly encourage you to employ the buy-and-hold mentality that I advocate throughout this book — don't hop in and out of ETFs. You should also only buy the ETFs that track the broader market indexes and that have the lowest expense ratios. Avoid those that track narrow industry groups or single, smaller countries. See Chapters 11 through 15 for specific ETFs that I like for specific situations.

If you're truly interested in investing in ETFs and you're a more advanced investor, make sure that you know which funds are the best ETFs. The best ETFs, like the best index funds, have low expense ratios. My top picks among the leading providers of ETFs include the following:

✔ **Vanguard:** Historically, Vanguard has been the low-cost leader with index funds and now has the lowest cost with their ETFs as well. If you're interested in finding out more about ETFs, be sure to examine Vanguard's ETFs. Vanguard also offers the Admiral Share class for bigger balance customers ($100K+) of its index funds that match the low expense ratio on their ETFs. (www.vanguard.com; ☎ 800-662-7447)

✔ **Wisdom Tree:** Developed by Wharton business professor Jeremy Siegel, this new family of indexes is weighted toward stocks paying higher dividends. These ETFs have higher fees but offer a broad family of index choices for investors seeking higher-dividend-paying stocks. *Note:* Other ETF providers do offer a number of value-oriented and higher-dividend-paying stock funds. (www.wisdomtree.com; ☎ 866-909-9473)

Two additional and large providers of ETFs include the following firms (beware that many of their ETFs are pricey or too narrowly focused):

✔ **iShares:** BlackRock has competitive expense ratios on some domestic ETFs based on quality indexes, such as Russell, Morningstar, S&P, Lehman, Dow Jones, and so on. (www.ishares.com; ☎ 800-474-2737)

✔ **State Street Global Advisors:** This group uses indexes from Dow Jones/Wilshire, S&P, Russell, and MSCI, among others. (www.ssgafunds.com; ☎ 866-787-2257)

Mimicking Closed-End Funds: Unit Investment Trusts

Unit investment trusts (UITs) have much in common with closed-end funds (discussed in Chapter 2). UITs take an amount of money (for example, $100 million) and buy a number of securities (such as 70 large-company United States stocks) that meet the objectives of the UIT. Unlike a closed-end fund (and mutual funds in general), however, a UIT does *not* make any changes to its holdings over time — it simply holds the same, fixed portfolio. This holding of a diversified portfolio can be advantageous because it reduces trading costs and possible tax bills.

With that said, UITs do suffer from the following major flaws:

✔ **Significant upfront commissions:** Brokers like to push UITs for the same reason that they like to pitch load mutual funds — for the juicy commission that they ultimately deduct upfront from your investment. Commissions are usually around 5 percent, so for every $10,000 that you invest into a UIT, $500 goes out of your investment and into the broker's pocket. Although UITs do have ongoing fees, their fees tend to be lower than those of most actively managed mutual funds — they're typically in the neighborhood of 0.2 percent per year. As an alternative, you can buy excellent no-load funds (see Chapter 7), which, because you're buying the fund directly from an investment company and without the involvement of a broker, charge you no commission. The best no-load funds also have reasonable management fees, and some charge even less than UITs charge (such as the index funds that I discuss in Chapter 10).

✔ **Lack of liquidity:** Especially in the first few years after a particular UIT is issued, you won't readily find an active market in which you can easily sell your UIT. In the event that you can find someone who's interested in buying a UIT that you're interested in selling, you may have to sell the UIT at a discount from its actual market value at the time.

✔ **Lack of ongoing management oversight:** Because UITs buy and hold a fixed set of securities until the UIT is liquidated (years down the road), they're more likely to get stuck holding some securities that end up worthless. For example, compared to the best bond mutual funds (see Chapter 12), bond UITs have had a greater tendency to end up holding bonds in companies that go bankrupt.

Customizing Your Own Funds Online

On some Web sites, various services pitch that you can invest in a chosen basket of stocks for a low fee — and without the high taxes and high fees that come with mutual fund investing. Like most political "Vote for me and not my opponent" ads, these services misrepresent both their own merits and the potential drawbacks of funds.

These "create your own funds" services pitch their investment products as a superior alternative to mutual funds. One such service calls its investment vehicles *folios,* charging you $29 per month ($290 if paid annually) to invest in folios, each of which can hold a few dozen stocks that are selected from the universe of stocks that this service makes available. The fee covers trading in your folios that may only occur during two time windows each day that the stock market is open. The folio service states that orders that are placed between 11 a.m. and 2 p.m. are processed starting at 2 p.m.; orders that are placed between 2 p.m. and 11 a.m. are processed starting at 11 a.m.

So, in addition to the burden of managing your own portfolio of stocks, you have virtually no control over the timing of your trades during the trading day. (You can place traditional orders at whatever time the market is open but you'll be assessed an additional fee of $3 per trade.)

The site also says, "Mutual funds impose fees that can be very high — and hard to calculate." I agree with that statement. However, without doing too much homework, an investor can easily avoid high-fee funds. For example, an investor can invest in the best index funds for an annual fee of 0.2 percent per year or less. Thus, an investor would need to have in excess of $150,000 invested through this folio service to come out ahead in terms of the explicit fees.

In addition, you need to be aware of additional fees. One folio service's Web site says (in fine print, of course) that it ". . . does charge for certain special services and does receive payment for order flow." You must be ready to shell out the dough if you

- ✔ Want to wire money out of your account — $30

- ✔ Need a copy of a prior statement or transaction — $10

- ✔ Hold any restricted securities (which are subject to SEC Rule 144) — $75

- ✔ Close out an account — $50

The site further warns, "Note: These are today's prices and fees, which are subject to change periodically."

You're simply not going to get the same level of service (and comfort) when dealing with a Web-site-based service as you do when dealing with the leading fund companies that I discuss in this book. The companies that I recommend have trained representatives available by phone. Understanding and evaluating the performance of self-created funds is difficult, and unlike mutual funds, these funds have no standards or easily accessible services that report and track the performance of your customized folio (see Chapter 17 for more information on adjusting your portfolio).

It seems to me that folio services are geared toward those people who want to hold individual stocks, who trade a lot, and who seek to cap their annual trading costs. Although I prefer investing in the best mutual funds, you can invest in stocks of your own choosing — as long as you do so with a long-term perspective. But if you were going to simply buy and hold individual stocks, why would you want to pay a Web-site-based service $290 per year?

Chapter 6

Hedge Funds and Other Managed Alternatives

*W*ealthier investors with large amounts to invest (typically well into the six figures) usually have more choices when it comes to investment vehicles. Some financial advisers and money management firms pitch alternatives to mutual funds to these folks.

The unbelievably wide variety of mutual funds enables you to invest in everything from short-term money market securities to corporate bonds, U.S. and international stocks, precious metals and other commodity companies, and even real estate funds. Although funds can fill many investing needs — as I discuss in Chapter 1 — you may be interested in and benefit from directly investing in things such as real estate, your own business, and many other investments.

During the early to mid 2000s, hedge funds were proliferating and promising high returns with less risk. In the prior edition of this book, I warned readers, "As with all sales pitches, you must separate fact from fiction and hype." This chapter can help you do just that if you're rolling in the dough. Plenty of hedge fund investors got burned during the financial market turmoil in the late 2000s.

Other types of privately managed investment accounts, such as wrap accounts, exist that have some things in common with mutual funds. The following sections provide some background that you need to know if you're going to consider these fund alternatives.

Hedge Funds: Extremes of Costs and Risks

Hedge funds, historically an investment reserved for big-ticket investors, are seemingly like mutual funds in that they typically invest in stocks and bonds. They have the added glamour and allure, however, of taking significant risks and gambles with their investments. Hedge funds may take risks by purchasing derivatives (see Chapter 2), or they may bet on the fall in price of particular securities by selling the securities short. (When you *short sell,* you borrow a security from a broker, sell it, and then hope to buy it back later at a lower price.) Some hedge funds even invest in other hedge funds.

This section takes a closer look at hedge funds and gives you a clear idea of what hedge funds are and what you need to know and do before you consider investing in one.

Getting the truth about hedge funds

In the prior edition of this book written in 2007, I warned, "Although hedge funds have recently been the buzz in some investment circles and some wealthier investors have been dropping money into them, they may not be the best choice for you. Hedge funds are typically a far riskier investment than your typical mutual fund. What's the hidden truth about these funds? The following list highlights some of hedge fund's dangers:"

Hedge funds have a much higher risk than mutual funds

When a hedge fund manager bets right, he can produce high returns. When he doesn't, however, the fund manager can have his head handed to him on an expensive silver platter. With short selling, because the value of the security that was sold short can rise an unlimited amount, the potential loss from buying it back at a much higher price can be horrendous. And even the most experienced investing professionals can also lose a pile of money in no time when they invest in derivatives. Hedge fund managers have also been clobbered when a previously fast rising commodity like natural gas or copper futures plunges in value.

A number of hedge funds have gone belly up when their managers guessed wrong. In other words, their investments did so poorly that investors in the fund lost all their money. As I discuss in Chapter 2, the odds of this happening with a mutual fund — particularly from one of the larger, more established companies — are nil.

Hedge funds have much higher fees than mutual funds

Hedge funds charge an annual management fee of about 1 to 2 percent and a performance fee, which typically amounts to a whopping 20 percent of a fund's profits. Veteran investment observer Jack Bogle said of hedge funds and the high fees that are extracted and paid to the hedge fund's managers (and not their customers), "Hedge funds are a compensation strategy not an investment strategy."

Hedge funds aren't subject to the same regulatory scrutiny

A *Forbes* 2004 article on the hedge fund industry entitled "The Sleaziest Show On Earth" referred to the industry as, ". . . a business rife with exorbitant fees, phony numbers, and outright thievery." During the severe stock market decline in the late 2000s, many hedge funds did poorly, and some went under or were exposed to be fraudulent Ponzi schemes, the most notorious being the fund run by the now jailed Bernie Madoff.

If that's still not enough to convince you from the perspective of one of the nation's best business magazines that caters to those affluent enough to invest in such funds, consider this: *Forbes* went on to say, "Hedge funds exist in a lawless and risky realm, exempt from the rules governing mutual funds, equities, and most other investments. Hedge funds aren't even required to keep audited books — and many don't. These risky funds often are guilty of inadequate disclosure of costs, overvaluation of holdings to goose reported performance and manager pay, and cozy ties between funds and brokers that often shortchange investors." For more about insufficient regulatory oversight of hedge funds, please see the "Investigating hedge funds" section later in this chapter.

Hedge funds have lower returns compared to mutual funds

Objective studies which I have seen, such as the one conducted by Princeton University's Burton Malkiel, present an unflattering perspective on hedge fund industry returns. In short, hedge funds have produced lower average annual returns when compared with similar mutual funds.

If you want riskier investments, you can find aggressive mutual funds, or you can buy mutual funds *on margin* through a brokerage account, meaning that you make a down payment but control a larger investment (such as when you purchase a home with a mortgage). See Chapter 16 for more about the risks and rewards of buying on margin.

Investigating hedge funds

Unfortunately, hedge funds aren't subject to the same regulatory scrutiny from the Securities and Exchange Commission (SEC) that mutual funds are. However, if you go against my advice and consider investing in a hedge fund, I suggest that you adhere to the advice the SEC offers. The following guidelines for evaluating hedge funds can help.

Read all the important documents

Take the time to read the fund's prospectus or offering memorandum and all related materials. Doing so discloses the fees, managers, and overall investment strategy.

Make sure you understand the level of risk involved in the fund's investment strategies and ensure that they're suitable to your personal investing goals, time horizons, and risk tolerance. As with any investment, the higher the potential returns, the higher the risks you must assume.

Understand how a fund's assets are valued

Funds of hedge funds and hedge funds may invest in *highly illiquid* securities (not easily and quickly converted into cash) that may be difficult to value. Moreover, many hedge funds give themselves significant discretion in valuing securities. You should understand a fund's valuation process and know the extent to which a fund's securities are valued by independent sources.

Ask questions about fees

Fees impact your return on investment. Hedge funds typically charge an asset management fee of 1 to 2 percent of assets, plus a performance fee of 20 percent of a hedge fund's profits. A *performance fee* could motivate a hedge fund manager to take greater risks in the hope of generating a larger return. Funds of hedge funds typically charge a fee for managing your assets, and some may also include a performance fee based on profits.

These fees are charged in addition to any fees paid to the underlying hedge funds. If you invest in hedge funds through a fund of hedge funds, you'll pay two layers of fees: the fees of the fund of hedge funds and the fees charged by the underlying hedge funds.

Understand any limitations on redeeming your shares

Hedge funds typically limit opportunities to redeem, or cash in, your shares (for example, to four times a year), and often impose a "lockup" period of one year or more, during which you can't cash in your shares. (By contrast, mutual funds offer daily liquidity). These should be disclosed in the hedge fund's prospectus.

Research the backgrounds of hedge fund managers

Know with whom you're investing. Make sure hedge fund managers are qualified to manage your money and find out whether they have a disciplinary history within the securities industry. You can get this information (and more) by reviewing the adviser's Form ADV. You can search for and view a firm's Form ADV by using the SEC's Investment Adviser Public Disclosure (IAPD) Web site (`www.adviserinfo.sec.gov/IAPD/Content/IapdMain/iapd_SiteMap.aspx`).

You also can get copies of Form ADV for individual advisers and firms from the investment adviser, the SEC's Public Reference Room, or (for advisers with less than $25 million in assets under management) the state securities regulator where the adviser's principal place of business is located. If you don't find the investment adviser firm in the SEC's IAPD database, be sure to call your state securities regulator or search the NASD's BrokerCheck database for any information they may have.

Don't be afraid to ask questions

You're entrusting your money to someone else. You should know where your money is going, who is managing it, how it's being invested, how you can get it back, what protections are placed on your investment, and what your rights are as an investor.

The SEC goes on to provide the following comments and suggested protections for those purchasing a hedge fund:

- ✔ **Hedge fund investors don't receive all the federal and state law protections that commonly apply to most registered investments.** For example, you won't get the same level of disclosures from a hedge fund that you'll get from registered investments. Without the disclosures that the securities laws require for most registered investments, it can be quite difficult to verify representations you may receive from a hedge fund. You should also be aware that, while the SEC may conduct examinations of any hedge fund manager that is registered as an investment adviser under the Investment Advisers Act, the SEC and other securities regulators generally have limited ability to check routinely on hedge fund activities.

- ✔ The SEC can take action against a hedge fund that defrauds investors and has brought a number of fraud cases involving hedge funds. Commonly in these cases, hedge fund advisers misrepresented their experience and the fund's track record. Other cases were classic "Ponzi schemes," where early investors were paid off to make the scheme look legitimate. In some of the cases, the hedge funds sent phony account statements to investors to camouflage the fact that their money had been stolen. *That's why it's extremely important to thoroughly check out every aspect of any hedge fund you might consider as an investment.*

✔ If you encounter a problem with your hedge fund or fund of hedge funds, you can send your complaint by using the SEC's online complaint form at www.sec.gov/complaint.shtml.

Wrap (Or Managed) Accounts: Hefty Fees

Brokerage firms (Prudential, Merrill Lynch, Salomon Smith Barney, PaineWebber, and Morgan Stanley Dean Witter) that used to sell investment products on commission now offer investment management services for an ongoing fee rather than commissions. This change is an improvement for investors because it reduces some of the conflicts of interest caused by commissions.

Wrap accounts, or *managed accounts,* go by a variety of names, but they're the same in one crucial way: For the privilege of investing your money through their chosen money managers, they charge you a percentage of the assets that they're managing for you. These accounts are quite similar to mutual funds except that the accounts don't have the same regulatory and reporting requirements as do mutual funds.

Wrap accounts management expenses are high. In fact, they're up to 2 to 3 percent per year of assets under management. Remember that stocks have historically returned about 10 percent per year before taxes. So if you're paying 2 to 3 percent per year to have the money managed in stocks, 20 to 30 percent of your return (before taxes) is siphoned off. You pay a good chunk of money in taxes on your 10 percent return. So a 2 to 3 percent wrap fee actually ends up depleting up to half of the profits that you get to keep after you pay taxes — ouch!

No-load (commission-free) mutual funds offer investors access to the nation's best investment managers for a fraction of the cost of wrap accounts. You can invest in dozens of top-performing funds for an annual expense of 1 percent per year or less. Many excellent funds are available for far less — 0.1 to 0.5 percent annually.

So why do people invest through wrap accounts if they're such a poor investment? Brokerage firms hoodwink investors into paying so much more for access to investment managers with clever marketing — slick, seductive, deceptive, misleading pitches.

The following are the key components of brokerage firms' pitch for wrap accounts — and then the real truth behind the pitch:

✔ *"You're accessing investment managers who normally don't take money from small-fry investors like you."* Not a single study shows that the performance of money managers has anything to do with the minimum account size they handle. Besides, no-load mutual funds hire many of the same managers who work at other money management firms. In fact, Vanguard, the nation's largest exclusively load-free investment firm, contracts out to hire money managers who typically handle only multimillion-dollar private-client accounts to run many of their funds. A number of other mutual funds are managed by private money managers who typically have high entrance requirements for their individual private clients.

✔ *"You'll earn a higher rate of return, so the fees are worth it."* Part of the bait brokers use to hook you into a wrap account is the wonderful rates of returns that these accounts supposedly generate. You could've earned 18 to 25 percent per year, they say, had you invested with the "Star of Yesterday" investment management company. The key word here is "could've." History is history. As I discuss in Chapter 7, in the money management business, many of yesterday's winners become either tomorrow's losers or its mediocre performers.

You must also remember that, unlike mutual funds, whose performance records are audited by the SEC, wrap account performance records include marketing hype. The SEC doesn't audit wrap accounts. The most common ploy is showing the performance of only selected accounts — which turn out to be (you got it) only the ones that performed the best!

The expenses you pay to have your investments managed have an enormous impact on the long-term growth of your money. If you can have your money managed for 0.5 to 1 percent per year rather than 2 to 3 percent, you have an enormous performance advantage already.

✔ *"A wrap account is tailored to your personal needs."* Thousands of different mutual funds are available out there, covering every possible combination of investments and degree of risk. You can find a mutual fund and develop a portfolio of funds that meets your objectives and risk tolerance. Some wrap accounts have only funds that are managed by a particular brokerage firm, making it impossible for you to invest in the best from the universe of all funds.

Moreover, if your portfolio ever begins to drift from your objectives, buying into a new mutual fund is much easier than ending a relationship with a broker who sold you the wrap account.

✔ *"There's little difference in cost between wrap accounts and mutual funds."* The worst and most inefficient mutual funds can have total costs approaching that of a typical wrap account. But you're informed, right? You're not going to invest in the highest-cost funds. Chapters 11 through 14 detail which mutual funds offer both top performance and low cost.

Private Money Managers: One-on-One

In the world of money management, added benefits — snob appeal and ego stroking for many — come with having your own private money manager. First of all, you generally need big bucks, often $1 million or more, to gain entrance. A *private money management* company allows you to sit down and visit with a personal representative and perhaps even the investment manager. The company may lavish you with attention and glossy brochures. You hear how your money not only receives individualized and personalized treatment but also how superb the investment manager's performance has been in prior years.

Even if you have big bucks, you probably don't need a private money manager for two simple reasons:

- ✔ **The best, average, and worst private money managers earn returns comparable to their counterparts in the mutual fund business.** And as I mention earlier in this chapter, some mutual fund firms contract out to or are themselves private money managers. This gives you the best of both worlds: the SEC oversight of a mutual fund and access to some money managers that you may not otherwise be able to use.

- ✔ **You pay high fees to use these money manager's services.** One bank CEO, speaking at a banking conference about future sources of revenue growth, said private money management for the wealthy, along with the credit card business, are two "high-return, low-risk businesses" in the financial world. Knowing that you're getting soaked with high fees like the average credit card customer shouldn't make you feel so special about having a private money manager!

If you're considering investing through private investment firms, make sure that you

- ✔ Ask to see independently audited rates of return. Private managers' holdings and performances aren't subject to the same scrutiny and reporting as mutual funds are.

- ✔ Check many references.

- ✔ Compare the performance and costs of the private money manager with similar mutual funds in this book.

For more ideas about evaluating money managers, see the criteria for selecting mutual funds in Chapter 7.

Part III
Separating the Best from the Rest

The 5th Wave   By Rich Tennant

"Oh, look! Mr. Peepers just picked the very same mutual funds your investment software did!"

In this part . . .

In this part, I cover the difficult process of narrowing down the multitude of funds to the best funds for your situation. I also discuss how to utilize fund company reports: prospectuses and annual reports. In addition to explaining proven selection techniques, I name names and highlight the best firms with which to conduct your fund investing.

Chapter 7

Finding the Best Funds

· ·

In This Chapter

▶ Keeping your investment from being whittled away by fees

▶ Looking at a fund's past and knowing how much risk a fund takes

▶ Getting to know the fund manager and fund family expertise

· ·

*W*hen you go camping in the wilderness, you can do a number of things to maximize your odds of happiness and success. You can take maps and a GPS navigator to stay on course, good food to keep you nourished, proper clothing to stay dry and warm, and some first-aid stuff in case something awful happens, such as an outbreak of mosquitoes. But no matter how much preparation you do, you still may not have the best of times. You may get sick, trip over a rock and break your leg, or face inclement weather.

And so it is with mutual funds. Although funds can help you reach your financial goals, they come with no guarantees. You can, however, use a number of simple, common-sense criteria to greatly increase your chances of investment success. The issues in this chapter are the main ones you should consider when trying to separate the funds most likely to succeed from those most likely to perform poorly. The mutual funds that I recommend in Chapters 11 through 14 meet these criteria.

Evaluating Gain-Eating Costs

A survey conducted by the Investment Company Institute asked mutual fund buyers what information they reviewed about a fund *before* purchasing it. Fifth on the list, mentioned by only 43 percent of the respondents, were fees and expenses. Therefore, the majority of fund buyers surveyed — a whopping 57 percent — did *not* examine the fees and expenses for the funds that they bought.

Additionally, only 27 percent of fund buyers surveyed bothered to look at how much of a load or sales charge was levied by the fund. At the other end of the spectrum, past fund performance was the most cited information reviewed by fund buyers (with 75 percent considering).

Such survey results don't surprise me. I've witnessed investors looking first — and sometimes only — at the prior performance of a fund while completely ignoring fees. Doing so is generally a major mistake.

The charges you pay to buy or sell a fund and the ongoing fund-operating expenses have a big impact on the rate of return you ultimately earn on your investments because fees are deducted from your investment returns. All other things being equal, high fees and other expenses depress your returns. You can and should examine a fund's expenses and fees *before* you buy into it. In contrast, past performance is actually a relatively poor indicator of a fund's likely future returns. (Later in this chapter, I discuss how many of yesterday's star funds turn into tomorrow's losers or mediocre performers.) You just can't know what tomorrow will bring.

Although you have no idea how much of a return you'll make, you *can* find out, before buying a fund, how much the fund has been charging in fees — both upfront (in the form of sales commissions) and ongoing (in the form of fund operating expenses). Factor these known reductions in returns into your fund-buying decisions.

Losing the load: Say no to commissions

When the Securities and Exchange Commission (SEC) deregulated brokers' commissions in 1975, the vast majority — more than 85 percent — of all mutual funds were sold through brokers. The funds they sold are known as *load funds. Load* simply means *commission*. When you purchase a load fund through a broker (who often calls himself something other than a broker), the broker is paid a commission (typically ranging from 4 percent to 8.5 percent) out of the amount that you invest.

Thanks in part to the deregulation of brokerage commissions and to the technological revolution that's taken place over recent decades, the growth of the *no-load* (commission-free) mutual fund industry took off. Technology provided fund companies with a cost-effective way to handle thousands of accounts for folks like you who don't have millions of dollars to invest. This fact also enabled fund companies to sell no-load funds directly to investors. Today, no-load funds account for the majority of investors' mutual fund holdings.

Loads deducted from your investment money are an additional and unnecessary cost when you're in the market for the best mutual funds. The best no-load funds are every bit as good, if not better, than the best load funds. Today, you can stick with the no-load funds and keep more of your investment dollars working for you.

Not surprisingly, those who have a vested interest in sales loads argue in favor of funds that carry sales loads. Over the years, I've heard the content of these broker pitches through readers who write to me or visit my Web site and in counseling clients who came to me for advice.

Be wary of brokers or planners pitching house brands — for example, a Morgan Stanley broker recommending Morgan Stanley mutual funds. The fund industry scandal in the early 2000s further shined the light on this problematic practice. Salespeople often get higher commissions by pushing house brands.

Refuting myths about loads

Brokers have much to say about paying loads, and you should be aware of the arguments they use. Here are a few examples:

- ✔ ***Don't concern yourself with commissions — I get paid by the mutual fund company.*** It's true that the mutual fund company pays the broker's commission. But where do you think this money comes from? From your investment dollars — that's where. Brokers like to imply that you're not effectively paying for the commission because it comes from the mutual fund company.

- ✔ ***You get what you pay for — load funds have better fund managers.*** Bunk! Every objective study that I've seen shows that paying a load doesn't get you a better fund manager. Remember, loads wind up in the pockets of the selling brokers and don't go toward the management of the fund.

  What the studies have shown is that on average load funds underperform no-loads. Why? It's simple: Those commissions paid to the brokers come out of the fund's returns, although you may not know that from a fund's published rankings. Some published mutual fund rankings and ratings services completely ignore sales commissions in their calculations of funds' returns (see Chapter 20).

- ✔ ***No-loads have higher ongoing fees.*** Investment salespeople imply or state that no-loads have to make it up somewhere if they aren't charging you a sales commission. Although this may sound logical, remember that sales commissions go to the broker, not toward the expenses of managing the fund. Fact is, the reverse is true: Load funds, on average, have higher, not lower, annual operating expenses than no-load funds.

All funds have to spend money to market themselves. Load funds spend money to market themselves both to brokers and to the investing public like you and me. And the better no-load companies, such as those recommended in Chapter 9, benefit from the thousands of investors who call, based on word-of-mouth or other recommendations (such as through this book!), seeking to invest.

✔ *No-loads have hidden costs.* In this case, a half-truth doesn't make a whole. Both no-load *and* load funds incur brokerage transaction costs when securities are bought and sold in the fund. These costs aren't really "hidden." They're disclosed in a fund's Statement of Additional Information (discussed in Chapter 8), which is part of the fund's prospectus; however, they're not included in the calculated annual operating costs for any type of mutual fund, either load or no-load.

✔ *No-loads are for do-it-yourself types. People who need help buy load funds.* This either/or mentality is trumpeted not only by investment brokers but also by some financial writers and others in the media who sometimes parrot what brokers say to them. If you need advice, you have options. One alternative is to hire a financial adviser and pay a fee for her time to recommend specific no-load mutual funds. No-loads are hardly just for do-it-yourself types (see Chapter 9 for the different types of advisers you may hire), although you can see from this book (after you finish reading it) that you have what it takes to just do it yourself.

✔ *I'll do a financial plan for you to determine your needs.* Try as they may, investment salespeople can't perform objective, conflict-free financial planning. (You should *never* pay for a "financial plan" from an investment salesperson.) The problem with sales loads is the power of self-interest (discussed in Chapter 9). This issue is rarely talked about, but brokers' self-interest is even more important than the extra costs you pay. When you buy a load fund through a salesperson, you miss out on the chance to objectively assess whether you should buy a mutual fund at all. Maybe you'd be better off paying debts or investing in something entirely different. But salespeople almost never advise you to pay off your credit cards or your mortgage — or to invest through your company's retirement plan — instead of buying an investment through them.

I've seen too many people get into investments without understanding what they're buying and what the risks are. People who sell mutual funds usually sell other investments, too. And some of those other products — vehicles such as limited partnerships, cash-value life insurance, annuities, futures, and options — hold the allure (for the salespeople) of high commissions. Salespeople tend to exaggerate the potential rewards and obscure the risks and drawbacks of what they sell and often don't take the time to educate investors.

✔ *I can get you those funds that you're interested in from the same no-load companies, such as Fidelity.* Brokers like to imply that they can sell you basically the same funds that you could buy on your own through no-load companies. However, top no-load companies, such as Vanguard, for example, don't sell any load funds through brokers. Fidelity sells a series of load funds, called Fidelity Advisor funds, through commission-based brokers. These funds carry hefty upfront sales charges and/or much higher ongoing fees — up to a full 1 percent more per year — than their no-load counterparts.

In recent years, increasing numbers of brokerage firms are offering their customers access to some no-load mutual funds through a service known as a *wrap* (or *managed*) *account.* To get into these funds, you must agree to pay the brokerage firm an annual investment management fee on top of the fees the underlying mutual funds charge. (I explain in Chapter 6 why high-fee wrap accounts aren't in your best interest.)

✔ *The no-loads won't call you to tell you when to get out of the market or switch funds.* True. But far from being a disadvantage, not getting a call to switch funds is actually a plus. Although mutual funds offer daily liquidity, funds are meant to be a longer-term investment.

A broker who stands to gain financially when you trade is hard pressed to be a source of objective advice of when to trade funds. (In Chapter 17, I explain how to evaluate whether to continue holding the funds you own by applying the criteria discussed in this chapter.)

✔ *No-loads are impersonal organizations.* When you call a no-load fund's toll-free number, you'll surely get a different representative every time. Visiting a fund's Web site is even less personal. If it's important for you to have a relationship with someone at these firms, however, some representatives give you their names and extensions (just ask) so you can reach them in the future. (Higher balance customers at some fund companies can be assigned a dedicated representative, so inquire.)

A broker can be a personal contact who asks you about your golf game, how your family is doing, and . . . by the way . . . "What's the phone number of your rich Uncle Johnny?" Independent financial counselors who charge a fee for their time can serve the same role. Likewise, discount brokerage firms such as Charles Schwab, TD Ameritrade, and Fidelity maintain branch offices that offer a personal, local touch if you need and want it.

Hidden loads in alphabet soup: ABCD shares

Over the years, investors have learned about the sales loads that are deducted from their investments in load mutual funds. Perhaps you just discovered this yourself. Well, the companies that specialize in selling load funds have, with the unwitting assistance of government regulators, developed various types of funds that make finding the load much harder.

Just as some jewelers flog fake diamonds on late-night TV commercials, some brokers are selling funds that they *call* no-loads, when they're really *not* no-loads. By any other name, these funds are load funds: The only difference is that, with these funds, someone has taken the time to hide the sales commission.

For a given load fund, some fund companies have introduced different classes of shares, usually labeled by the letters A, B, C, or D. No matter what letter they slap onto it, remember that you're getting the same fund manager and the same fund. The only difference is how much the company's charging you to own it.

Shares with the traditional front-end load are usually sold as Class A shares. Class B, C, and D shares are the classes that the mutual fund marketers deploy tricky techniques such as *back-end loads* or ongoing commissions known as *12b-1 fees*. These commissions often end up being more expensive than the old upfront loads.

Take the back-end sales load, for example, which is the typical technique of Class B shares. Instead of assessing a load when you purchase these shares, you're charged a load when you sell them. But wait, the broker tells you, the more years you hold on to the shares, the lower the sales charge when you sell. In fact, if you hold on to the shares long enough — usually five to seven years — the load disappears altogether. This deal sounds a lot better than the Class A shares, which charge you an upfront load no matter what. Not so fast. The broker selling the Class B shares still gets a commission. The company simply raises the fund's operating expenses (much higher than on Class A shares) and pays the broker commissions out of that. One way or another, the broker gets his pound of flesh from your investment dollars.

Remember: You can easily avoid these hidden loads. Don't buy funds through salespeople. Buy no-loads, such as those recommended in this book.

Exposing loads

The only way to be sure that a fund is truly no-load is to look at the prospectus for the fund. Only there, in black and white and absent of all marketing hype, must the organization tell the truth about its sales charges and other fund fees. (Check out Chapter 8.)

Figure 7-1 is a sample of a typical fee table from a fund prospectus for a load fund. Note that the Class A shares have an upfront 6.5 percent sales commission that's deducted when you invest your money.

FEE TABLE

Shareholder Transaction Expenses:	Class A Shares	Class B Shares
Maximum Sales Charge Imposed on Purchase (as a percentage of offering price)	6.50%	None
Sales Charge Imposed on Dividend Reinvestments	None	None
Deferred Sales Charge	None	4.0% during the first year, decreasing 1.0% annually to 0.0% after the fourth year
Exchange Fee	None	None

Annual Fund Operating Expenses (as a percentage of average net assets):

	Class A Shares	Class B Shares
Management Fee	1.00%	1.00%
12b-1 Fees	None	1.00%
Other Expenses	0.25%	0.35%
Total Fund Operating Expenses	1.25%	2.35%

Example:

	Cumulative Expenses Paid for the Period of:			
	1 Year	3 Years	5 Years	10 Years

You would pay the following expenses on a $1,000 investment, assuming a 5% annual return, and redemption at the end of the period:

	1 Year	3 Years	5 Years	10 Years
Class A	$78	$106	$137	$229
Class B	$64	$93	$124	$265

You would pay the following expenses on the same $1,000 investment, assuming no redemption at the end of the period:

	1 Year	3 Years	5 Years	10 Years
Class A	$78	$106	$137	$229
Class B	$24	$73	$124	$265

Figure 7-1:
How to spot load funds.

The Class B shares don't have an upfront commission but instead have a deferred sales charge, which decreases over time. *However,* note that this class can charge you up to an extra 1 percent per year (12b-1 marketing expense fees). Class B shares in this example (as in most real cases) cost you more in the long run because you pay this cost each year as long as you own the fund. Check out the "Hidden loads in alphabet soup: ABCD shares" sidebar earlier in this chapter for even more details on this game of hide the load.

Considering a fund's operating expenses

One cost of fund ownership that you simply can't avoid is *operating expenses.* Every mutual fund — load and no-load — has operational costs: paying the fund manager and research assistants, employing people to answer the phone lines and operate a Web site, printing and mailing prospectuses, buying technology equipment to track all those investments and customer-account balances, and so on.

Running a fund business costs money! Fund fees also include a profit for the fund company. (The brokerage costs that a fund pays to buy and sell securities aren't included in a fund's operating expenses. You can find this information in a fund's Statement of Additional Information, which I discuss in Chapter 8.)

A fund's operating expenses are quoted as a percentage of the fund's assets or value. The percentage represents an annual fee or charge. In the case of load funds, this fee is in addition to the stated load. You can find this number in the expenses section of a fund's prospectus, usually denoted by a line, such as *Total Fund Operating Expenses.* Or you can call the mutual fund's toll-free number and ask a representative or dig for the information on most fund companies' Web sites. I detail what the operating expenses are for the funds recommended in this book.

Some people ask me how the expenses are charged and whether they're itemized on your fund statement. The answer is that a fund's operating expenses are essentially invisible to you because they're deducted before you're paid any return. Because these expenses are charged on a daily basis, you don't need to worry about trying to get out of a fund before these fees are deducted.

Although all funds must charge operating expenses, some funds charge much more than others. By picking the right funds, you can minimize the operating expenses you pay. And minimize them you should: Operating expenses come right out of your returns. Higher expenses translate into a lower return to you.

Expenses matter on all types of funds but more on some and less on others:

- ✔ **Expenses are critical on money market mutual funds and are very important on bond funds.** These funds are buying securities that are so similar and so efficiently priced in the financial markets. In other words, your expected returns from similar bond and money funds are largely driven by the size of a fund's operating expenses. This fact has been especially true in recent years when interest rates have gotten low.

- ✔ **With stock funds, expenses are a less important (but still important) factor in picking a fund.** Don't forget that, over time, stocks have averaged returns of about 10 percent per year. So, if one stock fund charges 1.5 percent *more* in operating expenses than another, you're giving up an extra 15 percent of your expected annual returns.

Some people argue that stock funds that charge high expenses may be justified in doing so — *if* they're able to generate higher rates of return. *But there's no evidence that high-expense stock funds do generate higher returns.* In fact, funds with higher operating expenses, on average, tend to produce *lower* rates of return. This makes sense because operating expenses are deducted from the returns that a fund generates.

But how high is high? You should generally shun a money market or bond fund that charges more than 0.5 percent per year, a U.S. stock fund that charges more than 1 percent per year, or an international or specialty fund that charges more than 1.3 percent per year. Steel yourself against clever marketing brochures and charming salespeople. Read the fine print and walk the other way to a better fund if costs are too high.

If a given fund's expenses are much higher than its peers, one of two things is usually happening: Either the fund has little money under management — and therefore has a smaller group of investors to bear the management costs — or the fund owners are greedy. Another possibility could be that the fund company is inefficiently managed. (Maybe the company rents high-cost, big-city office space and its telephone reps spend half the day talking with friends!) In any case, you don't want to be a shareholder of such a fund.

These high-expense funds have another insidious danger built in: In order to produce returns comparable to those of similar funds with lower costs, the manager of such a high-cost fund may take extra risks to overcome the performance drag of high expenses. So on top of reducing a fund's returns, higher expenses may expose you to greater risk than you desire.

In some cases, a fund (particularly a newer one that's trying to attract assets) will "reimburse" a portion of its expense ratio in order to show a lower cost. But if (or when) the fund terminates this reimbursement, you're stuck owning shares in a fund that has higher costs than you intended to pay.

All mutual fund fees — both loads and operating expenses — are disclosed in a fund's prospectus, which is why obtaining a fund's prospectus *before* you buy it is so important. Reviewing the prospectus is especially critical for funds pitched to you by brokers or by brokers who masquerade as "financial planners" and "consultants." I tell you how to decipher a fund prospectus later in this chapter.

Weighing Performance and Risk

Although a fund's *performance,* or its historic rate of return, is certainly an important factor to weigh when selecting a mutual fund, investors tend to overemphasize its importance. Choosing funds on simplistic comparisons of performance numbers is dangerous.

As all mutual fund materials are required to state, past performance is no guarantee of future results. Analysis of historic mutual fund performance proves that some of yesterday's stars may turn into tomorrow's skid row bums (as I discuss in the next section, "Star today, also-ran tomorrow").

Realize that funds with relatively high returns may achieve their results by taking on a lot of risk. Those same funds often take the hardest fall during major market declines. Remember that risk and return go hand in hand; you can't afford to look at return independent of the risk it took to get there. Before you invest in a fund, make sure you're comfortable with the level of risk the fund is taking on.

Star today, also-ran tomorrow

Some fund manager may have a fabulous quarter or year or two, ripping up the market with his little growth-stock fund. Suddenly, his face is plastered across the financial magazines; he's hailed as the next investing genius, and then hundreds of millions and perhaps billions of new investor dollars come pouring into his fund.

Short-term (one year is a short time period) fund performance numbers don't mean much — luck can be just as big a factor as skill. Also remember that earning much higher returns than other similar funds often means that the manager took a lot of risk. The greater the short-term returns for that fund and manager, the greater the odds of sharp slump.

The history of short-term mutual fund star funds confirms this: Of the number one top-performing stock and bond funds in each of the last 20 years, a whopping 80 percent of them subsequently performed worse than the average fund in their peer group over the next five to ten years! Some of these former number one funds actually went on to become the worst-performing funds in their particular category.

The following sections provide a historic sampling of the many examples of short-term stars becoming tomorrow's also-rans (and in some cases, downright losers).

Fidelity Growth Strategies

Launched in 1991, Fidelity Growth Strategies invests in medium-size growth companies. The fund performed a little better than the market averages in the early to mid-1990s, and then it dramatically outperformed its peer group in late 1990s.

So, Fidelity promoted the heck out of the fund, and investors piled into it to the tune of nearly $10 billion in 1999. And, Fidelity had some help from articles like the one that ran in the July 18, 1999, issue of *The New York Times*.

In a positively glowing profile of the fund, and its manager, Erin Sullivan, the *Times* called Sullivan ". . . the quintessential portfolio manager." And it added in the following material, which caused investors to send Ms. Sullivan's fund their investment dollars:

> *"Ms. Sullivan, 29, has been in charge of the $5.96 billion Fidelity Aggressive Growth fund since April 1997. In that time, the fund has posted total returns of 51.83 percent, annualized, versus 33.16 percent for the Standard & Poor's 500-stock index. . . . This year through July 15, the fund was up 44.34 percent, nearly tripling the 15.4 percent gain of the S.& P. 500.*
>
> *Ms. Sullivan goes about her business with the self-assurance of a Harvard graduate, the analytical rigor of a math theoretician, and the vigor of a marathon runner, all of which she is. But she has not entered a marathon race roughly since she took the reins of Aggressive Growth. 'It's hard to find time for anything else,' she said."*

Within months of the *Times* article, the fund's fortunes changed. Overloaded with overpriced technology stocks, the fund plunged 84 percent in value from early 2000 to late 2002. It was one of the worst performing funds of the decade just ended with its –9.9 percent per year annualized return.

Van Wagoner Emerging Growth fund

With a mere three years of stellar returns under his belt, Garrett Van Wagoner, manager of the Govett Smaller Companies Fund, decided to cash in on his exploding popularity and start his own money management firm — Van Wagoner Capital Management. Calling Van Wagoner the hottest small company stock picker around, several of the nation's largest financial magazines recommended investing in his new Emerging Growth fund. Investor cash came flooding in — more than a billion dollars in the fund's first six months of existence.

The Van Wagoner Emerging Growth fund (since renamed the Embarcadero Small Cap Growth fund) invests in high-flying smaller company growth stocks. In its first full year of operations (1996), the fund posted a respectable total return of nearly 27 percent, placing it within the top 20 percent of funds within its peer group.

In the next year, 1997, the fund dropped by 20 percent and dramatically underperformed its peer group and was among the worst of its peers. Money flowed out, and the fund was largely ignored until 1999 when Van Wagoner piled into technology stocks, which were zooming to the moon. In 1999, this fund produced a total return of a whopping 291 percent (making it the year's number one stock fund) while assets under management swelled from less than $200 million to nearly $1.5 billion!

Investors who came to Van Wagoner's party in 1999 were subsequently treated to one of the greatest collapses in the history of the fund industry. Following a drop of 20.9 percent in 2000, the fund posted horrendous losses in the next two years as well — losing 59.7 percent in 2001 and then 64.5 percent in 2002. In fact, the poor investors who bought in at or near the top during late 1999 through early 2000 experienced a stomach-wrenching plunge of more than 90 percent through September 2002. (The fund also had many horrendous years in the 2000s.) See Table 7-1 for how this fund has performed versus its relevant index — the Russell 2000 Growth Index.

Table 7-1	Comparing the Van Wagoner Emerging Growth Fund's Performance	
Year	Van Wagoner Emerging Growth Fund Total Return	Russell 2000 Growth Index Total Return
2000	−20.9%	−22.4%
2001	−59.7%	−9.2%
2002	−64.6%	−30.3%
2003	47.2%	48.5%
2004	−16.0%	14.3%
2005	−22.3%	4.1%
2006	10.8%	13.3%
2007	−7.8%	7.1%
2008	−56.8%	-38.5%
2009	12.6%	34.5%

Over the past decade, this fund has plunged in value by more than 94 percent! If you invested $10,000 in this fund at its inception in 1996, your investment would've shrunk to $1,841; whereas, the same investment in its average peer would've grown to $22,383!

Managers Intermediate Mortgage fund

Managed by portfolio manager Worth Bruntjen, Managers Intermediate Mortgage (MIM) was the darling of the moment for almost every mutual fund rating service in 1993. (I talk about rating services in Chapter 20.) It earned kudos because, in its seemingly boring investment universe — government-backed mortgage bonds — it produced an annual rate of return 3 percent higher than that of its peers (who came in it at just 10 percent per year) over the five-year period ending in 1993. By earning 13 percent per year rather than 10 percent, MIM's performance was about 30 percent better than its peers.

This fund received some of the highest ratings that most mutual fund rating companies allowed for performance, and, supposedly, MIM had "below average" risk. It earned a coveted five-star rating from a leading mutual fund rating service. When interest rates rose sharply in early 1994, the fund got clobbered. It produced a total return of –22 percent in the first half of 1994. This little six-month disaster was enough to bring the fund in dead last among 50 other mortgage bond funds for the five-year period ending June 30, 1994. And the disaster wiped out the above-average returns that this fund had generated over the five previous years.

This fund was able to achieve its temporarily high returns by taking a ton of risk. From where did all the danger come, you ask? The fund invested in complex *collateralized mortgage obligations* (CMOs), which are pieces of a mortgage. Buying CMOs is like buying chicken parts rather than a whole chicken at the supermarket. A mortgage gets chopped into the different years of principal and/or interest repayments. CMOs are incredibly complicated to understand, even if you surround yourself with computers and investment bankers.

Forbes magazine, which had written a glowing article praising fund manager Bruntjen on January 17, 1994, admitted that its earlier enthusiasm had been excessive — a rare and honorable thing for a financial magazine to do. *Forbes* said that the magazine had learned from the episode "not to be overly confident in historical statistics, especially those attached to complex investment products. In this case, a volatility measure calculated from a mostly bullish period turned out to be meaningless during a period when the market turned bearish."

Matterhorn Growth fund

This aggressive stock fund skyrocketed 184 percent in 1975 — the year following the end of one of the worst declines for the stock market since the Great Depression. Since the 1970s, however, this fund has been in the dog-house. It holds the dubious distinction of being the worst stock fund during the 1980s — one of the best decades ever for the stock market.

As money poured out of the fund, its annual operating expenses as a percentage of assets ballooned in excess of 4 percent per year! The fund was finally put out of its misery when it was merged into the CSI Equity fund in 2006.

Apples to apples: Comparing performance numbers

Remember back in school when the teacher handed back exams and you were delighted to get a 92 (unless you're from an overachieving family)? But then you found out that the average on the exam was a 95. You still may have been pleased, but a lot of air was let out of your balloon.

Mutual fund performance numbers are the same: They don't mean much until they're compared to the averages. A 15 percent return sounds great until you find out that the return from the relevant index market average (that invests in similar securities) was 25 percent during the same period.

The trick is picking the correct benchmark for comparison. Dozens of market indexes and fund category averages measure various components of the market. You always want to compare a fund's returns to its most appropriate benchmark. Comparing the performance of an international stock fund to that of a U.S. stock market index isn't fair, just as comparing a sixth-grader's test results on a given test to those of a tenth-grader taking the same test is unfair. (See Chapter 17 for a list of benchmarks and an explanation of what markets they measure.)

Context matters, and mutual fund companies realize this. So in their marketing literature, fund companies usually compare their funds' returns to selected benchmarks. Keep a wary eye on these comparisons. In the great American advertising tradition, fund companies often pick benchmarks that make it easy for their funds to look good. And in like manner, more than a few investment advisers who manage money do the same, as I discuss in Chapter 24.

Here's an example of how a fund can make itself look a lot better than it really is.

A number of years ago, the Strong Short-Term Bond Fund (subsequently acquired by Wells Fargo) ran ads claiming to be the number one, short-term bond fund. (I'd show you the ad, but Strong refused to grant permission to reprint it.) The ads featured a 12-month comparison graph that compared the Strong fund's yield to the average yield on other short-term bond funds. The Strong Short-Term Bond Fund, according to the graph, consistently outperformed the competition by 2 to 2.5 percent!

A bond fund must take a *lot* more risk to generate a dividend yield this much higher than the competition's. You should also be suspicious of any bond fund claiming to be this good with an annual operating expense ratio of 0.8 percent. With a yield and expenses that high (as I explain in Chapter 12), a fund has to take higher risks than supposedly comparable funds to make up for the drag of its expenses. And if the fund's taking that much more risk, then it needs to be compared to its true competition — which, in Strong's case, are other funds whose investments take similarly high risks. This fund isn't a bad fund, but it isn't nearly as good as the ad would've had you think.

This fund was on steroids! The Strong Short-Term Bond Fund wasn't comparable to most other short-term bond funds because

- ✔ **A high percentage of its bonds weren't high quality.** About 40 percent of its bonds were rated BBB or below. (I explain bond credit-quality ratings in Chapter 12.)

- ✔ **Many of its bonds weren't short-term bonds.** The Strong Fund invested in mortgage bonds that are more like intermediate-term bonds.

Strong's ad also claimed that its bond fund was ranked number one for the year. If a fund takes more risk than the funds it compares itself to, then sure, during particular, brief periods, it can easily end up at the top of the performance charts. But how strong of a long-term performer is this "number one" fund? Over the five years before this ad ran, even including the year the ad was so proud of, Strong's fund had *underperformed* most short-term bond funds.

Recognizing Manager Expertise

Much is made of who manages a specific mutual fund. Although the expertise of the individual fund manager is important, a manager isn't an island unto himself (or herself — more women are becoming fund managers nowadays). (And if the fund manager leaves or retires from the company, you're left holding the fund.) Earlier in this chapter (see "Star today, also-ran tomorrow"), I explain how a star fund can flare for its moment of investor glory and then easily twinkle down to become just another average or worse-than-average fund. Too many of us seem to want to believe that, in every field of endeavor — sports, entertainment, business — there are superhumans who can walk on water.

It's true that in the investment world some people shine at what they do. But compared to other fields, the gap between the star investment manager and the average one, over long time periods, typically is small.

If the stocks of large U.S. companies, for example, have increased an average of 13 percent per year over a decade, the money manager focusing on such securities may vault to star status if his fund earns 15 percent over the same time period. Don't get me wrong: An extra 2 percent per year ain't nothin' to sneeze at — especially if you have millions invested. But a 2 percent higher return is a lot smaller than what most people think they can achieve with the best investment managers.

Therefore, the resources and capabilities of the parent company should be equally important in your selection of which funds to invest in. Different companies have different capabilities and levels of expertise with different types of funds. In Chapters 11 through 14, I detail which firms have great reputations in various fund categories. I also recommend individual funds from these various companies.

Avoid fund companies with little mutual fund management experience and success. If you need surgery, you place your trust with a surgeon who's successfully performed the operation hundreds of times, not to a rookie who's only seen it on the local cable station. Avoid novelty funds as well. Mutual funds have been around for many decades. Yet not a week goes by without some newfangled fund coming out with a new concept. Most of these ideas come from the fund company's marketing department, which in some companies has too much clout. Instead of coming up with investments that meet investors' needs, they come up with gimmicky funds that involve extra risk and that almost always cost extra in their high annual operating expenses.

Chapter 8

Using Fund Publications

*F*und companies produce a lot of materials. Even with the growth and usage of the Internet, plenty of paper and trees get trashed annually.

While much of what funds publish isn't worth much of your time, some of it is and can address important questions you may have (or should have) about particular funds. You can learn about fund fees (including so-called hidden brokerage costs), strategies, investment holdings, risks, to name just a few. So, in this chapter, I walk you through three of the most important fund documents published for each and every mutual fund: the prospectus, annual report, and statement of additional information.

Reading Prospectuses — the Important Stuff, Anyway

Securities laws require every fund to issue a prospectus, and the U.S. SEC reviews the details of every single one (which probably keeps plenty of coffee and eyeglass companies in business). A *prospectus* is usually written and edited by an attorney who wouldn't know a lively and comprehensible sentence if it clobbered him on the head. You can safely skip most of what's said in a prospectus, but be on the lookout for a few things you should check out.

The most valuable information — the fund's investment objectives, costs, and performance history — is summarized in the first few pages of the prospectus. Read these. Skip most of the rest. The rest only tells you more than you could possibly want to know about how the fund is administered. Do you really want to know whether employees are paid monthly or weekly? Which brand of paper shredders they recently bought for the accounting department?

If you find prospectuses to be positively lethal in their tediousness, let me suggest a friendlier alternative: Just jump ahead to the fund recommendations in Chapters 10 through 13 of this book. I've already checked them out for you, and they meet the criteria for good funds that I list in this book. However, if you're going to be assessing funds for purchase other than those presented in this book, you need to be able to read and understand a prospectus.

In the pages that follow, I walk you through the more useful and relevant parts of a well-done prospectus for one of Vanguard's funds, the Wellington Fund. This fund has been in existence for more than 80 years. Consider that it was launched on July 1, 1929, right before the onset of the Great Depression. So to say that it has stood the test of time and tough times would be an understatement! Since its inception, the Wellington Fund has produced annualized returns of more than 8 percent per year, which demonstrates the value of diversification in stocks and bonds. (Remember, the specifics about the fund have since changed, so be sure to get a new prospectus if you want to invest in the Wellington Fund.)

Cover page

The prospectus is dated (see Figure 8-1) so that you know how recent its information is. Don't sweat it if the prospectus is several months old; in general, fund companies update prospectuses annually.

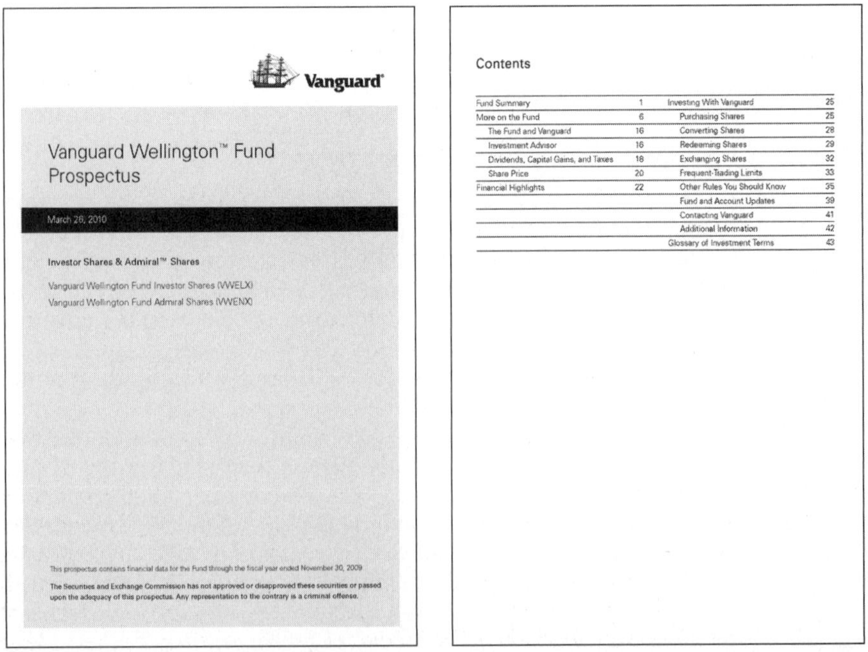

Figure 8-1: The Table of Contents shows you what's covered in the prospectus.

Source: The Vanguard Group. Reprinted with permission.

The table of contents is a sure sign that the prospectus is too long — but then lawyers seldom use 1 word where 50 will do. The table of contents helps you navigate the prospectus to find whatever information you want. To illustrate here, I cover a portion of this prospectus (most of the good stuff is near the front).

Some prospectuses describe more than one fund in a particular fund family. (This prospectus covers two different "Share Classes" — "Investor Shares" and "Admiral Shares," which are identical except that the Admiral Shares have far larger initial investment requirements and lower expenses.) This practice can save a fund company printing and mailing charges when it has funds with very similar investment objectives and/or funds run by the same investment management team.

Fund profile

The fund profile pages (beginning with Figure 8-2) contain a synopsis of the main attributes of the fund, such as a description of the fund's investment objectives and the *strategies* (the types of securities the fund invests in) that it employs to accomplish its objectives. The Wellington Fund seeks current income from its investments and modest appreciation. It invests the majority of its assets in stocks that pay decent dividends (for income as well as appreciation potential) and its remaining assets in high-quality bonds (for income).

Thankfully, funds are required to present, in a standardized format, the costs that you'll incur for the privilege of owning a fund. The first list of expenses shows the fees you pay when you buy and sell shares. These fees are deducted at the time a transaction occurs; unfortunately, they're rarely itemized. Because a no-load fund such as the Wellington Fund doesn't charge any sales commissions or redemption fees, you see the word *None* repeated throughout this section.

Here, you also find a list of the main risks that come with investing in this fund. All funds, especially those which invest in stocks and bonds (as this one does), come with risk. Don't let this list scare you away — let it make you feel better. You're hiring a knowledgeable and experienced fund manager who can do a much better job navigating these potential perils than you can.

On the second page of the fund profile section, you find a description of the fund's performance chart and table (see Figure 8-3). In the chart, you can see the yearly total return that an investor in this fund has earned over the past decade. (Below the chart is a description of the best and worst quarters — three-month periods.) Because this fund invests in a mixture of bonds and stocks, you shouldn't be surprised to see fluctuations — in some years, you see fairly large positive returns (in some cases, more than 20 percent), and in other years, you see a negative return. The performance information also shows the impact of taxes (which assumes the deduction of taxes at the highest federal rates) and comparison of the fund's returns to relevant market indexes.

Fund Summary

Investment Objective
The Fund seeks to provide long-term capital appreciation and reasonable current income.

Fees and Expenses
The following tables describe the fees and expenses you may pay if you buy and hold Investor Shares or Admiral Shares of the Fund.

Shareholder Fees
(Fees paid directly from your investment)

	Investor Shares	Admiral Shares
Sales Charge (Load) Imposed on Purchases	None	None
Purchase Fee	None	None
Sales Charge (Load) Imposed on Reinvested Dividends	None	None
Redemption Fee	None	None
Account Service Fee (for fund account balances below $10,000)	$20/year	None

Annual Fund Operating Expenses
(Expenses that you pay each year as a percentage of the value of your investment)

	Investor Shares	Admiral Shares
Management Expenses	0.31%	0.21%
12b-1 Distribution Fee	None	None
Other Expenses	0.03%	0.02%
Total Annual Fund Operating Expenses	0.34%	0.23%

Examples
The following examples are intended to help you compare the cost of investing in the Fund's Investor Shares or Admiral Shares with the cost of investing in other mutual funds. They illustrate the hypothetical expenses that you would incur over various periods if you invest $10,000 in the Fund's shares. These examples assume that the Shares provide a return of 5% a year and that operating expenses remain the same. The results apply whether or not you redeem your investment at the end of the given period. Although your actual costs may be higher or lower, based on these assumptions your costs would be:

	1 Year	3 Years	5 Years	10 Years
Investor Shares	$35	$109	$191	$431
Admiral Shares	$24	$74	$130	$293

Portfolio Turnover
The Fund pays transaction costs, such as commissions, when it buys and sells securities (or "turns over" its portfolio). A higher portfolio turnover rate may indicate higher transaction costs and may result in higher taxes when Fund shares are held in a taxable account. These costs, which are not reflected in annual fund operating expenses or in the previous expense example, affect the Fund's performance. During the most recent fiscal year, the Fund's portfolio turnover rate was 28% of the average value of its portfolio.

Primary Investment Strategies
The Fund invests 60% to 70% of its assets in dividend-paying and, to a lesser extent, non-dividend-paying common stocks of established, medium-size and large companies. In choosing these companies, the advisor seeks those that appear to be undervalued but have prospects for improvement. These stocks are commonly referred to as value stocks. The remaining 30% to 40% of the Fund's assets are invested mainly in fixed income securities that the advisor believes will generate a reasonable level of current income. These securities include investment-grade corporate bonds, with some exposure to U.S. Treasury and government agency bonds, and mortgage-backed securities.

Primary Risks
The Fund is subject to the risks associated with the stock and bond markets, any of which could cause an investor to lose money. However, because stock and bond prices can move in different directions or to different degrees, the Fund's bond and short-term investment holdings may counteract some of the volatility experienced by the Fund's stock holdings.

- With approximately 60% to 70% of its assets allocated to stocks, the Fund is proportionately subject to stock risks: *stock market risk*, which is the chance that stock prices overall will decline; and *investment style risk*, which is the chance that returns from mid- and large-capitalization value stocks will trail returns from the overall stock market. Historically, mid-cap stocks have been more volatile in price than the large-cap stocks that dominate the overall market, and they often perform quite differently.

- With approximately 30% to 40% of its assets allocated to bonds, the Fund is proportionately subject to bond risks: *interest rate risk*, which is the chance that bond

Figure 8-2:
The fund summary provides a digest of the fund's key features.

Source: The Vanguard Group. Reprinted with permission.

Annual Total Returns—Investor Shares

2000	2001	2002	2003	2004	2005	2006	2007	2008	2009
10.40	4.19	-6.90	20.75	11.17	6.82	14.57	8.34	-22.30	22.20

During the periods shown in the bar chart, the highest return for a calendar quarter was 13.12% (quarter ended June 30, 2009), and the lowest return for a quarter was −11.04% (quarter ended September 30, 2002).

Average Annual Total Returns for Periods Ended December 31, 2009

	1 Year	5 Years	10 Years
Vanguard Wellington Fund Investor Shares			
Return Before Taxes	22.20%	4.79%	6.15%
Return After Taxes on Distributions	21.13	3.52	4.69
Return After Taxes on Distributions and Sale of Fund Shares	14.70	3.67	4.67
Comparative Indexes			
(reflect no deduction for fees, expenses, or taxes)			
Standard & Poor's 500 Index	26.46%	0.42%	-0.95%
Wellington Composite Index	21.30	2.06	1.89

	1 Year	5 Years	Since Inception (May 14, 2001)
Vanguard Wellington Fund Admiral Shares			
Return Before Taxes	22.34%	4.91%	5.64%
Comparative Indexes			
(reflect no deduction for fees, expenses, or taxes)			
Standard & Poor's 500 Index	26.46%	0.42%	0.59%
Wellington Composite Index	21.30	2.06	2.78

Figure 8-3:
The fund profile summarizes performance data.

Source: The Vanguard Group. Reprinted with permission.

If a so-called financial adviser pitches a fund, but you're not sure whether she gets paid for selling it to you, *always* get a prospectus and check out the fund expense section. That way, you can see if commissions will erode your returns. In this case, you'd see that if an adviser recommended this fund, she isn't paid any commission — a good sign. (Refer to Chapter 7 for an example of a typical load-fund fee table.)

Operating expenses are fees charged on a continuous basis by all mutual funds; they cover the expenses of running a fund and include the fund company's management fee — out of which it earns its profit. In this case, they total a reasonable 0.34 percent (even less for the Admiral shares). Because these fees are deducted from the fund's returns before your returns are paid to you, lower operating expenses translate into higher returns for you.

In addition to showing you the fund expenses as a percentage of the amount an investor has in the fund, the prospectus also shows you the total expense dollars that an investor will incur over the years by investing a hypothetical amount ($10,000) in the fund.

Other fund information

The next section of the prospectus (see Figure 8-4) presents you with a hodgepodge of facts about the fund, some of which may be important to you: who manages the fund, how long the fund has been in existence, what the fund's total assets are, what its minimum initial investment amount is, and how to purchase and redeem shares.

Investment objectives and risks

This next section on investment strategies explains in detail what the fund is trying to accomplish and what risks the fund is subject to. In Figures 8-5 through 8-7, I show you the first few pages of this section. The Wellington Fund seeks both moderate growth of capital and current income. It tries to accomplish these objectives by investing in stocks that pay decent dividends and bonds (fixed-income securities). (The Plain Talk sections within this prospectus — see the shaded boxes — explain important fund-investing concepts. The Plain Talk section isn't required, and you won't necessarily find it, or the equivalent, in every prospectus.)

Actual after-tax returns depend on your tax situation and may differ from those shown in the preceding table. When after-tax returns are calculated, it is assumed that the shareholder was in the highest individual federal marginal income tax bracket at the time of each distribution of income or capital gains or upon redemption. State and local income taxes are not reflected in the calculations. Please note that after-tax returns are shown only for the Investor Shares and will differ for each share class. After-tax returns are not relevant for a shareholder who holds fund shares in a tax-deferred account, such as an individual retirement account or a 401(k) plan. Also, figures captioned *Return After Taxes on Distributions and Sale of Fund Shares* will be higher than other figures for the same period if a capital loss occurs upon redemption and results in an assumed tax deduction for the shareholder.

Investment Advisor
Wellington Management Company, LLP

Portfolio Managers

Edward P. Bousa, CFA, Senior Vice President and Equity Portfolio Manager of Wellington Management. He has managed the stock portion of the Fund since 2002.

John C. Keogh, Senior Vice President and Fixed Income Portfolio Manager of Wellington Management. He has managed the bond portion of the Fund since 2006.

Purchase and Sale of Fund Shares
You may purchase or redeem shares online through our website at *www.vanguard.com*, by mail (The Vanguard Group, P.O. Box 1110, Valley Forge, PA 19482-1110), or by telephone (800-662-2739). The following table provides the Fund's minimum initial and subsequent investment requirements.

Account Minimums	Investor Shares	Admiral Shares
To open and maintain an account	$10,000	$100,000
To add to an existing account	$100 by check, exchange, wire, or electronic bank transfer (other than Automatic Investment Plan, which has no established minimum)	$100 by check, exchange, wire, or electronic bank transfer (other than Automatic Investment Plan, which has no established minimum)

Tax Information
The Fund's distributions may be taxable as ordinary income or capital gain.

Financial Intermediary Compensation
The Fund and its investment advisor do not pay financial intermediaries for sales of Fund shares or related services.

5

Figure 8-4:
Important details about the fund.

Source: The Vanguard Group. Reprinted with permission.

You can think of the investment policies or objectives as a broad set of rules or guidelines (for example, the major type of securities that the fund invests in) that the fund operates under when investing your money. This hopefully protects you from most major surprises. And if a fund violates these guidelines — for instance, if this fund puts all its money into international stocks — the SEC would spank, reprimand, and penalize Vanguard. Unethical fund companies may be willing to pay this small price if they can seduce more people into their funds by showing higher returns that result from taking poorly disclosed risks.

If you've taken the time to look at how much money this fund has made for investors, you owe it to yourself to understand this fund's risks, too. This section of the prospectus does an excellent job of discussing the Wellington Fund's risks, using examples from past decades instead of just from recent years, which were generally good years for the financial markets.

Plain Talk About Costs of Investing

Costs are an important consideration in choosing a mutual fund. That's because you, as a shareholder, pay the costs of operating a fund, plus any transaction costs incurred when the fund buys or sells securities. These costs can erode a substantial portion of the gross income or the capital appreciation a fund achieves. Even seemingly small differences in expenses can, over time, have a dramatic effect on a fund's performance.

The following sections explain the primary investment strategies and policies that the Fund uses in pursuit of its objective. The Fund's board of trustees, which oversees the Fund's management, may change investment strategies or policies in the interest of shareholders without a shareholder vote, unless those strategies or policies are designated as fundamental. Note that the Fund's investment objective is not fundamental and may be changed without a shareholder vote.

Plain Talk About Balanced Funds

Balanced funds are generally "middle-of-the-road" investments that seek to provide some combination of income, capital appreciation, and conservation of capital by investing in a mix of stocks and bonds. Because prices of stocks and bonds can respond differently to various economic events and influences, a balanced fund should experience less investment risk than a fund investing exclusively in stocks.

Market Exposure

Stocks
Roughly 60% to 70% of the Fund's assets are invested in stocks.

> The Fund is subject to stock market risk, which is the chance that stock prices overall will decline. Stock markets tend to move in cycles, with periods of rising prices and periods of falling prices.

To illustrate the volatility of stock prices, the following table shows the best, worst, and average annual total returns for the U.S. stock market over various periods as measured by the Standard & Poor's 500 Index, a widely used barometer of market activity. (Total returns consist of dividend income plus change in market price.) Note that the returns shown do not include the costs of buying and selling stocks or other expenses that a real-world investment portfolio would incur.

7

Figure 8-5: Investment objectives and risks.

Source: The Vanguard Group. Reprinted with permission.

U.S. Stock Market Returns
(1926–2009)

	1 Year	5 Years	10 Years	20 Years
Best	54.2%	28.6%	19.9%	17.8%
Worst	–43.1	–12.4	–1.4	3.1
Average	11.8	10.1	10.7	11.3

The table covers all of the 1-, 5-, 10-, and 20-year periods from 1926 through 2009. You can see, for example, that although the average return on common stocks for *all* of the 5-year periods was 10.1%, average returns for *individual* 5-year periods ranged from –12.4% (from 1928 through 1932) to 28.6% (from 1995 through 1999). These average returns reflect *past* performance of common stocks; you should not regard them as an indication of *future* performance of either the stock market as a whole or the Fund in particular.

Stocks of publicly traded companies and funds that invest in stocks are often classified according to market value, or market capitalization. These classifications typically include small-cap, mid-cap, and large-cap. It's important to understand that, for both companies and stock funds, market-capitalization ranges change over time. Also, interpretations of size vary, and there are no "official" definitions of small-, mid-, and large-cap, even among Vanguard fund advisors. The asset-weighted median market capitalization of the Fund's stock portfolio as of November 30, 2009, was $53.8 billion.

Bonds
The Fund invests the remaining 30% to 40% of its assets in bonds.

> The Fund is subject to interest rate risk, which is the chance that bond prices overall will decline because of rising interest rates. Interest rate risk should be moderate because the average term of the Fund's bond portfolio is generally intermediate-term, and because the Fund's bond holdings represent less than 40% of the Fund's assets.

Although bonds are often thought to be less risky than stocks, there have been periods when bond prices have fallen significantly because of rising interest rates. For instance, prices of long-term bonds fell by almost 48% between December 1976 and September 1981.

To illustrate the relationship between bond prices and interest rates, the following table shows the effect of a 1% and a 2% change (both up and down) in interest rates on the values of three noncallable bonds of different maturities, each with a face value of $1,000.

8

Figure 8-6: More investment objectives and risks.

Source: The Vanguard Group. Reprinted with permission.

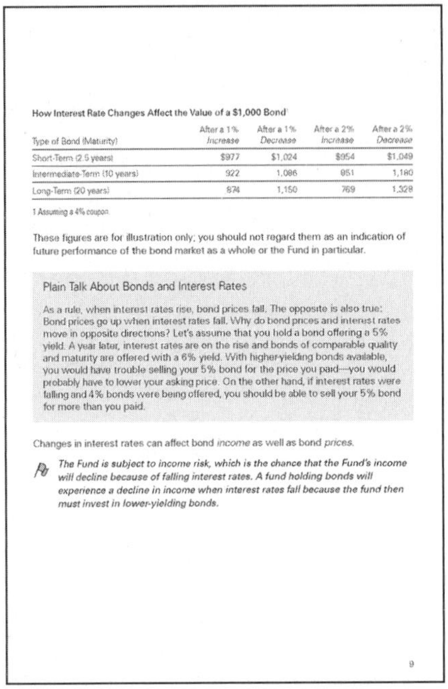

How Interest Rate Changes Affect the Value of a $1,000 Bond[1]

Type of Bond (Maturity)	After a 1% Increase	After a 1% Decrease	After a 2% Increase	After a 2% Decrease
Short-Term (2.5 years)	$977	$1,024	$954	$1,049
Intermediate-Term (10 years)	922	1,086	851	1,180
Long-Term (20 years)	874	1,150	769	1,328

1 Assuming a 4% coupon

These figures are for illustration only; you should not regard them as an indication of future performance of the bond market as a whole or the Fund in particular.

Plain Talk About Bonds and Interest Rates

As a rule, when interest rates rise, bond prices fall. The opposite is also true: Bond prices go up when interest rates fall. Why do bond prices and interest rates move in opposite directions? Let's assume that you hold a bond offering a 5% yield. A year later, interest rates are on the rise and bonds of comparable quality and maturity are offered with a 6% yield. With higher-yielding bonds available, you would have trouble selling your 5% bond for the price you paid—you would probably have to lower your asking price. On the other hand, if interest rates were falling and 4% bonds were being offered, you should be able to sell your 5% bonds for more than you paid.

Changes in interest rates can affect bond *income* as well as bond *prices.*

The Fund is subject to income risk, which is the chance that the Fund's income will decline because of falling interest rates. A fund holding bonds will experience a decline in income when interest rates fall because the fund then must invest in lower-yielding bonds.

9

Figure 8-7:
Still more
investment
objectives
and risks.

Source: The Vanguard Group. Reprinted with permission.

Investment adviser

This important section (see Figure 8-8) provides background about the investment adviser — the folks actually managing the investments of this fund. You can read about the firm (in this case, it's an outside money management company — Wellington Management Company) who make the fund's investment decisions.

Financial highlights

If you get a headache looking at all the numbers on financial pages, you're not alone. Figure 8-9 looks frightening, but this table is just a yearly summary of the value of the fund's shares and the distributions the fund has made. (I cover these subjects in detail in Chapters 17 and 18.)

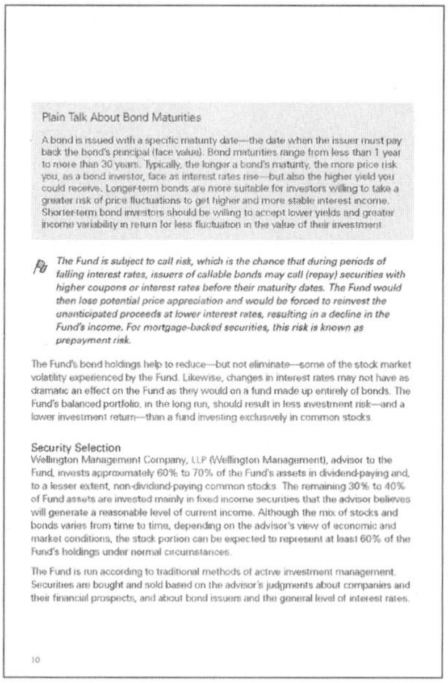

Plain Talk About Bond Maturities

A bond is issued with a specific maturity date—the date when the issuer must pay back the bond's principal (face value). Bond maturities range from less than 1 year to more than 30 years. Typically, the longer a bond's maturity, the more price risk you, as a bond investor, face as interest rates rise—but also the higher yield you could receive. Longer-term bonds are more suitable for investors willing to take a greater risk of price fluctuations to get higher and more stable interest income. Shorter-term bond investors should be willing to accept lower yields and greater income variability in return for less fluctuation in the value of their investment.

The Fund is subject to call risk, which is the chance that during periods of falling interest rates, issuers of callable bonds may call (repay) securities with higher coupons or interest rates before their maturity dates. The Fund would then lose potential price appreciation and would be forced to reinvest the unanticipated proceeds at lower interest rates, resulting in a decline in the Fund's income. For mortgage-backed securities, this risk is known as prepayment risk.

The Fund's bond holdings help to reduce—but not eliminate—some of the stock market volatility experienced by the Fund. Likewise, changes in interest rates may not have as dramatic an effect on the Fund as they would on a fund made up entirely of bonds. The Fund's balanced portfolio, in the long run, should result in less investment risk—and a lower investment return—than a fund investing exclusively in common stocks.

Security Selection

Wellington Management Company, LLP (Wellington Management), advisor to the Fund, invests approximately 60% to 70% of the Fund's assets in dividend-paying and, to a lesser extent, non-dividend-paying common stocks. The remaining 30% to 40% of Fund assets are invested mainly in fixed income securities that the advisor believes will generate a reasonable level of current income. Although the mix of stocks and bonds varies from time to time, depending on the advisor's view of economic and market conditions, the stock portion can be expected to represent at least 60% of the Fund's holdings under normal circumstances.

The Fund is run according to traditional methods of active investment management. Securities are bought and sold based on the advisor's judgments about companies and their financial prospects, and about bond issuers and the general level of interest rates.

10

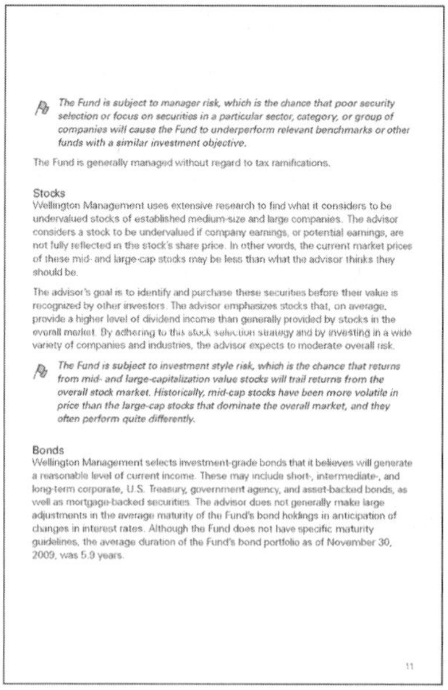

The Fund is subject to manager risk, which is the chance that poor security selection or focus on securities in a particular sector, category, or group of companies will cause the Fund to underperform relevant benchmarks or other funds with a similar investment objective.

The Fund is generally managed without regard to tax ramifications.

Stocks

Wellington Management uses extensive research to find what it considers to be undervalued stocks of established medium-size and large companies. The advisor considers a stock to be undervalued if company earnings, or potential earnings, are not fully reflected in the stock's share price. In other words, the current market prices of these mid- and large-cap stocks may be less than what the advisor thinks they should be.

The advisor's goal is to identify and purchase these securities before their value is recognized by other investors. The advisor emphasizes stocks that, on average, provide a higher level of dividend income than generally provided by stocks in the overall market. By adhering to this stock selection strategy and by investing in a wide variety of companies and industries, the advisor expects to moderate overall risk.

The Fund is subject to investment style risk, which is the chance that returns from mid- and large-capitalization value stocks will trail returns from the overall stock market. Historically, mid-cap stocks have been more volatile in price than the large-cap stocks that dominate the overall market, and they often perform quite differently.

Bonds

Wellington Management selects investment-grade bonds that it believes will generate a reasonable level of current income. These may include short-, intermediate-, and long-term corporate, U.S. Treasury, government agency, and asset-backed bonds, as well as mortgage-backed securities. The advisor does not generally make large adjustments in the average maturity of the Fund's bond holdings in anticipation of changes in interest rates. Although the Fund does not have specific maturity guidelines, the average duration of the Fund's bond portfolio as of November 30, 2009, was 5.9 years.

11

Figure 8-8: The investment adviser actually manages the fund's money.

Source: The Vanguard Group. Reprinted with permission.

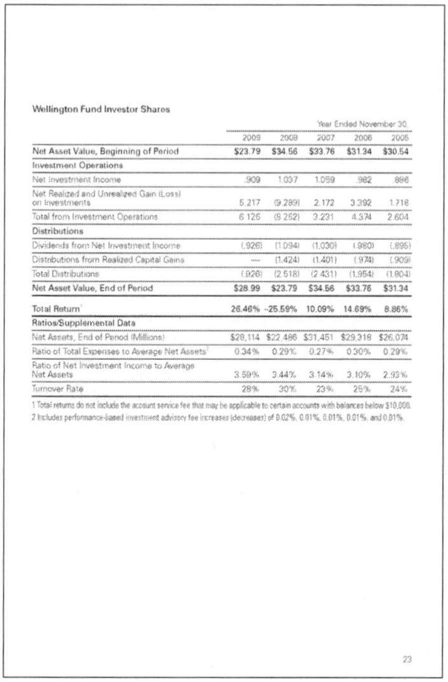

Wellington Fund Investor Shares

	Year Ended November 30,				
	2009	2008	2007	2006	2005
Net Asset Value, Beginning of Period	**$23.79**	**$34.56**	**$33.76**	**$31.34**	**$30.54**
Investment Operations					
Net Investment Income	.909	1.037	1.059	.982	.886
Net Realized and Unrealized Gain (Loss) on Investments	5.217	(9.289)	2.172	3.392	1.718
Total from Investment Operations	6.126	(8.252)	3.231	4.374	2.604
Distributions					
Dividends from Net Investment Income	(.926)	(1.094)	(1.030)	(.980)	(.895)
Distributions from Realized Capital Gains	—	(1.424)	(1.401)	(.974)	(.909)
Total Distributions	(.926)	(2.518)	(2.431)	(1.954)	(1.804)
Net Asset Value, End of Period	**$28.99**	**$23.79**	**$34.56**	**$33.76**	**$31.34**
Total Return[1]	**26.46%**	**-25.59%**	**10.09%**	**14.69%**	**8.86%**
Ratios/Supplemental Data					
Net Assets, End of Period (Millions)	$28,114	$22,486	$31,451	$29,318	$26,074
Ratio of Total Expenses to Average Net Assets[2]	0.34%	0.29%	0.27%	0.30%	0.29%
Ratio of Net Investment Income to Average Net Assets	3.59%	3.44%	3.14%	3.10%	2.93%
Turnover Rate	28%	30%	23%	25%	24%

1 Total returns do not include the account service fee that may be applicable to certain accounts with balances below $10,000.

2 Includes performance-based investment advisory fee increases (decreases) of 0.02%, 0.01%, 0.01%, 0.01%, and 0.01%.

23

Figure 8-9: Financial highlights.

Source: The Vanguard Group. Reprinted with permission.

The *Net Asset Value* (NAV) is the price per share of the fund. Tracking this value provides an incomplete, *terrible* measure of what you would've earned in the fund. Why? Just look at the distributions section, which details all the money paid out to shareholders each year. This fund has paid out total distributions (dividends and capital gains) of $9.63 per share over this five-year period. This per-share figure is an enormous amount when you consider that the share price actually decreased from $30.54 to $28.99 during the period — a 5.1 percent decrease. But if you add in the distributions to the change in share price, now you're talking about a 26.5 percent (or more) increase (if you'd reinvested these distributions, you would've had an even greater return).

The *Total Return* represents what investors in the fund have earned historically. The returns on this type of fund, which invests in stocks and bonds, bounce around from year to year. You can see how the total investments (*Net Assets*) in the fund have changed over time. Assets can increase from new money flowing into the fund as well as from an increase in the value of a fund's shares.

This section of a prospectus also shows you how a fund's annual operating expenses (*Ratio of Total Expenses to Average Net Assets*) have changed over time. They should decrease when a fund is growing. This fund's expense ratio of 0.29 percent in 2005 increased to 0.34 percent four years later. If operating expenses are high (not in this case) and don't decrease, their persistent levels may signal a company that maximizes its profits because of the fund's popularity. For funds that are only a few years old, expenses may remain higher because the fund is building its base of investors. (The slight increase for this fund isn't significant and was due in part to the high return of the most recent year, which increased the fund manager's performance fee payments.)

The line *Ratio of Net Investment Income to Average Net Assets* shows the annual dividends, or yield, that the fund has paid. (This figure is especially important for retired people, who need income to live on.) In this example, the downward trend merely reflects the overall decline in interest rates during the period. If you looked at this ratio for a similar fund, you'd see the same trend for this period.

The *Turnover Rate* tells you how much trading takes place in a fund. Specifically, it measures the percentage of the portfolio's holdings that has been traded over the year:

- ✔ A low turnover number (less than 30 percent or so), such as the one for this fund, denotes a fund with more of a buy-and-hold strategy.

- ✔ A high turnover number (100 percent plus) indicates a fund manager who does a lot of trading. Rapid trading is costlier and riskier and may increase a fund's taxable distributions.

Reviewing Annual Reports

Funds also produce annual reports that discuss how the fund's been doing and provide details on the specific investments that a fund holds. Look at the annual report if, for instance, you want to know which countries an international fund is currently invested in.

 You can get answers to questions like what countries a fund invests in by calling a fund's toll-free number or by hunting around on a fund company's Web site. (Some fund companies enable you to access their fund's annual reports and prospectuses on their Web site.) Some of the mutual fund information sources that I recommend in Chapter 20 also report this type of information. (Or you could say, "Details, details. Just suggest some funds to buy for different needs." That's just what I do in Chapters 11 through 15.)

In this section, I review the pages from the annual report on the Vanguard Wellington Fund — the same fund whose prospectus I introduce you to in the preceding section. In addition to producing an annual report, each fund produces a semiannual report that (guess what?) comes out halfway between annual reports. The semiannual reports are usually a bit shorter than the full-year reports but contain the most up-to-date information on the fund's current investment holdings and performance.

 When you call a fund company to ask for applications, specifically request a fund's recent annual or semiannual reports. Unlike a prospectus, most funds don't automatically send you annual reports. (And, of course, most fund companies provide these reports on their Web sites.)

Chairman's letter and performance discussion

The Chairman's letter is supposed to explain how well the fund has performed recently and why (see Figure 8-10). In far too many reports, the fund's chief executive uses his or her letter to the stockholders merely as an opportunity to overhype how well the fund has done — during *good* periods in the financial markets. In tougher times, too many fund execs blame subpar performance on the market. It's like fishing: On a successful day, you talk about your uncanny casting ability, your brilliant choice of lures, and your ability to keep still and quiet. When you come home empty handed, the fish just weren't biting.

Dear Shareholder:

For the fiscal year that ended November 30, 2009, Vanguard Wellington Fund's Investor Shares and Admiral Shares both returned about 26%, a strong performance driven by the stock market's turnaround and the fund advisor's expert stock selection. By comparison, the fund's benchmark, the unmanaged Wellington Composite Index, returned about 24%.

While stocks in a variety of industries made solid contributions as markets rallied during the dramatic recovery, the fund's health care and materials holdings were especially impressive. Wellington Management Company, the fund's advisor, also made wise decisions in the consumer staples, energy, and industrial sectors.

All ten equity sectors in the fund had positive returns, and only the utilities and telecommunication services groups returned less than double digits. The fixed income portion of the fund also outperformed the fund's fixed income benchmark.

If you hold the Wellington Fund in a taxable account, you may wish to review the section on the fund's after-tax returns later in this report.

Stock markets worldwide produced double-digit returns
For the 12 months ended November 30, U.S. stocks posted significant gains, as the steep losses suffered during the first

President's Letter

Figure 8-10:
President's
letter.

Source: The Vanguard Group. Reprinted with permission.

A good annual report like Vanguard's will detail the performance of the fund and compare it to relevant benchmarks and comparable funds. You hope that your fund will meet or exceed the performance of comparable funds (and perhaps even of the benchmark, too) in most periods. Don't worry if your fund periodically underperforms a little. Especially with stock and bond funds, you invest for the long haul, not just for six months or a year.

Unfortunately, as I discuss earlier in this chapter, more than a few fund companies use benchmarks (indexes) as comparisons for their funds' performances so that their funds look as if they perform better than they really do. This ruse is similar to a financially savvy adult like, say, me, comparing his mutual fund selection abilities to those of, say, a child. I'm at something of an unfair advantage (at any rate, I'd better be). As you review a fund's annual report, keep in mind this tendency of some funds to fudge comparisons. In Chapter 17, I discuss ways you can make sure that you're comparing a fund's performance to an appropriate benchmark.

In addition to discussing the fund's performance during the year, an annual report also covers how the overall financial markets were feeling. If you're used to a steady diet of the daily news, an overview like this can help you to better see and understand the big picture (and maybe you won't be so shocked that one of your funds lost, say, 2 percent last year when you see that the benchmark index most relevant to that fund lost 5 percent).

A good annual report is educational and honest. As you can see, Vanguard's is both. The report does a nice job of providing a historical context for understanding this fund's performance. It also clearly explains that a surging stock market the past year propelled this fund's returns.

The comparisons to competitors help you make sure that you're comparing your fund to the Wellington Fund's true peers — apples to apples. These comparisons are even more valuable and useful when applied over longer periods (see Figure 8-11). You can see how the Wellington Fund performed against its competitors ("average balanced fund") and the benchmark composite index. The Wellington Fund handily beat the competition and the benchmark index. (The "Composite Index" is a mythical investment, which has the advantage of not having any costs deducted from it.)

In the world of stocks and bonds, one year is too short a period to evaluate a fund. In this section, the chairman also looks forward and prudently reminds you that the future will likely contain both good and bad periods.

Figure 8-11: Long-term performance discussion.

low months were erased by the rally that began in March. The stock market's rebound seemed to anticipate an improvement in the broader economy, which began to show signs of growth in the second half of the period.

The story was similar in many international markets. They collapsed in late 2008 and early 2009, then rebounded at a startling rate. The recovery was especially swift and powerful in emerging markets, many of which came out of the financial crisis in better fiscal and economic shape than their developed-market counterparts.

Despite the strong performance seen since March, the longer-term returns of most stock market indexes bear witness to the trials suffered by many investors in the not-so-distant past. Over the past three years, for example, both U.S. and international stock indexes have declined. Five-year annualized returns for U.S. stocks as of November 30 were mostly positive, but far from impressive. Stock markets abroad fared better over this longer period, posting average annual returns of almost 7%.

For bonds, a period of panic was followed by robust returns

Volatility was also a theme in the fixed income market over the past 12 months. At the peak of the credit crisis in late 2008, investors shunned just about any security not issued by the U.S. Treasury. This stampede to quality led to the widest gap between the very low yields of Treasuries and the much higher yields of corporate bonds since the Great Depression.

In early spring, "green shoots" began to emerge—signs that aggressive fiscal and monetary policies were getting the global economy back on its feet. Investors' appetite for risk returned to more normal levels and the demand for corporate bonds increased, raising their prices and bringing down their yields. For the 12 months ended November 30, taxable and municipal bonds each notched double-digit results, returning about 12% and 14%, respectively.

Shorter-term savings vehicles, including money market funds, didn't fare as well. They became casualties of the Fed's dramatic cuts in short-term interest rates, which were intended to nurse the economy back to health. In December 2008, the Fed reduced its target for the federal funds rate, a benchmark for the interest rates paid by money market instruments and other very short-term securities, to between 0% and 0.25%. The target has stayed there ever since. After its meeting in early November, the Fed said it expected to maintain the target at this level "for an extended period."

Stocks and bonds contribute to success

The Wellington Fund's fiscal year began amid extreme volatility in the financial markets and the deepest recession since the 1930s. As the stock market skidded toward its bottom in March, however, investment opportunities arose. Wellington Management Company has distinguished itself over the years with its value-oriented

Market Barometer

	Average Annual Total Returns Periods Ended November 30, 2009		
	One Year	Three Years	Five Years
Stocks			
Russell 3000 Index (Large-caps)	27.38%	–5.71%	1.02%
Russell 2000 Index (Small-caps)	24.53	–8.26	–0.46
Dow Jones U.S. Total Stock Market Index	28.06	–5.65	1.24
MSCI All Country World Index ex USA (International)	47.13	–2.73	6.78
Bonds			
Barclays Capital U.S. Aggregate Bond Index (Broad taxable market)	11.63%	8.40%	5.45%
Barclays Capital Municipal Bond Index	14.17	4.17	4.50
Citigroup 3-Month Treasury Bill Index	0.20	2.36	2.91
CPI			
Consumer Price Index	1.84%	2.40%	2.52%

Expense Ratios[1]
Your Fund Compared With Its Peer Group

	Investor Shares	Admiral Shares	Mixed-Asset Target Allocation Growth Funds Average
Wellington Fund	0.35%	0.22%	1.06%

[1] The fund expense ratios shown are from the prospectus dated March 29, 2010, and represent estimated costs for the current fiscal year based on the fund's net assets as of the prospectus date. For the fiscal year ended November 30, 2009, the fund's expense ratios were 0.34% for Investor Shares and 0.21% for Admiral Shares. The peer-group expense ratio is derived from data provided by Lipper Inc. and captures information through year-end 2008.

Investment adviser's thoughts

The "Advisor's Report" is where the portfolio managers of the fund (in this case, the Wellington Management Company) explain how the economic environment affected the fund's performance. They also look ahead and discuss what the future may hold and what investment strategy they plan to take in the near future (see Figure 8-12). I especially like how this report highlights not only their successes but also their less-than-stellar performers.

Figure 8-12: Investment advisor's insights and reflections.

Advisor's Report

Vanguard Wellington Fund's Investor Shares returned about 26% for the fiscal year ended November 30, 2009. The performance exceeded the return for the composite index, which is weighted 65% in large-capitalization stocks and 35% in high-quality corporate bonds, as well as the average return of mixed-asset target allocation growth funds.

The investment environment

Stocks gained just over 25%, as measured by the S&P 500 Index, for the 12-month period ended November 30, 2009. U.S. equities snapped back in November, rising for the eighth time in the past nine months. Markets closed modestly off their peak levels as news of debt problems in Dubai briefly sparked a rise in risk aversion toward the end of the period. While the news shook global markets, equity markets finished the period significantly higher than their March 2009 lows, with emerging markets continuing their dominance over developed markets as investors favored higher-risk assets.

Recent actions taken by banks and other financial services companies to increase their capital strength, in addition to the broader rally in equity prices, appear to have taken the risk of further severe economic decline off the table. However, the most recent economic news has been mixed. As consumers improve their balance sheets, confidence remains low amid a worsening unemployment rate and sluggish housing market.

The return of growth to the U.S. economy has been uneven and, for the most part, government-assisted, but the return of liquidity and risk appetite to the bond market has been nothing short of dramatic. Lower Treasury yields have allowed other borrowing costs to decline. Drops in mortgage rates, swap rates, and the cost of borrowing between banks (as represented by the London Interbank Offered Rate, or LIBOR) have provided relief for some mortgage and nonfinancial corporate borrowers. However, year-end profit-taking and fears that Dubai's debt restructuring announcement would have negative systemic implications halted the advances of nongovernment fixed income markets toward the end of the period.

Our successes

Strong stock selection was the main driver of overall equity performance for the period. Select holdings in the health care, energy, materials, consumer staples, and industrials sectors added to results. Top absolute contributors during the period included IBM, Schering-Plough, JPMorgan Chase, Wells Fargo, and International Paper.

IBM's solid earnings in a tough environment led to outperformance for the period. Schering-Plough's stock price jumped significantly following news that it would combine with Merck as part of a reverse merger. JPMorgan Chase shares surged in May after the bank announced that it planned to repay the money it received under the Troubled Asset Relief Program (TARP) without raising capital. More recently shares have benefited from improved earnings. We added to our holding in International Paper in April after the company strengthened its balance sheet through a debt refinancing. The company's shares gained as earnings per share and cash flow generation were better than the market expected, further improving the company's balance sheet. Wells Fargo benefited from a stock offering that helped secure the company's financial position and focused investors' attention on the company's future earnings power.

8

The fund's bond portfolio also performed well. Security selection within the corporate sector, particularly holdings in insurance and consumer cyclicals and noncyclicals, was the primary driver of outperformance for the period.

Our shortfalls

Within the equity portion of the fund, security selection in the information technology and telecommunication services sectors detracted modestly from results. Also detracting from returns were meaningfully underweighted positions to the information technology and consumer discretionary sectors and overweighted positions in the utilities and telecommunication services sectors. Absolute detractors for the period included Bank of America, Capital One, and General Electric.

Bank of America shares declined after the company posted its first quarterly loss of the year. Steeper consumer and commercial loan losses more than offset a boost in revenue from Bank of America's acquisition of Merrill Lynch and strong trading profits. Capital One saw a rapid escalation in credit card losses as a result of the economic slowdown. We eliminated our position early in the period. General Electric, the industrial and financial services giant, saw shares tumble on missed first-quarter earnings, concerns over the stability of its GE Capital finance unit, and the subsequent rating downgrade by both Moody's and Standard & Poor's. We reduced our exposure to GE, starting late in 2008, but not before the fund had borne the brunt of the share-price decline. Shares of General Electric gained more recently on news that the company was in talks to sell its stake in NBC Universal to Comcast (the companies announced that they had reached an agreement shortly after the close of the fiscal period).

Within fixed income, our U.S. Treasury holdings, which we maintain for potential liquidity needs, underperformed higher-risk assets during the period.

The fund's positioning

We continue to search diligently for attractively valued companies with strong operating characteristics. We are particularly interested in the stocks of companies whose business fundamentals are poised to improve. As always, an above-average dividend is central to our stock selection process.

9

Source: The Vanguard Group. Reprinted with permission.

Performance and its components

The performance page looks like a terrible overload of numbers, but it actually contains valuable information (see Figure 8-13).

For example, this table shows you how the Wellington Fund has performed each year. As you can see in the *Cumulative Performance* table, although the fund has produced an *average* annual return of 6.20 percent per year over the past ten years, its return varies much from year to year. In 2008 (fiscal year, which in this case ends November 30), for instance, its return was –25.6 percent, but the return was 26.5 percent in 2009. If a swing in returns such as this makes you reach for your motion sickness prescription, you'd better skip investing in the fund.

To earn better returns, you have to take risks.

Wellington Fund

Performance Summary

All of the returns in this report represent past performance, which is not a guarantee of future results that may be achieved by the fund. (Current performance may be lower or higher than the performance data cited. For performance data current to the most recent month-end, visit our website at www.vanguard.com/performance.) Note, too, that both investment returns and principal value can fluctuate widely, so an investor's shares, when sold, could be worth more or less than their original cost. The returns shown do not reflect taxes that a shareholder would pay on fund distributions or on the sale of fund shares.

Cumulative Performance: November 30, 1999–November 30, 2009
Initial investment of $10,000

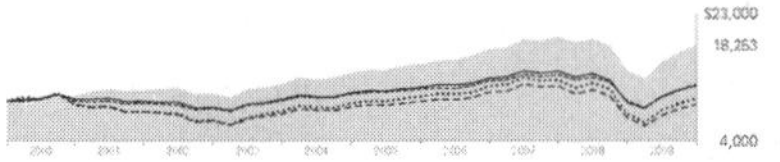

	Average Annual Total Returns Periods Ended November 30, 2009			Final Value of a $10,000 Investment
	One Year	Five Years	Ten Years	
Wellington Fund Investor Shares[1]	26.46%	5.26%	6.20%	$18,253
Dow Jones U.S. Total Stock Market Index	28.06	1.24	0.27	10,278
S&P 500 Index	25.39	0.71	–0.57	9,443
Wellington Composite Index[2]	23.87	2.42	2.15	12,375
Mixed-Asset Target Allocation Growth Funds Average[3]	26.23	1.86	2.06	12,266

	One Year	Five Years	Since Inception[4]	Final Value of a $100,000 Investment
Wellington Fund Admiral Shares	26.57%	5.40%	5.66%	$159,951
Dow Jones U.S. Total Stock Market Index	28.06	1.24	1.44	112,985
S&P 500 Index	25.39	0.71	0.37	103,246
Wellington Composite Index[2]	23.87	2.42	2.71	125,651

1 Total returns do not include the account service fee that may be applicable to certain accounts with balances below $10,000.
2 Weighted 65% S&P 500 Index and 35% Lehman U.S. Long Credit AA or Better Index through February 29, 2000, and 65% S&P 500 Index and 35% Barclays Capital U.S. Credit A or Better Bond Index thereafter.
3 Derived from data provided by Lipper Inc.
4 Performance for the fund's Admiral Shares and comparative standards is calculated since the Admiral Shares' inception: May 14, 2001.
See Financial Highlights for dividend and capital gains information.

15

Figure 8-13: Total investment returns, year by year.

Source: The Vanguard Group. Reprinted with permission.

Investment holdings

The *Statement of Net Assets* section lists every investment the fund owns. Here's where you get the details that tell you exactly where your money is invested. You can see here the incredible diversification your money gets in a mutual fund; you actually own a tiny sliver of each of these securities if you invest in this fund (see Figure 8-14). For example, in this first section, you can see that this fund (as of November 30, 2009) was 65 percent invested in stocks, which are presented here by industry.

Reviewing a fund's specific investment holdings is important. Sometimes, a fund's name is misleading relative to what the fund actually holds; often, the *Objective* section of a prospectus doesn't provide insight into important factors, such as the sizes of the companies that it owns.

For each security, you also can see how much each investment was worth at the end of the most recent year. (Do you need to know, should you care, and will it be on the test? No, no, and no!)

Continuing on in the report, you see more of the investments that the fund owns. Figure 8-15 shows you some of the bonds the fund owns. These bonds are listed by issuer (government versus corporate) and the corporate bonds by industry and specific companies.

Figure 8-14:
Investment holdings of the fund.

Wellington Fund

	Coupon	Maturity Date	Face Amount ($000)	Market Value* ($000)	Percentage of Net Assets
U.S. Government and Agency Obligations					
U.S. Government Securities					
United States Treasury Note/Bond	1.000%	7/31/11	1,143,000	1,152,203	2.5%
United States Treasury Note/Bond	1.000%	9/30/11	525,000	529,937	1.1%
United States Treasury Note/Bond	2.750%	2/15/19	202,000	195,467	0.4%
				1,870,697	4.0%
Agency Bonds and Notes					
Bank of America Corp.	3.125%	6/15/12	50,000	52,461	0.1%
General Electric Capital Corp.	2.000%–3.000%	12/9/11–9/28/12	98,985	101,857	0.2%
John Deere Capital Corp.	2.875%	6/19/12	50,000	52,134	0.1%
JPMorgan Chase & Co.	3.125%	12/1/11	25,000	26,117	0.1%
PNC Funding Corp.	2.300%	6/22/12	13,580	14,510	0.0%
Wells Fargo & Co.	3.000%	12/9/11	19,000	19,811	0.1%
Agency Bonds and Notes—Other †				113,184	0.2%
				379,674	0.8%
Conventional Mortgage-Backed Securities †				10,975	0.0%
Total U.S. Government and Agency Obligations (Cost $2,242,950)				2,267,346	4.8%
†Asset-Backed/Commercial Mortgage-Backed Securities (Cost $19,945) †				20,043	0.0%
Corporate Bonds					
Finance					
Banking					
BAC Capital Trust VI	5.625%	3/8/35	90,180	66,816	0.1%
Bank of America Corp.	4.375%	12/1/10	10,000	10,268	0.0%
Bank of America NA	5.300%–6.000%	3/15/17–10/15/36	96,000	96,027	0.2%
Bank One Corp.	7.875%	8/1/10	40,000	41,396	0.1%
Golden West Financial Corp.	4.750%	10/1/12	10,000	10,597	0.0%
Goldman Sachs Group Inc.	5.000%–6.750%	1/15/11–10/1/37	322,995	337,998	0.7%
JPMorgan Chase & Co.	3.700%–7.900%	2/1/11–12/29/49	264,835	278,028	0.6%
Merrill Lynch & Co. Inc.	5.770%–6.875%	7/25/11–9/15/26	186,000	194,129	0.4%
National City Bank of Pennsylvania	7.250%	10/21/11	20,000	21,509	0.1%
National City Bank	7.250%	7/15/10	25,000	25,843	0.1%
National City Corp.	6.875%	5/15/19	13,950	15,228	0.0%
PNC Bank NA	4.875%	9/21/17	50,000	48,933	0.1%
PNC Financial Services Group Inc.	6.250%	5/21/49	44,000	42,690	0.1%
Wachovia Bank NA	6.000%	1/15/08	65,000	64,927	0.1%
Wachovia Corp.	5.500%	5/1/13	25,000	37,391	0.1%
Wells Fargo & Co.	3.750%–6.375%	8/1/11–9/15/16	143,000	150,417	0.3%
Wells Fargo Bank NA	6.450%	2/1/11	5,000	5,306	0.0%
Wells Fargo Capital XIII	7.700%	12/29/49	45,145	41,082	0.1%
Wells Fargo Financial Inc.	5.500%	8/1/12	20,000	21,866	0.1%
Banking—Other †				2,122,952	4.5%
Brokerage †				10,655	0.0%
Finance Companies					
General Electric Capital Corp.	5.250%–6.750%	2/22/11–8/7/37	252,200	265,275	0.5%
Finance Companies—Other †				225,279	0.5%
Insurance †				1,236,194	2.6%
Other Finance †				66,544	0.1%
Real Estate Investment Trusts †				254,203	0.8%
				5,680,095	12.0%

19

Figure 8-15: Bond holdings of the fund.

Source: The Vanguard Group. Reprinted with permission.

Investigating the Statement of Additional Information (SAI)

The brokerage fees that a fund pays to buy and sell securities for the fund are *not* included in the annual operating expense numbers that a fund reports. Brokerage costs reduce a fund's returns just the same as a fund's operating expenses and are ultimately reflected in the fund's annual rate of return.

Although fund brokerage costs are typically far less than the fund's operating expenses, funds that frequently trade or "turn over" their holdings can have significant brokerage expenses. These costs are disclosed in a fund's *Statement of Additional Information (SAI)*. More trades mean more costs draining your returns, which may also lead to more taxable distributions. Rest assured that the funds recommended in this book have relatively low overall expenses including brokerage fees.

In case you're curious, for the Vanguard Wellington fund, the brokerage expenses amount to about 0.07 percent annually — a small fraction of the funds' annual operating expense ratio.

Chapter 9

Buying Funds from the Best Firms

In This Chapter

▶ Becoming familiar with the best and worst places to buy funds

▶ Letting discount brokers work for *you*

▶ Knowing when hiring an adviser is appropriate

*H*undreds of investment companies offer thousands of fund options. However, only a handful of these fund companies offer many top-notch funds, so in this chapter, I tell you which companies are the best places for your fund investing.

Some other good individual funds are run by companies not mentioned in this chapter. (I recommend specific funds in Part IV of this book.) In addition to recommending the best parent fund companies, I also recommend the best discount brokers. Although these guys are slightly more expensive, discount brokers make buying the best funds from different fund companies and holding all the funds in a single account a lot easier.

Finding the Best Buys

When studying the different mutual funds companies, you may see a lot of different funds. Some are better than others. Using the criteria in Chapter 7, this chapter presents the best buys. In this section, I discuss the best companies through which to invest in funds directly. Check out the Appendix for each company's contact information. *Note:* In the fund company descriptions, I devote more space to those companies whose funds I recommend the most in this book. Some good funds are offered by companies not on this short list — please see Chapters 11 through 14 for all the specific fund picks.

The Vanguard Group

The Vanguard Group is now the largest mutual fund company in America, having surpassed Fidelity. Vanguard's significant growth since the early 1990s has been somewhat of a vindication for a company that was underrated for many years. (At the time that I wrote the first edition of this book in 1994, I went on record as saying that Vanguard, overall, was the best mutual fund company around and wasn't getting the recognition it deserved. My praise led some folks to ask whether I had a vested interest in praising Vanguard and the answer then is the same as today — no!)

One of the reasons for Vanguard's underrating is the fact that its funds are almost never at the very tiptop of the performance charts for their respective categories. As I discuss in Chapter 7, this sign is actually good, because many number-one-performing funds are rarely even above average over the long haul. Although Vanguard offers a broad spectrum of funds in terms of risk, it doesn't take excessive risks with the funds it offers; thus, its funds rarely are ranked number one over short time periods.

Because of Vanguard's unique shareholder-owned structure (see the nearby sidebar "Vanguard's roots: The Bogle difference"), the average operating-expense ratio of its funds — 0.22 percent per year for U.S. stock funds, 0.29 percent for international stock funds, and 0.14 percent for bond funds — is lower than that of any other fund family in the industry. In fact, the average fund family's expense ratio is a whopping four times higher than Vanguard's. Vanguard also offers its Admiral series of funds with lower expense ratios for higher balance customers and low-cost exchange-traded funds (see Chapter 5).

A pioneer in the field, Vanguard was the first to offer to the public *index funds,* which are unmanaged portfolios of the securities that comprise a given market index. Many fund companies have since added index funds to their lists of offerings. But Vanguard is still the indexing leader with the broadest selection of index funds and the lowest operating expenses in the business. (I talk more about the advantages of index funds in Chapter 10.)

Vanguard's low expenses translate into superior performance. Especially with money market and bond funds (markets in which even the best fund managers add relatively little value), Vanguard's funds are consistently near the head of the class.

Vanguard is best at funds appealing to safety-minded investors — those who want to invest in money market, bond, and conservative stock funds. However, Vanguard also offers aggressive stock funds with solid performance and low-expense ratios (see Chapter 13 for the list). In managing stock funds, where performance is supposed to be more closely tied to the genius of the fund manager, Vanguard's thriftiness enhances performance.

Vanguard's roots: The Bogle difference

In the early 1970s when Vanguard was formed, John Bogle, its founder and former CEO, made the big decision that to this day clearly differentiates Vanguard from its competition: Vanguard distributes funds and provides shareholder administration on an *at-cost basis* — that is, with no markup.

Bogle insisted that the management of most of the stock funds be contracted out to private money management firms, from whom Vanguard would negotiate the best deals. Thus, Vanguard's mutual fund investors would own the management company. Contrast this arrangement to that of traditional fund companies, in which the parent management company receives the profits from managing the funds.

Bogle felt that this unique corporate structure ensured that fund shareholders would obtain the best deals possible on money managers. "Funds ought to be run for the benefit of shareholders, not for the fund managers," Bogle reasoned. History has proven Bogle not only to be right but also to be a mutual fund investor's best advocate.

Fidelity Investments

Fidelity Investments is the second largest mutual fund company in America. A mutual fund Goliath, Fidelity offers hundreds of funds. As evidence of Fidelity's enormous buying power, representatives from dozens of companies visit its Boston offices every day. Most mutual fund managers have to travel to the companies they're interested in researching; if you're a Fidelity mutual fund manager, however, many companies come to you.

Fidelity's roots trace back to the 1940s, when Edward C. Johnson II took over the then-fledgling Fidelity Fund from its president, who felt that he couldn't make enough money as the head of an investment fund! Johnson's son, Ned (Edward C. Johnson III), assumed Fidelity's top position in 1972 and has clearly proven that you can make a truckload of money operating mutual funds: He's personally worth billions.

If you're venturing to do business with Fidelity on your own, you have your work cut out for you. One of the biggest problems novice investors have at Fidelity is discerning the good funds from the not-so-good ones. (My book separates the best from the rest and highlights which Fidelity funds are worthy of your investment dollars.)

I specifically advise shunning the following types of funds at Fidelity:

- ✔ **Bond funds:** Relative to the best of the competition, Fidelity's bond funds charge higher operating expenses that depress an investor's returns. (*Note:* For larger balance customers, Fidelity offers a decent series of bond funds known as Spartan funds that have lower operating expense ratios — see Chapter 11.)

Funds with branch offices: Even better?

Many mutual fund companies have their offices in one location. If you happen to live in the town or city where they're located and want to do business with them, you can visit them in person. However, odds are that, unless you maintain several homes, you won't be living near the fund companies with which you want to do your fund-investing business.

Some fund companies, such as Fidelity, have greater numbers of branch offices, which are located primarily in densely populated and more affluent areas. You may feel more comfortable dropping a check off or speaking to an investment representative face to face instead of being navigated through an automated voice message system or mouse-clicking through a Web site. However, there's no sound *financial* reason that you need to go in person to a fund company —you can do everything you need to do by phone, mail, or computer.

In most cases, you pay a cost for doing your fund investing through firms with branch offices. Operating all those branch offices in areas where rent and employees don't come cheaply costs a good chunk of money. Ultimately, firms that maintain a large branch network need to build these extra costs into their funds' fees. Higher fees lower your investment returns.

A counterargument that fund companies with many branch offices make is that if the branch offices succeed in enticing more investors to use the funds offered by the company, more total money is brought in. Having more money under management helps to lower the average cost of managing each dollar invested.

- ✔ **Adviser funds:** Fidelity sells this family of load funds through investment salespeople; these funds carry high sales loads or high ongoing fees.

- ✔ **Sector funds:** You should also avoid Fidelity's sector funds (Select), which invest in just one industry — such as air transportation, insurance, or retailing. These funds have rapid changeover of managers. Being industry focused, these funds are poorly diversified (highly concentrated) and quite risky. Fidelity, unfortunately, encourages a trader mentality with these funds.

One of Fidelity's strengths is its local presence — it operates 100+ branch offices throughout the United States and staffs its phones 24 hours a day, 365 days a year.

Dodge & Cox

Dodge & Cox is a San Francisco–based firm that has been in the fund business since the Great Depression. It's best known for its conservatively managed funds with solid track records and modest fees.

Unfortunately for new investors, from time to time, Dodge & Cox has closed some of its funds. The company did so to keep funds from becoming too bloated with assets to manage, which could undermine the performance of those funds. Thanks to the severe stock market decline in the late 2000s, all its funds were reopened and remain so as of this writing. However, if any of its funds appeal to you, you should establish an account in case it shuts any of its funds again to new investors.

Oakmark

Harris Associates, which has managed money since 1976, is the investment management company that oversees the management of Oakmark, this value-oriented Chicago-based family of funds.

As with the Dodge & Cox funds (see the preceding section), a number of the best Oakmark funds have closed from time to time to new investors. As of this writing, all its funds are open. Be aware that when some of its funds have closed in the past, investors who establish accounts directly with Oakmark can still buy some of the closed funds.

T. Rowe Price

Founded in 1937, T. Rowe Price is one of the oldest mutual fund companies — named after its founder, T. (Thomas) Rowe Price, who's generally credited with popularizing investing in growth-oriented companies. The fund company has also been a fund pioneer in international investing.

T. Rowe Price remained a small company for many years, focusing on its specialties of U.S. growth stocks and international funds. That stance changed in recent decades as the company offered a comprehensive menu of different fund types. It offers 401(k) retirement plans specifically for smaller companies. The fund company also offers a series of lower cost money market and bond funds called Summit funds with a minimum initial investment of $25,000.

TIAA-CREF

This nonprofit organization provides an array of investment services to education, hospitals, and other nonprofit organizations and offers a solid family of funds to the general public. Its funds have low operating expense ratios and are conservatively managed.

Headquartered in New York City, the company has major operations in Charlotte, North Carolina, and Denver, Colorado, as well as about 60 local offices. The organization got its start in 1918 when Andrew Carnegie and his Carnegie Foundation established a pension system for professors. Funding initially came from grants from the foundation and Carnegie Corporation of New York, and regular contributions from participating institutions and individuals. Today, TIAA-CREF invests more than $400 billion on behalf of investors.

The funds' low minimums make them a good choice for investors with smaller sums to invest. They have no-minimum-investment IRAs with no annual administrative fees.

Other fund companies

With so many companies offering mutual funds, the number of them competing for your mutual fund dollars far exceeds those that are worthy of your consideration. But here are some additional noteworthy fund companies:

- ✔ **Artisan:** This small family of well-managed stock funds is headquartered in Milwaukee, Wisconsin. Unfortunately, as the popularity of some of its funds has grown over the years, some of them have closed. As of this writing, the Artisan International Small Cap Fund, Artisan Mid Cap Fund, Artisan Mid Cap Value Fund, and Artisan Small Cap Value Fund are closed to new investors.

- ✔ **Harbor:** Based in Toledo, Ohio, Harbor Funds contracts with outside money managers who manage money for affluent individuals and institutions. Although Harbor fund managers don't take great risks, their funds are expected to — and are generally able to — outperform comparable market indexes.

- ✔ **Masters' Select:** The investment advisory firm of Litman/Gregory, which manages money for affluent individuals and institutions, developed this unique and small family of funds in 1997. Each of the funds within this family, which is based in Orinda, California, contracts out the actual management of the investment dollars to a handful of top fund managers.

- ✔ **USAA:** Headquartered in San Antonio, Texas, USAA is a conservative family of efficiently managed mutual funds (and generally low-cost, high-quality insurance). Although you (or a family member) need to be a military officer, enlistee, or military retiree to gain access to its homeowner and auto insurance, anyone can buy its mutual funds. USAA also offers investors, with small amounts to invest (minimum of $50 monthly) and without several thousand dollars required to meet fund minimum requirements, the ability to invest via electronic monthly transfers. For more info on USAA's funds, check out its Web site at `www.usaa.com/inet/ent_utils/McStaticPages?key=investments_mutual_funds_main`.

Hundreds of mutual fund companies offer thousands of funds. Many aren't worth your consideration because they don't meet the common-sense selection criteria outlined in Chapter 7. So if you're wondering why I didn't mention a particular fund family, it's probably because the record shows that its funds are high cost, low performance, managed in a schizophrenic fashion, or all of the above. Check them out against the criteria in Chapter 7 to see for yourself. (***Note:*** In Part IV, where I recommend specific funds in varying fund categories, I also mention some other funds offered by companies that aren't specifically written up in this chapter.)

One of the beauties of all the fund choices out there is that you don't have to settle for mediocre or inferior funds. If you're wondering what to do with such funds that you already own, please read Chapter 17.

Discount Brokers: Mutual Fund Supermarkets

For many years, you could only purchase no-load mutual funds directly from mutual fund companies. If you wanted to buy some funds at, say, Vanguard, Oakmark, T. Rowe Price, and Dodge & Cox, you needed to call these four different companies and request each firm's application. So you ended up filling out four different sets of forms and mailing them in with a separate check to each of the companies.

Soon, you received separate statements from each of the four fund companies reporting how your investments were doing. (Some fund companies make this even more of a paperwork nightmare by sending you a separate statement for each individual mutual fund that you buy through them.)

Now suppose that you wanted to sell one of your T. Rowe Price funds and invest the proceeds at Oakmark. Doing so was also a time-consuming pain in the posterior, because you had to contact T. Rowe Price to sell, wait days for it to send you a check for the sale's proceeds, and then send the money with instructions to Oakmark. Shopping this way can be tedious. Imagine wanting to make a salad and having to go to a lettuce farm, a tomato farm, and an onion farm to get the ingredients. That's why we have supermarkets!

In 1984, Charles Schwab came up with the idea to create a supermarket for mutual funds. Charles Schwab is the discount broker pioneer who created the first mutual fund supermarket (which other discount brokers have since copied) where you can purchase hundreds of individual funds from dozens of fund companies — one-stop mutual fund shopping.

The major benefit of such a service is that it greatly simplifies the paperwork involved in buying and selling different companies' mutual funds. No matter how many mutual fund companies you want to invest in, you need to complete just one application for the discount broker. And instead of getting a separate statement from each company, you get one statement from the discount broker that summarizes all your mutual fund holdings. (***Note:*** You still must maintain separate nonretirement and IRA accounts.)

Moving from one company's fund into another's is generally a snap. The discount broker can usually take care of all this with one phone call from you. Come tax time, you receive just one 1099 statement summarizing your fund's taxable distributions to record on your tax return.

You weren't born yesterday, so you know that all this convenience must have a catch. Here's a hint: Because discount brokers serve as intermediaries for the buying and selling of funds and the time and money spent sending you statements, they expect to make some money in return. So guess what? It costs you more to use a discount broker. Discount brokers charge you a transaction fee whenever you buy or sell most of the better funds that they offer. Leading discount brokers typically charge a flat fee of around $35.

Buying direct versus discount brokers

Buying funds directly from fund companies versus buying funds through a discounter's mutual fund supermarket isn't inherently better. For the most part, it's a trade-off that boils down to personal preference and individual circumstances.

Why to buy funds direct

Many reasons exist to buy funds directly from the company. Here are a few:

- ✔ **You're thrifty.** And you can take that as a compliment. Being vigilant about your investing costs boosts your returns. By buying direct from no-load fund companies, you avoid the discount brokerage transaction costs.

- ✔ **You don't have much money to invest.** If you're investing less than $5,000 per fund, the minimum transaction fees of a discount broker will gobble up a large percentage of your investment. You don't have to hassle with transaction fees when you buy direct from a no-load fund company.

- ✔ **You're content investing through one of the bigger fund companies with a broad array of good funds.** For example, if you deal directly with one mutual fund company that excels in all types of funds, you can minimize your fees and maximize your investment returns. Given the breadth and depth of the bigger companies' fund selections, you should feel content centralizing your fund investments through one of the better companies. However, if you sleep better at night investing through multiple fund companies' funds, I won't try to change your mind.

Given the fact that most of the major fund companies, such as Vanguard, Fidelity, and T. Rowe Price, have discount brokerage divisions offering mutual funds from companies other than their own, you could use one of these companies as your base and have the best of both worlds. Suppose, for example, that you want to invest a large portion but not all your money in Fidelity funds. By establishing a discount brokerage account at Fidelity, all your Fidelity fund purchases would be free of transaction fees; then through that same account, you could also buy other fund companies' funds.

Why to buy through a discount broker

Here are the main reasons to go with a discount broker:

- ✔ **You want to invest in funds from many fund companies.** In general, different fund companies excel in different types of investments: You may want to build a portfolio that draws on the specific talents of various companies. Although you can buy directly through each individual fund company, the point eventually comes where the hassle and clutter just aren't worth it. The one-stop shopping of a discount broker may well be worth the occasional transaction fee.

- ✔ **You hate paperwork.** For those of you out there whose disdain of paperwork is so intense that it keeps you from doing things that you're supposed to do, a discount broker is for you.

- ✔ **You want easy access to your money.** Some discount brokerage accounts offer such bells and whistles as debit cards and unlimited check-writing privileges, making it simple for you to tap in to your money. (That can be a bad thing if this tempts you to spend your money!)

- ✔ **You want to buy into a high-minimum fund.** One unique feature available through some discount broker's fund services is the ability to purchase some funds that aren't normally available to smaller investors.

- ✔ **You want to buy funds on margin.** Another interesting but rarely used feature that comes with a brokerage account is that you can borrow *on margin* (take out a loan from the brokerage firm) against mutual funds and other securities (which are used as collateral) held in a nonretirement account. Borrowing against your funds is generally lower cost than your other loan options, and it's potentially tax deductible. That said, buying and holding funds on margin can be costly and risky, and you may be forced to sell some funds or add cash to your account if the value of your investments declines too much.

You have a way (that involves hassle) to buy and sell your funds and use a discounter but reduce the total transaction fees: Purchase your funds initially from the mutual fund company and then transfer the shares at no charge into a discount brokerage account. Conversely, when you're ready to sell shares, you can transfer shares from the discounter to the mutual fund company before you're ready to sell. (See Chapter 16 for details about transfer forms.)

Debunking "No Transaction Fee" funds

After several years of distributing funds for all these different fund companies, discount brokers came up with another innovation. Discount brokers were doing a lot for mutual fund companies (for instance, handling the purchase and sale of funds, as well as the ongoing account recordkeeping and reporting), but they weren't being paid for all their work.

In 1992, Charles Schwab & Company negotiated to be paid an ongoing fee to service and handle customer accounts by some mutual fund companies. Today, through Schwab and other discount brokers who replicated this service, you can purchase hundreds of funds without paying any transaction fees (that is, you pay the same cost as if you'd bought the funds through the mutual fund company itself). These are called *No Transaction Fee (NTF) funds.*

On the surface, this idea certainly sounds like a great deal for you — the mutual fund investor wanting to buy funds from various companies through a discount brokerage account. You get access to many funds and one account statement without paying transaction fees.

The no-transaction fee fund is a case of something sounding much better than it really is. Although some discount brokers say or imply that NTF funds are free, they're hardly free. Discount brokers are able to waive the transaction costs only because the participating fund companies have agreed to foot the bill. In a typical arrangement, the participating fund company shares a portion of its operating expense ratio with the discount broker handling the account. But as you know if you read Chapter 7, annual operating expenses are drawn from the shareholders' investment dollars. So in the end, you're still the one paying the transaction costs.

As a group, NTF funds are inferior to the best no-load funds that you pay the discounters a transaction fee to purchase because NTF funds tend to

✔ Have higher operating expenses than non-NTF funds

✔ Be offered by smaller, less experienced fund companies who may be struggling to compete in the saturated mutual fund market

You'll notice that big, well-established fund companies (including the ones discussed earlier in this chapter, such as Vanguard, Fidelity, and T. Rowe Price) don't participate in NTF programs. They don't have to; the demand for their funds is high even with transaction costs.

In their rush to sign up more NTF funds, some discounters have ignored the quality of the NTF funds they offer. Some financial publications encourage and effectively endorse this lack of quality control by giving higher ratings (in articles purporting to review and rate various discount brokers) to those discounters offering more "free" funds to customers. As with a restaurant meal, more isn't always better — quality counts as well!

Whenever you make a mutual fund investment decision through a discount broker, try not to be influenced by the prospect, or lack thereof, of a transaction fee. In your efforts to avoid paying a small fee today, you can end up buying a fund with high ongoing fees and subpar performance. If you're so concerned about paying additional fees, deal directly with mutual fund companies and bypass the discount brokers and their transaction fees.

Using the best discount brokers

Although I've spoken of mutual fund companies and discount brokers as separate entities, the line between them has greatly blurred in recent years. For example, Schwab started as a discount broker but later began selling its own mutual funds. Other companies started selling mutual funds but have now moved into the discount brokerage business. The most obvious example is Fidelity, which offers brokerage services through which you can trade individual securities or buy many non-Fidelity mutual funds.

Vanguard and T. Rowe Price have excellent discount brokerage divisions that offer an extensive array of funds from other leading fund companies and charge competitive transaction fees. Vanguard charges $35 per trade and $3 for regularly scheduled dollar-cost averaging trades (minimum of $100); T. Rowe Price charges $35 per trade.

The discount brokerage services of Fidelity, Vanguard, or T. Rowe Price make a lot of sense if you plan on doing the bulk of your fund investing through their respective funds. Remember, you only have to pay brokerage transaction fees on funds offered by other fund companies. You won't pay for buying a Fidelity fund from Fidelity or a Vanguard fund from Vanguard or a T. Rowe Price fund from T. Rowe Price.

If you're already wondering how to get in touch with the companies that I recommend in this chapter, check out the Appendix, which includes the phone numbers, Web sites, and mailing addresses for all these companies. But before you put the cart before the horse, I strongly recommend that you at least read through Part IV of this book. That's where I recommend specific funds and discuss how to assemble a top-notch portfolio of funds.

Places to Pass By

Don't base your investment decisions on your gut: Some mutual fund companies have plush offices and they charge relatively high fees for their funds (to pay for all their overhead costs) or sell poorly performing funds — or both. What types of places are likely to make you feel comfortable but lead you astray? Many people do their fund investing through a list of wrong places:

- **The First Faithful Community Bank:** Many people feel comfortable turning their money over to the friendly neighborhood banker. You've done it for years with your checking and savings accounts. The bank has an impressive-looking branch close to your home, complete with parking, security cameras, and a vault. And then there's that FDIC insurance that guarantees your deposits. So now that your bank offers mutual funds, you may feel comfortable taking advice from the "investment specialist" or "consultant" in the branch (and may erroneously believe that the funds it sells carry FDIC coverage).

  Well, the branch representative at your local bank is probably a broker who's earning commissions from the mutual funds he's selling you. Bank funds generally charge sales commissions and higher operating expenses and generally have less-than-stellar performance relative to the best no-load funds. And because banks are relatively new to the mutual fund game, the broker at your bank may have spent last year helping customers establish new checking accounts and may have little knowledge and experience with investments and mutual funds. Remember, if he's working on commission, he's a salesperson, not an adviser. And the funds he's selling are load funds. You can do better.

- **Plunder and Pillage Brokerage Firm:** Brokers work on commission, so they can and will sell load funds. They may even try to hoodwink you into believing that they can do financial planning for you. Don't believe it. As I discuss in Chapter 7, purchasing a load fund has no real benefit; you have better alternatives.

- **Fred, the Friendly Financial Planner:** You may have met Fred through a free seminar, adult education class, or a cold call that he made to you. Fred may not really be a financial planner at all; instead, he could be a salesperson/broker who sells load funds. (If you want to hire an objective planner or adviser for investing in funds, see the next section.)

✔ **Igor, Your Insurance Broker:** Igor isn't just selling insurance anymore. He now may sell mutual funds, as well, and may even call himself a financial consultant. (See the preceding remarks for brokers.)

✔ **The Lutheran-Turkish-Irish-Americans-Graduated-from-Cornell-and-Now-Working-in-the-Music-Business Fund:** Hoping to capitalize on the booming fund business, special interest groups everywhere have been jumping in to the fray with funds of their own. Don't be surprised if your church, your alma mater, or your ethnic group makes a passionate pitch to pool your money with that of like-minded individuals in the hands of a manager who truly understands your background.

Although something can possibly be said for group solidarity, I suggest leaving your nest egg alone. Such special-interest funds carry loads and high operating fees and, because they have relatively little money to manage, are usually managed by money managers with little experience.

Hiring an Adviser: The Good, Bad, and Ugly

Dealing directly with various fund companies or simply selecting funds from among the many offered through a discount brokerage service may seem overwhelming to you. But don't hire an adviser until you've explored the real reasons why you want to hire help. If you're like many people, you may hire an adviser for the wrong reason. Or you'll hire the wrong type of adviser, an incompetent one, or one with major conflicts of interest. Check out the following sections for the highlights of why you should and why you shouldn't hire an adviser for overall advice.

The wrong reason to hire an adviser

Don't hire an adviser because of what I call the *crystal ball phenomenon.* Although you know you're not a dummy, you may feel that you can't possibly make informed and intelligent investing decisions because you don't closely follow or even understand the financial markets and what makes them move. Don't believe any advisor who claims he saw particular events (for example, the early 2000s bear market, the late 2000s financial crisis) coming in advance and perfectly positioned his clients' investment portfolio.

No one who you hire has a crystal ball. No one can consistently predict future movements in the financial markets to know which types of investments will do well and which ones won't. Investing intelligently in mutual funds isn't that complicated. You bought this book, so read it, and you find out all you need to know to invest wisely in funds.

The right reasons to hire an adviser

Consider hiring an adviser if

✔ You're too busy to do your investing yourself.

✔ You always put off investing because you don't enjoy doing it.

✔ You're uncomfortable making investing decisions on your own.

✔ You want a second opinion.

✔ You need help establishing and prioritizing financial goals.

Beware of conflicts of interest

The field of investment and financial planning is booby-trapped with land mines awaiting the naive investor. A particularly dangerous one is the enormous conflict of interest that's created when "advisers" sell products that bring them commissions.

If a *financial planner* or *financial consultant* sells products and works on commission, he's a salesperson, not a planner — just as a person who makes money selling real estate is a real estate broker, not a housing consultant! There's nothing wrong with salespeople — you just don't want one spouting suggestions when you're looking for objective investment and financial-planning advice.

Here are some of the problems created by commission-based advice:

✔ **Investments that carry commissions can pit your interests against those of the broker selling them.** The bigger the commission on a particular investment product, the greater the incentive the broker/planner/adviser has to sell it to you.

✔ **Investments that carry commissions mean that you have fewer dollars working in the investments you buy.** Commissions are siphoned out of your investment dollars. When it comes to returns, non-commission investments have a head start over commission ones.

✔ **Investments that carry the highest commissions also tend to be among the costliest and riskiest financial products available.** They're inferior products; that's why they need high commissions to motivate salespeople to sell them.

✔ **Planners who work on commission have an incentive to *churn* your investments.** Commissions are paid out whenever you buy or sell an investment (every time you make a trade). So some commission-greedy brokers/planners encourage you to trade frequently, attributing the need to changes in the economy or the companies in which you've invested. Not only does heavy trading fatten the broker/adviser's wallet at your expense, but also it's a proven loser as an investment strategy. (See Chapter 10 for more about investment strategies and your portfolio.)

✔ **Planners who work on commission may not keep your overall financial needs in mind.** You may want to fund your employer-sponsored retirement plan or pay off your mortgage or credit card debt before you start investing. The commission-based and money-managing planner has no incentive to recommend such strategies for you; that would give you less money to invest through them.

✔ **Planners who work on commission may create dependency.** They may try to make it all so complicated that you believe you can't possibly manage your finances or make major financial decisions without them.

Your best options for help

You must do your homework *before* hiring any financial adviser. First, find out as much as you can about the topic you need help with. That way, if you do hire someone to help you make investment and other financial decisions, you're in a better position to evaluate his or her capabilities and expertise.

Realizing that you need to hire someone to help you make and implement financial decisions can be a valuable insight. Even if you have a modest income or modest assets, spending a few hours of your time and a few hundred dollars to hire a professional can be a good investment. The services that advisers and planners offer, their fees, and their competence, however, vary tremendously.

Financial advisers make money in one of three ways:

✔ From commissions based on sales of financial products

✔ From fees based on a percentage of your assets that they're investing

✔ From hourly consultation charges

If you read the preceding section, you already know why the first option is the least preferred choice. (If you really want to or are forced to work with an investment broker who works on commission, be sure to read the last section in this chapter — "If you seek a salesperson.")

A generally better choice than a commission-based broker is a planner who works on a fee basis. In other words, the planner is paid by fees from clients such as you, instead of from the investments and other financial products that he or she recommends that you buy. This compensation system removes the incentive to sell you products with high commissions and churn your investments through a lot of transactions to generate more commissions. However, this system still has potentially significant conflicts of interest.

Many of the leading discount brokerage and mutual fund companies now offer advisory services (either in-house or through referrals), which typically perform mutual fund management for a percentage of assets under their care. With their in-house asset management, you probably won't be able to get the hand-holding, handshakes, and eye-to-eye contact that you would by hiring a local financial-planning firm. However, if you're looking at hiring a financial adviser, I encourage you to consider and interview the advisory divisions of the firms discussed in this chapter. Just be sure to put them through the questions that I recommend in Chapter 24.

The most cost-effective method is to hire an adviser who charges an hourly fee and doesn't sell investment and other financial products. Because he doesn't sell any financial products, his objectivity should be greater. He doesn't perform money management, so he can help you get your financial house in order and make comprehensive financial decisions, including selecting good mutual funds.

Your primary concern in selecting a planner, hourly based or otherwise, is hiring one who's competent. You can address this by checking references and discovering the difference between good and bad financial advice. You have further risk if you and the adviser don't clearly define the work to be done and the approximate total cost before you begin. Don't forget to set your parameters upfront.

A drawback of an entirely different kind occurs when you don't follow through on your adviser's recommendations. You paid for this work but didn't act on it: The potential benefit is lost. If part of the reason that you're hiring an adviser in the first place is that you're too busy or not interested enough to make changes to your financial situation, then you should look for this support in the services you buy from the planner.

If you just need someone as a sounding board for ideas or to recommend some specific no-load mutual funds, hire an hourly based planner for one or two sessions of advice. You save money by doing the legwork and implementation on your own. Just make sure that the planner is willing to give you specific enough advice that you can implement it on your own. Some planners charge for developing a financial plan and then will withhold specific investing advice and recommendations to create the need for you to hire them to do more, perhaps even to manage your money.

If you have a lot of money that you want managed among a variety of mutual fund investments, you can hire a financial adviser who charges a percentage of your assets under management. Some also offer financial-planning services. Some just manage money in mutual funds and other investments.

In the chapters ahead, I give you enough information for you to make wise mutual fund investing decisions. You owe it to yourself to read the rest of the book *before* deciding whether to hire financial help. Also, be sure to pay extra close attention to Chapter 24, which covers the ten issues to consider and questions to ask when hiring an adviser to help with mutual fund investing.

If you seek a salesperson

Despite the additional (and hence, avoidable) sales charges that apply when you purchase a load fund instead of a no-load fund, you may be forced to, or actually want to, buy a load fund through a salesperson working on commission. Perhaps you work for an employer that set up a retirement plan with only load funds as the investment option. Or your Uncle Ernie, who's a stock-broker, will put you in the family doghouse if you transfer your money out of his firm and into no-load funds. Maybe you really trust your broker because of a long-standing and productive investment relationship (but ask yourself this: Is your success because of the broker or the financial markets?).

Protect yourself

If you're comfortable and willing to pay commissions from 4 percent up to as much as 8.5 percent to invest in mutual funds, you have a number of ways to protect your money and well-being when working with brokers:

- ✔ **Be aware that you're working with a broker.** Unlike the real estate profession in which an employee's title — real estate broker or agent — clearly conveys how she makes her money, many investment sales-people today have labels that obscure what they do and how they make money. Common misnomers include financial planner, financial consultant, or financial adviser as names for salespeople who used to be called stock, securities, or insurance brokers.

- ✔ **Make sure that you've already decided what money you want to invest and how it fits into your overall financial plans.** This point is one of the most important things for you to do first if you're going to invest through a commission-based investment salesperson. Guard against being pushed into dollar amounts and/or investments that aren't part of your financial plan.

Make sure you get the best funds

If you've optimized the structuring of your finances and you have a chunk of money that you're willing to pay as a sales charge to invest in load funds, make sure that you're getting the best funds for your investment dollars. The criteria to use in selecting those load funds are no different from those used to select no-load funds:

- ✔ Invest in funds managed by mutual fund companies and portfolio managers that have track records of expertise that take a level of risk that fits your needs, and that charge reasonable annual operating expenses.

- ✔ Pay attention to the annual operating expenses that both load and no-load funds charge. These fees are deducted from your funds' returns in much the same way that IRS taxes are deducted from your paycheck, with one critical difference: Your pay stub shows how much you pay in taxes, whereas your mutual fund account statement doesn't show the fund's operating expense charges. You need the prospectus for that, and even then it won't show you what you paid in dollars for that.

- ✔ Never invest in a mutual fund without knowing all the charges — sales charges, annual operating expenses, and any annual maintenance or account fees. You can find all these in a fund's prospectus (see Chapter 8 for the scoop on how to decipher a prospectus).

Part IV
Crafting Your Fund Portfolio

The 5th Wave   By Rich Tennant

"You may want to talk to Phil — he's one of our more aggressive fund managers."

In this part . . .

You start building a portfolio of funds to help you meet your goals. I explain the fundamentals of putting a portfolio together, including such concepts as asset allocation, buy and hold versus market timing, and selecting tax-appropriate funds. I recommend the best money market, bond, and stock funds for the job. And just to make sure that I don't leave you hanging, I pull it all together for you in a chapter that shows you how real people construct fund portfolios and fit funds into their overall financial plans. The last chapter of this part walks you through the paperwork you need to fill out to build your fund portfolio.

Chapter 10

Perfecting a Fund Portfolio

*A*lthough *portfolio* usually describes a collection of funds, it doesn't have to. For certain goals, one or two funds may be all that you need (for example, a short-term bond fund and a money market fund for a home down payment). Even for a long-term goal, such as retirement, you may select just one fund; some mutual fund companies offer funds of funds, which, as the name suggests, are mutual funds comprised of other mutual funds. (See Chapter 13 for details on such funds.) And although a portfolio is sometimes held inside one account, it doesn't have to be. The funds that make up your retirement portfolio, for example, could be in numerous accounts from different investment companies.

This chapter shows you how to draw up a blueprint for your investing goals that includes all the key considerations, including *asset allocation* (how you divvy up your portfolio among different investments), tax implications (especially for portfolios held outside of tax-sheltered retirement accounts), and some mutual fund investing strategies. I then help you execute your plan.

Asset Allocation: An Investment Recipe

Asset allocation simply describes the proportion of different investment types (stocks, bonds, international investments, and so on) that make up your mutual fund portfolio. So if someone asks, "What's your asset allocation?" a typical response may be, "I have 60 percent in stocks, a third of which is in foreign stocks, and 40 percent in bonds."

You may hear a mutual fund nerd spout off about his allocation using more detailed terminology including *large-cap* and *small-cap* stocks, or between *growth funds* and *value funds.* Don't worry about these terms for now. (Check out Chapter 13 for more information about these terms.)

Allocating to reduce your risks

You wouldn't have to worry about asset allocation if it weren't for a simple investment truth: *The greater an investment's potential return, generally the greater the chance and magnitude of a short-term loss.* If there were no chance of loss, you could throw asset allocation out the window. No matter what your savings goal, you could put all your money into stocks. After all, in comparison to bonds and money market investments, stocks should give you the biggest long-term returns (see Chapter 1 for more details). If you had no chance of loss when investing in stocks, every dollar you saved would go to creating wealth in stocks. Your net worth would balloon.

In the real world, stocks are a volatile investment. Although providing the highest long-term gains, stocks also carry the greatest risk of short-term loss (compared with putting your money in bonds or money market accounts).

Asset allocation, then, is all about striking the right balance between your desire for higher returns and your ability to withstand a short-term loss. All things being equal, all people prefer higher returns. And although everyone has a different personality and temperament about accepting risk, your realistic ability to withstand a loss depends primarily on your time horizon.

Looking toward your time horizon

The *time horizon* of a financial goal is the length of time between now and the time when you expect to need the money to accomplish that goal. If you're currently 30 years old and want to retire by age 60, then the time horizon of your retirement investments is 30+ years from now (even though you'll begin to use some of your retirement money at age 60, some of it won't be spent until later in your retirement). If you're saving to buy a home by the time you're 35 years old, then the time horizon of that goal is five years from now.

The longer your time horizon, the more able you are to withstand the risk of a short-term loss. For example, if you have a 30-year time horizon for retirement investments, then a short-term loss isn't a big deal — your investments have plenty of time to recover. Thus, you probably want more of your retirement dollars in growth investments, such as stocks.

Short-term goals

Asset allocation for goals with short time horizons is quite simple:

- ✔ **Less than two years:** If you have less than two years, you're generally best off sticking to money market funds. Stocks and bonds are volatile, and although you have the potential for earning higher returns in stocks and bonds, a money market fund offers the combination of terrific safety and some returns. See Chapter 11 for more on money market funds.

- ✔ **Between three and seven years:** If your time horizon is between three and seven years, then consider using shorter-term bond funds. (If you have between two and three years, you can use both money market and short-term bond funds.) When you're able to keep your money in an investment for several years, then the extra potential returns from low-risk bonds begin to outweigh the risk of short-term loss from possible bond market fluctuations. See Chapter 12 for more on bond funds.

- ✔ **Seven or more years:** If your time horizon is seven years or more, I think that you have a long enough time horizon to start investing in stocks as well as longer-term bonds.

Some market pundits and those involved with money management refer to extended periods such as the 2000s as the *lost decade.* These people will point to a market index such as the Dow Jones Industrial Average and exclaim that from the end of 1999 through the end of 2009, that index of 30 large U.S. company stocks essentially treaded water and ended the decade at about the same level it began the decade. This statement is highly misleading and inaccurate. During that decade, numerous U.S. and foreign stock indexes posted healthy returns of between 5 and 10 percent annually. Bond investors did well over that period as well. And, you should also remember that these folks are over-looking the dividend payments stock investors earn and that are not reflected in the quoted level of a given market index. While some commentators are simply ignorant of these facts, others, especially those managing money, selling newsletters, and advocating market timing, have an agenda to convince you that buying and holding don't work and that you need their services to time the market. Please see the section "Timing versus buy-and-hold investing," later in this chapter, as well as Chapter 20, which discusses market forecasters.

Retirement and other long-term goals

Long-term goals, such as retirement and college tuition, require more complex asset allocation decisions than those demanded by short-term goals. If you plan to retire in your 60s, your retirement portfolio needs to fund your living expenses for 20 or more years. That's a tall order. Unless you have vast wealth in comparison to your spending desires, the money you've earmarked for retirement needs to work hard for you. That's why you should heavily weight a portfolio that you're investing for your future retirement, particularly during your earlier working years, toward investments with appreciation potential like stocks.

Your current age and the number of years until you retire should be the biggest factors in your retirement asset allocation decision. The younger you are and the more years you have before retirement, the more comfortable you should be with growth-oriented investments, such as stock funds.

As you approach retirement age, however, you should gradually scale back the risk and volatility of your portfolio. That's why, as you get older, bonds should become an increasingly bigger piece of your portfolio pie. Although their returns are generally lower, bonds are less likely to suffer a sharp downswing in value that could derail your retirement plans.

Table 10-1 in the next section lists some guidelines for allocating money you've earmarked for long-term purposes, such as retirement. All you need to figure out is how old you are (I told you investing was easier than you thought!) and the level of risk you're comfortable with.

Factoring in your investment personality

In Table 10-1, I add a new variable to the asset allocation decision: your *investment personality,* or tolerance for risk. Even if you and another investor are the same age, and you both have the same time horizon for your investments, you could very well have different tolerances or desires to accept and deal with risk. Some people are more apt to lose sleep over their investments, just as some people are scared by roller coasters, whereas other people get a thrill from them.

Table 10-1	Asset Allocation Guidelines for the Long Haul	
Your Investment Attitude	**Bond Allocation (%)**	**Stock Allocation (%)**
Play it safe	Age	100 – age
Middle of the road	Age – 10	110 – age
Aggressive	Age – 20	120 – age

Be honest with yourself and invest accordingly. If you're able to accept who you are instead of fighting it, you'll be a happier and more successful investor. Here's my advice for how to categorize yourself:

✔ **Play it safe:** Indicators of this investment personality include little or no experience or success investing in stocks or other growth investments, fear of the financial markets, and risk-averse behavior in other aspects of life. You may desire to be conservative with your investments if you have enough saved to afford a lower rate of return on your investments.

✔ **Middle of the road:** Indicators of this investment personality include some experience and success investing in stocks or other growth investments, and some comfort with risk-taking behavior in other aspects of one's life.

✔ **Aggressive:** Indicators of this investment personality include past experience and success investing in stocks or other growth investments — and a healthy desire and comfort with sensible risk-taking behavior in other aspects of one's life. You may also want to be more aggressive if you're behind in saving for retirement and you want your money to work as hard as possible for you.

What does it all mean, you ask? Consider this example. According to Table 10-1, if you're 35 years old and don't like a lot of risk but recognize the value of striving for some growth to make your money work harder (a middle-of-the-road type), you should put 25 percent (35 – 10) into bonds and 75 percent (110 – 35) into stocks.

Divvying up your stocks between home and abroad

Your next major asset allocation decision is to divvy up your stock investment money between U.S. and international stock funds. This step is an important one for keeping your portfolio properly diversified. Although some consider international markets risky, putting all your stock market money into just one country is even riskier, even if the country is relatively large and familiar, such as the United States.

When the U.S. market slumps, some markets do better. Moreover, developing countries have the potential for greater economic growth and stock market returns than the U.S. market. Here's the portion of your stock allocation that I recommend investing overseas, guided by your investment attitude:

✔ **Play it safe:** 20 percent

✔ **Middle of the road:** 33 percent

✔ **Aggressive:** 40 to 50 percent

So if you're a 35-year-old, middle-of-the-road type who's investing 75 percent of your portfolio in stocks, you'd then put 33 percent of that stock money into international stock funds. Multiplying 33 percent by 75 percent works out to about 25 percent of the entire portfolio. So you'd put 25 percent in bonds, 50 percent in U.S. stocks, and 25 percent in international stocks.

Gradual change is better than abrupt change. If you've had little or no experience or success investing in stocks, you're better to start with the play-it-safe allocation and then work your way to riskier allocations as you develop more comfort and knowledge.

College savings goals

Be careful when investing money for your child's college education. Doing so the wrong way can harm your child's chances of getting needed financial aid and increase your tax burden (see Chapter 3 for more information).

The strategy for allocating money in a college savings portfolio can be similar to that used for retirement money. Assuming that your child is young, the goal is relatively long term, so the portfolio should emphasize growth investments, such as stocks. However, as the time horizon decreases, bonds should play a bigger role. The big difference, of course, between investing for your retirement and investing for your child's college costs is that the time horizon for college depends not on your age, but on the age of the child for whom you're investing.

Here's my rule for investing college money for your kids. To figure how much money you should put in bonds, take the following numbers:

- ✓ **Play it safe:** 60 + child's age
- ✓ **Middle of the road:** 45 + child's age
- ✓ **Aggressive:** 30 + child's age

The rest of your college investment should go into stocks (with at least a third in stocks overseas). Use this rule to adjust the mix as your child gets older. For example, suppose that you have a 5-year-old, and you want to follow a middle-of-the-road approach when investing her college money. In this case, you could invest approximately 50 percent (45 + 5) in bonds, with the remaining 50 percent in stocks, one-third of which you'd invest overseas.

Taxes: It's What You Keep That Matters

Like asset allocation, tax implications are a fundamental consideration in portfolio construction. When you're constructing a mutual fund portfolio outside of a tax-sheltered retirement account, Uncle Sam gets to grab a share of your returns. Part of what makes up a mutual fund's returns are dividend distributions and capital gains, which are subject to taxation.

For this reason, when you're investing outside of tax-sheltered retirement accounts, you must distinguish between pre-tax and post-tax returns. Think of it as the business world difference between revenue and profit. Revenue is what a business collects from selling products and services; profit is what a business gets to keep after paying all of its expenses, and in the end, that's what really matters to a business. Likewise, your after-tax return, not your pre-tax return, should matter most to you when you invest your money.

Unfortunately, all too many investors (and often their advisers) ignore the tax consequences and invest in ways that increase their tax burdens and lower their effective returns. For example, when comparing two similar mutual funds, most people prefer a fund that earns returns of 13 percent per year on average to a fund that earns 12 percent. But what if the 13 percent per year fund causes you to pay a lot more in taxes? What if, after factoring in taxes, the 13 percent per year fund nets you just 9 percent, while the 12 percent per year fund nets you an effective 10 percent return?

In the following sections, I help you plan how funds fit in your portfolio, given your current tax bracket, and how to ensure that the tax bite is as painless as possible. Check out Chapter 18 for all the ins and outs of accounting for your funds when filing your tax return.

Fitting funds to your tax bracket

Fortunately, you can pick your funds to minimize the federal and state governments' shares of your returns. Some funds, for example, are managed to minimize highly taxed distributions, and certain government bond funds focus on investments that generate tax-free income.

Understanding ordinary (marginal) income tax rates

To choose the right funds for your investment purposes, you must know your *marginal tax rate,* which is the rate you pay on the last dollar you earn. For example, if you earned $50,000 last year, the marginal rate is the rate you paid on the dollar that brought you from $49,999 to $50,000. The government charges you different tax rates for different parts of your annual income.

You pay less tax on your *first* dollars of earnings and more tax on your *last* dollars of earnings. For example, if you're single and your taxable income totaled $50,000 during 2010, you paid federal tax at the rate of 10 percent on the first $8,375 of taxable income, 15 percent on the income from $8,375 to $34,000, and 25 percent on income above $34,000 (see Table 10-2). The rate you pay on those last dollars of income (25 percent) is your marginal rate.

Your marginal tax rate allows you to quickly calculate how much tax you owe on additional salary and certain types of nonsalary income, such as

✔ Interest from taxable bonds

✔ Interest from taxable money market funds

✔ Short-term capital gains (that is, gains from investments sold after being held for one year or less)

Suppose that on top of your $50,000 salary you have some bond funds that pay taxable interest in a nonretirement account that distributed $1,000 of dividends. Because you know your marginal tax rate — 25 percent — you know that Uncle Sam gets $250 of that $1,000 distribution ($1,000 × 25 percent). Note that states generally also levy income taxes. Table 10-2 shows federal tax rates for singles and for married couples filing jointly.

Table 10-2	2010 Federal Income Tax Brackets and Rates	
Singles' Taxable Income	**Married-Filing-Jointly Taxable Income**	**Federal Tax Rate**
Less than $8,375	Less than $16,750	10%
$8,375 to $34,000	$16,750 to $68,000	15%
$34,000 to $82,400	$68,000 to $137,300	25%
$82,400 to $171,850	$137,300 to $209,250	28%
$171,850 to $373,650	$209,250 to $373,650	33%
More than $373,650	More than $373,650	35%

Lower tax rates on stock dividends and long-term capital gains

In 2003, a major federal tax bill significantly lowered the tax rate applied to

✔ Dividends paid by corporations (domestic or foreign) on their stock

✔ Long-term capital gains (from profits on appreciated investments sold after being held for more than one year)

For those in the four highest federal income tax brackets listed in Table 10-2 (25, 28, 33, and 35 percent), the tax rate on stock dividends and long-term capital gains is just 15 percent. And, get this, stock dividends and long-term capital gains are tax-free for taxpayers in the 10 and 15 percent federal income tax brackets!

Although the income paid on bond funds and money market funds is called a *dividend,* such income doesn't qualify for the new, lower federal income rates on stock dividends. Dividend income that you receive from mutual funds holding stocks qualifies for the lower dividend tax rate.

Minimizing your taxes on funds

Now that you're equipped with knowledge about your tax bracket and tax rates on various fund distributions (if you don't have a clue and skipped the preceding section, you may want to visit it before continuing here), the following sections enable you to understand how to select tax-friendly mutual funds when investing outside of retirement accounts.

Use tax-free money market and bond funds

Certain kinds of money market and bond funds invest only in bonds issued by governments, and depending on the type of government entity they invest in, their dividends may not be subject to state and/or federal tax.

Such funds are typically identified by the words *Treasury* or *municipal* in their fund titles:

✔ A *Treasury fund* buys federal-government-issued Treasury bonds (also called *Treasuries*), and its dividends — although federally taxable — are free of state taxes.

✔ The dividends of a *municipal bond fund,* which invests in local and state government bonds, are free of federal tax, and if the fund's investments are limited to one state and you live in that state, the dividends are free of state taxes as well.

Because Treasuries and municipal bonds aren't subject to complete taxation, the governments issuing these bonds can pay a lower rate of interest than, say, comparable corporate bonds (the dividends on which are fully taxable to bondholders). Therefore, before taxes are taken into account, tax-free bond and money market funds yield less than their taxable equivalents.

However, after taxes are taken into account, you may find that with tax-free money market or bond funds, you come out ahead of comparable taxable funds if your tax bracket is high enough. Because of the difference in taxes, the earnings from tax-free investments *can* end up being greater than what you're left with from comparable taxable investments. If you're in the 28 percent federal bracket or higher (see Table 10-2), see Chapters 11 and 12 for details on tax-free money market and bond funds.

Don't buy tax-free funds inside retirement accounts. Your returns inside a retirement account are already sheltered from taxation. Ignore the taxability of funds and go for the highest yields.

Invest in tax-friendly stock mutual funds

Unfortunately, stock mutual funds don't have a tax-free version like bond and money market funds do. Unless they're held inside a retirement account, stock fund distributions are taxable. However, as discussed in the previous sections, not all stock distributions and returns are treated equally from an income tax standpoint. With stock funds, more than any other type of fund, investors often focus exclusively on the pre-tax historical return, ignoring the tax implications of their fund picks.

You can invest in stock funds that are *tax friendly* — in other words, funds whose investing style keeps highly-taxed distributions to a minimum. Here's how stock funds can minimize taxable distributions:

✔ **Buy-and-hold investing:** Dividends and capital gains are two types of stock fund distributions. Capital gains distributions are generated when a fund manager sells a stock for a profit; that profit must then be given out to the shareholders annually. Some fund managers engage in frequent trading, which can cause their funds to produce more distributions. But other fund managers are buy-and-hold investors. These managers tend to produce fewer capital gains distributions than their peers who trade frequently.

Index mutual funds and exchange-traded funds tend to produce fewer capital gains distributions because they hold their securities longer. (For more on indexing, see "Fund Investing Strategies" later in this chapter, as well as Chapter 13 for more details on stock index funds.)

✔ **Long-term capital gains:** Although no capital gains' distributions are best for minimizing taxes, a good manager ultimately sells some stocks at a profit when he sees better opportunities elsewhere. When a fund manager does sell stocks at a profit, you pay a far lower tax rate when these realized gains are long term — from stocks held more than one year. (See the section "Lower tax rates on stock dividends and long-term capital gains," earlier in this chapter.)

✔ **Offsetting gains with losses:** If a fund manager sells some stock for a gain of $10,000 but sells other stock for a loss of $10,000, the capital gains net out to zero. Some funds, managed specifically to minimize distributions, employ this offsetting technique to lower their capital gains. I identify the best of these tax-managed stock funds in Chapter 13.

Watch the calendar

When purchasing stock mutual funds outside of tax-sheltered retirement accounts, consider the time of year at which you purchase shares in funds. December is the most common month in which mutual funds make capital gains distributions. Most funds also make a dividend distribution around that time as well. (Dividends are also sometimes distributed at other times of the year, especially on bond funds.)

Don't invest in a fund just before it makes a large distribution. You're not reaping any rewards from the capital gains distribution because, right after such a distribution, the fund's share price decreases to reflect the size of the payout. You are, however, effectively making yourself liable for taxes on gains you didn't share in.

When making purchases late in the year, find out whether and when the fund may make a significant capital gains and dividend distribution. Fund companies can usually tell you, in advance of the actual capital gains and dividend distribution, approximately how much they expect the distribution to be.

Fund Investing Strategies

In this section, I discuss some of the different investing strategies and philosophies that you can use to direct a mutual fund portfolio, and I also explain which ones are best for you and which ones to avoid. Having an overarching strategy is vital for many reasons. Without a clear plan and approach, you'll have less success, more anxiety, and more temptation to fall prey to sales pitches and unsound approaches.

Timing versus buy-and-hold investing

Over the past two centuries, stocks have produced an average return of about 9 to 10 percent per year. Some individual years are better, with stocks returning up to 20 or even 30 percent or more; other years are worse, with stocks losing 20 percent or more in value. But when taken over a period of decades, the up years and the down years historically net out to returns of about 9 to 10 percent per year.

Despite the long-term healthy returns stocks generally produce, it's disconcerting to some people to invest their money into something that can decline. Many newsletters, advisers, and the like claim to predict the future movement of the financial markets. On the basis of such predictions, these folks advocate timing the purchase and sale of securities, such as stocks, to maximize returns and minimize risks.

Although market timing sounds good in theory, a wealth of studies and evidence shows that market timing simply doesn't work in practice. (In Chapter 20, I discuss the historically poor track record of investment newsletters that attempt market timing.) In fact, those who try to time the markets inevitably do worse than those who simply buy and hold, because they too often miss the right times to buy and sell.

Market timing is based on that age-old investment mantra, "Buy low, sell high." It sounds so simple and logical; perhaps that's what makes it such an attractive concept. One fundamental problem, however, destroys the logic: Recognizing a low or a high comes only with hindsight; market movements, especially in the short term, are unpredictable. Telling someone to buy low and sell high is similar to telling someone that it's okay to drive his car if he expects not to have an accident and that he should stay out of his car if he expects to have an accident!

If buying and holding had an investment mantra, it would be "Buy now, sell much later." Instead of betting on short-term market movements, buy-and-hold investors do their homework and select solid funds and rely on long-term trends and aren't so concerned with *when* to get in and out of the market as much as *how long* they're actually in there. Buy-and-hold investors know that if they hang in there through the inevitable tough times, the good years outnumber the bad, and they come out ahead.

Don't jump in and out of funds. After you've bought into a decent fund, you have few good reasons to move out of it (see Chapter 17). Not only does buy-and-hold investing offer better returns, but also it's less work and hassle.

Active versus index fund managers

Unlike other mutual funds, in which the portfolio manager and a team of analysts scour the market for the best securities, an index fund manager passively invests to match the performance of an index. *Index funds* are funds that can be (and, for the most part, are) managed by a computer, with intelligent human oversight. An index fund manager invests the fund's assets so as to replicate an underlying index, such as Standard & Poor's 500 index — 500 large-company U.S. stocks. An S&P 500 index fund generally buys and holds the same 500 stocks, and in the same approximate amounts, that comprise the S&P 500 Index.

Index funds are underrated — they don't get the credit they deserve. Index funds are a little bit like Jaime Escalante, that Garfield High School math teacher of poor children in the ghettos of Los Angeles (see the terrific movie, *Stand and Deliver,* about him). In a school where kids often dropped out and were lucky to learn some algebra, Escalante got his kids to master calculus. In fact, he got *entire classes* to work hard and pass the college advanced placement exam for calculus. (The College Board that administers the AP test couldn't believe that so many kids from this school could pass this exam, so the kids were investigated for cheating — that's how Escalante's story was discovered, and he finally got credit for all the great work that he did.)

Low-cost index funds work hard by keeping expenses low, staying invested, and holding on to a relatively fixed list of stocks. So, like Escalante's kids, index funds are virtually guaranteed to be at the top of their class. Over long periods (ten years or more), index funds outperform about three-quarters of their actively-managed peers investing in the same types of securities! Most actively managed funds can't overcome the handicap of high operating expenses that pulls down their funds' rates of return. Because significant ongoing research doesn't need to be conducted to identify companies to invest in, index funds can be run with far lower operating expenses. (Please also see Chapter 5 for a discussion of the exchange-traded funds, which are index funds you can buy and sell on a stock exchange.)

The average U.S. stock fund has an operating expense ratio of 1.5 percent per year. (Some funds charge expenses as high as 2 percent or more per year.) That being the case, a U.S. stock index fund with an expense ratio of just 0.2 percent per year has an average advantage of 1.3 percent per year. A 1.3 percent difference may not seem like much, but in fact, the difference is significant. Because stocks tend to return about 10 percent per year, you're throwing away about 13 percent of your expected stock fund returns when you buy a non-index fund. If you factor in the taxes that you pay on your fund profits, these higher expenses gobble even more of your after-tax profits.

Another often overlooked drawback to actively managed stock funds: Your fund manager can make costly mistakes, such as not being invested when the market goes up, being too aggressive when the market plummets, or just being in the wrong stocks. An actively managed fund can easily underperform the overall market index that it's competing against. An index fund, by definition, can't.

Table 10-3 lists the worst-performing U.S. stock funds over the past decade. Note how much worse these bowser funds performed versus the broad U.S. stock market index. The past decade was one of the worst for U.S. stocks in history for sure, but you can clearly see that the worst funds underperformed relevant market indexes by about 12 to 30 percent per year over this decade long time span!

Table 10-3	Worst Performing U.S. Stock Funds versus Market Indexes
Fund	**Annualized Total Return**
Embarcadero Absolute Return	–26.4% per year
Embarcadero Market Neutral	–19.2% per year
First American Mid Cap Select A	–15.5% per year
BlackRock Focus Growth A	–12.8% per year
Apex Mid Cap Growth	–11.9% per year
Stock Market Indexes	**Annualized Total Return**
Russell 2000	+3.8% per year
DJ Wilshire 5000 Index	0.0% per year

Source: Morningstar, Inc.

When you invest in broadly diversified index funds, you never see your funds in the list of the top-performing funds — but then you never see your funds in the list of the worst-performing funds, either. Don't overestimate your ability to pick *in advance* the few elite money managers who manage to beat the market averages by a few percentage points per year in the long run. And then don't overestimate the pros' ability to consistently pick the right stocks.

Index funds make sense for a portion of your investments, especially when investing in bonds and larger more-conservative stocks, where it's difficult for portfolio managers to beat the market. Index funds also make sense for investors who are concerned that fund managers may make big mistakes and greatly underperform the market.

As for how much you should use index versus actively managed funds, it's really a matter of personal taste. If you're happy knowing that you can get the market rate of return and knowing that you can't underperform the market, you can index your entire portfolio. On the other hand, if you enjoy the game of trying to pick the better managers and want the potential to earn better than the market level of returns, don't use index funds at all. A happy medium is to do some of both.

Putting Your Plans into Action

Constructing a mutual fund portfolio is a bit like constructing a house: There's a world of difference between designing a plan and executing it. If you're the architect, your world is all clean lines on white paper. But if you're the general contractor responsible for executing the plan, your circumstances are generally messier; you may face such challenges as inclement weather, unsuitable soil, and undependable construction workers.

Like the contractor, you're bound to meet challenges in the execution of the plan — in your case, constructing a mutual fund portfolio instead of a house. Some of these challenges come from the funds themselves; your personal circumstances are the source of others. With patience, persistence, and a healthy helping of my advice, all are surmountable. Investing in funds is much, much easier than building a house — which is why you can do it yourself if you so desire.

Determining how many funds and families to use

Suppose that you've used the discussion earlier in this chapter to nail down an asset allocation for your retirement portfolio: 25 percent in bonds, 50 percent in domestic stocks, and 25 percent in international stocks. That's all quite specific except for the fact that these percentages tell you nothing about how many funds and how many fund families you should use to meet these percentages. (I introduce the concept of fund families in Chapter 2).

You could do all your investing through one family of funds, given the sheer number and quality of funds that the larger and better fund companies. Centralizing your investments in one family saves on administrative hassles by cutting down on the number of applications to complete, envelopes to open, statements to file, tax statements to deal with, and so on. Plus, you're more likely to find your way around better at a company that you spend more of your time interacting with. Consider a good argument against investing through one family of funds, though: Even the best mutual fund companies don't offer the best of every type of fund. By not spreading out your funds over different fund families to take advantage of their particular strengths, you may be sacrificing a little bit of return.

Discount brokerage services offer some of the best of both approaches. You get one-stop shopping and one statement for all your holdings, but you also have access to funds from many families. The downside: You pay small transaction fees to purchase many of the better funds through discounters. (I discuss discount brokerage services in detail in Chapter 9.)

You won't find *one* right answer to how many fund families to work with and whether to use a discount brokerage account. Choose the approach that works best for your needs. I use a combination of these approaches by maintaining accounts through a large mutual fund company while also using discount brokerage services to buy funds from some of the smaller fund families that are more of a hassle to work with. This strategy allows me to maximize centralization while minimizing transaction fees.

As for the number of individual funds to hold in your portfolio, again, there's no one correct answer. The typical mutual fund is quite diversified to begin with, so you needn't invest in too many. In fact, because some funds invest across different types of investments (known as hybrid funds) or even across other funds (known as funds of funds), you may be able to achieve your desired asset allocation by investing in just one fund.

At a minimum, I recommend that you own enough funds so that you're able to diversify not only across the general investment types (stocks, bonds) that you've targeted but also across different types of securities within those larger categories — bonds of various maturity lengths, stocks of various-size companies. (I explain these concepts in Chapters 12 and 13.)

As your savings allow, I generally recommend that you invest at least $3,000 to $5,000 per fund. If you're investing outside of a retirement account, most of the better mutual funds require an initial investment of this magnitude anyway. Inside a retirement account, you may invest less — typically only $500 or $1,000 per fund — to start. However, because most retirement accounts annually ding you about $10 per fund as an account maintenance fee, you should aim to invest the higher amounts so you don't have your small investment devoured by high relative fees. (A $10-per-year fee diminishes a $500 investment by 2 percent each year.) Some fund companies waive this fee if you keep more than a certain amount — $5,000, for example — in their funds.

As you have larger sums to invest, it makes sense to use more funds. Suppose that you have $300,000 and want to divide it equally among bonds, U.S. stocks, and international stocks. You *could* put $100,000 into each of three funds: one bond fund, one U.S. stock fund, and one international stock fund. But with that much money to invest, why not use at least two of each of the different types of funds? That way, if the one international stock fund you've chosen does poorly, all of your money earmarked for overseas investing isn't doing poorly in that fund. There's no reason that you can't use even three different funds within each category. The more money you have, the more sense diversifying across two or three funds per category makes.

And one more point: Don't invest in more funds than you have time to track. If you can't find the time to read your funds' semiannual and annual reports, that's a sign that you have too many funds. Extra diversification won't make up for a lack of monitoring.

Matching fund allocation to your asset allocation

One thing that can trip up your asset allocation plans is the fact that mutual funds have their own asset allocations. For example, a hybrid fund may invest 60 percent in stocks and 40 percent in bonds. Perhaps you, on the other hand, want to invest 75 percent in stocks and 25 percent in bonds. How the heck do you fit that kind of fund into your portfolio?

One option is to shun hybrid funds. Take Thoreau's advice to simplify your (investing) life: Avoid funds that invest in different investment types. Buy purebreds — stock funds that are 100 percent (or close to 100 percent) invested in stocks, bond funds that invest only in bonds, and international stock funds that are entirely invested overseas. That way, your asset allocation calculations stay simple.

Take the desired mix of the hypothetical 35-year-old from earlier in this chapter: 25 percent in bonds, 50 percent in U.S. stocks, and 25 percent in international stocks. If she has $10,000 to invest and sticks to purebred funds, figuring out how much money to put into each kind of fund is a simple matter of multiplying the desired allocation percentage by the $10,000 total to invest. In this case, she should put $2,500 in a pure bond fund (25 percent × $10,000), $5,000 in a U.S. stock fund, and $2,500 in an international stock fund.

If that seems a little too easy, you're right. Even if they label themselves as purebreds, plenty of mutual funds are given leeway in their charters to dabble in other investment types. Read the annual report of some so-called U.S. stocks funds and you may find that up to 20 percent of their assets are invested in bonds or international stocks.

Some hybrid funds are excellent funds, and eliminating them simply to avoid a math problem seems a bit silly. Although I encourage you to focus on purebred funds, fitting a hybrid fund, or a hybrid disguised as a purebred, into your portfolio occasionally makes sense.

Take the example of a 35-year-old investor — one who wants a portfolio of 25 percent bonds, 50 percent U.S. stocks, and 25 percent international stocks. Suppose that she's picked out three funds she wants to buy: a U.S. stock fund (100 percent stocks), an international stock fund (100 percent international stocks), and a hybrid fund (60 percent U.S. stocks, 40 percent bonds). Because the hybrid fund is the only one with bonds, the investor needs to figure out how much to put into the hybrid fund so that she ends up with about 25 percent (overall) in bonds. Because 40 percent of the hybrid fund is invested in bonds, the arithmetic looks like this:

$$0.4 \ (40 \text{ percent}) \times \text{Amount to be invested in fund} = 0.25$$

$$\text{Amount to be invested in fund} = 0.25 \div 0.4$$

$$\text{Amount to be invested in fund} = 0.625 \ (\text{or } 62.5 \text{ percent})$$

I like nice, round numbers, so I rounded 62.5 off to 60. Here's how much money she should put into each fund to get her desired investment mix:

60 percent hybrid fund (60 percent in U.S. stocks, 40 percent in bonds)

15 percent U.S. stock fund (100 percent in stocks)

25 percent international stock fund (100 percent in international stocks)

Allocating when you don't have much to allocate

If you're just starting out, you may have little money to allocate. Here you've spent all this time exploring how to design a terrific portfolio, and then, thanks to minimum initial investment requirements, you may realize that you only have enough money to buy one of the five funds you've selected!

Fear not. This problem has several answers:

✔ Buy a hybrid fund or a fund of funds (see Chapter 13) whose asset allocation is similar to your desired mix. Don't sweat the fact that you can't find a fund with the exact mix you want. For now, getting close is good enough. When you're able to afford it, you can, if you so desire, move out of the hybrid fund and into the funds you originally chose.

✔ Buy your desired funds — one at a time — as you're able to afford them. I call this little trick *diversifying over time,* and it's perfectly legit.

One twist on this strategy that tests and perhaps improves your mutual fund investing habits is to start by investing in the type of fund (bond or international stock, for example) that's currently doing the most poorly — that is, buy when shares are on sale. Then the next year, add the fund type that's doing the most poorly at *that* time. (Make sure to buy the better funds within the type that's doing poorly!)

For more ideas, see Chapter 15 for sample portfolios for beginning investors.

Investing large amounts: To lump or to average?

Most people invest money as they save it. If you're saving through a company retirement plan, such as a 401(k), this option is ideal: It happens automatically, and you're buying at different points in time, so even the world's unluckiest person gets to buy some funds at or near market bottoms.

But what if you have what to you seems like a whole *lot* of money that's lolly-gagging around in a savings or money market fund? Maybe it's just piled up because you're thrifty, or maybe you recently inherited money or received a windfall from work. You're discovering more about how to invest this money, but after you decide what types of investments you'd like to purchase, you may be terrified at the thought of actually buying them.

Some people in this situation feel a sense of loss, failure, or even guilt for not making better use of the money than just letting it sit in a savings or money market account. Always remember one important thing: At least you're earning a positive return in the bank or money fund, and it beats the heck out of rushing into an investment that you don't understand and in which you may lose 20 percent or more. Of course, you have every reason to find the best parking spot that you can for your money. (See Chapter 11 for recommendations of the best money market funds.)

So how do you invest your lump? One approach is to *dollar-cost average* it into the investments you've chosen. This means that you invest your money in equal chunks regularly, such as once a month or per quarter. For example, if you have $50,000 to invest and you want to invest it once per quarter over one year, you'd invest $12,500 per quarter until it's all invested. Meanwhile, the money that's awaiting future investment happily continues accumulating interest in a good money market fund. Take a look at the pros and cons of this method of investing a large sum:

- ✔ **Thumbs up:** The attraction of dollar-cost averaging is that it allows you to ease into riskier investments instead of jumping in all at once. The benefit may be that, if the price of the investment drops after some of your initial purchases, you can buy some later at a lower price. If you invest all your money at once and then the financial markets get walloped, it's human to think, "Why didn't I wait?"

History has proven that dollar-cost averaging is a great risk-reducing investment strategy. If you'd used dollar-cost averaging during the worst decade for stock investors in the last century (1928 to 1938), you still would've averaged 7 percent per year in returns despite the Great Depression and a sagging stock market.

- ✔ **Thumbs down:** The flip side of dollar-cost averaging is that if your investments do what they're supposed to and increase in value, you may wish that you'd invested your money faster. Another possible drawback of dollar-cost averaging is that you may get cold feet continuing to put money in an investment that's dropping in value. Some folks who are attracted to dollar-cost averaging are afraid to continue boarding what appears to be a sinking ship.

Dollar-cost averaging also can cause headaches with your taxes when it's time to sell investments held outside retirement accounts. If you buy an investment at many different times and prices, the accounting is muddied as you sell portions of the investment. Also, remember to try not to purchase funds, particularly stock funds that have had a good year, late in the year because most of these funds distribute capital gains in December.

In my opinion, dollar-cost averaging is most valuable when the money you want to invest represents a large portion of your total assets and you can stick to a schedule. Making it automatic is best so that you're less likely to chicken out and discontinue investing if your initial investment purchases have declined in value from when you bought them.

Most mutual fund companies offer automatic exchange services. Pick a time period that makes sense. I like to do dollar-cost averaging once per quarter early in the quarter (the first of January, April, July, and October). If you feel comfortable investing and want to get on with the program, averaging your money over one year is fine, but it's riskier. If you have big bucks to invest and you're cautious, you may prefer to average the money over two to five years. (In this case, you can use some CDs or Treasury bills as holding places in order to get a better return than on the money market fund.)

Sorting through your existing investments

A final question that people who want to start a comprehensive mutual fund investment program, but who also have existing portfolios, frequently ask me is what to do with their existing investments. Here are my thoughts:

✔ **Keep the good nonfund investments.** Although I'm a fan of mutual funds, there's no compelling reason for you to invest all your money in funds. If you enjoy investing in real estate or securities of your own choosing, go right ahead. You may have inherited other assets that have done well over the long term, and you shouldn't rush into selling them, especially if prodded to do so by a self-serving investment advisor or broker. Take your time and evaluate what you have. You can account for these other investments when you tally up your asset allocation. As for evaluating the mutual funds you may already own, see Chapter 17.

✔ **Get rid of high-fee, poorly performing investments.** As you understand more about the best mutual fund investments, you may come to realize by comparison how lousy some of your existing investments are. I won't stand in your way of dumping them!

✔ **Pay attention to tax consequences.** When you're considering selling a nonretirement account investment, especially one that has appreciated considerably since its original purchase, be mindful of taxes. Assets held for more than 12 months are eligible for the more favorable capital gains tax rates (see Chapter 10).

Chapter 11

Money Market Funds: Beating the Bank

In This Chapter

▶ Distinguishing money market funds from other mutual funds

▶ Choosing the right fund for you

▶ Getting a glimpse of the best money market funds around

*B*ack in the days when Richard Nixon was President, folks had hundreds of alternatives for safely investing their spare cash — they could schlep around and shop among banks, banks, and still more banks. Although it may seem that safe-money investors had many alternatives, they really didn't. As a result, yields weren't all that great compared with what a large institutional investor with millions of dollars to invest could obtain by purchasing ultrasafe short-term securities.

Then in the early 1970s, money market mutual funds were born. The concept was fairly simple. The money market mutual fund invested in the same safe, higher-yielding financial instruments (which I discuss in the section "Grasping what money funds invest in," later in this chapter) that only those with big bucks could buy. The money market fund then sells shares to investors who don't have vast sums to invest. By pooling the money from thousands of investors, the fund offers investors a decent yield (after charging a reasonable fee to cover the operational expenses and make a profit). In their first years of operation, these "people's" money funds had little cash flowing in. By 1977, less than $4 billion were in money market funds. But then interest rates rose sharply as inflation took hold. Soon, bank depositors found that the rates of interest they could earn could rise no more, because banks were limited by federal regulations to paying 5 percent interest.

As interest rates skyrocketed in the late 1970s and investors found that they could earn higher yields by switching from bank accounts to money market funds, money flooded into those funds. Within just four years, money market fund assets mushroomed more than fiftyfold to $200 billion. (Today, more than $1 trillion resides in retail money market funds.)

Money Market Funds 101

Money market mutual funds are a large and unique part of the mutual fund industry's offering. *Money market funds are the only type of mutual fund whose share price doesn't fluctuate in value.* The share prices of stock and bond mutual funds fluctuate from day to day depending on how the stock and bond markets are doing. Money market funds, in stark contrast, are locked in at $1 per share. This section gives you the lowdown on these funds.

Comparing money funds with bank accounts

You make money with money market funds by earning dividends, similar to the interest you earn on bank savings accounts. However, the best money market mutual funds offer several significant benefits:

- ✓ **Higher yields:** What first attracted investors (including me as a young adult) to money market funds (back when interest rates zoomed up in the late 1970s and early 1980s) still holds true today. The best money market mutual funds pay a higher yield than equivalent bank accounts, despite the deregulation of the banking industry.

- ✓ **Multiple tax flavors:** Besides their lower rate of return, another problem with bank savings accounts is that they come in one tax flavor: taxable. There's no such thing as a bank savings account that pays you tax-free interest. Money market funds, however, come in a variety of tax-free versions, paying dividends free of federal or state tax or both. So, if you're in a high federal or state (or both) income tax bracket, money funds offer you advantages that a bank savings account simply can't.

- ✓ **Check-writing privileges:** Money market mutual funds allow you to write checks, without charge, against your account. Most mutual fund companies require that the checks be written for larger amounts — typically at least $250 — and may limit the number that can be written per month. They don't want you using these accounts to pay all your small household bills because checks cost money to process.

- ✓ **Convenient access to other mutual funds:** After you've established a money market mutual fund at a particular fund company, investing in other funds offered by that company becomes a matter of placing a simple toll-free phone call or clicking your computer mouse. (And, as I discuss in Chapter 9, if your chosen fund company has a discount brokerage division, you may also be able to invest in mutual funds from other parent companies.) One centralized account eliminates the need to complete additional application forms every time and reduces the ongoing paperwork involved in tracking your funds. Paperwork nirvana!

How banks get away with paying less

How and why do banks continue to pay less interest than most money funds? Two reasons:

✔ Banks have a lot of overhead due to all the branch offices they operate.

✔ Banks know that they can get away with paying lower yields because many of their

depositors, perhaps including you, believe that the FDIC insurance that comes with a bank account makes it safer than a money market mutual fund. I dispel this myth in the section "I won't have FDIC insurance," later in the chapter.

✔ **No lines and traffic jams:** Because you can invest and transact in mutual funds online, over the phone, and through the mail, you can save yourself considerable hassle. Even though most banks are becoming more technologically savvy, some bank transactions, including opening an account, require you to drive to a bank branch. When you deal with a fund, you've also eliminated the risk of being part of a crime scene, as numerous bank branches today still suffer from robberies and holdups.

Sometimes, you get put on hold for a short time when you call a mutual fund company. The better companies (the ones I recommend in this book) generally won't leave you hanging for more than 15 to 30 seconds. If they do, please write me (you can drop me a note through my Web site at www.erictyson.com) and let me know so that together we can hassle them or delete them from the next edition!

Banks have developed money market deposit accounts (MMDAs) that are money fund wannabes. Banks set the interest rate on MMDAs, and it's generally lower than what you can get from one of the better money market mutual funds. Check writing on MMDAs, if it's available, is usually restricted to just a few checks monthly.

As latecomers to the mutual fund business, some banks now offer real money market mutual funds, including tax-free money funds. Again, the better money market mutual funds from mutual fund companies are generally superior (see my recommendations in the section "Finding the Recommended Funds," later in this chapter) to those offered by banks. The reason: Most bank money market funds have higher operating expenses and hence lower yields than the best money funds offered by mutual fund companies.

Finding uses for money funds

The best money market funds are the ideal substitute for a bank savings account — offering equivalent safety to a bank, but a much better yield. Money market funds are well suited for some of the following purposes:

✔ **Your emergency cash reserve:** Money market funds are a good place to keep your emergency cash reserve. Because you don't know what the future holds, you're wise to prepare for the unexpected — events such as job loss, unanticipated medical bills, or a leaky roof. Three to six months' worth of living expenses is a good emergency reserve target for most people (for example, if you spend $3,000 in an average month, keep $9,000 to $18,000 reserved).

You may be able to get by with just three months' living expenses if you have other accounts, such as a 401(k) or family members and close friends that you could tap for a loan. Consider keeping up to one year's expenses handy if your income fluctuates wildly. If your profession involves a high risk of job loss, and if finding another job could take a long time, you also need a significant cash safety net.

✔ **Short-term savings goals:** If you're saving money for a big-ticket item that you hope to purchase within the next couple of years — whether it's a fishing boat or a down payment on a home — a money market fund is a terrific place to accumulate and grow the money. With such a short time horizon, you can't afford to expose your money to the gyrations of stocks or longer-term bonds. A money market fund offers not only a safe haven for your principal but also a yield that should keep you a step ahead of the inflation rate.

✔ **A parking spot for money awaiting investment:** Suppose that you have a chunk of money that you want to invest for longer-term purposes but you don't want to invest it all at once for fear that you may buy into stocks and bonds just before a big drop. A money market fund can be a friendly home to the money awaiting investment as you purchase into your chosen investment gradually over time. (This technique is known as *dollar-cost averaging,* which I explain in Chapter 10.)

✔ **Personal checking accounts:** You can use money market funds with no restrictions on check writing for household checking purposes. Some discount brokerage services that offer accounts with a check-writing option downplay the fact that an investor is allowed to write an unlimited number of checks (in any amounts) on his or her account. You can leave your bank altogether — some money funds even come with debit cards that you can use at bank ATMs for a nominal fee! Later in this chapter (in the section "Finding the Recommended Funds"), I point out specific funds that offer unlimited check-writing privileges.

✔ **Business accounts:** You can also open a money market fund for your business. You can use this account for depositing checks received from customers and holding excess funds, as well as for paying bills by means of the check-writing feature. Some money funds allow checks to be written for any amount, and such accounts can completely replace a bank checking account.

You can also establish direct deposit with most money market funds. You can have your paycheck, monthly Social Security benefit check, or most other regular payments you receive from larger organizations zapped electronically into your money market mutual fund account.

Refuting common concerns

Investors new to money market mutual funds sometimes worry about what they're getting themselves into. It's good to be concerned and educated *before* you move your money into securities you've never invested in. Most people don't worry about the money they keep in the bank. They should — at least a little. First of all, banks get burglarized and defrauded more than mutual funds! (A thief created a bogus ID and visited five branches of my bank, posing as me, and succeeded in withdrawing $400 from my checking account. The bank covered the loss, but I chose to take my business elsewhere.)

The biggest risk of keeping extra money in a bank savings account is that inflation erodes your money's purchasing power because of the paltry interest you're getting. *Remember:* The FDIC insurance system is a government insurance system — not an ironclad, 100-percent safety guarantee. This section presents the concerns that I hear about money market funds, and the reasons I think that you shouldn't worry about them.

1 won't have FDIC insurance

Some people are nervous about money market mutual funds because they aren't "insured." (One exception: Government insurance covered money funds by during the late 2000s financial crisis. See the sidebar: "The one year money market funds had insurance".) Bank accounts, on the other hand, come with insurance that protects up to $250,000 you have deposited (assuming that your bank participates in the FDIC system). So, if a bank with FDIC insurance fails because it lends too much money to people and companies that go bankrupt or abscond with the funds, you should get your money back, up to $250,000.

But consider this: Part of the reason that money market funds aren't insured is that they don't really need to be. Mutual fund companies can't fail because they have a dollar invested in securities for every dollar you deposit in their money funds. Banks, on the other hand, are required to have available just 12 cents for every dollar you hand over to them; that's why they need insurance.

The one year money market funds had insurance

During the height of the financial crisis in 2008, in early September 2008, the share price of a money market fund, the Reserve Primary Fund, fell below $1 per share, the normally fixed price for all money funds. This fund actually declined 3 percent to $0.97 per share. While 3 percent is a small decline, especially compared with declines in the stock market, investors in money market mutual funds have enjoyed and expect that the share price of their money funds would hold constant at $1 per share. (Reserve lost some money on Lehman commercial paper that it owned that plunged in value when Lehman filed for bankruptcy.)

To calm nervous investors, then U.S. Treasury Secretary Henry Paulson announced a new insurance plan, which covered money market fund asset balances investors had in money funds, on September 19, 2008. A specific date was chosen as regulators didn't want investors, especially large institutional investors, continuing to move money around trying to game the system. Some banks also complained that with insurance coverage instituted on money funds, bank depositors might move money from banks to the higher yielding money market funds. If banks and money funds both had insurance, why leave your money in a lower yielding bank account?

The new money market fund insurance program was not intended as a long-term or permanent change for the money market mutual fund business. The insurance ended on September 18, 2009, one year after its inception.

Historically, since their inception in 1972, money market funds have been extremely safe. Only one other fund broke the buck (by 6 percent) and that was a fund run by and invested in only by a modest number of institutional investors. Today, assets in all money funds (both retail and institutional) total more than $3 trillion. Hundreds of trillions of dollars have flowed into and out of money funds over the decades without any retail investors losing principal.

Rather than boosting yield by keeping their expenses low, some money funds venture into riskier debt to boost their fund's yields. That's one of several reasons why I recommend that when you invest in money market funds, you do so with a larger and conservatively managed investment company that keeps expenses low, which is the only safe way to boost a money fund's yield. These firms don't generally stretch for a little extra yield by taking silly risks, and in the highly unlikely event that they ever bought something problematic, they would surely make good on the $1 per share price.

In the late 2000s, a couple dozen money fund owners have infused modest amounts of capital into their money funds to keep them from possibly breaking the buck when they held a security that may have had to be listed at a reduced value on the fund's books. Taking such action requires U.S. Securities & Exchange Commission (SEC) approval. Such requests have happened before, but their pace increased dramatically during the 2008 financial crisis. Among fund companies having to take such action were Allianz, HSBC Holdings, Legg Mason, Northern Trust, Ridgewood Investments, SEI Investments, TD Ameritrade, and Wells Fargo.

According to law professor and industry observer Mercer Bullard (who also was the technical reviewer for this edition of this book), the law is unclear as to whether fund companies ever need to disclose to their shareholders that they sought relief for their money funds and were blessed to do so by the SEC.

It's possible that a money market fund's investments may decline slightly in value — thus reducing the share price of the money market fund below a dollar. In a few cases, money market funds have held some securities that ended up tanking. However, in each and every case (except for one, which I discuss next), the money market fund was *bailed out* — that is, cash was infused into the money fund by the mutual fund company, thus enabling the fund to maintain a price of $1 per share.

One money market fund, however, did break the buck. A newspaper article dramatically headlined, "Investors Stunned as a Money Fund Folds," went on to say, "The fund's collapse is the latest blunder to shake investors' confidence in the nation's mutual fund industry." Although such hype may help to fill readers with anxiety (and perhaps sell more newspapers), it obscures several important facts. This particular money fund didn't collapse; it was liquidated because its investors, who were all small banks, owned the fund, and they decided to disband it. The fund didn't hold money from retail investors like you and me. If it had, the fund company surely would've bailed it out, as other fund companies have done. You should also know that only 6 percent of the investing banks' money was lost. Hardly a collapse — and I doubt that anyone was stunned!

If you have more than $250,000 in one bank and that bank fails, you can lose the money over the $250,000 insurance limit. I've seen more than a few cases where people had more than the insured amount— in one case, a person who came to me for advice had nearly $2 million — sitting in a bank account! Now that's risk! Since 1980, more than 3,000 banks have failed. Because the government has taken a hard line on not going beyond the insurance limits in the 2000s, bank depositors have lost hundreds of millions of dollars.

Stick with larger mutual fund companies if you're worried about the lack of FDIC insurance. They have the financial wherewithal and the most incentive to save a floundering money fund. Fortunately, the larger fund companies have the best money funds anyway.

The check may get lost or stolen

No one can legally cash a check made payable to you. Don't mistakenly think that going to your local bank in person is safer — you could slip on some dog droppings or get carjacked.

If you're really concerned about the mail, use a fund company or discount broker with branch offices. I don't recommend spending the extra money and time required to send your check by way of registered or certified mail. You know if your check got there when you get the statement from the fund company processing the deposit. (In those rare cases where a check does get lost, know that checks can be reissued.) And when you're depositing a check made payable to you, be sure to endorse the check with the notation "for deposit only" along with your account number under your signature.

When the bank or credit union may be better

Although I advocate use of the best money market funds, I realize that a bank or credit union savings account is sometimes the most practical place to keep your money. Your local bank, for example, may appeal to you if you like being able to do business face to face. Perhaps you operate a business where a lot of cash is processed; in this case, you can't beat the convenience and other services that a local bank offers. And, if you have only $1,000 or $2,000 to invest, a bank savings account may be your better option; the best money market funds generally require a higher minimum initial investment.

For investing short-term excess cash, you may first want to consider keeping it in your checking account. This option may make financial sense if the extra money helps you avoid monthly service charges because your balance occasionally dips below the minimum. In fact, keeping money in a separate savings account rather than in your checking account may *not* benefit you if service charges wipe out your interest earnings.

Don't forget to shop around for the best deals on your checking account because minimum balance requirements, service fees, and interest rates vary. Credit unions offer some of the best deals, although they usually don't offer extensive access to free ATMs. The largest banks with the most ATM machines — you know, the ones that spend gobs of money on advertising jingles and billboards — usually offer the worst terms on checking and savings accounts.

I may have trouble accessing my money

Although it may appear that you can't easily and quickly access your money market fund holdings, you can, in fact, efficiently tap your money market fund in a variety of ways (*Note:* You can use these methods at most fund companies, particularly the larger ones):

- ✔ **Check writing:** The most efficient way to access your money market fund is to write a check. Suppose that you have an unexpectedly large expense that you can't afford to pay out of your bank checking account. Just write a check on your money market mutual fund.

- ✔ **Electronic transfers:** Another handy way to access your money (which may be useful if your money fund checkbook is hidden under a mountain of papers somewhere in the vicinity of your desk) is to call the fund company and ask it to have money sent electronically from your money market fund to your bank account or vice versa. (Such transactions can also be done on some fund companies' Web sites.) Or if you prefer, you can have the fund company mail you a check for your desired amount from your money fund.

  If you need money regularly sent from your money market fund to, say, your local bank checking account, you can set up an automatic withdrawal plan. On a designated day of the month, your money market fund electronically sends money to your checking account.

✔ **Wiring:** If you need cash in a flash, many money market funds offer the option of wiring money to and from your bank. Both the money market fund and the bank usually assess a small charge for this service. Most companies also send you money via an overnight express carrier, such as Federal Express, if you provide them with an account number.

✔ **Debit cards:** Brokerage account money funds that offer debit cards allow access to your money through bank ATMs.

Chapter 16 explains how to establish these account features. Unlike when you visit a bank, you can't simply drop by the branch office of a mutual fund company and withdraw funds from your account. They don't keep money in branch offices because they're not banks. However, you can establish the preceding account features, if you didn't set them up when you originally set up your account, by mailing in a form or by visiting the fund's branch office.

Grasping what money funds invest in

Under the Securities and Exchange Commission (SEC) regulations, money market funds can invest only in the most credit-worthy securities, and their investments must have an average *maturity* (when the short-term bonds pay off) of less than 60 days per new rules released by the SEC in 2010. The short-term nature of these securities effectively eliminates the risk of money funds being sensitive to changes in (short-term) interest rates.

The securities that money market funds use are extremely safe. General-purpose money market funds invest in government-backed securities, bank certificates of deposits (CDs), and short-term corporate debt issued by the largest and most credit-worthy companies and the U.S. government (although that may not be much comfort to some of you). The following sections explain the major types of securities that money funds hold.

Commercial paper

Corporations, particularly large ones, often need to borrow money to help make their businesses grow and prosper. In the past, most companies needing a short-term loan had to borrow money from a bank. In recent decades, issuing short-term debt or IOUs — *commercial paper* — directly to interested investors has become easier. Money market funds buy high-quality commercial paper that matures typically within 60 to 90 days and is issued by large companies (such as Boeing, Exxon Mobil, Hewlett-Packard, Home Depot, Microsoft, and Wal-Mart), banks, and foreign governments.

If you had hundreds of thousands of dollars to invest, you could purchase commercial paper yourself instead of buying it indirectly through a money market fund. If you do have a lot of money to invest, I don't recommend this approach. You incur fees when you purchase commercial paper yourself, and you most likely lack the expertise to know how to evaluate credit risks and what a fair price to pay is. The best money funds charge a small fee to do all this analysis for you, plus they offer perks, such as check-writing privileges.

Certificates of deposit

You can go to your local bank and invest some money in a *certificate of deposit* (CD). A CD is nothing more than a specific-term loan that you make to your banker — ranging anywhere from a month to some number of years.

Money market funds can buy CDs as well. The only difference is that they invest a lot more money — usually millions — in bank CDs. Thus, they can command a higher interest rate than you can get on your own. Money funds buy CDs that mature within a few months. The money fund is only insured up to $250,000 per bank CD, just like the bank insurance that customers receive. As with other money fund investments, the money fund does research to determine the credit quality of banks and other institutions that it invests in. Remember that money funds' other investments aren't insured.

Money market funds may hold some other types of CDs. U.S. branches of foreign banks issue Yankee CDs. Foreign banks or the foreign branches of U.S. banks issue Eurodollar CDs.

Government debt

McDonald's has signs in many locations saying that billions and billions have been served. Well, the federal government also serves up trillions and trillions — of dollars in debt, that is — in the form of Treasury securities. A truckload of federal government debt is outstanding — about $12 trillion.

Most money market funds invest a small portion of their money in Treasuries soon to mature. Money funds also invest in short-term debt issued by government-affiliated agencies, such as the Federal Home Loan Bank, which provides funds to the nation's savings and loans.

Government agency debt, which money funds also invest in, unlike Treasuries, isn't backed by the "full faith and credit of the U.S. government." However, no federal agency has ever defaulted on its debt. The folks back in Washington are certain to avoid the loss of faith in government-issued debt that would surely follow should such a default be allowed to occur.

As I discuss in more detail later in the chapter, some money market funds specialize in certain types of government securities that distribute tax-free income to their investors. Treasury money market funds, for example, buy Treasuries and pay dividends that are state-tax-free, but federally taxable. State-specific municipal money market funds invest in debt issued by state and local governments in one state. The dividends on state money funds are federal- and state-tax-free (if you're a resident of that state).

Other types of securities

Other types of securities typically make up small portions of a money fund's holdings. These types include the following:

- ✔ *Repurchase agreements (repos)* are overnight investments that money funds send to *dealers* (banks and investment banks' securities divisions), and the money fund receives Treasury securities overnight as collateral.

- ✔ *Bankers' acceptances* are more complex: They're issued by banks guaranteeing corporation debt incurred from trade. For example, if Sony sends televisions from overseas to the United States by freight but doesn't want to wait for its money until the ship comes in and the stores pay for the televisions, Sony can get paid right away by borrowing from a bank based on the expected delivery of the televisions. The stores get the televisions and pay for them, and then Sony's loan gets repaid.

Choosing a Great Money Market Fund

A money market fund is probably the easiest type of mutual fund to select. To save you time and make you the most money, the following sections describe the major issues to consider when selecting money funds.

Why yield and expenses go hand in hand

Within a given category of money market fund (general, Treasury, or municipal), money fund managers are investing in the same basic securities. The market for these securities is pretty darned efficient, so superstar money fund managers may eke out an extra 0.1 percent of yield over their competitors but not much more.

However, money funds can differ significantly from one another in yield due to expenses. For money market funds more than for any other kind of fund, operating expenses are the single biggest determinant of return. All other conditions being equal (which they usually are with money market funds), lower operating expenses translate into higher yields for you.

For money market funds, you shouldn't tolerate annual operating expenses greater than 0.5 percent. Top quality funds charge 0.25 percent or less annually. Remember, lower expenses don't mean that a fund company is cutting corners or providing poor service. Lower expenses are possible in most cases because a fund company has been successful in attracting so much money to invest. As I discuss in Chapter 12, fund companies with consistently low expenses on their money funds also generally offer good bond funds.

Money funds 20 percent off!

Some money market mutual funds aren't above resorting to the marketing tricks that retailers use. Beware of money fund managers running specials or sales. They try to lure investors by temporarily waiving (also known as *absorbing*) operating expenses. These sales tricks create money fund yields that are a lot like muscles on steroids: artificially pumped up. When the fund managers start thirsting for profits — and with time they will, because these aren't charities — they simply reinstate operating expenses, and then you can watch the air go out of the yield balloon. Some bond mutual funds (see Chapter 12) engage in this deceptive practice as well.

Some fund companies run sales because they know that a major portion of the fund buyers lured in won't bother leaving (or knowing) when the operating expenses are jacked up. To get the highest long-term yield from money funds,

you're best off sticking with funds that maintain everyday low prices for operating expenses. You can ensure that your fund isn't running a special by asking what the current operating expense ratio is and whether the fund is waiving some portion of the expenses. You may also discern this status by checking the annual operating expense ratio in the fund's prospectus (see Chapter 8).

If you want to move your money to companies having specials and then move it back out when the special is over, you may come out a little ahead in your yield. If you have a lot of money and don't mind paperwork, this strategy may be worth the bother. But don't forget the value of your time, lost interest when a check is in the mail, and the chance that you may not stay on top of the fund's expense changes.

Looking at your tax situation

You've perhaps heard the expression, "It's not what you make; it's what you keep." What you keep on your investment returns is what's left over after the federal and state governments take their cut of your investment profits. If you're investing money held outside of a retirement account and you're in a high tax bracket (particularly the federal 28 percent or higher bracket), you may come out ahead by investing in *tax-free* money market funds instead of taxable ones. If you're in a high-tax state, a state-specific money market fund (if a good one is available in your state) may be a sound move. (See "Finding the Recommended Funds" section for specific fund recommendations.)

Tax-free refers to the taxability of the dividends paid by the fund. Don't confuse this term with the effective tax deductions you get on contributions to a retirement account, such as a 401(k).

Determining whether tax-free money market funds net you more

If you're in the highest federal tax brackets (see the federal tax rate chart in Chapter 10), you usually come out ahead in tax-free investments. The only way to know is to crunch the numbers.

In order to do the comparison properly, factor in federal as well as state taxes. Suppose, for example, that you call Vanguard, which tells you that its Prime Money Market fund currently yields 2.0 percent. The yield or dividend on this fund is fully taxable.

Suppose further that you're a resident of California and that Vanguard's California Money Market fund currently yields 1.4 percent. The California tax-free money market fund pays dividends that are free from federal *and* California state tax. Thus, you get to keep all 1.4 percent that you earn. The income you earn on the Prime Money Market, on the other hand, is taxed. So here's how you compare the two:

yield on tax-free fund ÷ yield on taxable fund

.014 (1.4 percent) ÷ .02 (2.0 percent) = 0.70

In other words, the tax-free fund pays a yield of 70 percent of that on the taxable fund. Thus, if you must pay more than 30 percent (1 − 0.70) in federal and California state tax, you net more in the tax-free fund. If you do this analysis comparing some funds today, be aware that yields bounce around. The difference in yields between tax-free and taxable funds widens and narrows a bit over time. Instead of simply comparing the current yield on a tax-free versus a taxable money fund, compare the two funds' yields over the past year.

One final and important point: Whenever a recession occurs, especially a severe one, some folks worry about the fiscal status of states that experience mushrooming deficits. California, for sure, was in the news a lot with its ballooning deficits due to the painful, late 2000s recession. Various commentators and talking heads referred to California as "bankrupt," which it most clearly was not. While I don't have a crystal ball for California or any other state, I can tell you that such fears have come and gone in the past. The conditions that lead to large budget deficits — declining tax revenue and rising state payments — inevitably reverse when the economy rebounds.

If you worry about being in a state-specific money market or bond fund due to the economic health of your state, then you probably should go with a nationally diversified fund to ease your fears. Either that, or tune out the fear-mongering talking heads (and visit my Web site at www.erictyson.com for an unbiased, level-headed view of recent news events).

Deciding where you want your home base

Convenience is another important factor in choosing where to establish a money market fund. For example, if you're planning on investing in stock and bond mutual funds at T. Rowe Price, that may be the best place for you to open up a money market fund as well. Although you may get a slightly higher money market yield from another fund company, opening up a separate account may not be worth the administrative hassle, especially if you don't plan on keeping much cash in the money fund.

If you don't mind the extra paperwork, you can go for the extra yield. Calculate (based on the yield difference) the costs of keeping a lower-yielding money fund. Every tenth (0.1) of a percent per $10,000 invested costs you $10 in lost dividends annually.

Keeping your investments close to home

Most mutual fund companies don't have local branch offices. Generally, maintaining few offices helps fund companies keep their expenses low and their yields higher. You may open and maintain your money market mutual fund through the fund's toll-free phone line, the mail, and the Internet.

Except for psychological security, selecting a fund company with an office in your area doesn't offer much benefit. But I don't want to downplay the importance of your emotional comfort level. Fund providers Fidelity, Schwab, TIAA-CREF, and TD Ameritrade have larger branch networks. Depending on where you live, you may be near one of the fund companies I recommend. (See the Appendix.)

Considering other issues

Most, but not all, money market funds offer other useful services, such as free check-writing privileges, fund exchange and redemption via telephone and the Internet, and automated, electronic exchange services with your bank account. The fund companies I recommend generally offer these features, so these shouldn't be deciding factors when debating among fund options. As I mention earlier in this chapter, most money funds require that you write checks for at least $250 or $500. Some funds don't have this restriction, which may be important if you want to pay smaller bills out of the account.

Another potentially important issue is the initial minimum investment required to open an account. Most funds require a minimum investment of $3,000 or so, although some require heftier amounts. If you drop below the minimum at most money market funds, it's no big deal, and no charge is assessed. Some money funds do, however, charge small fees for use of certain features. I discuss these fees in the next section.

Finding the Recommended Funds

In this section, I recommend the best money market funds, based on the criteria I discuss in the previous section,. Due to the financial crisis and severe recession in the late 2000s, short-term interest rates plummeted to near zero and continued that way into the new decade. As a result, the yield on many money market funds was near or even at zero. Many money funds had to absorb a portion of their fund's expenses so that the yield would not become negative. Some money funds closed to new investors because allowing new investors would have driven a fund's yield down even further because the fund manager would be forced to buy lower yielding bonds. Please see Chapter 12 for information on short-term bond funds as an alternative to low yielding money funds.

Taxable money market funds

Money market funds that pay taxable dividends are appropriate for retirement account funds awaiting investment as well as nonretirement account money when you're not in a high federal tax bracket *and* not in a high state tax bracket. Here are the best taxable money market funds to consider (call the fund companies for current yields):

✔ **Vanguard's Prime Money Market (VMMXX)** has an operating expense ratio of 0.25 percent per year. Like most Vanguard funds, it requires $3,000 to open. www.vanguard.com; ☎ 800-662-7447

✔ **TIAA-CREF Money Market (TIAXX)** has an annual expense ratio of 0.47 percent. Minimum to open an account is $2,500. www.tiaa-cref.org; ☎ 800-223-1200

✔ **Fidelity Cash Reserves (FDRXX)** has an operating expense ratio of 0.39 percent. $2,500 minimum initial investment. www.fidelity.com; ☎ 800-544-8888

✔ **T. Rowe Price Summit Cash Reserves** (TSCXX) has a minimum initial investment of $25,000 and an expense ratio of 0.47 percent per year. If you're doing the bulk of your investing through a fund company other than heavyweights Vanguard or Fidelity, it's your call whether you should do your money fund investing there as well. www.troweprice.com; ☎ 800-638-5660

U.S. Treasury money market funds

U.S. Treasury money market funds are appropriate if you're not in a high federal tax bracket but *are* in a high state tax bracket. Check out these funds:

✔ **Vanguard Admiral Treasury Money Market (VUSXX)** has a slim 0.12 percent annual expense ratio. Due to the very low yields on Treasury notes, this fund was closed to new investors in 2009. www.vanguard.com; ☎ 800-662-7447

✔ **USAA's Treasury Money Market (UATXX)** has a 0.44 percent operating cost and a $3,000 minimum initial investment. www.usaa.com; ☎ 800-531-8181

✔ **Fidelity's Government Money Market (SPAXX)** has an expense ratio of 0.45 percent. This fund's minimum initial investment is $25,000 for nonretirement accounts. This fund charges a $2 fee per check written (waived if your balance is greater than $50,000). www.fidelity.com; ☎ 800-544-8888

You can bypass Treasury money market funds and their operating fees by purchasing Treasury bills directly from your local Federal Reserve Bank for no fee. Buying Treasuries direct especially makes sense during periods of low interest rates like we had in the late 2000s and into the new decade. Although you save yourself expenses by going this route, you lose convenient access to your money. You have no check-writing privileges: If you need to tap the Treasuries before they mature, it's a bit of an administrative hassle and will cost you a brokerage fee. With Vanguard's expense ratios on their Treasury money funds, it costs you $12 per year with a $10,000 balance; $60 per year with a $50,000 balance.

Municipal tax-free money market funds

Municipal (also known as *muni*) money market funds invest in short-term debt issued by state and local governments. Dividends from municipal money funds are generally free of federal taxes. Those investors who limit their investing to just one state are generally free of state taxes as well (provided you live in that state).

You may be saying to yourself that state-specific muni funds are the way to go. Not so fast. You may not have to worry about shielding your dividends from state taxes if you live in a state that meets any of the following criteria:

✔ Doesn't impose any income tax, such as Florida (you lucky dog)

✔ Charges a lower income tax (less than 5 percent), such as Michigan

✔ Has a higher income tax but no decent state-specific money market funds to invest in

Understanding discount brokerage money fund options

As I discuss in Chapter 9, some discount brokers offer all-in-one accounts that combine unlimited check writing with investing. These accounts can certainly reduce the paperwork in your life: Everything from your monthly bill payments to your mutual fund holdings is consolidated on one account statement.

Comprehensive brokerage accounts are usually built around some kind of hub, a temporary holding place for the money that's waiting to be either spent or invested. This part is the portion of the account you can write checks against, funnel dividends into, and purchase investments with. You're usually given an option on how you want to hold this hub money. Look at your options carefully, and don't make the mistake of leaving your money in the default option.

With some all-in-one brokerage accounts, the hub may be called something like your *core account.* Your first option for the core account may be to keep it in cash. Although you do earn interest on it, that interest is fully taxable and offers a much lower yield than from a taxable money market fund.

Especially if you're in a higher tax bracket, the better choice may be to use a municipal money market fund that pays federally tax-free dividends. You also have the option to put your cash in a state-specific money market fund if you happen to live in a state in which the account provider offers such a fund: This strategy shields your dividends from state as well as federal taxes.

Of course, money funds outside of the core options don't give you features such as unlimited check writing, but you may be able to get a higher yield. You can always keep a small amount of money in one of the core options to cover any check-writing needs.

If you live in any of those states and if you're in a high federal tax bracket, you may be better off with a national money market fund, whose dividends are free of federal but not state tax. (Call the fund companies for current yields.) Check out these funds:

- ✔ **Vanguard Tax-Exempt Money Market (VMSXX)** has a 0.17 percent annual expense ratio and requires a $3,000 minimum initial investment to open. www.vanguard.com; ☎ 800-662-7447

- ✔ **T. Rowe Price Summit Municipal Money Market (TRSXX)** has a 0.47 percent annual expense ratio and requires a $25,000 minimum initial investment to open. www.troweprice.com; ☎ 800-638-5660

- ✔ **USAA Tax-Exempt Money Market (USEXX)** has a 0.51 percent annual expense ratio and requires a $3,000 minimum initial investment to open. www.usaa.com; ☎ 800-531-8181

State-specific money market funds, whose dividends are free of both federal and state taxes if you live in the specified state, are appropriate when you're in a high federal *and* state tax bracket. The major fund providers highlighted elsewhere in this chapter for having good money funds (Fidelity, USAA, Vanguard) offer competitive funds for states such as California, Florida, Massachusetts, Maine, New Jersey, New York, Ohio, Pennsylvania, and Virginia. If you can't find a good state-specific money fund for your state or you're only in a high federal tax bracket, you need to use one of the nation-wide muni money markets just described.

Chapter 12

Bond Funds: When Boring Is Best

*M*any investors, both novice and expert, think that the *b* in *bonds* is for *boring.* And they're partly correct. No one gets excited by bonds — unless she's an investment banker, money manager, or broker who deals in bonds and makes big bucks because of them.

But take the time in this chapter to get the whole scoop on bonds. They may seem boring, but they generally offer higher yields than bank and money market accounts with less volatility than stocks.

Understanding Bonds

So what the heck is a bond? Let me try to explain with an analogy. If a money market fund is like a savings account, then a bond is similar to a certificate of deposit (CD). With a five-year CD, for example, a bank agrees to pay you a predetermined annual rate of interest — say, 4.5 percent. If all goes according to plan, at the end of five years of earning the 4.5 percent interest, you get back the principal that you originally invested.

Bonds work about the same way, only instead of banks issuing them, corporations or governments issue them. For example, you can purchase a bond, scheduled to mature five years from now, from a company such as Walmart. A Walmart five-year bond may pay you, say, 6 percent. As long as Walmart doesn't have a financial catastrophe, after five years of receiving interest payments (also known as the *coupon rate*) on the bond, Walmart returns your original investment to you. (***Note:** Zero coupon* bonds pay no interest but are sold at a discounted price to make up for it.)

The worst thing that can happen to your bond investment is that if Walmart filed bankruptcy, then you may not get back *any* of your original investment, let alone the remaining interest.

You shouldn't let this unlikely but plausible scenario scare you away from bonds for these important reasons:

✔ **Bonds can be safer than you think.** Many companies need to borrow money (and thus issue bonds) and are good credit risks. If you own bonds in enough companies — say, in several hundred of them — and one or even a few of them unexpectedly take a fall, their *default* (failure to pay back interest or principal on time) affects only a sliver of your portfolio and wouldn't be a financial catastrophe. A bond mutual fund and its management team can provide you a diversified portfolio of many bonds.

✔ **You're rewarded with higher interest rates than comparable bank investments.** The financial markets and those who participate in them — people like you and me — aren't dumb. If you take extra risk and forsake FDIC insurance, you should receive a higher rate of interest investing in bonds. Guess what? Nervous Nellie savers who're comforted by the executive desks, the vault, the guard in the lobby, and the FDIC insurance logo at their local bank should remember that they're being paid less interest at the bank because of all those comforts.

If you like the government backing afforded by the FDIC program, you can replicate that protection in bond mutual funds that specialize in government-backed securities. (See the section "Eyeing Recommended Bond Funds," later in this chapter.)

In the last section of this chapter, "Exploring Alternatives to Bond Funds," I discuss some potentially higher yield alternatives to investing in bond funds. There, you see that with those higher yields comes greater risk. After all, there's no free lunch in the investing world.

Sizing Up a Bond Fund's Personality

Bond funds aren't as complicated and unique as people, but they're certainly more complex than money market funds. And thanks to some shady marketing practices by particular mutual fund companies and salespeople who sell funds, you have your work cut out for you in getting a handle on what many bond funds really are investing in and how they differ from their peers. But don't worry: I explain these important details for the good funds that I recommend later in this chapter.

After you know four key facts about bond funds — maturity, credit rating, the different entities that issue bonds, and, therefore, the tax consequences on those bonds — you can put the four together to understand how mutual fund companies came up with so many different types of bond funds. For example, you can buy a *corporate intermediate-term high-yield (junk) bond fund* or a *long-term municipal bond fund*. In the following sections, you see the combinations are many.

Maturity: Counting the years until you get your principal back

In everyday conversation, *maturity* refers to that quiet, blessed state of grace and wisdom that you develop as you get older (ahem). But that's not the kind of maturity I'm talking about here. *Maturity,* as it applies to bonds, simply refers to when the bond pays you back — it could be next year, 5 years from now, 30 years from now, or longer. Maturity is the most important variable by which bonds, and therefore bond funds are differentiated and categorized.

You should care *plenty* about how long a bond takes to mature because a bond's maturity gives you a good (although far from perfect) sense of how volatile a bond will be if interest rates change (see Table 12-1). If interest rates fall, bond prices rise.

Table 12-1	Interest Rate Increases Depress Bond Prices
Bond Type	*Price Change If Rates Suddenly Rise 1 Percent**
Short-term bond (2-year maturity)	–2 percent
Intermediate-term bond (7-year maturity)	–5 percent
Long-term bond (20-year maturity)	–10 percent

*Assumes that bonds are yielding approximately 7 percent. If bonds were assumed to be yielding more, then a 1 percent increase in interest rates would have less of an impact. For example, if interest rates are at 10 percent and rise to 11 percent, the price change of the 20-year bond is –8 percent.

Bond funds are portfolios of dozens — and in some cases, hundreds — of individual bonds. You won't need to know the maturity of *every* bond in a bond mutual fund. A useful summarizing statistic to know for a bond fund is the *average maturity* of its bonds. In their marketing literature and prospectuses, bond funds typically say something like, "The Turbocharged Intermediate-Term Bond Fund invests in high-quality bonds with an average maturity of 7 to 12 years."

Bond funds usually place themselves into one of three maturity categories:

- ✔ **Short-term bond funds:** These funds concentrate their investments in bonds maturing in the next few years.
- ✔ **Intermediate-term bond funds:** This category generally holds bonds that come due within five to ten years.
- ✔ **Long-term bond funds:** These funds usually own bonds that mature in 15 to 20 years or so.

These definitions aren't hard and fast. One long-term bond fund may have an average maturity of 14 years while another may have an average of 25 years.

You can run into problems when one intermediate-term fund starts bragging that its returns are better than another's. It's the old story of comparing apples to oranges. When you find out that the braggart fund has an average maturity of 12 years and the other fund has a maturity of 7, then you know that the 12-year fund is using the "intermediate-term" label to make misleading comparisons. The fact is, a fund with bonds maturing on average in 12 years *should* be generating higher returns than a fund with bonds maturing on average in 7 years. The 12-year fund is also more volatile when interest rates change.

The greater risk associated with longer term bonds, which suffer price declines greater than do short-term bonds when interest rates rise, often comes with greater compensation in the form of higher yields.

Most of the time, longer term bonds pay higher yields than do short-term bonds. You can look at a chart of the current yield ("today") of bonds of varying length maturities, which is known as a *yield curve.* Most of the time, this curve slopes upward (see Figure 12-1). Many leading financial publications and Web sites carry a current chart of the yield curve.

Duration: Measuring interest rate risk

If you're trying to determine the sensitivity of bonds and bond funds to changes in interest rates, *duration* may be a more useful statistic than maturity. A bond fund with a duration of ten years means that if interest rates rise by 1 percent, then the value of the bond fund should drop by 10 percent. (Conversely, if rates fall 1 percent, the fund should rise 10 percent.)

Trying to use average maturities to determine what impact a 1 percent rise or fall in interest rates will have on bond prices forces you to slog through all sorts of ugly calculations. Duration is no fuss, no muss — and it gives you one big advantage, too. Besides saving on number crunching, duration enables you to compare funds of differing maturities. If a long-term bond fund has a duration of, say, 12 years, and an intermediate fund has a duration of 6 years, the long-term fund should be about twice as volatile to changes in interest rates.

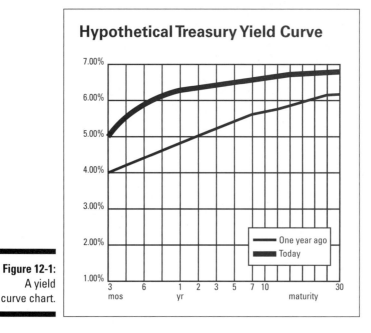

Hypothetical Treasury Yield Curve

Although duration is easier to work with *and* a better indicator than average maturity, you're more likely to hear about average maturity because a fund's duration isn't that easy to understand. Mathematically, it represents the point at which a bondholder receives half (50 percent) of the present value of her total expected payments (interest plus payoff of principal at maturity) from a bond. Present value adjusts future payments to reflect the fact that money received in the future has less value, primarily because of increases in the cost of living (inflation).

If you know a bond fund's duration, which you can obtain from the fund company behind the bond fund you're interested in, you know almost all you need to know about its sensitivity to interest rates. However, duration hasn't been a foolproof indicator: During particular periods when interest rates have risen, some funds have dropped more than the funds' durations predicted. But bear in mind that some heavy investing in unusual securities (such as derivatives) was required to make duration unreliable — so the duration values of the better funds, which I recommend in this chapter, usually work just fine as a guide. Also be aware that other factors — such as changes in the credit quality of the bonds in a fund — may affect the price changes of a bond fund over time.

Credit quality: Determining whether bonds will pay you back

Bond funds also differ from one another in terms of the creditworthiness of the bonds that they hold. That's just a fancy way of saying, "Hey, are they gonna stiff me or what?"

Every year, bondholders get left holding nothing but the bag for billions of dollars when their bonds default. You can avoid this fiasco by purchasing bonds that are unlikely to default, otherwise known as *high-credit-quality bonds.* Credit rating agencies — Moody's, Standard & Poor's, Duff & Phelps, and so on — rate bonds based on credit quality and likelihood of default.

The credit rating of a security depends on the company's (or the government entity's) ability to pay back its debt. Bond credit ratings are usually done on some sort of a letter-grade scale: For example, in one rating system, AAA is the highest rating, with ratings descending through AA and A, followed by BBB, BB, B, CCC, CC, C, and so on. Funds that mostly invest in

- ✔ **AAA and AA rated bonds** are considered to be *high-grade* or *high-credit-quality* bond funds; bonds of this type have little chance of default. These bonds are considered to be *investment quality* bonds.

- ✔ **A and BBB rated bonds** are considered to be *general* bond funds (*moderate-credit-quality*). Like AAA and AA rated bonds, these bonds are known as investment quality bonds.

- ✔ **BB or lower rated bonds** are known as *junk bond* funds (or by their more marketable name, *high-yield* funds). These funds expect to suffer more defaults — perhaps as many as a couple of percent of the total value of the bonds per year or more. *Unrated* bonds have no credit rating because they haven't been analyzed or evaluated by a rating agency.

Lower quality bonds are able to attract bond investors by paying them a higher interest rate. The lower the credit quality of a fund's holdings, the higher the yield you can expect a fund to pay (to hopefully more than offset the effect of potential defaults).

Issuer: Knowing who you're lending to

Bond funds and the bonds that they hold also differ according to which type of entity is issuing them. Here are the major options:

- ✓ **Treasuries:** These are IOUs from the biggest debtor of them all — the U.S. federal government. Treasuries include Treasury bills (which mature within a year), Treasury notes (which mature between one and ten years), and Treasury bonds (which mature in more than ten years). All Treasuries pay interest that's state-tax-free but federally taxable.

- ✓ **Municipals:** *Munis* are state and local government bonds that pay federally tax-free and state-tax-free interest to those who reside in the state of issue. The governments that issue municipal bonds know that the investors who buy municipals don't have to pay most or any of the income tax that normally would be required on other bonds — which enables the issuing governments to attract buyers at a lower rate of interest. Later in this chapter (in the section "How to obtain tax-free income"), I explain how to determine if you're in a high enough tax bracket to benefit from muni bonds.

- ✓ **Corporates:** Issued by companies such as General Mills and Hewlett Packard, corporate bonds pay interest that's fully taxable.

- ✓ **Mortgages:** You can actually get back some of the interest you're paying on your mortgage by purchasing a bond fund that holds it! Some bond funds specialize in buying mortgages and collecting the interest payments. The repayment of principal on these bonds is usually guaranteed at the bond's maturity by a government-sanctioned organization such as the Government National Mortgage Association (GNMA, also known as Ginnie Mae) or the Federal National Mortgage Association (FNMA or Fannie Mae).

- ✓ **Convertibles:** These are hybrid securities — bonds that you can convert into a preset number of shares of stock in the company that issued the bond. Although these bonds do pay interest, their yield is lower than nonconvertible bonds because convertibles offer you the upside potential of being able to make more money if the underlying stock rises.

- ✓ **International bonds:** Bond funds (and individual investors) can buy most of the preceding types of bonds from foreign issuers as well. In fact, international corporate and government bonds are the primary bonds that foreign bond mutual funds may hold. International bonds are riskier because their interest payments can be offset by currency price changes and may be riskier due to political instability and insufficient information.

Management: Considering the passive or active type

Some bond funds are managed like an airplane on autopilot. They stick to investing in a particular type of bond (such as high-grade corporate), with a target maturity (for example, an average of ten years). *Index funds* that invest in a relatively fixed basket of bonds — so as to track a market index of bond prices — are good examples of this passive approach. Exchange-traded funds (ETFs) of bonds are bond funds (generally index funds) that trade on a major stock exchange. See Chapter 5 for more on ETFs.

At the other end of the spectrum are aggressively managed funds. Managers of these funds have significant freedom to purchase bonds that they think will perform best in the future. For example, if a fund manager thinks that interest rates will rise, he'll buy shorter term bonds (remember that shorter term bonds are less sensitive to interest rate changes than longer term bonds) and keep more of a fund's assets in cash. The fund manager may be willing to invest more in lower credit-quality bonds if he thinks that the economy is going to improve and that more companies will prosper and improve their credit standing.

Aggressively managed funds gamble. If interest rates fall instead of rise, the fund manager who moved into shorter term bonds and cash suffers worse performance. If interest rates fall because the economy sinks into recession, lower credit-quality bonds suffer from a higher default rate and depress the fund's performance even further.

Some people think that predicting which direction interest rates and the economy are heading is fairly easy. The truth is that economic predictions are *difficult.* In fact, over long periods of time (ten or more years), meaningful predictions are almost impossible.

Investing some of your bond fund money in funds that try to be well positioned for changes in the economy and in interest rates may appear attractive. But remember that if these fund managers are wrong, you can lose more money. Over the long term, your best bet is efficiently managed funds that stick with a specific investment objective — such as holding intermediate-term, high-quality bonds — and don't try to time and predict the bond market.

Trying to beat the market can lead to getting beaten. Some bond funds have fallen on their faces after risky investing strategies backfired (see Chapter 7). Interestingly, bond funds that charge sales commissions (*loads*) and higher ongoing operating fees are the ones more likely to have blowups. This may be because these fund managers are under more pressure to try and boost returns to make up for these higher fees.

Inflation-indexed Treasury bonds

In 1997, the U.S. federal government introduced a new type of Treasury bond that's inflation proof: inflation-indexed Treasuries. These new Treasury bonds were designed to better meet the needs of inflation-fearing investors.

An investor with, say, $10,000 to invest could recently have purchased a ten-year, regular Treasury bond that yielded 4 percent interest, or about $400, annually. Now, contrast this regular Treasury bond with its new inflation-indexed brethren. The ten-year inflation-indexed bonds issued at the same time yielded about 1.5 percent. Before you think that this low yield is a rip-off, know that this is a real (as in not affected or eroded by inflation) rate of return of 1.5 percent.

The other portion of your return with these inflation-indexed bonds comes from the inflation adjustment to the $10,000 principal you invested. The inflation portion of the return gets added back into principal. So if inflation runs at, say, 2.5 percent, after one year of holding your inflation-indexed bond, your $10,000 of principal would increase to $10,250.

So, no matter what happens with the rate of inflation, the investor who bought the inflation-indexed bond, in my example, always earns a 1.5 percent return above and beyond the rate of inflation. If inflation leaps to 10, 12, or 14 percent, or more, as it did in the early 1980s, the holders of inflation-indexed Treasuries won't have the purchasing power of their principal or interest eroded by inflation. Holders of regular Treasury bonds, however, won't be as fortunate because at a continued double-digit annual inflation rate, holders of these 4 percent yield bonds would have a negative real (after inflation) return.

Because inflation-indexed Treasuries protect the investor from the ravages of inflation, they represent a less risky security. In the investment world, lower risk usually translates into lower returns.

Of course, the rate of inflation can and will change in the future. For the ten-year bonds chosen in my example, inflation needs to exceed 2.5 percent per year for the holders of the inflation-indexed bonds to come out ahead of those holding the regular Treasury bonds. If inflation were running at, say, 3 percent per year, the total return of inflation-indexed bonds would be 4.5 percent, exceeding the 4 percent on the regular Treasury bonds.

Income-minded investors need to know that the inflation-indexed Treasuries only pay out the real return, which in the preceding example was just 1.5 percent. The rest of the return, which is for increases in the cost of living, is added to the bond's principal. Thus, relative to regular Treasury bonds, which pay out all their returns in interest, the inflation-indexed Treasuries pay significantly less interest. Therefore, they don't make sense for nonretirement account investors who seek maximum income to live on.

For recommended inflation-indexed Treasury funds, please see the "Eyeing Recommended Bond Funds" section, later in this chapter. (Also know that regular bond fund managers may invest some of their fund's assets in inflation-indexed Treasuries if they appear attractive relative to other bonds.)

Investing in Bond Funds

It's time to get down to how and why you might use bonds. Bonds may be boring, but they can be more profitable for you than super-boring bank savings accounts and money market funds. Bonds generally pay more than these investments because they involve more risk: You're purchasing an investment that's intended to be held for a longer period of time than savings accounts and money market funds.

That doesn't mean that you have to hold a bond until it matures, because an active market for them does exist. You can sell your bond to someone else in the bond market (which is exactly what a bond fund manager does if he wants out of a specific bond he holds in the bond fund). You may receive more — or less — for the bond than you paid for it depending on what has happened in the financial markets since then.

As I discuss earlier, in the section "Maturity: Counting the years until you get your principal back," bond funds are riskier than money market funds and savings accounts because their value can fall if interest rates rise. However, bonds tend to be more stable in value than stocks (see Chapter 1).

Why you might (and might not) want to invest in bond funds

Investing in bonds is a time-honored way to earn a better rate of return on money that you don't plan to use within at least the next couple of years. As with other mutual funds, bond funds are completely liquid on a day's notice, but I advise you to view them as longer term investments. Because their value fluctuates, you're more likely to lose money if you're forced to sell the bond fund sooner rather than later. In the short term, the bond market can bounce every which way; in the longer term, you're more likely to receive your money back with interest.

Don't invest your emergency money in bond funds — use a money market fund instead (see Chapter 11). You could receive less money from a bond fund (and could even lose money) if you need it in an emergency.

Avoid using the check-writing option that comes with many bond funds. Every time you sell shares in a bond fund (which is what you're doing when you write a check), this transaction must be reported on your annual income tax return. When you write a check on a money market fund, by contrast, it isn't a so-called *taxable event* because a money fund has a fixed share price, so you're not considered to be adding to or subtracting from your taxable income when you sell these shares.

Aren't higher interest rates better if you need income?

In the early 2000s, after a multiyear drop, interest rates were at what seemed to be rock-bottom levels compared to those of earlier decades. Intermediate-term bonds were yielding around 4 percent — about one-third of what rates had been in the early 1980s.

Generally speaking, lower interest rates are great for the economy because they encourage consumers and businesses to borrow and spend more money. But if you were a retiree trying to live off the income being produced by your bonds, low interest rates seemed like the worst of all possible economic worlds.

For each $100,000 that a retiree invested in intermediate-term bonds, CDs, or whatever when interest rates were 12 percent, the retiree received $12,000 per year in interest or dividends. A retiree purchasing intermediate-term bonds in the early to mid 2000s after the fall in interest rates, however, received two-thirds less dividend income because rates on the same bonds and CDs were just 4 percent. So for every $100,000 invested, only $4,000 in dividend or interest income was paid.

If you're trying to live off the income being produced by your investments, a 67 percent reduction in that income may cramp your lifestyle. So higher interest rates are better if you're living off your investment income, right?

Wrong!

Never forget that the primary driver of interest rates is the expected future rate of inflation. Interest rates were much higher in the early 1980s because the United States had double-digit inflation. If the cost of living is increasing at the rate of 12 percent per year, why would you as an investor lend your money out (which is what you're doing when you purchase a bond or CD) at 4 percent? Of course, you *wouldn't* lend money at that rate — which is exactly why interest rates were so high in the early 1980s.

By the early 2000s, interest rates were low because the inflation dragon seemed to have been slain (and the economy was in a recession). So the rate of interest that investors could earn by lending their money dropped accordingly. Although low interest rates reduce the interest income, the corresponding low rate of inflation doesn't devour the purchasing power of your principal balance as quickly.

So what's an investor to do if she lives off the income from her investments but can't generate enough income because present interest rates are too low? A financially simple but psychologically difficult solution is to use up some of the principal to supplement the interest and dividend income. In effect, this situation is what happens anyway when inflation is higher — the purchasing power of the principal erodes more quickly. You also should educate yourself about the range of higher yielding (and quality) investment options available — this book helps you do just that.

You also shouldn't put too much of your longer term investment money in bond funds (for example, your retirement money if you're a young adult with many decades until you would retire). With the exception of those rare periods when interest rates drop significantly, bond funds won't produce the high returns that growth-oriented investments such as stocks, real estate, and your own business can.

Here are some common financial goals to which bond funds are well suited:

- ✔ **A major purchase:** But make sure that the purchase won't happen for at least two years, such as the purchase of a home. Short-term bond funds should offer a higher yield than money market funds. However, bond funds are a bit riskier, which is why you should have at least two years until you need the money to allow time for recovery from a dip in your bond fund account value.

- ✔ **Part of a long-term, diversified portfolio:** Because stocks and bonds don't move in tandem, bonds can be a great way to hedge against declines in the stock market. In fact, in a down economic environment, bonds may appreciate in value if inflation is declining. Different types of bond funds (high-quality bonds and junk bonds, for example) typically don't move in tandem with each other either, so they can provide an additional level of diversification. In Chapter 10, where I talk about asset allocation, I explain how to incorporate bonds into long-term portfolios for goals such as retirement.

- ✔ **Generating current income:** If you're retired or not working, bonds are better than most other investments for producing a current income stream.

How to pick a bond fund with an outcome you can enjoy

When comparing bond funds of a given type (for example, high-quality, short-term corporate bond funds), folks want to pick the one that's going to make the most money for them. But be careful; some mutual fund companies exploit your desire for high returns. These fund firms love to lure you into a bond fund by emphasizing high past performance and current yield, deflecting your attention away from the best predictor of bond fund performance: operating expenses.

Don't overemphasize past performance

A major mistake that novice bond fund investors make is to look at recent performance and assume that those are the returns they're going to get in the future. Investing in bond funds based only on recent performance is tempting right after a period when interest rates have declined, because declines in interest rates pump up bond fund total returns. Remember that an equal but opposite force is waiting to counteract pumped-up bond returns — bond prices fall when interest rates rise, which they eventually will.

Don't get me wrong: Past performance is an important issue to consider. But in order for performance numbers to be meaningful and useful, you must compare the same type of bond funds to each other (such as intermediate-term funds that invest exclusively in high-grade corporate bonds) and against the correct bond market index or benchmark (which I discuss in Chapter 17).

Be careful with yield quotes

A bond fund's *yield* measures how much the fund is currently paying in dividends; it's quoted as a percentage of the fund's share price — say, 5.2 percent. This statistic certainly seems like a valid one for comparing funds. Unfortunately, some fund companies have abused it.

Don't confuse a bond fund's yield with its return. Dividends are just one part of a fund's return, which also includes capital gain distributions and changes in the bond fund's share price. Over a given period of time, a bond fund could have a positive yield but a negative overall return, particularly if interest rates have increased or the credit quality of bonds in its portfolio has deteriorated.

Some unscrupulous fund companies try to obscure the difference between yield and return. For example, consider an advertisement sent by the Fundamental U.S. Government Strategic Income Fund. In huge type on the cover of this brochure, the fund boasted of its 11.66-percent yield, an impressive number because 30-year Treasury bonds were yielding less than 8 percent at the time. One can only assume that the designers of this promo piece hoped that you wouldn't check out the back cover, where the small print stated that the fund's total return for the previous year was –15.7 percent.

Mutual fund companies can play a few games to fatten a fund's yield. Such sleight of hand makes a fund's marketing department happy because higher yields make hawking the bond funds easier for salespeople. But remember that yield-enhancing shenanigans can leave you disappointed when a bond fund fails to perform well after you buy it based on the allure of a swollen yield. Here's what to watch out for:

 ✔ **Lower quality:** You may compare one short-term bond fund to another and discover, for example, that one pays 0.5 percent more and, therefore, looks better. But, if you look a little further, you see that the higher yielding fund invests 20 percent of its assets in *junk* bonds (a BB or less credit-quality rating), whereas the other fund is fully invested in *high-quality* bonds (AAA and AA rated). In other words, the junk bond fund isn't necessarily better; given the risk it's taking, it should be yielding more.

✔ **Lengthened maturities:** Bond funds can usually increase their yield just by increasing maturity a bit. (Insiders call this ploy *going further out on the yield curve.*) So when comparing yields on different bond funds, be sure that you're comparing them for funds of similar maturity. Even if they both call themselves "intermediate-term," if one bond fund invests in bonds maturing on average in seven years, while another fund is at ten years for its average maturity, comparing the two is a classic case of comparing apples to oranges. Because longer term bonds usually have higher yields (due to increased risk), the ten-year average maturity fund should yield more than the seven-year average maturity fund.

✔ **Giving your money back without your knowledge:** Some funds return a portion of your principal in the form of dividends. This move artificially pumps up a fund's yield but depresses its total return. Investors in this type of bond fund are rudely awakened when, after enjoying a healthy yield for a period of time, they examine the share price of their bond fund shares and find that they've declined in value.

When you compare bond funds to each other by using the information in the prospectuses (see Chapter 8), make sure that you compare their total return over time (in addition to making sure that the funds have comparable portfolios of bonds and similar durations).

✔ **Waiving of expenses:** Some bond funds, particularly newer ones, waive a portion or even all of their operating expenses to temporarily inflate the fund's yield. Yes, you *can* invest in a fund that's having a sale on its operating fees, but you also have the hassle of monitoring the fund to determine when the sale is over. Bond funds engaging in expense waiving often end such sales quietly when the bond market is doing well. Don't forget that if you sell a bond fund (held outside of a retirement account) that has appreciated in value, you owe taxes on your profits.

Do focus on costs

Like money market funds, bond fund returns are extremely sensitive to costs. After you've identified a particular type of bond fund to invest in, expenses — sales commissions and annual operating fees — should be your number-one criterion for comparing funds.

For bond funds, you should generally shun funds with operating expenses higher than 0.5 percent.

The marketplace for bonds is fairly efficient. For any two bond managers investing in a particular bond type — say, long-term municipal bonds — picking bonds that outperform the other's over time is difficult. But if one of those bond funds charges lower fees than the other, that difference provides the low-fee fund with a big head start in the performance race.

How bond funds calculate their yields

When you ask a mutual fund company for a bond fund's yield, make sure you understand the time period that the yield covers. Fund companies are supposed to report the *Securities and Exchange Commission (SEC) yield,* which is a standard yield calculation that allows for fairer comparisons across bond funds. The SEC yield reflects the bond fund's so-called yield to maturity. This yield is the best to use when you compare funds because it captures the effective rate of interest an investor will receive going forward.

Funds also calculate a yield that only looks at the recently distributed dividends relative to the share price of the fund. Funds can pump up this number by purchasing particular types of bonds. For just that reason, yield based on recently distributed dividends isn't nearly as useful a yield number to look at (although some brokers who sell bond funds love to use it because they push funds that are pumping up their yields).

You can earn a higher return from a bond fund by investing in funds that

✔ Hold longer term bonds

✔ Hold lower credit-quality bonds

✔ Have lower operating expenses

Please note that the first two ways of earning a higher bond fund yield — using longer term and lower credit-quality bonds — increase the risk that you're exposed to. Stick with no-load funds that have low annual operating expenses as a risk-free way to boost your expected bond fund returns.

How to obtain tax-free income

Just as money market funds can produce taxable or tax-free dividends (see Chapter 11), so too can bond funds. In order to produce tax-free income, a bond fund invests in municipal bonds (also called *muni bonds* or *munis*) issued by state or local governments.

As long as you live in the United States, generally, municipal bond fund dividends are federally tax-free to you. Funds that specialize in muni bonds issued just in your state pay dividend income that's typically free of your state's taxes as well.

When you're investing in bonds inside retirement accounts, use taxable bonds. If you're investing in bonds outside retirement accounts, the choice between taxable versus tax-free depends on your tax bracket. If you're in a high tax bracket (28 percent or higher for federal) and you want to invest in bonds outside of tax-sheltered retirement accounts, you may do better in a muni fund than in a bond fund that pays taxable dividends (see Chapter 10 to determine your tax bracket).

Eyeing Recommended Bond Funds

If you've read through this chapter, you now know more about bond funds than you probably ever imagined possible, so now it's time to get down to brass tacks: selecting bond funds for a variety of investing needs.

Using the logic laid out earlier in this chapter, I present you with a menu of choices. Although thousands of bond funds are available — few are left to consider after you eliminate the high-cost ones (loads and ongoing fees), low-performance funds (which are often the just-mentioned high-cost funds), and funds managed by fund companies and managers with minimal experience investing in bonds.

I've done the winnowing for you, and the funds I present in the sections that follow are the best of the best for meeting specific needs. I've organized the funds by the average maturity and duration of the bonds that they invest in, as well as by the taxability of the dividends that they pay.

Use the following funds only if you have sufficient money in your emergency reserve (see Chapter 3). If you're investing money for longer term purposes, particularly retirement, come up with an overall plan for allocating your money among a variety of different funds, including stock and bond funds. For more on allocating your money, be sure to read Chapter 10.

Short-term bond funds

Short-term bond funds, if they live up to their name, invest in short-term bonds (which mature in a few years or less). Of all bond funds, these are the least sensitive to interest rate fluctuations. Their stability makes them the most appropriate bond funds for money on which you want to earn a better rate of return than a money market fund could produce for you. But with short-term bond funds, you also have to tolerate the risk of losing a few percent in principal value if overall interest rates rise.

Even lower fees: High-balance funds and exchange-traded funds

Throughout this chapter, I highlight the best bond funds. Among other positive attributes, those funds have low fees. That said, you may be able to lower your bond fund fees even further in two additional ways. Some mutual fund companies will offer a lower fee version of a given bond fund to investors who are able to invest a larger amount into the fund.

For example, many Vanguard bond funds now offer "Admiral" versions with even lower operating expenses (and thus higher yields) for big balance customers. For example, Vanguard's Short-Term Investment-Grade Admiral shares (VFSUX), which sports a $100,000 minimum to invest, have an expense ratio of just 0.14 percent. The regular share class, which has a $3,000 minimum, has an expense ratio of 0.26 percent. You may qualify to convert your regular shares

(also known as "Investor" shares) in Short-Term Investment-Grade into Admiral shares if you've been a longer term customer but lack $100,000. If you've held the Investor shares at least ten years, you need a balance of $50,000. Where relevant in this chapter, I note attractive options for high-balance investors.

Another potentially attractive and low-cost option is exchange-traded funds (ETFs). However, as I discuss in Chapter 5, don't get blindly suckered into the pitch that ETFs are universally superior due to low costs. The vast majority of ETFs have higher costs than the best mutual funds recommended in this book. Interestingly and perhaps not surprisingly, the best bond ETFs come from Vanguard and where appropriate, I recommend some of their ETFs in this chapter.

Short-term bonds work well for investing money to afford major purchases that you expect to make in a few years, such as a home, a car, or a portion of your retirement account investments that you expect to tap in the near future.

Taxable short-term bond funds

Bond funds that pay taxable dividends are appropriate for nonretirement accounts if you're not in a high tax bracket (no more than 28 percent federal) and for investing inside retirement accounts. (Call the fund companies for current yields.)

Vanguard Short-Term Investment-Grade (VFSTX) invests the bulk of its portfolio in high- and moderate-quality, short-term corporate bonds. (The average credit rating is AA.) Typically, it keeps a small portion in U.S. Treasuries. It may even stray a bit overseas and invest several percent of the fund's assets in promising foreign bonds. This fund maintains an average maturity of two to three years, and duration currently is two years.

Robert Auwaerter has managed Vanguard's Short-Term Corporate fund since the early 1980s. Gregory Nassour, who had been an investment manager since 1994, was added as co-manager in 2008. All told, this fund invests in more than 1,000 bonds. (Imagine having to keep track of all of them on your own!) This fund's operating expense ratio is just 0.26 percent (0.14 percent for its Admiral share class discussed in the adjacent sidebar). It has a $3,000 minimum. (Investors are advised to keep at least $10,000 in this fund or register their accounts at Vanguard's Web site for electronic delivery of statements and fund reports; otherwise, you pay a $20 annual fee.) ☎ 800-662-7447.

Vanguard offers an ETF similar to this fund: **Short-Term Corporate Bond ETF (VCSH)**. It's expense ratio is just 0.15 percent.

U.S. Treasury short-term bond funds

U.S. Treasury bond funds are appropriate if you prefer a bond fund that invests in U.S. Treasuries (which have the safety of government backing) or if you're not in a high federal tax bracket (no more than 28 percent), but you *are* in a high state tax bracket (5 percent or higher). I don't recommend Treasuries for retirement accounts because they pay less interest than fully taxable bond funds. (Call the fund companies for current yields.)

Vanguard Short-Term Treasury (VFISX) invests in U.S. Treasuries maturing within two to three years — you can't get much safer than that. Duration currently is two years. This fund has been managed by David Glocke since 2000, who has been an investment manager since 1991. Although the fund has that lean Vanguard expense ratio of 0.22 percent annually (0.12 percent for the Admiral share class), don't forget that you can buy Treasuries direct from your local Federal Reserve Bank if you don't need liquidity. The minimum initial investment is $3,000. (Investors are advised to keep at least $10,000 in this fund or register their accounts at Vanguard's Web site for electronic delivery of statements and fund reports; otherwise, you pay a $20 annual fee.) ☎ 800-662-7447.

Municipal tax-free short-term bond funds

Short-term bond funds that are free of both federal and state taxes are scarce. However, some good short-term funds are free of federal, but not state, taxes. These are generally appropriate if you're in a higher federal bracket (more than 28 percent) but in a low state bracket (less than 5 percent).

If you live in a state with high taxes, consider a state money market fund, which I cover in Chapter 11. (Call the fund companies for current yields.)

Vanguard Short-Term Tax-Exempt (VWSTX) invests in the *crème de la crème* of the federally tax-free muni bonds issued by state and local governments around the country. (Its average credit rating is AA.) The fund's average maturity ranges from one to two years, and duration is about one year.

Vanguard Limited-Term Tax-Exempt (VMLTX) does just what the short-term fund does (and has the same manager), except that it does it a while longer. This fund's average muni bond matures in two to five years (with a duration of about three years), although its average credit rating is a respectable AA.

Both the short-term and limited-term funds have a miserly annual operating expense ratio of 0.20 percent and require a $3,000 minimum initial investment. Admiral shares, with a 0.12 percent expense ratio, are available for both these funds. (Investors are advised to keep at least $10,000 in this fund or register their accounts at Vanguard's Web site for electronic delivery of statements and fund reports; otherwise, you pay a $20 annual fee.) ☎ 800-662-7447.

Intermediate-term bond funds

Intermediate-term bond funds hold bonds that typically mature within a decade or so. They're more volatile than shorter term bonds but should be more rewarding. The longer you can own an intermediate-term bond fund, the more likely you are to earn a higher return on it than on a short-term fund, unless interest rates keep rising over many years.

You shouldn't purchase an intermediate-term fund unless you expect to hold it for a minimum of three to five years — or longer, if you can. Therefore, the money you put into this type of fund should be money that you don't expect to use during that period. (Call the fund companies for current yields.)

Taxable intermediate-term bond funds

If you invest in these funds in a nonretirement account, be sure that you're not in a high tax bracket — more than 28 percent federal.

Dodge & Cox Income (DODIX) is run by a conservative management team at an old San Francisco investment firm that has been managing money for private accounts since 1930 and running mutual funds since 1931. This fund, which focuses on government securities and high-grade corporate debt, has an average bond credit rating of AA, an average maturity of five to ten years, and a duration of about four to five years. This fund is team managed with the managers having an average tenure of about 14 years. The operating expense ratio is a reasonable 0.43 percent: $2,500 is the minimum initial investment ($1,000 for retirement accounts). ☎ 800-621-3979.

Harbor Bond (HABDX) is a more aggressive intermediate-term bond fund. The fund invests mostly in corporate bonds, as well as in mortgage bonds with average maturities of up to ten years (duration is about five years), depending on fund manager William Gross's outlook for inflation and the economy.

Gross, who's managed this fund since 1987, has three plus decades of experience managing money in the bond market. He makes relatively wide swings in strategy and, during periods of rising interest rates, has bulked up the fund with money market securities to protect principal. At times, Gross has also ventured small portions of the fund into foreign bonds, junk bonds, and even a sprinkling of derivatives such as futures and options to slightly leverage returns. (The fund has an average credit rating of AA.) Despite its aggressiveness, the fund has had low volatility. Although this fund's expense ratio is a tad on the high side (0.57 percent), Gross has delivered high enough long-term returns to justify the slightly higher costs. The minimum initial investment is just $1,000. ☎ 800-422-1050.

Vanguard Total Bond Market Index (VBMFX) is an index fund that tracks the index of the entire bond market, the Lehman Brothers Aggregate Bond Index. The fund is managed Kenneth Volpert, Gregory Davis, and a computer. It uses a sampling to mirror the index so it doesn't actually invest in every bond in the index. Investment-grade corporate bonds and mortgages make up the majority of the fund's investments; the rest are U.S. government and agency securities. The fund's average maturity is about seven years, with a duration of about five years. (Average bond credit rating is AA.) Annual operating expenses are a paltry 0.22 percent (0.14 percent for Admiral shares). (Investors are advised to keep at least $10,000 in this fund or register their accounts at Vanguard's Web site for electronic delivery of statements and fund reports; otherwise, you pay a $20 annual fee.) You need a $3,000 minimum initial investment to open. ☎ 800-662-7447.

Vanguard Total Bond Market ETF (BND) is an ETF similar to this fund. Its expense ratio is 0.14 percent.

Vanguard GNMA (VFIIX) invests in residential mortgages that people just like you take out when they purchase a home and borrow money from a bank. Like other GNMA funds, this one has very low credit risk. (Its average credit rating is AAA.) Why? Because the principal and interest on GNMAs is guaranteed by the U.S. government. All GNMA funds have prepayment risk. (If interest rates fall, mortgage holders refinance.) But this GNMA fund has less risk than most because it minimizes the purchase of mortgage bonds that were issued at higher interest rates — and are, therefore, more likely to be refinanced and paid back early.

This fund is managed by Thomas Pappas at Wellington Management, a private money management firm that Vanguard uses for some of its other funds. GNMA doesn't invest in some of the more exotic mortgage securities and derivatives that are abused by other firms' bond funds. Like all other bond funds, this one has interest rate risk, though it's comparable to other intermediate-term bond funds despite the longer maturity of most of this fund's holdings. Duration is generally around four years, and the fund's yearly operating expense ratio is 0.23 percent: $3,000 is the minimum initial investment. (Investors are advised to keep at least $10,000 in this fund or register their accounts at Vanguard's Web site for electronic delivery of statements and fund reports; otherwise, you pay a $20 annual fee.) ☎ 800-662-7447.

Vanguard Mortgage-Backed Securities ETF (VMBS) is an ETF similar to this fund. Its operating expense ratio is 0.15 percent.

Vanguard High Yield Corporate (VWEHX) invests in lower quality (junk) corporate bonds. These pay more and are for more aggressive investors stretching for greater yield. Intermediate-term junk bonds are volatile: They not only are interest rate sensitive, but also they're susceptible to changes in the economy. For example, this fund lost more than 10 percent of its principal value in 1989, 1990, and 1994 and more than 25 percent in 2008. (Dividends payments, of course, mitigated some of this principal erosion.)

Unlike other high-yield funds, this fund invests little (if any) of its funds in lower rated junk bonds; it invests in the best of the junk (its average credit rating is BB). The average maturity of this fund is seven years, with a duration of five years. Michael Hong, who has been an investment manager since 1997, at Wellington Management has managed this fund since 2008. The fund has been around since 1978 — a degree of longevity that makes it one of the longest and best-performing junk bond funds. Yearly operating expenses are 0.32 percent: $3,000 is the minimum initial investment. (Investors are advised to keep at least $10,000 in this fund or register their accounts at Vanguard's Web site for electronic delivery of statements and fund reports; otherwise, you pay a $20 annual fee.) ☎ 800-662-7447.

U.S. Treasury intermediate-term bond funds

U.S. Treasury bond funds are appropriate if you prefer a bond fund that invests in U.S. Treasuries (which have the safety of government backing) and if you're not in a high federal tax bracket (no more than 28 percent), but you *are* in a high state tax bracket (5 percent or higher). I don't recommend Treasuries for retirement accounts because they pay less interest than fully taxable bond funds. (Call the fund company for current yields.)

Vanguard Intermediate-Term Treasury (VFITX) invests in U.S. Treasuries maturing in five to ten years. (See the description for the short-term U.S. Treasury funds for minimum initial investment and expense ratio.) ☎ 800-662-7447.

Vanguard Inflation-Protected Securities (VIPSX) fund is a new breed of fund, which I cover in the "Inflation-indexed Treasury bonds" section in this chapter. With a low operating expense ratio of 0.25 percent (0.12 for the Admiral share class), this fund is a good one for inflation-skittish investors to consider. It has a $3,000 minimum initial investment. (Investors are advised to keep at least $10,000 in this fund or register their accounts at Vanguard's Web site for electronic delivery of statements and fund reports; otherwise, you pay a $20 annual fee.) ☎ 800-662-7447.

Municipal tax-free intermediate-term bond funds

Consider *federally* tax-free bond funds if you're in a high federal bracket (28 percent and up) but a relatively low state bracket (less than 5 percent). (Call the fund company for current yields.)

If you're in the market for a state *and* federally tax-free bond fund, the problem is that the ones available (and there aren't all that many) have high expenses. High expenses are always a problem but are especially so in a low interest rate environment (like has been around for years) because little of a fund's yield will be left to pay out. So, if you're in high federal (28 percent and up) *and* high state (5 percent or higher) tax brackets, you're better off using the nationwide Vanguard municipal bond fund that I describe at the end of this section.

Fidelity Intermediate Municipal Income (FLTMX) invests in high-credit-quality (average rating is A) municipal bonds that generally mature within ten years. This fund's average maturity is usually around eight years, with a duration of about five to six years. The expense ratio is a competitive 0.38 percent, and the minimum initial investment is $10,000. ☎ 800-544-8888.

Vanguard Intermediate-Term Tax-Exempt (VWITX) does what Vanguard's short-term muni funds do, except that it invests in slightly longer term muni bonds. (Duration is generally about six years, and the average credit rating is AA.) The annual operating expense ratio is a mere 0.20 percent (0.12 for the Admiral share class); $3,000 is the minimum initial investment. Investors are advised to keep at least $10,000 in this fund or register their accounts at Vanguard's Web site for electronic delivery of statements and fund reports; otherwise, you pay a $20 annual fee. ☎ 800-662-7447.

Long-term bond funds

Long-term bond funds are the most aggressive and volatile bond funds around. If interest rates on long-term bonds increase substantially, the principal value of your investment could decline 10 percent or more.

Long-term bond funds generally are used for retirement investing in one of two situations:

✔ For investors not expecting to tap their investment money — ideally — for a decade or more

✔ For investors wanting to maximize current dividend income and who are willing to tolerate volatility

Don't use these funds for investing money that you plan to use within the next five years, because a bond market drop could leave your portfolio with a bit of a hangover. (Use intermediate-term and short-term bond funds instead.) And don't use the taxable funds in a nonretirement account if you're in a high tax bracket — especially higher than 28 percent federal. (Call the fund companies for current yields.)

Taxable long-term bond funds

Bond funds that pay taxable dividends are appropriate for nonretirement accounts if you're not in a high tax bracket (no more than 28 percent federal) and for investing inside retirement accounts. (Call the fund companies for current yields.)

Vanguard Long-Term Investment-Grade (VWESX) is comprised mostly of high-grade corporate bonds, but it sometimes holds around 10 percent in Treasuries and foreign and convertible bonds. (Average credit rating is A.) Long-term bonds such as these (the fund's average maturity is 20+ years, with a duration of 10+ years) can produce wide swings in volatility. For example, this fund lost more than 12 percent of its principal value in 1999, its worst year in a generation. The dividends of 6.3 percent paid that year brought the fund back to produce a total return of –6.2 percent. Wellington Management's Lucius Hill has managed the fund since 2008, and he has been an investment manager since 1993. Wellington itself has managed this fund since its inception in 1973. It has an annual operating expense ratio of 0.28 percent (0.16 percent for Admiral shares), with a $3,000 minimum initial investment. (Investors are advised to keep at least $10,000 in this fund or register their accounts at Vanguard's Web site for electronic delivery of statements and fund reports; otherwise, you pay a $20 annual fee.) ☎ 800-662-7447.

An ETF version of this fund is available and is called **Vanguard Long-Term Corporate Bond ETF (VCLT)**. Its expense ratio is 0.15 percent.

U.S. Treasury long-term bond funds

U.S. Treasury bond funds are appropriate if you prefer a bond fund that invests in U.S. Treasuries (which have the safety of government backing) and if you're not in a high federal tax bracket (no more than 28 percent), but you *are* in a high state tax bracket (5 percent or higher). I don't recommend Treasuries for retirement accounts because they pay less interest than fully taxable bond funds. (Call the fund companies for current yields.)

Vanguard Long-Term Treasury (VUSTX) invests in U.S. Treasuries with average maturities around 20 years. Duration is about 12 years. (See the description in the section "U.S. Treasury short-term bond funds" for minimum initial investment and expense ratio.) Investors are advised to keep at least $10,000 in this fund or register their accounts at Vanguard's Web site for electronic delivery of statements and fund reports; otherwise, you pay a $20 annual fee. ☎ 800-662-7447.

Municipal tax-free long-term bond funds

Consider *federally* tax-free bond funds if you're in a high federal bracket (28 percent and up) but a relatively low state bracket (less than 5 percent). (Call the fund company for current yields.)

Vanguard Long-Term Tax-Exempt (VWLTX) does what Vanguard's short-term muni funds do, except that it invests in long-term muni bonds. (The average credit rating is AA.) This fund has an operating expense ratio of 0.20 percent. This fund has a $3,000 minimum initial investment. Investors are advised to keep at least $10,000 in this fund or register their accounts at Vanguard's Web site for electronic delivery of statements and fund reports; otherwise, you pay a $20 annual fee. ☎ 800-662-7447.

State and federally tax-free bond funds may be appropriate if you're in high federal (28 percent and up) *and* high state (5 percent or higher) tax brackets. The fund providers Fidelity, T. Rowe Price, and Vanguard offer competitive funds for states such as California, Connecticut, Florida, Maine, Maryland, Michigan, Minnesota, New Jersey, New York, Ohio, and Pennsylvania. If you can't find a good state-specific bond fund for your state, or if you're only in a high federal tax bracket, use the nationwide Vanguard Municipal bond funds I describe in this section. (Call the fund companies for current yields.)

Exploring Alternatives to Bond Funds

Bond mutual funds are just one way to lend your money and get paid a decent yield. In the following sections, I discuss the advantages and disadvantages of other alternatives, some of which have acronyms that you can impress your friends and family with — or confirm that you're an investments geek. Regardless of which investment type(s) you end up purchasing, do your big-picture thinking first: What do you plan to use the money for down the road? How much risk are you willing and able to take? What's your tax situation?

Most of these bond fund alternatives have one thing in common: They offer psychological solace to those who can't stomach fluctuations in the value of their investments. After I tell you more about these alternatives (including information that you're not likely to hear in a marketing pitch from the company or person who's trying to sell you on them), low-cost bond funds may look more attractive.

Certificates of deposit

For many decades, bank certificates of deposit (CDs) have been the *safe* investment of choice for folks with some extra cash that they don't need in the near term. The attraction is that you get a higher rate of return on a CD than on a bank savings account or money market fund. And unlike a bond fund, a CD's principal value doesn't fluctuate. Of course, you also enjoy the peace of mind afforded by the government's FDIC insurance program.

All these advantages of CDs aren't nearly as attractive as they may seem on the surface. I start with the FDIC insurance issue. Bonds and bond mutual funds aren't FDIC-insured. The lack of this insurance, however, shouldn't trouble you on high-quality bonds because these bonds rarely default. Even if a fund held a bond that defaulted, it probably would be a tiny fraction (less than 1 percent) of the value of the fund, so it would have little overall impact.

You may believe that there's no chance you'll lose money on a CD — but banks have failed and will continue to fail. Although you're insured for $100,000 in a bank, if the bank crashes, you'll likely wait a while to get your money back — and you'll probably have to settle for less interest than you expected, too.

Here's another myth about CDs: The principal value of your CD doesn't fluctuate. Sure it does; you just don't see the fluctuations! Just as the market value of a bond drops when interest rates rise, so too does the "market value" of a CD — and for the same reasons. At higher interest rates, investors expect a discounted price on fixed-interest-rate CDs because they always have the alternative of purchasing a new CD at the higher prevailing rates. Some CDs are actually bought and sold among investors — on what's known as a *secondary market* — and they trade and behave just like bonds.

So a lot of those advantages CDs seem to have aren't as impressive as some may believe. In fact, compared to bonds, CDs have a number of drawbacks:

✔ **Early withdrawal penalties:** Money in a CD isn't accessible unless you pay a fairly big penalty — typically, six months' interest. With a no-load (commission-free) bond fund, if you need some or all of your money next month, next week, or even tomorrow, you can access it without penalty.

✔ **Restricted tax options:** Another seldom-noted drawback of CDs is that they come in only one tax flavor — taxable. Bonds, on the other hand, come both in tax-free (federal and/or state) and taxable flavors. So if you're a higher tax-bracket investor, bonds offer you tax-friendly options that CDs can't.

✔ **Lower yield:** For a comparable maturity, CDs yield less than a high-quality bond. Often, the yield difference is 1 percent or more. If you don't shop around — if you lazily purchase CDs from the bank that you use for your checking account, for example — you may be sacrificing 2 percent or more in yield.

Don't forget about the unfriendly forces of inflation and taxes. They may gobble up all the yield that your CD is paying, thus leaving you no real growth on your investment. An extra percentage point or two from a bond can make a big difference in the long term.

You'll earn more over the years and have better access to your money in bond funds than in CDs. And bond funds make particular sense if you're in a higher tax bracket and would benefit from tax-free income on your investments. If you're not in a high tax bracket and you get gloomy whenever your bond fund's value dips, then consider CDs.

CDs may make the most sense if you know, for example, that you can invest your money for one year, after which you'll need the money for some purchase you expect to make. Just make sure that you shop around to get the best interest rate. If what attracts you to CDs is the U.S. government backing that comes with FDIC insurance, consider Treasuries, which are government-backed bonds. Treasuries often pay more interest than the better CDs available.

Individual bonds

Maybe you've had thoughts like these:

✔ Why buy a bond fund and pay all those ongoing management fees, year after year, when I can buy high-rated bonds that pay a higher yield than that fund I'm looking at?

✔ I can create my own portfolio of bonds and purchase bonds with different maturities. That way, I'm not gambling on where interest rates are headed, and I won't lose principal as I may in a bond fund.

Or more likely, you've listened to a broker — who was trying to sell individual bonds to you — make these sorts of remarks. Does the purchase of individual bonds make sense for you? Although the decision depends on several factors, I can safely say that most types of individual bonds probably are *not* for you. (Treasuries that you can buy directly from a local Federal Reserve Bank without charge are notable exceptions to my comments that follow.)

Here are some solid reasons why a good bond mutual fund beats individual bonds:

- ✓ **Mutual funds allow for better diversification.** You don't want to put all your investment money into a small number of bonds of companies in the same industry or that mature at the same time. Building a diversified bond portfolio with individual issues is difficult unless you have a hefty chunk (at least several hundred thousand dollars) that you desire to invest in bonds.

- ✓ **You want to save on commissions.** If you purchase individual bonds through a broker, you're going to pay a commission. In most cases, it's hidden; the broker quotes you a bond price that includes the commission. Even if you go through a discount broker, transaction fees take a healthy bite out of your investment. The smaller the amount invested, the bigger the bite. On a $1,000 bond, the fee can equal up to 5 percent.

- ✓ **Adjusting bond holdings as percentage of your portfolio is easy.** Good investment management includes monitoring and adjusting your overall bond/stock mix. Adding to or subtracting from your bond holdings by using individual bonds, however, can be inconvenient and costly.

- ✓ **Life's too short.** Do you really want to research bonds? You have better things to do with your time. Bonds and the companies that stand behind them aren't that simple to understand. For example, did you know that some bonds can be "called" before their maturity date? Companies often do this to save money if interest rates drop significantly. After you purchase a bond, you need to do the same things that a good bond fund manager would need to do, such as tracking the issuer's creditworthiness and monitoring other important financial developments.

In terms of costs, you can purchase terrific bond funds with yearly operating expense ratios of just 0.2 percent (or less). And remember, a bond mutual fund provides you tons of diversification and professional management so that you can spend your time doing activities you're good at and enjoy. You can increase your diversification by purchasing bond funds with different maturity objectives (short, intermediate, and long) or an index bond fund that covers the range.

If you already own individual bonds and they fit your financial objectives and tax situation, you can hold them until maturity because you've already incurred a commission (which some brokers instead call a *markup*) when they were purchased; selling them now would just create an additional fee. When the bond(s) mature(s), think about moving the proceeds into bond funds if you want to continue owning bonds.

Don't mistakenly think that your current individual bonds are paying the same yield as when they were originally issued. (That yield is the number listed on your brokerage account statement in the name of the bond.) As the market level of interest rates changes, the actual yield of your bonds fluctuates to rise and fall with the market level of rates. So if rates have fallen since you bought your bonds, the value of those bonds has increased — which in turn reduces the effective yield that you're currently earning.

Guaranteed-investment contracts

Guaranteed-investment contracts (GICs) are sold and backed by an insurance company. Typically, they quote you a rate of return projected one or a few years forward. So, like that of a CD, a GIC's return is always positive and certain. With a GIC, you experience none of the uncertainty that you normally face with a bond fund that fluctuates in value with changing interest rates and other economic upheavals.

The attraction of GICs is that your account value doesn't fluctuate (at least, not that you can see). For people who panic the moment a bond fund's value slips, GICs soothe the nerves. And they usually provide a higher yield than a money market or savings account.

As a rule, the insurance company invests GIC money mostly in bonds and usually a small portion in stocks. The difference between the amount these investments generate for the insurer and the amount they pay in interest is profit to the insurer. The yield is usually comparable to that of a bond fund. Typically, once a year, you'll receive a new statement showing that your GIC is worth more — thanks to the newly added interest.

Some employers offer GICs in their retirement savings plans as a butt-covering option or because an insurance company is involved in the company's retirement plan. More and more companies are eliminating GICs as investment options because of the greater awareness about GICs' drawbacks. First, insurance companies (like banks) have failed and will continue to fail. Although failed insurers almost always get bailed out — usually through a merger into a healthy company — you can take a haircut on the promised interest rate if your GIC is with a failed insurance company. Second, by having a return guaranteed in advance, you pay for the peace of mind in the form of lower long-term returns.

Mortgages

Another way that you can invest your money for greater dividend income is to lend your money via mortgages and second mortgages. Mortgage brokers often arrange these "deals." They appeal to investors who don't like the volatility of the stock and bond markets. With a mortgage, you don't have to look up the value every day in the newspaper; a mortgage seems safer because you can't watch your principal fluctuate in value.

What's amazing is that people who invest in these types of mortgages don't realize that they're getting a relatively high interest rate *only because they are accepting relatively high risk.* The risk is that the borrower can default, which would leave you holding the bag. More specifically, you could get stuck with a property that you may need to foreclose on. And if you don't hold the first mortgage, you're not first in line with a claim on the property.

If a property buyer could obtain a mortgage through a conventional bank, he would. Banks offer the lowest interest rates. So if a mortgage broker is offering you a deal to lend your money at 12 percent when the going bank rate is, say, 8 percent, that means you'll be lending money to people who the bank considers high risk. If a bank, with its vast assets on hand, isn't willing to lend money to somebody, ask yourself whether you should. Mortgage investments also carry interest rate risk: If you need to "sell" the mortgage early, you'll probably have to discount it, perhaps substantially if interest rates have increased since you purchased it.

If you're willing to lend your money to borrowers who carry a relatively high risk of defaulting, check out high-yield bond funds, which I discuss earlier in the chapter (under "Taxable intermediate-term bond funds"). With such funds, you at least diversify your money across many borrowers, and you benefit from the professional review and due diligence of the fund management team. If the normal volatility of a bond fund's principal value makes you queasy, then don't follow your investments so closely!

When you're selling some real estate and are willing to act as the bank and provide the financing to the buyer in the form of a first mortgage, consider that a viable investment. Be careful to check the borrower's credit, employment, and income situation; get a large down payment (at least 20 percent); and try not to lend so much money that it represents more than, say, 10 percent of your total investments.

Exchange-traded bond funds

In 2007, Vanguard launched four different bond ETFs:

- ✔ Total bond market ETF
- ✔ Short-term bond ETF
- ✔ Intermediate-term bond ETF
- ✔ Long-term bond ETF

These funds track respective Lehman Brothers bond indexes. The expense ratio of these new ETFs is 0.11 percent. Check out Chapter 5 for more information on ETFs.

Chapter 13

Stock Funds: Meeting Your Longer Term Needs

In This Chapter

▶ Growing your money in the stock market

▶ Investing in stocks through mutual funds

▶ Getting some stock fund recommendations

*M*ost stock market investors who don't manage money for a living and who make money do so not because they're pouring over daily market commentaries or are luckier or more clairvoyant than anyone else. They make money by simply being patient and using three simple investment methods:

✔ Invest in a diversified portfolio of stocks.

✔ Continue to save money and add to investments.

✔ Don't try to time the market.

A small number of extraordinary investors — Warren Buffett being a famous one who's frequently in the news — generate exceptional returns. Buffett and these other elite investors do the above three things *and* have a talent for identifying and investing in undervalued businesses before most others see that value. The good news for you is that you can earn handsome long-term stock market returns without having Buffett's talent. (And, you can some fun and make more money investing with the best fund managers who are able to post above-average, long-term returns.)

People who get soaked in the stock market are those who make easily avoidable mistakes. An *investment mistake* is a bad decision that you could've or should've avoided, either because better options were available, or because the odds were heavily stacked against you making money. Investment mistakes result from the following:

✔ Not understanding risk and how to minimize it

✔ Ignoring taxes and how investments fit into overall financial plans

✔ Paying unnecessary and exorbitant commissions and fees

✔ Surrendering to a sales pitch (or salesperson)

✔ Trading in and out of the market

Give up the search for a secret code — there isn't one. Focus on avoiding major gaffes.

The stock market isn't the place to invest money that you need to tap in the near future (certainly not money you need to use within the next five years). If your stock holdings take a dive, you don't want to be forced to sell when your investments have lost value. So come along for the ride — but only if you can stay for a while!

The Stock Market Grows Your Money

Stocks represent a share of ownership in a company and its profits (see Chapter 1). As companies (and economies in general) grow and expand, stocks enable investors to share in that growth and success. Over the last two centuries, investors holding diversified stock portfolios earned a rate of return averaging about 9 to 10 percent per year, which ended up being about 6 to 7 percent higher than the rate of inflation. Earning such returns may not seem like much (especially in a world with gurus and brokers claiming returns of 20 percent, 50 percent, or more per year). But don't forget the power of compounding: At 9 to 10 percent per year, your invested dollars doubles about every seven to eight years. The purchasing power of your money growing 6 to 7 percent more per year than the rate of inflation doubles about every 10 to 12 years.

Contrast this return with bond and money market investments, which have historically returned just a percent or two per year over the rate of inflation. At these rates of return, the purchasing power of your invested money takes several decades or more to double.

Your investment's return relative to the rate of inflation determines the growth in purchasing power of your portfolio. What's called the *real growth rate* on your investments is the rate of return your investments earn per year *minus* the yearly rate of inflation. If the cost of living is increasing at 3 percent per year and your money is invested in a bank savings account paying you 3 percent per year, you're treading water — your *real* rate of return is zero. (When you invest money outside of a tax-sheltered retirement account, you end up paying taxes on your returns, which could lead to a *negative* real "growth" in your money's purchasing power!)

Be patient

The 9 to 10 percent annual historic return in stocks (quoted in the preceding section) isn't guaranteed to be the same in the future. Consider some of the unexpected storms that hammered the stock market over the past 110 or so years (see Table 13-1).

Table 13-1	Great Plunges (20 Percent or More) in the Dow Jones Industrial Average Index of Large-Company Stocks		
Years	*Percent Decline**	*Years*	*Percent Decline**
1890–1896	47%	1961–1962	27%
1899–1900	32%	1966	25%
1901–1903	46%	1968–1970	36%
1906–1907	49%	1973–1974	45%
1909–1914	29%	1976–1978	27%
1916–1917	40%	1981–1982	24%
1919–1921	47%	1987	36%
1929–1932	89%	1998	20%
1937–1942	52%	2000–2003	40%
1946–1949	24%	2007–2009	55%

*The returns that stock market investors earned during these periods differ slightly from the above figures, which ignore dividends paid by stocks that mitigate some of the above declines. The returns also ignore changes in the cost of living, which normally increase over time and make these drops seem even worse. The Great Depression is the exception to that rule: The cost of living decreased then.

As you see in Table 13-1, the stock market can sometimes take a beating. But before you let the chart convince you to avoid the stock market, look at the time periods during which those great plunges occurred — notice how relatively short most of them are. During the last century, major stock market declines have lasted less than two years on average. Some of the 20-percent-plus declines lasted less than one year. The longest declines (1890–1896, 1909–1914, 1929–1932, 1937–1942, 1946–1949, and 2000–2003) lasted from three to six years.

Also remember that these declines are from an absolute peak to an absolute bottom. While we all know folks who don't seem to be possess good luck, no investor invests all their money at a precise peak of the stock market — and then would be hapless enough to sell at the exact bottom!

Table 13-1 tells less than half the story. True, the stock market can suffer major losses. But over the long haul, stocks make more money than they lose. That's how they end up with that 9 to 10 percent average annual long-term return I've been telling you about. Stock market crashes may be dramatic, but consider the powerful advances in Table 13-2 that have happened after big market declines.

Table 13-2	Great Surges in the Dow Jones Industrial Average after Major Market Declines
Years	*Percent Increase*
1896–1899	173%
1914–1916	114%
1932–1937	372%
1942–1946	129%
1949–1956	222%
1962–1966	86%
1970–1973	67%
1974–1976	76%
1987–1998	450%
2003–2007	98%
2009-2010*	71%

*Increase may continue and add to the stated number

In each and every one of the cases, subsequent stock market increases more than made up for the previous declines. In other words, wait long enough, and time will bail you out! (Hence, why stocks are for long-term investors and long-term goals.) If you're going to invest in stocks, you must have the time on your side to wait out a major market decline. If you don't, you face the risk of selling your stocks for a loss. Don't keep your emergency money in stocks. Only invest money that you don't plan on using for at least five years — preferably ten or more.

Add regularly to your stock investments

Although the stock market may be able to double the purchasing power of your money on average every 10 to 12 years, the real key to creating wealth with stocks is investing in them regularly. Put $1,000 into stocks, and seven years later, you'll probably have $2,000. But if you put $1,000 into stocks *every year* for seven years, you end up with nearly $9,500 — that's nearly five times more. Remember the power of combining these two simple but powerful financial concepts: *Regular savings* and *investing in growth-oriented investments* lead to simply amazing long-term results.

Another advantage of buying in regular chunks (some call this *dollar-cost averaging,* a subject I cover in Chapter 10) is that it softens the blow of a major decline. Why? Because you can make some of your stock investments as the market is heading south; perhaps you may even buy at or near the bottom. After the market rebounds, you show a profit on some of those last purchases you made, which helps soothe the rest of your portfolio — as well as your bad feelings about the decline. If you used dollar-cost averaging during the worst decade for stock investors last century (1928–1938), you still averaged 7 percent per year in returns despite the Great Depression and a sagging stock market.

Using Mutual Funds to Invest in Stocks

The best stock funds offer you diversification and a low-cost way to hire a professional money manager. In Chapter 4, I discuss at length why purchasing individual stocks on your own doesn't make good financial sense. (If you haven't read Chapter 4 yet and you believe that buying individual stocks is the best route for you to take, please read it.)

Reducing risk and increasing returns

When you invest in stocks, you expose yourself to risk. But that doesn't mean that you can't work to minimize unnecessary risk. One of the most effective risk-reduction techniques is *diversification* — owning numerous stocks in many industries to minimize the damage of any one stock's decline. Diversification is one reason why mutual funds are a proven way to own stocks.

Unless you have a lot of money to invest, you can only cost-effectively afford to buy a handful of individual stocks. If you end up with a lemon in your portfolio, it can devastate the returns of your better-performing stocks. Companies go bankrupt. Even those that survive a rough period can see their stock prices plummet by huge amounts — 80 percent or more — and sometimes in a matter of weeks or months.

Even during the 1990s bull market (a *bull market* is one in which stock prices are rising; its opposite is a *bear market*), certain individual stocks took it on the chin. A good example is Iomega, a darling of Internet message boards in the mid-1990s. After zooming to more than $135 per share in 1996, it plunged and languished below $5 per share (adjusting for splits). It was finally acquired by EMC for just under $4 per share

Of course, owning any stock in a company that goes bankrupt and stays that way means that you lose 100 percent of your investment. If this stock represents, say, 20 percent of your holdings, the rest of your stock selections must increase about 25 percent in value just to get your portfolio back to even.

Stock mutual funds reduce your risk by investing in many stocks, often 50 or more. If a fund holds 50 stocks and one drops to zero, you lose only 2 percent of the value of the fund if the stock was an average holding. If the fund holds 100 stocks, you lose 1 percent, and a 200-stock fund loses only 0.5 percent if one stock goes under. And don't forget another advantage of stock mutual funds: A good fund manager is more likely to sidestep investment disasters than you are.

Another way that stock funds reduce risk (and thus their volatility) is by investing in different types of stocks across various industries. Some funds also invest in both U.S. and international stocks.

Different types of stocks don't always move in tandem. So if smaller company stocks are being beaten up, large-company stocks may be faring better. If growth companies are sluggish, value companies may be in vogue. If U.S. stocks are in the tank, international ones may not be. (I discuss these different types of stock funds later in this chapter.)

You can diversify into various types of stocks by purchasing several stock funds, each of which focuses on different types of stocks. This diversification has two potential advantages. First, not all your money is riding in one stock fund and with one fund manager. Second, each of the different fund managers can focus on and track particular stock investing opportunities.

Making money: How funds do it

When you invest in stock funds, you can make money in three — count 'em, three — ways:

- **Dividends:** Some stocks pay dividends. Many companies make profits and pay out some of these profits to shareholders in the form of dividends. Dividends are taxed at a far lower income tax rate than ordinary income. (Find the lowdown on fund investments and taxes in Chapter 18.) As a mutual fund investor, you can choose to receive your fund's dividends as cash or reinvest them by purchasing more shares in the mutual fund.

  Unless you need the income to live on (if, for example, you're retired), reinvest your dividends into buying more shares in the fund. If you do this outside of a retirement account, keep a record of those reinvestments because those additional purchases should be factored into the tax calculations you make when you sell the shares.

- **Capital gains distributions:** When a fund manager sells stocks for more than she paid for them, the resulting profits, known as *capital gains,* must be netted against losses and paid out to the fund's shareholders. As with dividends, your capital gains distributions can be reinvested back into the fund. Gains from stock held for more than one year are known as *long-term capital gains* and are taxed at a much lower rate than your regular income (see Chapter 18).

- **Appreciation:** The fund manager isn't going to sell all the stocks that have gone up in value. Thus, the price per share of the fund should increase (unless the fund manager made poor picks or the market as a whole is doing poorly) to reflect the gains in unsold stocks. For you, these profits are on paper until you sell the fund and lock them in. Of course, if a fund's stocks decline in value, the share price depreciates. Hold the fund for more than one year and you qualify for low long-term capital gains tax rates when you sell.

If you add together dividends, capital gains distributions, and appreciation, you arrive at the *total return* of a fund. Stocks (and the funds that invest in them) differ in the proportions that make up their total returns, particularly with respect to dividends.

Seeing your stock fund choices

Stock mutual funds, as their name implies, invest in stocks. These funds are often referred to as *equity funds. Equity* (not to be confused with equity in real estate) is another word for stocks.

Stock funds and the stocks that they invest in usually are classified into particular categories based on the types of stocks they focus on. Categorizing stock funds often is tidier in theory than in practice, though, because some funds invest in an eclectic mix of stocks. Funds and the stocks that they hold differ from one another in three major ways:

- **Size of the company:** You can purchase stock in small, medium, and large companies. The size of a company is defined by the total market value (capitalization) of its outstanding stock. Small companies are generally defined as those that have total market capitalization of less than $2 billion. Medium-sized companies have market values between $2 billion and $10 billion. Large-capitalization companies have market values greater than $10 billion. These dollar amounts are somewhat arbitrary. (***Note:*** The term *capitalization* is routinely shortened to *cap,* as in small-cap company or large-cap stock.)

What do all those other names mean?

If small and large, value and growth, U.S. and international haven't created enough mind-numbing combinations of stock fund options, here are a few more names that you'll come across.

Start with all the variations on growth. *Aggressive growth* funds are, well, more aggressive than the other growth funds. Not only does an aggressive growth fund tend to invest in the most growth-oriented companies, but also the fund may engage in riskier investing practices, such as making major shifts in strategy and trading in and out of stocks frequently (turning over the fund's investments several times or more during the year).

Then consider *growth-and-income* funds and *equity-income* funds. Both of these fund types invest in stocks (equities) that pay decent dividends, thus offering the investor the potential for growth and income. Growth-and-income and equity-income are basically one and the same. The only real difference between them is trivial: Equity-income funds tend to pay slightly higher dividends (although some growth-and-income funds have higher dividends than equity-income funds!). They may pay higher dividends because they invest a small portion of their portfolios in higher-dividend securities, such as bonds and convertible bonds.

Income funds tend to invest a healthy portion (but by no means all) of their money in higher-yielding stocks. Bonds usually make up the other portion of income funds. As I explain later in this chapter, other fund names (such as

balanced funds) designate those funds investing in both stocks and bonds. Income funds are really quite similar to some balanced funds.

The term *international* typically means that a fund can invest anywhere in the world except the U.S. The term *worldwide* or *global* generally implies that a fund can invest anywhere in the world, including the U.S. I generally recommend avoiding worldwide or global funds that have just one manager for three reasons:

- ✔ It's difficult for a fund manager to thoroughly follow the companies and financial markets across a truly global investment landscape. (It's hard enough to follow either solely U.S. or solely international markets.)

- ✔ Most of these funds charge high operating expenses — often well in excess of 1 percent per year — that drag down investors' returns.

- ✔ The proportion of U.S. and foreign stocks within a global fund may vary a lot, which can make it difficult for you to have a set long-term allocation between foreign and domestic stocks.

Don't get bogged down in the names of funds. Remember that funds sometimes have misleading names and don't necessarily do what their names may imply. What matter are the fund's investment strategies and typical investments. I tell you what these strategies are for the funds I recommend in this book, and I show you how to combine great funds together into a portfolio in Chapter 15.

Why should you care what size companies a fund holds? Because smaller companies behave differently than larger companies do. Historically, smaller companies pay lower dividends (yields) or none at all, but may appreciate more. Their share prices, although more volatile, tend to produce greater total returns. Larger companies' stocks tend to pay greater dividends and on average are less volatile, but they produce slightly lower total returns than small-company stocks. Medium-sized companies, as you may suspect, fall between the two. Investing in companies of varying sizes can generally reduce a portfolio's risk and volatility.

✔ **Growth or value:** Stock fund managers and their funds are further categorized by whether investments are made in growth or value stocks.

- *Growth* stocks are public companies that are experiencing rapidly expanding revenues and profits and whose stocks are relatively costly in relation to the assets and profits of the company. These firms tend to reinvest most of their earnings in the company to fuel future expansion; thus, these stocks pay low dividends.

- *Value* stocks are public companies that are priced cheaply in relation to the company's assets and profits. Such a company could possibly be a growth company, but that's unlikely because growth company stocks tend to sell at a premium compared to what the company's assets are worth.

✔ **Geography:** Stocks and the companies that issue them are further categorized by the location of their main operations and headquarters. Is a company based in the United States or overseas? Funds that specialize in U.S. stocks are (surprise, surprise) called U.S. stock funds; those focusing internationally are typically called "international" or "overseas" funds.

By putting together two or three of these major classifications, you can start to appreciate all those silly and lengthy names that mutual fund companies give to their stock funds. You can have funds that focus on large-company value stocks or small-company growth stocks. These categories can be further subdivided into more fund types by adding in U.S., international, and worldwide funds. For example, you can have international stock funds focusing on small-company stocks or growth stocks.

The Best Stock Funds

Using the selection criteria outlined in Chapter 7, the following sections describe the best stock funds worthy of your consideration. The recommended funds differ from one another primarily in terms of the types of stocks they invest in. Keep in mind as you read through these funds that they also differ from each other in their tax friendliness (see Chapter 10). If you're investing inside a retirement account, you don't need to bother with this issue.

Because stock funds are used for longer-term purposes, the subject of stock funds usually raises another important issue: How do you divvy up your loot into the different types of investments for purposes of diversification and to make your money grow? Chapter 10 also answers that question.

Mixing it up: Recommended hybrid funds

Hybrid funds invest in a mixture of different types of securities. Most commonly, they invest in both bonds and stocks. These funds are usually less risky and less volatile than funds that invest exclusively in stocks; in an economic downturn, bonds usually hold up better in value than stocks do.

Hybrid funds make it easier for investors who're skittish about investing in stocks to hold stocks while they avoid the high volatility that normally comes with pure stock funds. You *could* place 60 percent of your investment moneys into a pure stock fund and the other 40 percent into a pure bond fund — but you can do just that by investing in one hybrid fund that has the same overall 60/40 mix. Because bonds and stocks often don't fluctuate in unison, movements of one can offset those of the other. Hybrid funds are excellent choices for retirement account investing, particularly when an investor doesn't have much money to start with.

Hybrid mutual funds come in two flavors:

- ✔ **Balanced funds:** Balanced funds try to maintain a fairly constant percentage of investment in stocks and bonds. For example, a balanced fund's objective may be to keep 60 percent of its investments in stocks and 40 percent in bonds. (Some balanced funds are exceptions to this rule and will, like asset allocation funds, adjust their mix over time.)

- ✔ **Asset allocation funds:** These funds adjust the mix of different investments according to the portfolio manager's economic expectations. Essentially, the fund manager keeps an eye on the big picture — watching both the stock and bond markets — and moves money between them in an *attempt* to get the best value. For example, if the manager thinks stocks are highly valued and bonds are not, he may move more money into bonds and out of stocks.

You should note, however, that most managers have been unable to beat the market averages by shifting money around instead of staying put in sensible investments. (See Chapter 10 for more on index funds.)

One of the brighter spots on the mutual fund landscape is the best mutual funds that invest in a variety of different funds offered by their parent companies. They're known as *funds of funds,* and they're the ultimate couch-potato way to invest! Later in this section, I discuss specific best funds of funds.

Because hybrid funds hold taxable bonds and, therefore, pay decent dividends, they aren't appropriate for many investors who're purchasing funds outside tax-sheltered retirement accounts. If you're in a higher tax bracket (federal 28 percent and higher), bonds that you hold outside a retirement account should probably be tax-free. With the exception of the Vanguard Tax-Managed Balanced Fund (see the sidebar, "A tax-friendly hybrid"), you should avoid the hybrid funds if you're in this situation. Buy separate tax-friendly stock funds (which I cover later this chapter) and tax-free bond funds (see Chapter 12).

The following sections describe some terrific hybrid funds. They're loosely ordered from those that generally take less risk to those that take more. Higher risk hybrid funds tend to hold greater positions in stocks and/or make wider swings and changes in their investments and strategies over time.

Vanguard Wellesley Income

The Vanguard Wellesley Income is among the most conservative and income oriented of the hybrids. This fund typically has about 60 percent of its assets in high-quality bonds, with the remaining assets in high-yielding, large-company stocks. Since its inception in 1970, the majority of this fund's returns have come from dividends. Like many of the other conservative Vanguard funds, this one is managed by Wellington Management and the duo of John Keogh and Michael Reckmeyer, who have more than five decades of investment experience between them.

This fund is ideal for people who've either retired or are on the verge of retiring — or anyone else who wants a high rate of current income but also wants/has some potential for growth from their investments. Its stocks are value oriented and among the more stable of stocks. Its high-quality bonds, which tend to be intermediate term, also don't go through the gyrations that junk bonds do. Expense ratio is 0.31 percent (0.21 percent for the Admiral share class which requires a $100,000 minimum). Minimum initial investment is $3,000. The fund charges a $20 annual low-balance fee for account balances below $10,000 unless you register your account on Vanguard's Web site for electronic delivery of statements and fund reports. ☎ 800-662-7447.

Vanguard's funds of funds

A *fund of funds* is simply a mutual fund that invests in other individual mutual funds. Although the concept isn't new, it's become increasingly attractive to investors who either are overwhelmed by the number of fund choices out there or who want to diversify. Vanguard offers some excellent funds of funds.

Begun in 1985 — and thus the oldest of the funds of funds — the **Vanguard Star** fund is diversified across 11 different Vanguard funds: 6 U.S. stocks, 2 foreign stocks, and 3 bonds. Its targeted asset allocation is about 65 percent in stocks and 35 percent in bonds. The Star fund's diversification comes cheap: The expense ratio of the underlying funds is 0.32 percent. (There's no additional charge for packaging them together.) The initial investment requirement is just $1,000.

A tax-friendly hybrid

Vanguard Tax-Managed Balanced is the one hybrid fund that's tax friendly enough to be considered for investments held outside tax-sheltered retirement accounts. Why? Because the bonds that it holds (typically half of this fund's investments) are federally tax-free municipal bonds. Be forewarned, though, that this fund has a steep initial minimum of $10,000 and is intended for investors who can hold the fund for at least five years. Otherwise, a 1 percent transaction fee is charged against your sale proceeds and paid into the fund. The fund's annual expense ratio is a mere 0.15 percent.

The bond portion of the portfolio is composed of high-quality and generally intermediate term municipal bonds. The stocks in this fund try to replicate the Russell 1000 index of the 1,000 largest company stocks in the United States, although the fund emphasizes stocks with lower dividends to reduce taxable distributions. Selling of stocks with capital gains is also minimized to reduce those taxable distributions as well.

Because this fund shuns dividend paying stocks, it's not a good choice for conservative, value-oriented investors seeking current investment income on which to live.

If you live in a high-tax state, instead of buying this Vanguard fund, you may be better off buying a state and federally tax-free municipal bond fund, if a good one's available for your state (see Chapter 12 to find out), and pairing it with a tax-friendly stock fund. Contact Vanguard investor and client information at (800) 662-7447.

Realizing that in the case of asset allocation, one size doesn't fit all, Vanguard introduced the LifeStrategy series of funds in 1994. Although each of the four LifeStrategy funds draws from numerous Vanguard stock and bond funds, they differentiate themselves by their target asset allocations. The **LifeStrategy Income** fund, the most conservative of the bunch, has 70 to 80 percent in bonds and 20 to 30 percent in stocks, whereas the **LifeStrategy Growth** portfolio, at the other end of the risk spectrum, invests 80 to 90 percent in stocks and 10 to 20 percent in bonds. The asset allocations of the **LifeStrategy Conservative Growth** and the **LifeStrategy Moderate Growth** funds fall somewhere in between. (If you want a fund that gradually scales back its risk as you get closer to retirement, take a look at Vanguard's Target Retirement fund series.)

By relying more heavily on index funds than the Star fund does, the LifeStrategy funds come through with an even lower average expense ratio of 0.22 percent. Minimum initial investment is $3,000, and these funds charge a $20 annual low-balance fee for account balances below $10,000 unless you register your account on Vanguard's Web site for electronic delivery of statements and fund reports. ☎ 800-662-7447.

The **Dodge & Cox Balanced** fund is one of the oldest and best-balanced funds, having started in 1931. Like Dodge & Cox itself, this fund is conservatively run, investing primarily in medium- and large-company U.S. value stocks and high-quality, intermediate-term bonds. Typically, it invests about 60 to as much as 70 percent in stocks and the rest in bonds.

This fund has always been managed by using a team approach, so if you like to be able to rattle off the name of a star fund manager who's investing your money, this fund isn't for you (although you can impress others by saying that the minimum account size that Dodge & Cox normally accepts is several million dollars). This fund has a low 0.53 percent expense ratio.

Vanguard Wellington

The **Vanguard Wellington** is the oldest hybrid fund: It dates back to the summer of 1929 (which means that it even survived the Great Depression!). This fund typically invests about 60 to 65 percent in larger company value-oriented stocks, with the remainder in high-quality, intermediate- to longer-term bonds. In recent years, approximately 10 to 15 percent of this fund's stocks were overseas.

This fund is co-managed by Wellington Management's Edward Bousa and John Keogh, who together have more than 55 years of investment management experience. The fund's expense ratio is 0.35 percent (0.23 for Admiral shares that require a $100,000 minimum). Minimum initial investment is $10,000. The fund charges a $20, annual low-balance fee for account balances below $10,000 unless you register your account on Vanguard's Web site for electronic delivery of statements and fund reports. ☎ 800-662-7447.

Fidelity Puritan

One of the company's oldest funds (it began in 1947), the **Fidelity Puritan** fund is co-managed by Ramin Arani and George Fischer, who have a combined four decades with Fidelity in investment research and management. Puritan typically has about 60 percent in stocks that tend to be large company and value oriented. In recent years, the fund has been investing about 10 percent of its stock allocation overseas.

Most of the bonds are intermediate term, and a modest portion of them are junk bonds. The expense ratio is 0.67 percent. Minimum initial investment is $2,500. The fund charges a $12 annual low-balance fee for nonretirement account balances below $2,000. ☎ 800-544-8888.

Fidelity's Freedom funds of funds

Fidelity offers 12 Freedom funds of funds: Freedom Income, Freedom 2000, Freedom 2005, Freedom 2010, Freedom 2015, Freedom 2020, Freedom 2025, Freedom 2030, Freedom 2035, Freedom 2040, Freedom 2045, and Freedom 2050. The **Freedom Income** fund is the most conservative, targeting 40 percent of its assets to fixed income funds, 40 percent to money market funds, and 20 percent to equity funds. At the other end of the scale is the **Freedom 2050** fund, the most aggressive, with about 90 percent of its assets in equity funds and 10 percent in fixed-income funds. The asset allocations of the other funds fall between these extremes. (The higher the number in the fund title, which is theoretically the customer's approximate retirement date, the greater its percentage of stock funds.)

All the Freedom Funds draw from a fixed pool of Fidelity funds, such as Capital & Income, Strategic Real Return, Investment Grade Bond, Blue Chip Growth, Disciplined Equity, Equity-Income, Growth Company, Large Cap Value, Diversified International, and Fidelity Overseas.

The combined operating expenses of the underlying funds within the Freedom Funds typically ranges from 0.7 to 0.8 percent. The Fidelity Freedom funds charge a $12 annual low-balance fee for nonretirement account balances below $2,000. ☎ 800-544-8888.

T. Rowe Price offerings

T. Rowe Price Balanced invests mainly in large-company stocks within the United States and has about one-quarter of its stocks overseas and 10 to 15 percent of its bonds in junk. The expense ratio is 0.69 percent. **T. Rowe Price Personal Strategy Balanced** is another fine hybrid fund, which typically holds 60 percent stocks of companies of varying sizes and has 20 to 25 percent of its stocks overseas. The expense ratio is 0.86 percent. Minimum initial investment for both of these funds is $2,500 ($1,000 for retirement accounts).

T. Rowe Price also has a series of target-date retirement funds, with names such as **T. Rowe Price Retirement** 2040, that are funds of funds. On the conservative end of the spectrum, it has T. Rowe Price Retirement Income and T. Rowe Price Retirement 2005, with expense ratios around 0.6 percent. At the most aggressive end of the spectrum, it has T. Rowe Price Retirement 2055, with an expense ratio of 0.79 percent. These funds gradually reduce their stock exposure and risk as you near the retirement date in the fund's name. ☎ 800-638-5660.

Letting computers do the heavy lifting: Recommended index funds

Index funds are passively managed — that means an index fund's money is invested, using computer modeling, to simply track the performance of a particular market index, such as the Standard & Poor's 500. When you buy into an index fund, you give up the possibility of outperforming the market, but you also guarantee that you won't much underperform the market either.

Beating the market is extremely difficult; most actively managed funds are unable to do it. The best index funds, however, have an advantage — the lowest operating expenses in the business. In Chapter 10, I further discuss the virtues of index funds and the role they should play in your portfolio.

Exchange-traded funds (ETFs) are index funds that are the newer kids on the block. ETFs trade on a stock exchange, and the best of them have low expense ratios like Vanguard's index funds. In fact, many of the best ETFs come from Vanguard. Where relevant, I have included recommended stock ETFs in this chapter. For more information about ETFs, including their pros and cons, please see Chapter 5.

Vanguard's index funds are generally the best stock index funds available. John C. Bogle, Vanguard's founder and former CEO, was the first person to take the idea of indexing to the mutual fund investing public; he's been a tireless crusader for index funds ever since. Today, Vanguard continues to be the index fund leader with the lowest operating expenses (which directly translates into higher index fund returns) and the biggest index fund selection around.

The flagship of Vanguard's index fleet, the **Vanguard Index 500** fund invests to replicate the performance of the popular stock market index — the Standard & Poor's 500 index — which tracks the stocks of 500 large companies in the United States. These 500 stocks typically account for about three-quarters of the total value of stocks outstanding in the U.S. market. I don't enthusiastically recommend this fund because you miss out on medium- and smaller-sized companies. Also, because it's weighted by the market value of the stocks in its index, you end up over-investing in sectors of the market (for example, technology stocks in the late 1990s and financial services stocks in the mid-2000s) that are bloated and due for a more substantial correction. The expense ratio on this fund is a razor-thin 0.18 percent, and if you invest $100,000 in the fund, you can use the Admiral share class with its ultra-low 0.09 percent expense ratio.

A more diversified and tax-friendlier fund than Vanguard's Index 500 is the **Vanguard Total Stock Market Index,** which replicates the performance of the MSCI US Broad Market Index, comprising 99.5 percent or more of the total market capitalization of all of the U.S. common stocks regularly traded on the New York and American Stock Exchanges, and the NASDAQ over-the-counter market. This index comprises the entire U.S. market of large-, medium-, and small-company stocks. This fund, which holds more than 3,400 stocks, also has a wafer-thin expense ratio of 0.18 percent and also offers Admiral shares with a 0.09 percent expense ratio.

Value-oriented indexes generally are a little less volatile, produce more dividend income, and offer slightly higher long-term total returns. Among U.S. index funds and exchange-traded funds I like is **iShares Russell 1000 Value ETF**, which invests in large cap U.S. stocks. For smaller cap stocks, check out **iShares Russell 2000 Value ETF**, **Vanguard Small Cap Value Index** fund, and **Vanguard Small Cap Value ETF**.

Taxes on stock funds

For mutual funds held outside of retirement accounts, you have to pay income tax on dividends and capital gains that are distributed. Stock dividends and long-term capital gains are taxed at far lower income tax rates relative to ordinary income (see Chapter 10). If your circumstances lead you to have money that you want to invest in stock funds outside of retirement accounts, by all means do it. But pay close attention to the taxable distributions that funds make (especially short-term capital gains distributions that aren't eligible for the lower tax rates). (I've indicated in this chapter which funds are tax friendly.)

In addition to the tax-friendly index and stock funds I note in the chapter, also check out the **Vanguard Tax-Managed Capital Appreciation** fund, which invests in the universe of the 1,000 largest company stocks in the U.S. stock market. (Vanguard actually selects and samples from among the 1,000 companies.) This fund seeks to minimize capital gains distributions by holding on to appreciating stock and, if it needs to sell some stocks at a profit, offsetting those sales by selling other stocks at a loss. Vanguard also offers a **Tax-Managed Growth and Income** fund, **Tax-Managed Small-Cap** fund, and a **Tax-Managed International** fund.

You shouldn't go into the Vanguard Tax-Managed funds unless you plan to hold your investment for five years because you'll get clipped with a transaction fee of 1 percent for such an early exit. The minimum initial investment is a hefty $10,000.

Vanguard Total International Stock Index seeks to replicate a combination of two international indexes: the Morgan Stanley Capital International Index (which is comprised of established economies) and the Select Emerging Markets Index. This fund is actually a fund of funds, as it includes Vanguard's index funds for Europe, the Pacific, and Emerging Markets. At 0.34 percent, this fund's expense ratio is a bargain for an international fund.

Vanguard FTSE All-World ex-US ETF is also a solid core international fund worth considering.

For nonretirement accounts, the minimum initial purchase for Vanguard index funds is $3,000. Vanguard's index funds charge a $20 annual low-balance fee for account balances below $10,000 unless you register your account on Vanguard's Web site for electronic delivery of statements and fund reports. ☎ 800-662-7447.

Keeping it local: Recommended U.S.-focused stock funds

This section focuses on the better actively managed funds that invest primarily in the U.S. stock market. I say *primarily* because some "U.S." funds venture into overseas investments. The only way to know for sure where a fund is currently invested (or where the fund may invest in the future) is to ask. You can start by calling the toll-free number of the mutual fund company that you're interested in. You can also read the fund's annual report (which I explain how to do in Chapter 8). A prospectus, unfortunately, won't give you anything beyond the general parameters that guide the range of investments: It won't tell you what the fund is currently investing in or has invested in.

Of all the different types of funds offered, U.S. stock funds are the largest category. To see the forest amidst the trees, remember the classifications I cover earlier in the chapter. Stock funds differ mainly in terms of the size of the companies they focus on and whether those companies are considered "growth" or "value" companies.

I highly recommend another of the fine but few funds offered by Dodge & Cox, the **Dodge & Cox Stock** fund, which focuses on large- and medium-company value stocks, including about 10 to 20 percent in foreign shares.

Unlike most U.S. stock funds today, this fund does little trading, often less than 15 percent of its portfolio annually. Like the Dodge & Cox Balanced Fund, this fund is managed by a team and doesn't try to time the markets. Its annual expense ratio is a low 0.52 percent.

Fairholme Fund

You may think that a fund that was started in late 1999, right before the peak of a long bull market and just before U.S. stocks in general suffered their worst decade was destined for trouble. But, you'd be wrong in the case of the **Fairholme Fund.** Fund managers Bruce Berkowitz and Charles Fernandez scour the world stock markets for undervalued stocks, primarily in medium- and larger size companies. This firm started out in the private money management business — Fairholme Capital Management — in 1997, which required a $1 million initial investment. The Fairholme fund's expense ratio is 1 percent. Initial minimum investment is $2,500; $1,000 for retirement accounts. ☎ 866-202-2263.

Fidelity Low-Priced Stock

The **Fidelity Low-Priced Stock** fund specializes in investing in small- and medium-company value stocks. As of this writing, about one-third of its stocks are overseas. As you may guess from its name, it buys stocks that have low share prices. Lower priced stocks tend to coincide with smaller companies, but not always: The price per share of a stock may bear little resemblance to the size of the issuing company because companies can "split" their stock and issue more shares, which cuts the price per share. This fund has been managed since its inception in 1989 by Joel Tillinghast, an amazing run given the turnover of managers at many funds, especially at Fidelity. Annual operating expenses are 1 percent. The minimum initial investment requirement is $2,500 for all accounts. ☎ 800-544-8888.

Sequoia

A conservatively managed fund with a long history (dating back to 1970) of success, **Sequoia** got a boost from Warren Buffett who closed an investment fund in 1969 and recommended that investors invest with the newly formed Sequoia, which was managed by Bill Ruane.

The fund generally focuses on larger company stocks. This fund is co-managed by Robert Goldfarb and David Poppe. Its expense ratio is 1 percent. Minimum initial investment is $5,000, $2,500 for retirement accounts. ☎ 800-686-6884.

Vanguard Primecap

Vanguard Primecap is one of the few growth-oriented stock funds that doesn't trade its portfolios heavily, trading typically less than 20 percent of its fund per year. It invests in companies of all sizes and even invests a small portion overseas. This fund has been managed since its inception by Howard Schow and Theo Kolokotrones of Primecap Management, a Southern California investment management company. Joel Fried was added as a co-manager in 1993; several additional co-managers were added in recent years. The expense ratio for this reasonably tax-friendly fund is a competitive 0.49 percent. (*Note:* This fund is currently closed to new investors.) Although this fund is closed, you can, however, still tap in to the investment expertise of Primecap Management through the **Primecap Odyssey Growth** fund ($2,000 minimum, 0.73 percent expense ratio). ☎ 800-662-7447 for Vanguard; ☎ 800-729-2307 for Odyssey.

Vanguard Selected Value

James Barrow and Mike Giambrone, who have nearly six decades of investment management experience between them, are principals in the money management firm of Barrow, Hanley, Mewhinney, & Strauss, which have managed most of this fund since 1999. A portion of this fund has also managed by Donald Smith & Company since 2005. **Vanguard Selected Value** focuses on mid-size value stocks and invests a small portion overseas. The fund's expense ratio is a low 0.45 percent. Unfortunately, Vanguard raised the minimum investment amount on this excellent fund to $25,000, so those with smaller balances to invest will need to look elsewhere. ☎ 800-662-7447.

Vanguard Strategic Equity

Using models honed by Gus Sauter and Joel Dickson of Vanguard's Quantitative Equity Group, this fund has invested in small- and medium-sized U.S. companies since 1995. This fund, too, has a higher minimum: $10,000. Expenses are a low 0.30 percent. ☎ 800-662-7447.

Being worldly: Recommended international funds

As I discuss in Part I, for diversification and growth potential, funds that invest overseas should be part of an investor's stock fund holdings. Normally, you can tell you're looking at a fund that focuses its investments overseas if its name contains words such as *international, global, worldwide,* or *world.*

Generally, you should avoid foreign funds that invest in just one country. As with investing in a sector fund that specializes in a particular industry, this lack of diversification defeats the whole purpose of investing in funds. Funds that focus on specific regions, such as Southeast Asia, are better but are generally problematic because of poor diversification and higher expenses than other, more-diversified international funds.

In addition to the risks normally inherent in stock fund investing, international securities and funds are also influenced by changes in the value of foreign currencies relative to the U.S. dollar. If the dollar declines in value, the value of foreign stock funds goes up. Some foreign stock funds hedge against currency changes. Although hedging helps to reduce volatility a bit, it costs money to do, so I wouldn't worry about it if I were you. Remember, you're investing in stock funds for the long haul. And in the long haul, your international stock funds' performance will largely be driven by the returns generated on foreign stock exchanges, not currency price changes.

The following sections offer my picks for diversified international funds that may meet your needs. Compared to U.S. funds, fewer established international funds exist, and they tend to have higher annual expense ratios. So I've listed fewer options for you. (Don't forget the **Vanguard Total International Stock Index** fund and the **Vanguard Tax-Managed International** fund, which I discuss earlier in this chapter.)

Vanguard International Growth

The **Vanguard International Growth** fund invests primarily in large companies with growth potential, mainly in established countries. It also invests a modest 15 to 20 percent in emerging markets.

International Growth is primarily managed by London-headquartered Schroder Capital Management, which has research offices around the world focused on specific countries and has managed this fund since its inception in 1981. In 2003, James Anderson of Baillie Gifford was added to manage a portion of this large fund. This fund has an expense ratio of 0.53 percent and has been reasonably tax friendly. Initial minimum investment is $3,000

(Admiral shares of this fund have a $100,000 minimum and levy 0.34 percent in annual expenses). The fund charges a $20 annual low-balance fee for account balances below $10,000 unless you register your account on Vanguard's Web site for electronic delivery of statements and fund reports. ☎ 800-662-7447.

Dodge & Cox International

This excellent private money management firm also offers a handful of excellent mutual funds and manages the **Dodge & Cox International** fund, a foreign stock offering, which focuses on larger company, value-oriented stocks. The fund is managed by a team of investment managers, most of whom have been with the firm for 20+ years. Expenses are a low 0.64 percent. Minimum initial investment is $1,000 for retirement accounts; $2,500 for other accounts. ☎ 800-621-3979.

Masters' Select International Equity

Like a fund of funds, **Masters' Select International Equity** has some of the best fund managers each managing a portion of fund. Some of these top fund managers manage funds that are closed to new investors. Although each manager has a somewhat different investment orientation, collectively this fund invests in foreign companies of all sizes, including those in emerging markets.

Masters' Select International's expenses are 1.07 percent. (Unfortunately this fund is closed to new investors.) If you sell shares in this fund within six months of purchase, you must pay a 2 percent redemption fee. Minimum initial investment is $10,000 ($1,000 for retirement accounts). ☎ 800-960-0188.

Expanding your horizon: Recommended global stock funds

A select number of stock funds invest globally (overseas as well as in the United States) and do so well and cost-effectively; I detail those funds in this section.

Oakmark Global

The **Oakmark Global** fund invests in an eclectic mix of companies worldwide. Oakmark is one of a very short list of fund firms that has successfully managed a global stock mutual fund. While the fund commenced operations in 1999, fund manager Clyde McGregor has been with the Oakmark Funds parent company (Harris Associates) since 1981 and co-manager Robert Taylor has been with Harris since 1994. Together, McGregor and Taylor have five decades of experience in money management. While expenses are a little high at 1.23 percent. Minimum initial investment for all account types is $1,000. ☎ 800-625-6275.

T. Rowe Price Spectrum Growth

ERIC'S PICKS

T. Rowe Price offers a number of good stock funds, both U.S. and international, and the **Spectrum Growth** fund of funds offers a simplified way to invest in them. The U.S. stock funds in this fund cover the entire range of company sizes. Spectrum Growth also invests about 25 percent of its assets overseas.

This fund of funds is managed by regular meetings of a committee made up of fund managers within the company. Slight changes in allocations among the different funds are made based on expectations of how particular types of stocks (for example, growth versus value, larger versus smaller company) will fare in the future. The expense ratio of the funds in this fund come to about 0.82 percent, and the company doesn't charge an additional fee for the fund's packaging. Minimum initial investment is $2,500 ($1,000 for retirement accounts). ☎ 800-638-5660.

Tweedy Browne Global Value

ERIC'S PICKS

Tweedy Browne Global Value invests in value stocks of companies of all sizes worldwide, primarily in established countries. Although it can invest in the United States, its U.S. holdings are generally 10 to 15 percent of the fund. The parent company has an excellent reputation, managing money privately since the 1920s; this fund itself has been in existence since 1993 and has done well. Operating expenses, consistently lowering as the fund grows in size, are still a bit on the high side at 1.4 percent. Initial minimum investment is $2,500 ($500 for retirement accounts). ☎ 800-432-4789.

Vanguard Global Equity

This excellent fund is co-managed by three leading private money management firms: Marathon Asset Management, Acadian Asset Management, and AllianceBernstein. U.S. stocks currently comprise about 40 percent of the fund. The expense ratio of 0.47 is low for a global fund. Minimum initial investment is $3,000. The fund charges a $20 annual low-balance fee for account balances below $10,000 unless you register your account on Vanguard's Web site for electronic delivery of statements and fund reports. ☎ 800-662-7447.

Chapter 14

Specialty Funds: One of a Kind

. . . .

In This Chapter

▶ Looking into real estate investment trust (REIT) funds

▶ Getting the scoop on precious metals and commodities funds

▶ Reviewing utility funds

▶ Doing good with socially responsible and market neutral funds

. . . .

*I*n the other chapters in this part of the book, I explain the three major types of funds: money market, bond, and stock. Specialty funds, which tend to be stock funds, are often known as *sector* funds because they tend to invest in securities in specific industries. But, as you see in this chapter, some specialty funds hold securities in a variety of industries but engage in unusual strategies that separate them from their peers.

In addition to real estate and precious metals funds, other types of sector-focused funds I discuss in this chapter are commodity funds, and utility funds, which are popular with some investors who want more conservative stock investments. In addition, I cover specialty funds that engage in unusual strategies and invest in a wide range of industries — socially responsible funds and market neutral funds.

Sector Funds: Should You or Shouldn't You Invest in Them?

In most cases, you should avoid specialty or sector funds. Investing in stocks of a single industry defeats a major purpose of investing in mutual funds — you give up the benefits of diversification. Also, just because the fund may from time to time be dedicated to a *hot* sector (a sector fund or two is often at the top of short-term performance charts), you can't assume that the fund will pick the right stocks within that sector.

Another good reason to avoid sector funds is that they tend to carry much higher fees than other mutual funds do. Many sector funds also tend to have high rates of trading or turnover of their investment holdings. Investors holding these funds outside of retirement accounts may have to turn over a tidy portion of their returns to the IRS.

The only types of specialty funds that may make sense for a small portion (10 percent or less) of your investment portfolio are funds that invest in real estate or precious metals. These types of funds can help diversify your portfolio because they can do better during times of higher inflation — which often depresses general bond and stock prices. Don't feel obligated to invest in these sector funds, however, because diversified stock funds tend to hold some of these specialty investments.

Landlording Made Easy: Real Estate Investment Trust (REIT) Funds

Do you want to invest in real estate without the hassle of being a landlord? Invest in *real estate investment trusts (REITs),* which are stocks of companies that invest in real estate. These funds typically invest in properties, such as apartment buildings, shopping centers, and other rental properties. Of course, evaluating REIT stocks is a hassle, but you can always (you guessed it) invest in a mutual fund of REITs!

REITs are small-company stocks and usually pay decent dividends. Sorry, but these dividends aren't eligible for the lower dividend tax rates for other stock funds. As such, REITs aren't appropriate for higher-tax-bracket investors investing money outside of retirement accounts. Most of the larger, diversified U.S. stock funds that I recommend in Chapter 13 have a small portion of their fund's assets invested in REITs, so you'll have some exposure to this sector without investing in a REIT-focused fund.

Here are some solid REIT funds from which to choose:

- ✔ **Cohen & Steers Realty Shares** has been managed by Martin Cohen and Robert Steers since the fund began in 1991. (Two additional comanagers have recently been added.) The minimum initial investment is steep at $10,000. Discounters also may offer it without transaction charges. Annual operating expenses are 1.00 percent. ☎ 800-437-9912.

- ✔ **Fidelity Real Estate Investment,** the oldest REIT mutual fund, is managed by Steven Buller, who's been with Fidelity since 1992 and managed this fund since 1998. This fund has expenses of 0.92 percent per year. Initial minimum investment is $2,500 ($500 for retirement accounts). ☎ 800-544-8888.

- ✔ **T. Rowe Price Real Estate** has been managed since its inception by portfolio manager David Lee. 0.75 percent, $2,500 minimum ($1,000 for retirement accounts). ☎ 800-638-5660.

- ✔ **Vanguard REIT Index,** yet another of Vanguard's long line of index funds, has minimal expenses of just 0.21 percent. Although this fund will never be a star in its category, its low expenses should ensure its long-term success. Minimum investment amount is $3,000. The fund charges a $20, annual low-balance fee for account balances below $10,000 unless you register your account on Vanguard's Web site for electronic delivery of statements and fund reports. ☎ 800-662-7447.

Profiting from What Everyone Needs: Utility Funds

Utility funds tend to attract older folks who want to earn good dividends and not have the risk of most stock investments. And that's what utility funds are good for. But this once-staid industry has been shaken up by increased competition.

In a sense, utility funds are superfluous. Most diversified stock funds contain some utilities, and those investors who want income can focus on better income-producing funds, such as Wellesley Income in the hybrid group and the value-oriented stock funds that I discuss in Chapter 13.

Arming for Armageddon: Precious Metals Funds

Gold and silver have been used by many civilizations as mediums of exchange because these metals have unique physical properties and rarity. These precious metals are used not only in jewelry but also in less frivolous applications, such as manufacturing.

With a paper-based currency, such as the U.S. dollar, the government can always print more currency to pay off its debts. This process of casually printing more and more currency can lead to a currency's devaluation — and to inflation.

Holdings of gold and silver can provide a so-called hedge against inflation. In the United States during the late 1970s and early 1980s, inflation rose dramatically. This rise depressed stocks and bonds. Gold and silver, however, soared in value, rising more than 500 percent (even after adjusting for inflation) from 1972 to 1981.

Over the long term, however, precious metals are lousy investments. They don't pay any dividends, and their price increases just keep you up with, but not ahead of, increases in the cost of living. Although investing in precious metals is better than keeping cash in a piggy bank or stuffed in a mattress, it's historically not been as good as bonds, stocks, and real estate.

Don't purchase precious metals futures contracts. *Futures* aren't investments; they're short-term gambles on which way prices of an underlying investment (in this case, gold or silver) may head over a short period of time (see Chapter 1). You also should stay away from firms and shops that sell coins and *bullion* (not the soup, but bars of gold or silver). Even if you can find a legitimate firm (which isn't an easy task), storing and insuring gold and silver are costly. You don't get good value for your money.

Gold and silver can help to diversify a portfolio, but if you want to invest in precious metals, you're wise to do so through mutual funds. For more information about determining how these types of funds may fit with the rest of your investments and how to buy them, be sure to read Chapter 12.

Vanguard Precious Metals and Mining fund, like most gold and precious metals funds, invests in mining companies' stocks worldwide because many are outside the United States in countries such as South Africa and Australia. This fund, which also invests in other metals such as platinum and nickel, has one of the best track records among precious metals funds and has been around since 1984. Annual operating expenses for this tax-friendly fund are 0.40 percent. At the time this book went to press, this fund was closed but will likely reopen, probably when this market sector isn't overheated as it has been recently. Minimum initial investment is $3,000. The fund charges a $20, annual low-balance fee for account balances below $10,000 unless you register your account on Vanguard's Web site for electronic delivery of statements and fund reports. ☎ 800-662-7447.

If you expect high inflation or if you just want an inflation hedge in case you expect the end of civilization, you could invest in a gold and precious metals fund. But these funds have wild swings and aren't for the faint of heart or for the majority of your portfolio. To illustrate why, consider this: In 1993, the Vanguard Precious Metals and Mining fund rocketed up 93 percent, whereas in 1997, it lost almost 39 percent. From 2000 through 2007, it increased in value more than 600 percent! But, then in 2008, this fund lost a whopping 56 percent.

In 2009, it jumped 76.5 percent. For an alternative, less volatile (and lower return) inflation hedge, consider investing in inflation-protected Treasury bonds (which I discuss in Chapter 12).

Commodity Funds

Precious metals are but one type of commodity. The major commodities that trade include energy commodities (such as oil, gasoline, and natural gas), grains and other agriculture commodities, industrial metals (such as titanium, aluminum, stainless steel, nickel, and copper), and livestock.

A number of mutual funds invest so as to track or beat various broadly diversified commodity indexes. Here are the notable attributes of commodities as an investment class:

- **Modest returns:** Long-term commodity returns are comparable to those on bonds but certainly less than stocks.

- **High volatility:** Commodities tend to be at least as volatile as stock prices without offering as high long-term returns.

- **Diversification value:** Historically, commodities have posted their best returns when stocks and bonds have done poorly. For example, this situation happened during a portion of the 1970s, when commodities did well during times of increasing inflation. Thus, commodities add some diversification to a portfolio.

Plenty of poor commodity funds, including exchange-traded funds, are out there. In addition to high fees, funds in this space are often plagued by poor long-term returns due to excessive risk taking that doesn't pan out.

Commodity funds should never be used for more than a small portion (say, 10 percent) of your portfolio, you should primarily use them for their diversification value. Because of their volatility, commodity funds are best used over several or more years, as you would use a stock fund.

Here's a short list of some of the better commodity funds available:

- Credit Suisse Commodity Real Return Strategy
- Fidelity Global Commodities
- Harbor Commodity Real Return Strategy
- PIMCO Commodity Real Return Strategy

Hedging: Market Neutral (Long-Short) Funds

In Chapter 6, I discuss hedge funds. As I have in prior editions of this book, I warn investors about the many dangers of such funds, which lure investors with the promise of expected high returns and the possibility of doing well even when the stock market is doing poorly. Many hedge funds sell stocks short — a strategy that makes money when stock prices fall, but that typically leads to losing money. Often overlooked are the high fees, big risks, and relatively poor to mediocre long-term performance of most hedge funds.

The mutual fund industry developed *market neutral funds,* also known as *long-short funds,* as yet another answer to investor fears about falling stock market prices. A typical market neutral fund invests in stocks, which its fund manager believes will rise in value, but also shorts some stocks that the fund manager thinks will fall in value. (When you *sell short,* you borrow a security from a broker, sell it, and then hope to buy it back later at a lower price.) Supposedly, such funds shine during a volatile market because plenty of stocks should be rising and falling, and a smart manager, so the theory goes, should be able to invest in those that will rise and short those that will fall.

Well, this category of funds has generally failed to deliver for investors, which is why I haven't recommended these funds in prior editions of this book. Consider the following issues with market neutral funds:

- **High expenses:** The average expense ratio is a whopping 2.07 percent. One reason is the high costs involved in short selling. Paying more than 2 percent per year in fees is a major drag on your potential long-term returns.

- **Lack of track records:** Of the 235 funds engaging in this strategy, only 65 have a five-year track record, only 19 have 10-year track records, and only 8 have 15-year track records.

- **Mediocre returns:** In the five-year period ending April 7, 2010, which includes a fairly volatile period of rising and falling markets, the average market neutral fund posted an annual average return of just 1.9 percent. Over this same period, diversified funds generally returned double to triple that amount.

If you're skittish about investing in stocks, then you need to develop an overall investment plan which includes holding a diversified portfolio. Ultimately, if you're uncomfortable putting any money in stocks, then don't do so. Investing in funds that short stocks is even more dangerous and risky.

Matching Morals to Investments: Socially Responsible Funds

Socially responsible mutual funds appeal to investors who want to marry their investments to their social principles and avoid supporting causes that they feel are harmful. These funds attempt to look at more than a company's bottom line before deciding to commit their investors' capital. Many of these funds consider such factors as environmental protection, equal employment opportunity, the manner in which a company's employees are treated, and the level of honesty that a company displays in its advertising.

I can certainly understand the desire to put your money where your mouth is; unfortunately, socially responsible funds fail to bridge the gap between theory and practice. If you blindly plunk down your money on such a fund, you may be disappointed with what you're actually getting. Bear with me as I explain.

Evil is in the eye of the beholder

The biggest problem is that the term *socially responsible* has different meanings for different people. Sure, most socially conscious investors can agree on some industries as being "bad." The tobacco industry, associated with hundreds of thousands of deaths and billions of dollars of healthcare costs, is an obvious example, and socially responsible funds avoid them. But most industries aren't so easy to agree on.

For example, McDonald's is the world's largest fast-food (hamburger) company, as well as a stock that some socially responsible funds hold. McDonald's is deemed socially responsible because of its support for children's charities, participation in recycling programs, hiring and promotion of women and minorities, and purchase of hundreds of millions of dollars in goods and services from woman- and minority-owned businesses.

But how socially responsible is a company whose business depends on beef? It's certainly not the best for people's health, and raising cattle is tremendously land and water intensive. Moreover, some may also question the screening and awarding of contracts based on gender and ethnicity. Others may blame McDonald's for running small local restaurants out of business and contributing to the sterile strip-mall culture of our communities.

Or consider Toys "R" Us, the giant toy retailer and another stock that's widely held by socially responsible funds for many of the same reasons that McDonald's is. But this company sells widely criticized violent video games that keep kids away from homework. Thus, some investors might consider Toys "R" Us a socially *ir*responsible company — and that's before you consider the heaps of plastic (made from petroleum) and the drive toward overconsumption that the toy industry generates.

Pick any company, put it under a magnifying glass, and you can find practices that are objectionable to somebody's (perhaps your) moral consciousness. Of course, that's a poor argument for throwing in the towel. I'm simply warning you that you may be hard-pressed to find a fund manager whose definition of social responsibility is closely enough aligned to yours. A mutual fund, by its very nature, is trying to please thousands of individual investors. That's a tall order when you throw moral consciousness into the picture.

Even if you can agree on what's socially irresponsible (such as selling tobacco products), funds aren't always as clean as you'd think or hope. We live in a global economy where it's increasingly difficult to define a company's sphere of influence. Although a socially responsible fund may choose to avoid tobacco manufacturers, it may invest in retailers that sell tobacco products, or the paper supplier to the tobacco manufacturer, or the advertising agency that helps pitch tobacco to consumers.

Ways to express your social concerns

Some funds that aren't labeled "socially responsible" still meet many investors' definitions of socially responsible. These other funds usually carry lower fees and produce better returns. For example, GNMA bond funds invest in mortgages that allow people to purchase their own homes. Municipal bond funds buy bonds issued by local governments to fund projects that most would consider good — such as building public transportation, libraries, and schools. See Chapter 10 for my specific bond fund recommendations.

If you consider investing in socially responsible funds, look well beyond a fund's marketing materials. When you find a socially responsible fund that interests you, call the fund company and ask it to send you a recent report that lists the specific investments that the fund owns. Otherwise, you may be blissfully ignorant, but not as socially responsible as you may like to believe.

You can always consider alternative methods of effecting social change, such as through volunteer work and donations to causes that you support. You can also exercise a means of change that people the world over are dying for, a means that is guaranteed to all U.S. citizens by the Constitution and is exercised today by only a minority of American adults — the right to voice your opinion and vote.

Chapter 15

Working It Out: Sample Portfolios

*T*his chapter is where the rubber hits the road. If you read the other chapters in this part of the book, where I discuss the details of money market, bond, and stock funds and everything in between, the concepts and individual funds may be swirling around your brain like random pieces of paper in a city alley during a windstorm. (Chapter 10 covers several important investment selection topics as well, including asset allocation. If you haven't read that chapter, please do so now — otherwise, you may be less able to make use of the guidance in this chapter.)

In this chapter, I talk through some real live cases. (Of course, the names and details have been changed to protect the innocent!) This chapter should bring a lot of things together for you; I at least hope that it calms the whirlwind.

My goal in going through these cases is to illustrate useful ways to think about investing in funds and to provide you with ideas and specific solutions to investment situations. You may think that you'll benefit most from reading only those cases that seem closest to your current situation, but I encourage you to read as many cases as your time allows — perhaps even all of them. Each situation raises somewhat different issues, and your life and your investing needs will change in the years ahead.

Don't worry if your circumstances don't perfectly match one of these cases; in fact, it probably won't be a complete match. After all, you're uniquely you. However, the principles illustrated here are general enough to be tailored to just about anyone's specific situation.

Throughout these cases, I explain

- ✔ How your investing decisions fit within the context of your overall finances
- ✔ How to consider the tax impact of your investing decisions
- ✔ How to recognize situations in which you may need to make other financial moves prior to (and maybe even instead of) investing in mutual funds

Determine where you stand with regard to your own important financial goals, such as retirement planning (the fund-related ins and outs of which I cover in Chapter 3), before you put together your investment portfolio. The examples in this chapter are arranged from the simpler cases to the more complex.

Getting Started

If you're just starting to get your financial goals together, you're hardly alone. If you're still in school or otherwise new to the working world, *good for you* if you want to get on the right investing road now! Regardless of your age, though, remember that it's never too late. Just get started.

Starting from square one: Melinda

Melinda is in her 20s, works as an architect, earns decent money, lives in New Jersey, and has no debt and no savings yet because she just started her first job. Financially speaking, she's a blank slate, but because she made a New Year's resolution to get her finances in order, she wants to do something.

Her employer offers her health and disability insurance and a profit-sharing retirement plan, which only her firm may contribute to, but to which small contributions have been made in the past. She wants to invest in mutual funds but doesn't want hassle in either paperwork or complications on an ongoing basis.

On a monthly basis, she figures that she can save $600. She wants to invest for growth. With her money earmarked for long-term future needs, such as retirement, she sees no need to invest conservatively (even though she does want some of her investments more conservatively invested). She's in the 28 percent federal tax bracket now, but as her experience in her field increases, she expects to earn more.

Recommendations: Melinda should consider investing $5,000 annually in a Roth IRA (see Chapter 3). In her case, a regular IRA contribution won't be tax deductible because her employer offers a retirement plan under which she's considered covered and because she earns more than is allowed to make a tax-deductible contribution to a regular IRA.

Melinda could invest in a fund of funds, such as Vanguard LifeStrategy Growth, Fidelity Freedom 2050, or T. Rowe Price Spectrum Growth (all covered in Chapter 13), which all offer the simplicity of one-stop shopping and reduced annual account fees.

Like everyone else, Melinda should have an emergency source of cash. Although the mutual funds that she's investing in outside her retirement account are liquid and can be sold any day, she runs a risk that an unexpected emergency could force her to sell when the markets are hung over.

With family to borrow from if needed, she could make do with, say, a cushion equal to three months' living expenses. She could even postpone building an emergency fund until after she funds her IRA. (Normally, I'd recommend establishing the emergency fund first, but because she has family she can borrow from, I believe that it's okay to go for the long-term tax benefits of funding the IRA account.) Because she won't keep a large emergency balance, she could keep her emergency fund in her local bank account, especially if the balance helps keep her checking account fees down. Given her current tax bracket, if Melinda wanted a money market mutual fund, she could invest in a taxable fund, such as Fidelity Cash Reserves or others described in Chapter 11.

For longer term growth, Melinda could invest her monthly savings as follows:

> 60–70 percent in Vanguard Total Stock Market Index

> 30–40 percent in Vanguard Total International Stock Index

(These funds are reasonably tax friendly, which is important because she's investing outside a retirement account and is in a reasonably high tax bracket.)

These funds generally make low taxable distributions and make especially low distributions, such as short-term capital gains, that are highly taxed. They require a $3,000 minimum initial investment, so Melinda needs to save the minimum before she can invest. After the minimum is met and invested in each fund, she can have money deducted electronically from her checking account and invested in these mutual funds.

Silencing student loans: Stacey the student

Stacey is a 25-year-old graduate student in psychology with three years to go before she gets her well-deserved degree. She's hoping that all this education will fetch her a solid income when she finally gets out of school.

Her current income amounts to about $19,000 per year. She's also sitting under $25,000 of student debt from her undergraduate days. Both of her loans are in deferment, so she's not obligated to make payments until she finishes graduate school: One is incurring interest at 7 percent per year; the other is subsidized (the government is paying the interest until she gets out of school).

Fortunately, Stacey has the starving-student-thing down cold. She's so savvy at living cheap that despite her low income she has an extra $150 to play with at the end of every month. (Stacey has an emergency reserve already in place.)

Stacey wants to be debt-free sooner, so her first instinct is to use that money to start paying down those student loans. But Stacey is also excited about investing for her future. Because half of her student loan interest is subsidized, she's wondering if she'd come out ahead by using her extra money to open and invest in an IRA account.

Recommendations: Stacey should be proud of herself. Living below her means on such a small income, as well as thinking about her financial future, is commendable. She's asking good questions. Her decision comes down to a comparison of the student loan interest rate to the potential return of her IRA investments. Because she'll be investing for retirement, which is decades away for a 25-year-old, Stacey's time horizon is long enough to focus largely or almost entirely on stocks. As I discuss in Chapter 1, stocks historically have returned about 9 to 10 percent per year. Measured against the 7 percent interest she's paying on her unsubsidized student loan, Stacey can perhaps come out a little ahead by holding off on student loan payments and investing in stocks through an IRA account. (She can deduct up to $2,500 per year in student loan interest on her tax return; her investment returns would ultimately be taxed).

I say that it's really Stacey's call as to which option — paying down the 7 interest student loan or investing in good stock mutual funds through an IRA — makes her feel more comfortable. Financially, the choice is a tossup. It's worth noting, however, that the annual savings of 7 percent that comes from paying down the student loan is *a sure thing,* whereas the stock market annual average returns of 9 to 10 percent are an expectation and in no way guaranteed. For this reason, I'd be inclined to pay down the student loans at 7 percent.

Getting started with just $50 per month

Although most mutual funds' minimum initial investment amount of a couple of thousand dollars is quite small compared to that of private money managers, who have six-figure to several-million-dollar entrance requirements, the amount may still loom large if you're just starting to save and invest. You want to get on with the program, and you don't want to risk giving in to the temptation to spend your savings if they're sitting around in your bank account until you can save enough for high-fund minimums.

Here's a way around the problem. Some fund companies (for example, TIAA-CREF and T. Rowe Price) allow you to invest in their funds without meeting the minimum initial investment

requirements as long as you enroll in an automatic investment program. You can do the trick with these by having a small amount per month deducted from your bank account and sent electronically to the fund company. Call the fund family's toll-free number to see if it offers an automatic investment plan for a fund you're interested in.

Also remember that fund retirement account minimums are significantly lower — often as low as $50 per month, some even less. A final strategy is to save for several months until you have enough for some of the funds recommended in Chapters 11, 12, and 13 that have lower minimums.

If Stacey decides to go the IRA route, because she has such a long time horizon, her fund(s) should focus almost entirely on stocks. Ideally, her fund(s) should be diversified across large-, medium-, and small-company stocks as well as international investments. Stacey's situation is ideally suited for a fund of funds (such as the ones I recommend to Melinda in the preceding section). Alternatively, if she wants to get going with investing $150 per month and not wait to save enough to meet a fund's minimum, she could invest monthly in an automatic investment plan (AIP) through a company such as TIAA-CREF or T. Rowe Price that waives fund minimums if you sign up for an AIP (see the sidebar "Getting started with just $50 per month").

Living month to month with debt: Mobile Mark

Mark is a 42-year-old renter who says that he has no desire to own a home. He doesn't want the feeling of being tied down in case he ever wants to move — something he's done a lot of over the years. Currently, he lives in California. Feeling that he's hitting middle age, Mark wants to start socking away money regularly into investments. He has a large folder filled with mutual fund ads and prospectuses but finds most of the material confusing and intimidating. He has about $5,000 in a bank IRA invested in a certificate of deposit.

Mark feels insecure living month to month and being so dependent on his paycheck. One of the reasons he's feeling some financial pressure is that, in addition to his monthly rent, he has an auto loan payment of about $300 per month and total credit card debt of $6,000. He also doesn't have any family he can depend on for money in an emergency.

Recommendations: Although Mark has the best of intentions, he's a good example of someone who's managed to get his financial priorities *out* of order. Mark's best and most appropriate investment now is to pay off his credit card and auto loan debt and forget about fund investing for a while. These debts have interest rates of 10 to 15 percent, and paying them off is actually his best investment.

Like millions of others, Mark got into these debts because credit is so easily available and encouraged in our society. Such easy access to borrowing has encouraged Mark to spend more than he's been earning. Thus, one of the first things he should do is figure just where his money goes in a typical month. By using his credit card statement, checkbook register, and memory of items he's bought with cash, Mark can determine how much he's spending on food, clothing, transportation, and so on. He needs to make some tough decisions about which expenditures he'll cut so that he can pay off his debts.

Like Melinda (the 20-something architect in the first example), Mark should also build an emergency reserve. If he ever loses his job, becomes disabled, or whatever, he'd be in real financial trouble. Mark has no family to help him in a financial pinch, and he's close to the limits of debt allowed on his credit cards. Because he often draws his checking account balance down to a few hundred dollars when he pays his monthly bills, building up his reserve in his checking or savings account to minimize monthly service charges makes the most sense for him now. Recently, Mark eliminated about $100 per year in service charges by switching to a bank that waives these fees if he direct deposits his paycheck.

By mainly going on a strict financial program — which included sacrifices such as dumping his expensive new car and moving so that he could walk or bike to work — within three years, Mark became debt-free and accumulated several thousand dollars in his local bank. Now he's ready to invest in mutual funds.

Because his employer offers no retirement savings programs, Mark should annually contribute $5,000 to an individual retirement account (IRA). Mark doesn't want investments that can get clobbered: He thinks that he's been late to the saving game and doesn't want to add insult to injury by losing his shirt in his first investments. Being a conservative sort, Mark thinks that Vanguard makes sense for him. For his IRA, he can divide his money between a hybrid fund, such as Vanguard Wellington (70 percent), and an international stock fund, such as Vanguard International Growth (30 percent). In addition to his new $5,000 contribution, Mark also should transfer his $5,000 bank CD IRA into these funds. In the event that he isn't eligible for a tax deduction on a regular IRA, he should definitely fund a Roth IRA.

Now debt-free, Mark thinks that he can invest about $400 per month in addition to his annual IRA contribution. His income is moderate, so he's in the 28 percent federal tax bracket. He wants diversification, but he doesn't have a lot of money to start his investing program. He has set up an automatic investment plan whereby each month the $400 is invested in the T. Rowe Price Personal Strategy Balanced or T. Rowe Price Retirement 2035 ($50 per month minimum with an automatic investment plan).

Competing goals: Gina and George

George works as a software engineer, and his wife Gina works as a paralegal. They live in Virginia, are in their 30s, and have about $20,000 in a savings account, to which they currently add about $1,000 per month. This money is tentatively earmarked for a home purchase that they expect to make in the next few years. They figure they need a total of $40,000 for a down payment and closing costs; they're in no hurry to buy because they plan to relocate after they have children in order to be closer to family. (The allure of free baby-sitting is just too powerful a draw!)

Justifiably, they're pleased with their ability to save money — but they're also disappointed with themselves for leaving so much money earning so little interest in a bank. They figure that they need to be serious about investments because they want to retire by age 60, and they recognize that kids cost money.

George's company, although growing rapidly, doesn't offer a pension plan. In fact, the only benefits his company does offer are health insurance and a 401(k) plan that George isn't contributing to because plan participants can't borrow against their balances. Gina's employer offers health insurance, $50,000 of life insurance, and disability insurance — but, like George's employer, Gina's employer doesn't offer a retirement savings plan.

Recommendations: Deciding between saving for a home or funding a retirement account and immediately reducing one's taxes is often a difficult choice. In George and Gina's case, however, they can and should do some of both. At a minimum, George can save 10 percent of his income in his company's 401(k) plan. Wanting to be somewhat aggressive and considering his age, George could invest about 80 percent in stock funds with the balance in bonds among his 401(k) plan's mutual fund investment options.

Here are his 401(k) plan options and how he should invest:

0 percent in the money market fund option

20 percent in Vanguard Total Bond Market Index

20 percent in Fidelity Contrafund

25 percent in Dodge & Cox Stock

35 percent in Oakmark International

0 percent in a so-called guaranteed investment contract (GIC) that isn't a mutual fund but a fixed-return insurance contract (see the sidebar on "Investing money in company-sponsored retirement plans" for a discussion of these investment options)

If George contributes the maximum amount through his employer's 401(k) and he and Gina still want to invest more in retirement accounts, they can invest $5,000 each, per year, into an IRA.

Gina shouldn't worry that, if she and George divorce, George would get all the money in his 401(k) plan. As with nonretirement account assets, these assets can be split between a divorcing husband and wife. A more significant concern would occur if, say, George is an isolated dunce and refuses to talk to Gina about the investment of this money for their retirement and makes some not-so-smart moves, such as frequently jumping from one fund to another. (Try discussing this issue with your spouse. If you don't get anywhere with your spouse, pay a visit to your local marriage counselor.)

What about their $20,000 that's sitting in a bank savings account? They should move it, especially because George is a fan of USAA, having benefited from their terrific insurance programs as a member of a military family. Initially, he and Gina can establish a tax-free money market fund, such as the USAA VA Money Market fund, as an emergency reserve.

Because they don't plan to need the down payment money for the home for another three to five years, they can invest some of their savings — perhaps as much as half — in the USAA Tax-Exempt Intermediate-Term Bond fund. Even though they'll pick up a little more yield, they need to know that the bond fund share price declines if interest rates rise. (For that weighty subject, see Chapter 12.)

George should get some disability insurance to protect his income. (It turns out that his employer offers a cost-effective group coverage plan.) Before Gina becomes pregnant, George and Gina should also purchase some term life insurance.

Investing money in company-sponsored retirement plans

In some company-sponsored plans, such as 401(k)s, you're limited to the predetermined investment options your employer offers. In most plans, the mutual funds are decent and make you happy that you didn't have to do the research. Plans differ in the specific options they offer, but these basic choices are common:

✔ **Money market funds:** These funds offer safety of principal because they don't fluctuate in value. But you run the risk that your investment won't keep up with or stay ahead of inflation and taxes (which are due upon withdrawal of your money from the retirement account). *In most cases, skip this option.*

If you use the borrowing feature that some retirement plans allow, you may need to keep money in the money market investment option. For regular contributions coming out of your paycheck, money funds make little sense.

✔ **Bond mutual funds:** This option pays higher yields than money funds but carries greater risk because the value can fall if interest rates increase. However, bonds tend to be more stable in value than stocks. Aggressive, younger investors should keep a minimum amount of money in these funds, whereas older folks who want to invest more conservatively may want to invest more money this way.

✔ **Guaranteed-investment contracts (GICs):** Backed by an insurance company that typically quotes you an interest rate a little lower than on bond funds, GICs have no volatility (that you can see). The insurance company, however, normally invests your money mostly in bonds and a bit in stocks. GICs are generally better than keeping your retirement money in a money market

or savings account, both of which usually pay a couple of percent less in yield (see Chapter 11).

✔ **Balanced mutual funds:** Invest in a mixture primarily of stocks and bonds. This one-stop shopping concept makes investing easier and smoothes out fluctuations in the value of your investments — funds investing exclusively in stocks or bonds make for a rougher ride. These funds are solid options and can be used for the majority of your retirement plan contributions.

✔ **Stock mutual funds:** Invest in stocks, which usually provide greater long-term growth potential but also wider fluctuations in value from year to year. Some companies offer a number of different stock funds, including those investing overseas. Unless you plan to borrow (if your plan allows) against your funds — for example, for a home purchase — you probably should have a healthy helping of stock funds.

✔ **Employee Stock Ownership Plans (ESOPs):** Offer employees the option of investing in their company's stock (not all companies make these plans available). Generally, I'd avoid this option because your future income and other employee benefits are already riding on the company's success. If the company hits the skids, you may lose your job and your benefits. You certainly don't want the value of your retirement account to depend on the same factors. If you expect your company to conquer the competition, though, investing a portion of your retirement account is fine if you're a risk-seeking sort — but no more than 25 percent. If you can buy the stock at a discount compared to its current market value, that's so much the better.

If George and Gina had little or no money saved and couldn't save for both the home and get the tax benefits of their retirement account contributions, they'd have a tougher choice. They should make their decision based on how important the home purchase is to them. Doing some of both (saving for the home and in the retirement accounts) is good, but the option of not using the retirement account and putting all their savings into the home down payment "account" is fine, too.

Wanting lots and lotsa money: Pat and Chris

Pat and Chris earn good money, are in their 40s, and live in South Dakota. Pat is self-employed and wants to sock away as much as possible in a retirement savings plan. He figures that he can invest at least 10 percent of his income. Chris works for the government, which offers a retirement plan with the following options: a money market fund, a government (big surprise!) bond fund, and a stock fund that invests in large-company U.S. stocks only.

Pat and Chris want diversification and are willing to invest aggressively. They want convenience, and they're willing to pay for it. In addition to Pat's retirement plan, they want and are able to save additional money to invest for other purposes, such as Chris's dreams of buying a small business and investing in real estate. They currently own a home that has a mortgage that could easily be supported by one of their incomes. Neither depends on the other's income.

Pat also has an $8,000 IRA account, which is currently divided between a Class B growth stock fund and a Class A total return bond fund (both load funds). Pat hasn't contributed to the IRA for six years now. He also owns a universal life insurance plan, which he bought from the same broker who sold him the load mutual funds. He bought the life insurance plan five years ago when he no longer could make tax-deductible contributions to his IRA; the life insurance plan is better than an IRA, according to Pat's broker, because he can borrow from it. The broker told Pat last week that his life insurance plan is "paid up" (he need not put any more money into the plan to pay for the $20,000 of life insurance coverage) and has a cash value of $3,300, although he'd lose $1,200 (due to surrender charges) if he cashed it in now.

Recommendations: First, Pat should get rid of his load mutual funds and his current broker. The broker has sold Pat crummy mutual funds. The funds have high fees and dismal performance relative to their peers. He could transfer his fund monies into something like Vanguard Star.

Pat doesn't need life insurance because no one depends on Pat's income. Besides, it's a lousy investment. (For the compelling reasons why you're better off not using life insurance for investing, see Chapter 1.) Pat should dump the life insurance and either take the proceeds or roll them over into a variable annuity (which I explain later in this chapter).

Pat can establish a Keogh retirement savings plan and stash away up to 20 percent of his net self-employment income per year (See Chapter 3 for more on Keoghs). He could establish his Keogh plan through a discount brokerage account that offers him access to a variety of funds from many firms. Over the years, he could divide up his Keogh money as follows:

15 percent in Dodge & Cox Income or Harbor Bond

15 percent in Vanguard Total Bond Market Index

10 percent in Vanguard Total Stock Market Index

10 percent in Fairholme

20 percent in T. Rowe Price Spectrum Growth

15 percent in Oakmark Global

15 percent in Vanguard Total International Stock Index

Because Chris doesn't have international stock funds as an investment option, Pat can invest more in these than he normally should if he were investing on his own. In Chris's retirement plan, contributions could be allocated this way: approximately one-third into the bond fund and the remainder in the stock fund.

As for accumulating money for Chris to purchase a small business or to invest in real estate, Pat and Chris should establish a tax-free money market fund, such as the Vanguard Tax-Exempt Money Market fund, for this purpose. As could George and Gina earlier in this chapter, Pat and Chris can invest in a short- to intermediate-term tax-free bond fund if they anticipate not using this money for at least several years and want potential higher returns.

Changing Goals and Starting Over

Life changes, so your investing needs may change as well. If you have existing investments, some may no longer make sense for your present situation. Perhaps your investment mix is too conservative, too aggressive, too taxing, or too cumbersome given your new responsibilities. Or maybe you've been through a major life change that's causing you to reevaluate or begin to take charge of your investments. The following sections offer some examples sure to stimulate your thinking about an investing makeover.

Funding education: The Waltons

One of the biggest life changes that makes many adults think more about investing is the arrival of a child or two. And after contemplating all the fear-mongering ads and articles about how they're going to need a gazillion dollars to send their little bundles of joy off to college in 18 years, many a parent goes about investing in the wrong way.

The Waltons — Bill, 42, and Carol, 41, along with their two children, Ted, 3, and Alice, 5 — live in the suburbs of Chicago in a home with a white picket fence and a dog and cat. They own a home with a mortgage of $150,000 outstanding. Their household income is modest because they both teach.

The Waltons have $40,000 in five individual securities in a brokerage account they inherited two years ago. They also have $20,000 in two of that same brokerage firm's limited partnerships, now worth less than half of what they paid for them years ago. Bill and Carol prefer safer investments that don't fluctuate violently in value.

They have $25,000 invested in IRAs within a load domestic stock fund and $10,000 in a load foreign stock fund outside an IRA. Bill hasn't been pleased with the foreign fund, and Carol is concerned about supporting foreign countries when so many Americans are without jobs. Both of them like conservative, easy-to-understand investments and hate paperwork. They also have $10,000 apiece in custodial accounts for each of the kids, which Bill's dad has contributed for their educational expenses. Bill's dad wants to continue contributing money for the kids' college expenses.

Bill just took a new job with a university that offers a 403(b) retirement savings plan, which he can get with many of the major mutual fund companies. He wasn't saving through his old employer's 403(b) plan because, with the kids, they spend all their incomes. Carol's employer doesn't have a retirement savings plan.

Recommendations: First, Bill should be taking advantage of his employer's 403(b) plan. Though he may *think* that he can't afford to, he really can. If need be, he should dump the individual securities and use that money to help meet living expenses while he has money deducted from his paycheck for the tax-deductible 403(b) account. (Always consider the tax consequences if you consider selling securities held outside of a retirement account. In the Waltons' case, these securities have only been held for a couple of years and were worth approximately the amount of their tax cost basis — see Chapter 18 for more on tax basis.)

TIAA-CREF would be a fine choice for Bill's 403(b). He could allocate his money as follows:

100 percent in Fidelity Freedom 2030 or Fidelity Freedom 2035 (fund of funds)

or

100 percent in Vanguard LifeStrategy Moderate Growth (fund of funds)

Bill and Carol could hold onto their load domestic stock fund investment that they have in their IRAs: This fund has a solid track record and reasonable annual fees of 0.7 percent. Its only drawback is its sales load of 5.75 percent, which is water under the bridge for Bill and Carol because it was deducted when they first bought this fund.

Their foreign stock fund isn't a good fund and has high ongoing management fees. They should dump this fund and invest the proceeds in some better and more diversified international stock funds, such as those in Chapter 13. And regarding Carol's concerns about supporting foreign companies, many companies today have operations worldwide. If she's strongly against investing overseas, I suppose that she can choose not to invest her IRA money overseas, but her portfolio will likely be more volatile and less profitable in the long run. Foreign stocks don't always move in lock step with domestic ones, and some foreign economies are growing at a faster rate than our economy.

Regarding custodial accounts, Bill and Carol need to remember that the amount of financial aid their kids will qualify for decreases as more money is saved in the children's names. Bill's dad should hold on to the money himself or give it to Bill and Carol. (This latter option has the added benefit of increasing Bill's ability to fund his 403(b) account and take advantage of the tax breaks it offers.) Bill and Carol (and you as well, if you have children) should read Chapter 3, which has important information you should know before you invest in funds for college.

The limited partnerships are bad news. Bill and Carol should wait them out until they're liquidated and then transfer the money into some good no-load mutual funds.

Rolling over (but not playing dead): Cathy

It's a surprise to her as much as it is to her friends and family: Cathy has a new job. Although she was happily employed for many years with a respected software company, she got smitten with the entrepreneurial bug and signed on with a well-funded start-up software company. Her 401(k) plan investment of about $100,000 is invested in the stock of her previous employer. The company is waiting for Cathy's instructions for dealing with the money. It's been nine months since she got sucked into the vortex of the insane hours of a start-up company.

Nearing 40, tired but invigorated from those long days at her new company, Cathy has resolved to make some decisions about where to invest this money. She's comfortable investing the money fairly quickly after she thinks she has a plan. Cathy wants to invest somewhat aggressively: Although she enjoys working hard, she happily imagines a time when she doesn't need to work at all. She likes the idea of diversifying her investments across a few different fund families. She also wants to minimize her paperwork by setting up as few accounts as possible while at the same time minimizing transaction fees.

Recommendations: Cathy should sell her stock through her old employer and transfer cash. This sale will save on brokerage commissions. Having her retirement money in one company's stock like this is risky.

For the best of both worlds, Cathy can establish an IRA through Vanguard's brokerage divisions, which would give her access to all the great Vanguard funds, plus access for a small fee to non-Vanguard funds. She could invest the money as follows:

> 20 percent in Vanguard Total Bond Market Index
>
> 30 percent in Vanguard Total Stock Market Index
>
> 10 percent in Vanguard Selected Value or Fairholme or Sequoia
>
> 10 percent in Primecap Odyssey Growth
>
> 10 percent in Oakmark Global or Tweedy Browne Global Value
>
> 10 percent in Vanguard Total International Stock Index
>
> 10 percent in Masters' Select International or Dodge & Cox International

Wishing for higher interest rates: Nell, the near retiree

Nell is a social worker. Now 59 and single, she wants to plan for a comfortable retirement. In addition to owning her home without a mortgage, she has $225,000 currently invested as follows:

> $60,000 in a bank money market account
>
> $110,000 in Treasury bills that mature this month
>
> $55,000 in an insurance annuity that's invested in a "guaranteed investment contract" through her employer's nonprofit retirement savings 403(b) plan

Nell currently earns $40,000 per year and has received pay increases over the years that keep pace with inflation. She has $300 per month deducted from her paycheck for the annuity plan. Her employer allows investments in the retirement plan through almost any insurance company or mutual fund company she chooses. She's also saving about $800 per month in her bank account. She hates to waste money on anything, and she doesn't mind some paperwork.

Nell is concerned about outliving her money; she doesn't plan to work past age 65. She's terrified of investments that can decrease in value, and she knows a friend who lost thousands of dollars in the stock market. She says that her CDs and Treasuries were terrific in the 1980s when she was earning 10 percent or more on her money. She's concerned now, though. She keeps reading and hearing that many large, reputable companies are laying off thousands of workers, but the stock market seems to be once again rising to high levels. She wishes that interest rates would rise again.

Recommendations: First, Nell should stop wishing for higher interest rates. Interest rates are primarily driven by inflation, and high inflation erodes the purchasing power of one's money (see Chapter 12). The problem here is that Nell's portfolio is poorly diversified. All her money is in fixed-income (lending) investments that offer no real potential for growth and no real protection against further increases in the cost of living.

Even though she's planning to retire in six years, she's certainly not going to use or need all of her savings in the first few years of retirement. She won't use some of her money until her 70s and 80s. Thus, she should invest some money in investments that have growth potential.

Nell also could and should invest more through her employer's retirement savings plan because she's saving so much outside that plan and already has a large emergency reserve. In fact, she should invest the maximum amount allowed under her employer's plan: 20 percent of her salary. She also can do better to invest in no-load funds for her 403(b) plan instead of through an insurance annuity, which carries higher fees. Vanguard and its hybrid funds (which are far less volatile because they invest in many different types of securities) are logical choices for her to use for her 403(b). I'd recommend the following investment mix for Nell's 403(b):

> 25 percent in Vanguard Wellesley Income
>
> 25 percent in Vanguard Star
>
> 25 percent in Vanguard Wellington
>
> 25 percent in Vanguard LifeStrategy Moderate Growth

In addition to putting future money into these mutual funds, Nell should also decide whether she wants to transfer her existing annuity money into these funds as well. First, she should check her annuity account statement to see whether the insurance company would assess a penalty for transferring her balance. (Many insurance companies charge these penalties to make up for the commissions they have to pay to insurance agents for selling the annuities.)

If the penalty is high, she might delay the transfer a few years: These penalties tend to dissipate over time (because the insurer has use of your money long enough to compensate for the agent's commission). If, however, the annuity is a subpar performer (a likelihood, given its high fees), she may want to go ahead with the transfer despite a current penalty. (See Chapter 16 for how to do proper transfers.)

With the $170,000 in money outside of her retirement accounts, Nell can gradually invest (perhaps once per quarter over two years) a good portion of this money into a mix of funds that, overall, is more conservative than the mix she's using for her 403(b). She can be more conservative because she'd likely tap the nonretirement money first in the future. She should reserve $25,000 in Vanguard's U.S. Treasury money market fund, which pays more than her bank account. Nell wants to have her emergency reserve in an investment that's government backed.

Nell can use taxable funds for the other $145,000 because

- ✔ She's in a low-to-moderate tax bracket.
- ✔ She's nearing retirement.
- ✔ Investing solely in tax-friendly funds wouldn't meet her needs. (The stock funds would have to be growth oriented — increasing the risk beyond Nell's comfort level.)

I recommend that she invest the money as follows:

25 percent in Vanguard Total Bond Market Index

20 percent in Vanguard Wellington

25 percent in Fidelity Freedom 2020

20 percent in T. Rowe Price Retirement 2020

10 percent in Fidelity Puritan

If you're older than Nell, you can use a similar but more conservative mix of funds. For example, if you're in your 70s, for the 403(b), you could substitute the Vanguard LifeStrategy Income fund in place of the LifeStrategy Moderate Growth fund and invest 40 percent in that fund and 20 percent each in the other three funds (Wellesley Income, Star, and Wellington). For the nonretirement money, you could shift the Fidelity Puritan money to the Vanguard Total Bond Market Index fund.

Lovin' retirement: Noel and Patricia

Noel and Patricia, both age 65, are retired, healthy, and enjoying their long days unfettered by the obligations of work. They take long road trips together to pursue their hobbies. Noel is an avid fisherman, and Patricia is a wildlife photographer.

Together, they want about $4,500 per month to live on. Social Security provides $2,000 per month, and Noel's pension plan kicks in another $1,500 per month. That leaves an extra $1,000 per month that must come from their $400,000 nest egg, currently comprised of

$260,000 in bank CDs

$40,000 in a money market

$100,000 in IRAs, most of it in hybrid funds and bonds

They are in a low tax bracket.

Noel and Patricia have an outstanding $50,000 mortgage at 7 percent interest.

Recommendations: A good portfolio for a retiree must not only provide an income for today's expenses but also protect income for the years down the road. Noel and Patricia are managing to get by on the current income from their investments. However, with only 10 percent of their nest egg invested for growth in stocks, they've left themselves quite exposed to the ravages of inflation. Their retirement could easily last another 25+ years. Unless they allocate their assets more aggressively, their nest egg may not last that long.

They can accomplish all their goals if they're able to boost their portfolio's total average annual returns from 6 percent to 8 percent. (You have to crunch some numbers to figure out where you stand in terms of retirement planning; see Chapter 3.) Averaging 8 percent annual returns shouldn't prove difficult; Noel and Patricia can boost their stock allocation to about 50 percent.

First, however, when the CDs mature, Noel and Patricia should go ahead and pay off the remaining $50,000 of their mortgage. Even if they invested a bigger portion of their portfolio in potentially higher returning investments such as stocks, they can't easily expect to get an overall return that much better than 7 percent, the interest rate they're currently paying on the mortgage. True, the tax deductibility of mortgage interest effectively reduces that interest rate a bit, but don't forget that they must pay income tax on investment dividends and profits as well as on retirement account withdrawals, which effectively reduces the rate of return on their investments.

The dreaded d's: Downsizing, divorce, disability, and death

Life isn't always what we hope it'll be. Sometimes it changes suddenly. You lose your job, your health, or a loved one. Everyone reacts differently to these events. Some maintain a balanced and positive perspective. Others get depressed, panic, and make rash decisions. If you're making financial decisions that you haven't had to make before, you owe it to yourself to be educated about your options and the pros and cons of each. Be especially careful about hiring financial help because you're in danger of being too dependent and blindly following advice.

The only step you should rush to take is to raise an emergency reserve if you need one. Be careful about selling investments that show a profit, which could boost your tax bill. In one case, a client I had just started working with got laid off. From his perspective, the layoff came out of nowhere; it was a complete shock. He was married, and he and his wife were raising their two children. They were heavily in debt, having stretched to buy the most expensive home they could afford and having leased two expensive cars. They had decent savings, but all their money was in the stock market. Luckily for them, this scenario occurred when the market was doing well. His first move was to sell some of their stock to raise cash to tide them over if finding a job took a while. This move made sense and was all that he needed to do immediately. The rest of their investments could be left alone.

As evidenced by their current investment choices, Noel and Patricia are conservative, safety-minded investors. And although they could be more aggressive, Noel and Patricia can't be too aggressive, given their ages. Thus, paying off their mortgage, which carries a 7 percent interest rate, makes good sense. In addition to the psychological satisfaction of owning their home free and clear, by eliminating their monthly mortgage payment, Noel and Patricia will reduce their cost of living, taking pressure off their need to generate as much current investment income.

They can also afford to move quite a bit of money out of their money market fund into better yielding bond funds; $9,000 in the money market, enough to cover six months of expenses together with their Social Security and pension checks, is plenty.

So, after paying off the mortgage and withdrawing cash from the money market, they'll have $241,000 to invest in funds in a nonretirement account. They could invest it as follows:

    20 percent in Dodge & Cox Income or Vanguard Total Bond Market Index

    20 percent in Vanguard Wellesley

    20 percent in T. Rowe Price Balanced

    40 percent in Vanguard LifeStrategy Conservative Growth

Noel and Patricia need about $1,000 per month from this money, which works out to $12,000 per year on $241,000 invested in nonretirement accounts and $100,000 invested in IRAs. To get $12,000 per year from $341,000, those investments would need to produce an income of about 3.5 percent per year. The preceding mix of funds recently yielded about 3 percent, so they would need to use a small amount of principal to reach their annual income goal. For more details about how to plan retirement withdrawals to make your money last, please see my newly coauthored book, *Personal Finance for Seniors For Dummies* (Wiley).

With their IRAs, they could keep their financial affairs really simple and use a fund of funds, such as Vanguard's LifeStrategy Moderate Growth.

Dealing with a Mountain of Moola

Sometimes the financial forces are with you, and money *pours* your way. Hopefully, this windfall happens for good reasons instead of due to a negative event. Regardless, a pile of money may overwhelm you. The good news is that a lump sum gives you more financial options. The following sections describe the ways a couple of people handled their sudden wealth.

He's in the money: Cash-rich Chuck

Chuck is a successful Pennsylvania entrepreneur in his late 30s. Starting from scratch, he opened a restaurant eight years ago. Today, he's reaping the fruits of his labor. After several relocations and remodels, Chuck has built himself quite an operation, with 40 employees on the payroll. It's difficult for him to believe, but his restaurant's profit is now running at around $500,000 per year. Not surprisingly, money has been piling up at a fast rate. He now has about $800,000 resting in his business bank checking account paying next to no interest.

He owns a home with a mortgage of about $250,000 but has no money in retirement savings plans. Chuck doesn't want to set up a retirement savings plan at his company because he'd have to make contributions for all of his employees in a plan such as an SEP-IRA or a Keogh (which I cover in Chapter 3).

Chuck has been planning to open another location. He figures that a second location will cost around $400,000, but, as he says, "You just never know with construction work what the total tab may be." He considers himself a conservative investor.

Recommendations: The first thing Chuck should do is get his pile of money out of the bank and into a safer investment. Bank accounts are federally insured only up to $250,000 — so if his bank fails (and banks have and will continue to fail), he'll have a lot to cry over. Besides, money market funds pay much better interest than his checking account does.

Chuck has several options for investing his excess money. The first is to pay for the cost of a second location: With his savings, he can likely buy a second location with cash. But he faces a couple of drawbacks to using too much or all of his cash on a second location:

- ✔ **The issue of liquidity:** You can't write checks on a piece of real estate (unless you establish a home equity line of credit).

- ✔ **The issue of diversification:** If he doesn't use all his savings on a second location, he can invest in things other than his business.

Another option for Chuck is to pay off his home mortgage. Yes, he gets a decent tax deduction for his mortgage interest on Schedule A of his Form 1040 — although some of the tax write-off is lost because of his high income. However, because Chuck has all this extra cash, paying off the mortgage saves interest dollars. That would leave $550,000 in his money fund.

If he paid down his mortgage and didn't want to pay all cash for his second restaurant location, he could take out a business loan. However, that loan would likely be at a higher interest rate than the rate he pays on a mortgage for his home (because banks consider small-business loans riskier). Because some of the home mortgage interest isn't tax-deductible, the options are close to a financial wash in Chuck's case. So he could pay off the mortgage and perhaps use some of his remaining money to pay for part of the second location, and the rest could be financed with a business loan.

He should keep a good cushion — say, around $200,000 — for operating purposes for his business. (A bank line of credit may be useful to line up as well). Some entrepreneurs, including those who've gone on to achieve great success, have violated these principles — and more — by not only pouring all their savings into their business but also by borrowing heavily. I say: To each his own. There's nothing wrong with going for it if you're willing and able to accept the financial consequences. However, if the going gets tough and you don't have a safety net (such as family members who could help with a small short-term loan), you could get wiped out.

Because Chuck uses his current bank account for keeping his excess cash as well as for check writing, he could establish a tax-free money market fund with check-writing privileges. Some brokerage accounts, such as those offered by discount brokers (such as Fidelity, Vanguard, and TD Ameritrade), offer unlimited check writing. (See Chapter 11 for more on money funds.) Beyond the money market fund, Chuck could begin to invest some money ($100,000 to $200,000) in reasonably tax-friendly mutual funds through Vanguard:

20 percent in Vanguard PA Long-Term Tax-Exempt

35 percent in Vanguard Tax-Managed Capital Appreciation

15 percent in Vanguard Tax-Managed Small-Cap

15 percent in Vanguard Tax-Managed International

15 percent in Vanguard Total International Stock Index

In place of the previously mentioned stock funds, Chuck could use some exchange-traded funds (ETFs). For example, in place of the two domestic stock funds, he could invest in Vanguard's Total Stock Market ETF. In place of the foreign stock funds, he could use Vanguard's FTSE All-World ex-U.S. ETF.

Inheritances: Loaded Liz

About a year ago, Liz, who's in her 40s, received a significant inheritance. She received about $600,000; $150,000 of this sum was a portfolio of individual large-company, higher yielding stocks, and the balance came as cash. The stock portfolio is being managed by an out-of-state adviser, who charges 1.5 percent per year as an advisory fee and places trades through a brokerage firm. Despite the fact that the portfolio usually has only about eight stocks in it, trade confirmations come in about once per month.

Liz currently is a college professor and makes about $50,000 per year. She has approximately $40,000 invested in the TIAA-CREF retirement plan, with 80 percent in the plan's bond fund and 20 percent in its stock fund. She's saving and investing about $400 per month in the plan because that's the amount she can afford. Liz also has $110,000 in a bank IRA CD that will mature soon.

Liz currently owns a home and is happy with it. It has a mortgage of about $90,000 at a fixed rate of 7 percent. She wants to retire early, perhaps before age 60, so that she can travel and see the world. She's wary of risk and gets queasy over volatile investments, but she's open to different types of funds. She likes to use many different companies but doesn't want the headache of a ton of paperwork. Liz prefers doing business over the phone and through the mail because she's too busy to go to an office.

Recommendations: First, Liz should maximize her retirement contributions even though she thinks that she's saving all that she can afford. She has all this extra money now that she could draw upon and use to supplement her reduced take-home pay if maximizing her retirement contributions doesn't leave enough to live on.

This extra cash also affords Liz another good move — getting rid of the mortgage. It's costing her 7 percent interest pre-tax (around 5 percent after tax write-offs), and she'd have to take a fair amount of risk with her investments to better this rate of return.

Liz also needs to invest her money more aggressively, particularly inside her retirement accounts. All of her IRA and 80 percent of her employer's retirement plan money are in fixed-income investments. In the TIAA-CREF plan, she can invest 30 percent in the bond fund, 40 percent in its stock fund, and 30 percent in its global equities fund.

She could transfer her IRA account to a discount broker and invest it as follows:

40 percent in Vanguard Star

20 percent in Fidelity Freedom 2030

20 percent in T. Rowe Price Spectrum Growth

10 percent in Vanguard Total Stock Market Index or ETF

10 percent in Dodge & Cox International or Masters' Select International

After paying down the mortgage and keeping an emergency reserve of $40,000, as well as another $70,000 for remodeling, Liz would have $250,000 in cash plus the stocks. She should sell the stocks because their dividend income is taxable and she's paying 1.5 percent per year (plus commissions) to have her account managed. The account has underperformed the S & P 500 by an average of 3 percent per year over the past five years. She could transfer these shares to Vanguard's discount brokerage division and then sell them there to save on commissions as well as to have money at Vanguard to invest in its funds. Then Liz could invest the remaining $400,000 once per quarter over the next two to three years as follows:

20 percent Vanguard Intermediate-Term Tax-Exempt

40 percent Vanguard Tax-Managed Balanced

25 percent in Vanguard Total Stock Market Index or ETF

15 percent in Tweedy Browne Global Value or Oakmark Global

Getting Unstuck . . .

Some people feel overwhelmed when they're making investing decisions. If you're one of those people — and if you're willing to pay the price and put in the hours to interview and select the right person and firm — you can hire a financial adviser (see Chapter 24). But if you're not willing to put in that time and money, don't worry — you can still keep things simple (without sacrificing quality). Table 15-1 can help you establish and maintain a simple, yet solid, mutual fund portfolio by using funds of funds (which I discuss in Chapter 13).

Table 15-1 assumes that you're investing money for retirement and that you're willing to take on a moderate level of risk. (Remember that, because funds of funds hold thousands of individual securities, they're more than diverse enough to be used "exclusively.") When investing money in a retirement account (or if you're not concerned about taxable distributions, in a nonretirement account), use the recommended mix of funds for your age in the second column. When investing retirement money that happens to be in a nonretirement account, you can avoid taxable distributions by using the recommended selection of funds for your age in the third column.

Table 15-1	Eric's Keep-It-Simple Portfolio	
Your Age	**Suggested Vanguard Funds**	**Tax-Friendly Vanguard Fund Mix***
Less than 36	100% LifeStrategy Growth	54% Total Stock Market Index 26% Total International Stock Index 20% Intermediate-Term Tax-Exempt
36–45	50% LifeStrategy Growth 50% LifeStrategy Moderate Growth	47% Total Stock Market Index 23% Total International Stock Index 30% Intermediate-Term Tax-Exempt
46–55	100% LifeStrategy Moderate Growth	40% Total Stock Market Index 20% Total International Stock Index 40% Intermediate-Term Tax-Exempt
56–65	50% LifeStrategy Moderate Growth 50% LifeStrategy Conservative Growth	33% Total Stock Market Index 17% Total International Stock Index 50% Intermediate-Term Tax-Exempt
66–75	100% LifeStrategy Conservative Growth	27% Total Stock Market Index 13% Total International Stock Index 60% Intermediate-Term Tax-Exempt
76–85	50% LifeStrategy Conservative Growth 50% LifeStrategy Income	20% Total Stock Market Index 10% Total International Stock Index 70% Intermediate-Term Tax-Exempt
86 or more	100% LifeStrategy Income	13% Total Stock Market Index 7% Total International Stock Index 80% Intermediate-Term Tax-Exempt

* If you live in California, Florida, Massachusetts, New Jersey, New York, Ohio, or Pennsylvania, you can substitute the state-specific Vanguard bond fund appropriate for your state in place of the Intermediate-Term Tax-Exempt fund. Although the state-specific bond funds are more volatile because they invest in longer term bonds, they pay slightly higher yields.

* If you prefer to use the Vanguard Tax-Managed funds that I discuss in Chapter 13, simply substitute 67 percent Tax-Managed Capital Appreciation and 33 percent Tax-Managed Small Capitalization for Total Stock Market Index; and Tax-Managed International for Total International Stock Index.

* If you're investing larger balances and understand ETFs (see Chapter 5), you could use Vanguard's Total Stock Market Index ETF in place of the domestic stock funds in the table and Vanguard's FTSE All-World ex-US ETF in place of the foreign stock funds.

Chapter 16

Applications, Transfers, and Other Useful Forms

In This Chapter

▶ Explaining application basics

▶ Understanding nonretirement and retirement account forms

▶ Establishing an automatic investment program

▶ Asking for help

*W*hen you invest money, completing forms is unfortunately a requirement. But don't despair. If you truly detest paperwork and mailing
things, you'll be happy to know that you can now complete many application
forms online. In this chapter, I explain how to fill out fund application and
transfer forms.

Although the subject of this chapter may seem mundane, I explain some
extra-nifty things that perhaps you didn't know you could do with fund
investing. And, unlike dealing with IRS tax forms year after year, fund paperwork isn't unpleasant to deal with. You won't have much (if any) ongoing
paperwork to do, except for filing the taxes owed on mutual fund distributions held outside of retirement accounts (the subject of Chapter 18).

Taking the Nonretirement Account Route

As I discuss in Chapter 9, you can purchase most of the excellent mutual
funds that I recommend in this book either directly from the mutual fund
company responsible for them or through a discount brokerage firm. Though
you see many similarities between mutual fund company and discount broker
applications, you also see that brokerage account applications are a different
type of animal than mutual fund company applications. I show you how to
handle both in this chapter.

Filling in the blanks: Application basics

In years past, prospective customers called the fund company on its toll-free number and said, "Please send me your account application materials for your (fill-in-the blank) fund." Several days later, a packet arrived in the mailbox with enough density and heft to make a great flyswatter! Most of the content was marketing propaganda to convince people to send gobs of money. You had to hunt around for the document that said something like *Account Registration Form* or *New Account Application* or *Application.*

Thanks to the Internet, now you can open fund accounts online. In the past, although various fund companies allowed you to access and download account application forms on their Web sites, you still had to print the application, sign it, and drop it in the mail. But today, electronic signatures exist. *E-signatures,* as they're commonly referred to, are now legally equal to traditional pen-and-ink signatures on paper forms. You don't literally sign a form using your computer; you're simply assigned a code that serves as your very own e-signature. Fund companies ensure your account's security by requiring your Web browser to use sophisticated encryption technology and by mailing another code to the address that you provide in your application.

Here are the potential benefits of completing an account application online:

- ✔ You can get your new account open much faster, which may come in handy when you face a deadline for opening a particular type of account (such as a retirement account).

- ✔ You can save time completing forms through the same company. Most of the better fund-company Web sites remember your information when you've completed one form, which allows them to precomplete common portions of new forms when you come back to open more new accounts.

The following sections explain and show you how to complete the important portions of a typical new account application for a nonretirement account (I discuss the nuances of retirement account applications later in the chapter).

Account registration

In the *account registration* section (which usually comes first on an account application), you're asked to choose the appropriate box and enter the name of the individual or organization that's registering the account. Here are the common types of account registrations:

- ✔ **Individual or Joint Account:** Choose this option if you're opening the account for yourself or jointly for yourself and someone else. *Joint tenants with rights of survivorship* is generally the default classification for jointly registered accounts and establishes the following conditions:

- The person you've jointly registered the account with can do everything that you can do on the account, such as calling and inquiring about account balances, performing transactions, and writing checks. Neither party needs the other's permission (although it's possible to establish the account so that both signatures are required for check writing).

- Each account holder has an equal interest in the account.

- If you should die, the entire account balance goes to the other person registered on the account without the hassles and expense of going through probate.

A rarely used option is to register the account as tenants in common. To arrange a *tenancy in common,* you can have a legal document drawn up specifying that each tenant owns a certain percentage of the account. Unlike shares of ownership for joint tenants with rights of survivorship, the shares for tenants in common need not be equal. If you die, the account is restricted; your share of the account is distributed to the person whom you designated to receive it, and the surviving account holder is required to set up a new account for his share.

If you go to the trouble of setting up the account registration as tenants in common, just write in the margin in this section of the form that you want the account set up this way or attach a short letter that presents the same request. The fund company doesn't want or need to see the legal document (which you should keep with your will) or other important personal financial documents.

✔ **Gift or Transfer to Minor:** Use this section if you want to open (register) an account in your child's name. As the parent, you're the *custodian,* your child the *minor.* Your state's name is requested in this section because two different sets of laws govern custodial accounts: the Uniform Gift to Minors Act (UGMA) and the Uniform Transfer to Minors Act (UTMA). States allow one or the other. Your child is legally entitled to the money in the account when she reaches the so-called age of majority (which is, depending on the state, between 18 and 21). Read Chapter 3 before putting money into an account in your child's name because there are drawbacks.

✔ **Trust:** Generally, you know if you have a trust because you're either the one who sets it up or you're the recipient of assets that are part of a trust. There are many types of trusts. For example, some folks, by the time they get older, have set up a *living trust* that allows their assets to pass directly to heirs without going through probate. If you have a trust agreement, provide the pertinent details at this point in the form.

✔ **Corporation, Partnership, or Other Entity:** If you want to open a mutual fund account for your corporation or local Rotary Club, use this section. You need a taxpayer ID number. If your organization doesn't have one, call the IRS at 800-829-3676 (800-TAX-FORM) and request Form SS-4, or visit its Web site at www.irs.gov.

Your personal information

This part's easy. You may be wondering why some fund companies ask for your phone numbers, the name of your employer, and your occupation. The company wants your phone numbers so it can call you regarding account issues. The rest of this information is partly required by fund regulators and partly just desired by the fund company for its own market research; it wants to know about the people who invest in each of its specific types of funds. If you want to maintain your privacy, you can skip the employment stuff, and the fund company will still happily open your account.

Your investment

The investment section is where you tell 'em which fund you want. But be careful in this section. Most account applications offer a menu of fund choices, so you need to double-check that you've selected the fund that you have your heart set on.

To ensure that the money is deposited into the correct fund, check the account statement that you receive when you open your account. Although it doesn't happen often, fund companies (and you!) occasionally make mistakes.

Your method of payment

After you open an account, you're faced with the task of getting money into your new account in order to buy some mutual funds. You can put money into your account by mailing the fund company a check, having funds electronically transferred from an existing bank account, or transferring funds from an account you previously opened at the fund company.

Generally, you need to send a check to open a mutual fund account. If this is the case, make the check payable to the fund (if the company numbers its funds, include the fund number next to the fund company name). Don't worry about someone stealing the check or a mail thief cashing it (remember that you make the check payable to the fund).

After you open a money market fund account, you can do exchanges into other accounts by telephone. Exchanges save you the hassle of filling out more application forms every time you open new funds at the same company (although different account types, such as IRAs, do require separate account applications). Make sure that you have another source of cash during the time it takes for the fund company to open your money fund and send your first check. Sometimes people send in almost all their money and then, in a few days, they wish that they'd kept some back.

Dividend and capital gains payment options

Most mutual funds make dividend and capital gains payments. If you're not living off this income, it's usually best to reinvest these payments by purchasing more shares in the fund. To reinvest, just check the box indicating that you want to have the fund's dividend and capital gains reinvested. This strategy eliminates the hassle of receiving and cashing checks often and then figuring out where to invest the money (but it doesn't change the taxability of a fund's distributions).

On the other hand, if you're retired, for example, you may want the distributions on your fund sent to you so that you can spend it on early-bird restaurant specials. Most fund companies offer you the option of having the money from distributions sent to you as a check through the mail. Or, even better, the fund can electronically transfer the money to your bank account. This method gets you the money quicker and requires less mail to open and fewer checks to sign and schlep to the bank.

Wiring and automatic investment options

You're not required to have wiring and automatic investment options on an account. *Wire redemption* allows you to request that money be wired to your bank account. Use this feature if you might unexpectedly need money fast. Your mutual fund and your bank may charge for wiring services, though, so don't use wiring as your regular way to move money to and from your bank.

If you want to make regular deposits into one of your fund accounts, you can select an *automatic investment* plan, which authorizes the fund to instruct your bank to send a fixed amount on a particular day of the month (or some other time period). You can do the same in reverse by withdrawing money on a regular schedule, too. The minimum amount should be stated on the form.

Special purchases and redemptions is an electronic funds transfer — it's like a paperless, electronic check that allows you to move money back and forth between your bank and mutual fund accounts. This process usually takes a full two days to complete because, like a check, the transaction is cleared through the Automated Clearing House (wiring can typically be done the same day or next day). The fund and the bank shouldn't charge for the service because it's just like a check (which means that it costs less than wiring).

To establish these additional services, remember to attach a preprinted deposit slip or blank check (write "VOID" in large letters across the front of the check so that no one else can use it).

Check-writing option

Check writing is a useful feature to sign up for on a money market fund. But most money funds limit check writing to amounts of $250 or more.

I don't recommend establishing check writing for bond funds because each time you write a check on a bond fund, you must report the transaction on your annual tax return (because the price of the bond fund fluctuates, you'll be selling at different prices than you bought). Keep enough cash in your money fund and write your checks from there.

Opening multiple fund accounts quickly

Some of the larger fund companies have a number of good funds, so you may want to invest in multiple funds at one company. Through a comprehensive account application form, *most* fund companies let you invest in multiple funds without having to complete a mountain of paperwork. However, not all fund companies offer these comprehensive account application forms. You're supposed to fill out a separate application for each fund you plan to invest in, but you don't need to. Avoid this paperwork nightmare in several ways:

✔ Establish a money market fund first. Then you may do exchanges by phone into any other funds you want. When you call to order the money fund materials, ask for the prospectuses for the other funds that you're interested in. When you do telephone exchanges, fund companies are required by the SEC to ask if you've received the prospectus before they'll allow an exchange.

✔ Attach a separate piece of paper to one application with instructions to the fund company to open "identically registered accounts in the following funds" (but first make sure the company allows this shortcut). Next to each fund name, list the amount you want to invest. Don't forget to sign the page and attach your check.

✔ Open a discount brokerage account through a firm that allows telephone exchanges (see the "Buying in to discount brokerage accounts" section).

Buying in to discount brokerage accounts

As I discuss in Chapter 9, discount brokerage firms and the discount brokerage divisions of fund companies offer you the opportunity, through a single account, to invest in hundreds of funds from many fund companies. Brokerage firms are different from mutual fund companies. The first difference is that brokerage accounts allow you to hold and trade individual securities, such as stocks and bonds. This feature is handy if you hold individual securities and want them in the same account as your mutual fund.

Another difference is that, in addition to offering mutual funds, brokerage accounts allow you to invest in riskier types of securities and engage in riskier investing strategies. Many brokerage firms, for example, allow investing in options (see Chapter 1), which are volatile, short-term, gambling-type instruments. Keep your distance.

Most of the sections on a typical brokerage application are the same as those on a mutual fund application, which I describe in the "Filling in the blanks: Application basics" section, earlier in the chapter. The following sections explain the main differences that may give you cause for pause.

Borrowing money so you can invest: Margin accounts

Brokers offer (and sometimes encourage) *margin trading.* Just as you can purchase a home and borrow some money to finance the purchase when you can't afford to pay all cash, you can do the same with your investments. When you buy a home, most banks require that you make a 10 to 20 percent down payment on the purchase price. When you invest in a brokerage account, you need to make a 50 percent down payment.

Buying investments on margin isn't something I recommend because

✔ You pay interest. Although the rate is competitive — nothing approaching the worst credit cards — it still isn't cheap. Typically, the rate is a bit more than you'd pay on a fixed-rate mortgage on your home.

✔ If your investments fall significantly in value (25 to 30 percent), you get a *margin call,* which means that you need to add more cash to your account. If you can't or don't add more money to your account, you must sell some investments to raise the cash. Of course, if your securities' prices increase in value, you earn money not only on the down payment you invested but also on the borrowed money invested. (That's called *leverage.*)

✔ You can't invest on margin in retirement accounts, which is where you should be doing most of your investing (because of the tax benefits).

Borrowing on margin can be useful as a short-term source of money. Suppose you need more short-term cash than you have in a money fund. Instead of selling your investments, just borrow against them with a margin loan. This move makes sense especially if you'd have to pay a lot of tax on profits were you to sell appreciated investments.

Getting personal

Brokerage applications ask for financial information that most people consider to be confidential, such as your driver's license number, income, and net worth. "Why," you may rightfully ask, "are they being so nosy? Do they really need to know this stuff?"

All brokerage firms ask for this kind of information (although different firms ask different questions) because of the so-called know-your-customer rule imposed by regulators. Because brokerage accounts allow you to do some risky stuff, regulators believe that brokerage firms should make at least a modest effort to determine whether their clients know enough and have a sufficient financial cushion to make riskier financial investments.

Make your paperwork go faster and your investing less dangerous and skip this! If you're not signing up for the risky account features, such as margin and options trading, the brokerage firm doesn't need to know this info.

Accessing your cash: Checks and debit cards

Some brokerage accounts offer additional features, such as check writing and a debit card, that allow more convenient ways for you to access the money in your account. The only challenge is that you may have to request a different application for the special type of account that offers these features.

Debit cards look just like credit cards and are accepted by retailers the same way as credit cards. But, when you use your debit card, the money is generally sucked out of your account within a day or two. Using debit cards instead of credit cards may simplify your financial life by saving you from writing a check every month to pay your credit card bill. However, you give up the *float* — the free use, until the credit card bill is due, of the money that you owe — because debit cards quickly deduct the money owed from your account. You may also use your debit card to obtain cash from ATMs.

As with a money market mutual fund account, you may obtain checks to write against the money market fund balance in your brokerage account. Don't forget to complete the signature card for check writing.

Some brokerage accounts come with even more features that make organizing your finances easier, such as unlimited check writing and a bill payment service. These services cost more money, and you may have to put more money into your account, pay a monthly service fee, and/or pay an annual account fee if you don't place a specified minimum number of trades per year.

Transferring your dough into a new brokerage account

You may have cash, securities, and most mutual funds transferred into a new brokerage account that you establish. (If you haven't opened an account yet, you also need to complete an account application form.) All you need is an account transfer form for the brokerage firm into which you're transferring the assets. Using one of these forms saves you the hassle of contacting brokerage firms, banks, and other mutual fund companies from which you want to move your money. Using this form also saves you the bother and risk of taking possession of these assets. The following sections contain the info you need to know to complete a typical brokerage account transfer form.

Information about your (new) brokerage account

Your new brokerage firm needs to know into which account you want your assets transferred, so in this section you fill in your name as you have it on your account application or as it's currently listed on your account, if it's already open. If you're sending your account application with this transfer form, you won't have an account number yet, so just write *NEW* in the space for your account number.

Information about the account you're transferring

Here, you write the name of the brokerage, bank, or fund company that holds the assets you want to transfer and enter the account number of your account there. You may see the phrase *Title of account;* this simply means your name as it appears on the account you're transferring.

Brokerage account transfers

In this section, you indicate whether you want to transfer your entire brokerage account — which makes your administrative life easier by eliminating an account — or only a part of it. (Another advantage of closing accounts at firms such as Prudential, Merrill Lynch, and so on is that they generally charge an annual account fee.)

If you're doing a partial transfer, you generally just list the assets that you want to transfer — for example, IBM stock — and the number of shares, such as "50" or "All." With partial transfers that include the transfer of mutual funds, you may have to go through the hassle of completing a transfer form for each company whose funds you're moving. You may have to list these funds in a separate section.

You generally won't be able to transfer (into your new brokerage account) mutual funds that are unique (or *proprietary*) to the brokerage firm you're leaving. Funds that can't be transferred typically include funds such as Prudential, Merrill Lynch, and so on. If there are no adverse tax consequences, you're better off selling these funds and transferring the cash proceeds. Check out Chapter 17, which walks you through the issues to consider if you're debating whether to hold or sell a fund.

If you bought some of those awful limited partnerships, check with the discount brokerage firm to which you're transferring your account to see if it'll be able to hold them. Discounters will likely charge you a fee ($25 to $50) to hold LPs, but many of the lousy firms that sold them to you in the first place also charge you for the privilege of keeping your account open with them. If the costs are about the same, I'd move the LPs to your new account to cut down on account clutter. Another alternative is to speak with the branch manager of the firm that sold them to you and ask that it waives the annual account fee for continuing to hold your LPs there.

Mutual fund transfer forms

As I explain in the last section, you can only transfer certain companies' funds into a brokerage account. For each fund you're transferring, you typically list the fund name, your account number, and the amount of shares you want transferred or sold.

If you're transferring the fund as is instead of selling it, tell the new firm whether you want the fund's dividends and capital gains distributions reinvested. Unless you need this money to live on, I'd reinvest it.

Bank, savings and loan, or credit union transfers

A potential complication occurs when you're transferring money from a certificate of deposit. In that case, send in this form several weeks before the CD is set to mature.

If you're like most people and do things at the last minute, you may not think about transferring a CD until the bank notifies you by mail days before it's due to mature. Here's a simple way around your inability to get the transfer paperwork in on time: Instruct your bank to place the proceeds from the CD into a money market or savings account when the CD matures. Then you can have the proceeds from the CD transferred whenever you like.

Attach your account statement!

Don't forget to attach a copy of a recent statement of the account you're transferring as well as your account application if you haven't previously opened an account. At this point . . . you're done! Mail the completed application in the company's postage-paid envelope, and the transfer should go smoothly. If you have problems, see Chapter 19 for solutions.

Preparing for Leisure: Retirement Accounts

The applications for retirement accounts pose new challenges. But, remember that it will be worth the effort: Otherwise, how will you pay for dentures and your annual AARP membership? The first part of these applications is just like a nonretirement account application, except that it's easier to fill out. Retirement accounts are only registered in one person's name: You can't have jointly registered retirement accounts. Because mutual fund company retirement account forms are so similar to brokerage account retirement forms, I cover only the differences here.

Retirement account applications

Individual Retirement Accounts (IRAs) are among the most common accounts you may use at a mutual fund company. This section explains what you need to know to complete an IRA application. I also discuss the unique features of the other common retirement accounts — SEP-IRAs and Keoghs, which are used for the self-employed and small business owners. (For a detailed explanation of the various types of retirement accounts, see Chapter 3.)

If you plan to transfer money from a retirement account held elsewhere into the one you're opening, before you start, pay attention to two details:

✔ Make sure that the retirement account type you're opening (such as a SEP-IRA) matches the type you're transferring from (unless you're moving money from a 401(k) plan, in which case you'd be sending that money into an IRA because you can't open a 401(k) as an individual).

✔ If you want to transfer individual securities from a brokerage account, you need a *brokerage* account application for the type of retirement account you're opening, not a mutual fund account application.

Register for an account

Account registration is an easy section to fill out — but make sure that, if you're transferring IRA money from another firm into your mutual fund IRA, you list your name exactly as it appears on the account you're transferring. Otherwise, the firm that has your IRA may make a fuss, causing delays and making you complete yet more forms. ***Note:*** Some applications ask for your employer info. You don't have to provide this if you don't want to.

Choose your investment method

With an IRA, you can fund your account through three methods:

✔ **Annual contribution:** Select this option if you're opening up a new IRA with money previously held outside any kind of retirement account. You must specify which kind of fund(s) you want to buy, how much you'll be contributing (in 2010, up to $5,000; $6,000 if you're age 50 and older), which kind of IRA you want to open (traditional or Roth), and which tax year you're making your contributions. You have until the time you file your tax return (the deadline is April 15) to make a contribution for the previous year.

✔ **Transfer from an existing IRA:** If you want to move an IRA from another investment firm or bank into your new mutual fund IRA, select this option. You also need to complete an IRA transfer form (which I explain in the "What to do before transferring accounts" section). This option is the best way to move an existing IRA because it presents the least hassle and the fewest possibilities of a tax screw-up.

✔ **Rollovers:** Withdrawing the money from another IRA and sending it yourself to the new account isn't a good way to transfer your IRA. The big danger is that if you don't get the funds back into the new account within 60 days, you'll owe megataxes (income tax plus penalties).

TIP

Retirement plan applications for the self-employed and small business: SEP-IRAs and Keoghs

If you're self-employed or a small business owner, consider opening a SEP-IRA or Keogh plan. Most self-employed people can generally make larger tax-deductible contributions into these accounts than they can into a regular IRA. (I discuss the pros, cons, and contribution limitations of SEP-IRAs and Keoghs in Chapter 3.)

SEP-IRA applications are virtually identical to IRA applications, so just follow the instructions for the IRA applications in the section "Retirement account applications" (in fact, some firms use the same application form). At those firms that use SEP-IRA applications that differ from IRA applications, you may see references to "Employer Contribution" as the main difference. If you're the business owner, you, as the self-employed person, are your own employer. If you have other employees, they may be eligible for SEP-IRA contributions under your plan (the maximum waiting period is three years of service — a *year of service* is a year in which an employee earns $550). When employees become eligible for contributions, you set up accounts for them (with their names on them) — they don't establish accounts on their own.

Keogh account applications are more complicated. You must complete more paperwork, particularly if you set up the combined profit-sharing and money purchase pension plans that I explain in Chapter 4.

A few items appear on a Keogh application that you won't find on an IRA application. First, you must supply an *employer tax identification number.* If your business has obtained a tax identification number from the IRS, plug that in. Otherwise, most small business owners use their Social Security numbers. You also need the name(s) of the *plan administrator,* the person(s) responsible for determining which employees are eligible in the plan, making contributions into the accounts, and other tasks. If you're a sole proprietor, you're the administrator. In larger businesses, the administrator is the business owner(s).

The Keogh plan documents also ask whether your company operates, for tax purposes, on a calendar year (which ends on December 31) or a fiscal year (which has some other end date for the year). Employees are eligible to participate after they've completed two years of service. Different plans define a year of service differently, but most use 500 or 1,000 hours as the threshold.

If you're rolling over money from an employer-sponsored plan, such as a 401(k), you can select the option that's labeled something like *Traditional Rollover IRA.* Tax advisers usually recommend that money coming from your employer's plan should go into a rollover account. This choice allows you to someday transfer the money back into another employer's plan. Of course, you can choose investments in your IRA, so this may sound like a silly reason to use a rollover IRA. An advantage to establishing a contributory IRA, instead, is that you can add to it with future IRA contributions. You can also merge it with other IRAs.

Don't request that your employer issue you a check because your employer must withhold 20 percent for taxes. If you want to roll the full amount over — a wise move — you must come up with the missing 20 percent when you deposit the money into your IRA. Otherwise, you owe tax and penalties on it. Establish your IRA and then instruct your employer to send your money directly to that account.

Select your account service options

Most companies allow you to pick and choose from various service options that come with your IRA. Some of them, such as telephone/computer exchange, are automatically available with your account unless you specify otherwise. You can usually also set up an automatic investment plan; contributions to your IRA can be regularly deducted from either your bank checking account or your paycheck itself. Such plans generally have lower minimum initial investment requirements.

Designate your beneficiaries

In the beneficiaries section, you specify who gets all this retirement money if you work yourself into an early grave or haven't spent all of it by the time you go. In most cases, people name their spouses, kids, parents, or siblings. You may also list organizations such as charities that you want to receive some of your money; providing their tax identification number and address is a good idea (just include this info on a separate piece of paper).

If your children are under 18, they don't have access to the money. A guardian who you identify through your will controls the money. If you die without a will, the courts will assign a guardian. Your *primary beneficiaries* are first in line for the money, but if they've all crossed the finish line by the time you do, your *contingent beneficiaries* receive the money.

What to do before transferring accounts

If you have money in a retirement account in a bank, brokerage firm, other mutual fund company, or in a previous employer's retirement plan, you can transfer it to the mutual fund(s) of your choice. Here's a list of steps for transferring a retirement account. *Note:* If you're doing a rollover from an employer plan, please heed the differences indicated:

1. **Decide where you want to move the account.**

   See Chapter 9 for help with this decision.

2. **Obtain an account application and asset transfer form.**

   Call the toll-free number of the firm you're transferring the money to (or visit its Web site) and ask for an *account application and asset transfer form* for the type of account you're transferring to — for example, an IRA, SEP-IRA, Keogh, or 403(b).

You can tell which account type you currently have by looking at a recent account statement; the account type is given near the top of the form or in the section with your name and address. If you can't figure it out on a cryptic statement, call the firm that currently holds the account and ask a representative which type of account you have (just be sure to have your account number handy when you call).

3. **Figure out which securities you want to transfer and which you need to liquidate.**

Transferring existing investments in your account to a new investment firm can cause glitches because not all securities may be transferable. If you're transferring cash (money market assets) or securities that trade on any of the major stock exchanges, transferring isn't a problem.

If you own publicly traded securities, it's often better to transfer them *as is* to your new investment firm, especially if the new firm offers discount brokerage services. (The alternative is to sell them through the firm you're leaving, which may cost you more.)

If you own mutual funds unique to the institution you're leaving, check with your new firm to see whether it can accept them. If not, you need to contact the firm that currently holds them to sell them.

4. **(Optional) Let the firm from which you're transferring the money know that you're doing so.**

(You don't need to worry about this step if you're rolling money out of an employer plan.) If the place you're transferring from doesn't assign a specific person to your account, you definitely should skip this step. If you're moving your investments from a brokerage firm where you've dealt with a particular broker, though, the decision is more difficult. Most people feel obligated to let their rep know about the transfer.

In my experience, calling your representative with the bad news is usually a mistake. Brokers or others who have a direct financial stake in your decision to move your money will try to sell you on staying. Some may try to make you feel guilty, and badger you. The more that you feel personally obligated to continue doing business with a broker, the more likely it is that your personal relationship is getting in the way of your financial goals. Instead, write a letter if you want to let them know you're moving your account. It may seem the coward's way out, but writing usually makes your departure easier on both sides. With a letter, you can polish your explanation, and you don't run as much risk of putting the broker on the defensive. Just say that you've chosen to self-direct your investments.

But then again, telling an investment firm that its charges are too high or that it sold you a bunch of lousy investments that it misrepresented to you may help the firm to improve in the future. Don't fret this decision too much. Do what's best for you and what you're comfortable with.

Establishing retirement accounts quickly

Okay, so you procrastinate — you're human. Perhaps it's April 14 or 15, and you want to establish an IRA, but you need to do it, like, now. You don't have time to call a toll-free number, wait for days to get the application in the mail, and then wait even more days until the fund company receives your check. All isn't lost; get yourself out of your pickle in several proven ways:

✔ **Visit a branch office.** Companies such as Fidelity and TD Ameritrade have numerous branch offices. Call them to find the location of the one nearest you. You may also be near other companies' main offices. Check the Appendix of this book for contact information. And believe it or not, some branch offices are kept open late on tax day. (Some larger firms even keep some of their branches open until midnight.)

✔ **Visit a Web site.** Most fund companies provide downloadable account applications on the Internet — and increasing numbers of fund providers allow you to complete these applications online using e-signatures (which I discuss in the section "Filling in the blanks: Application basics"). Most likely, however, you'll have to print and mail a form. And to get your money into your newly opened account, you need to wire or electronically transfer funds (or employ one of the other strategies that I discuss in this sidebar).

✔ **Use an express mail service.** Although not a low-cost option, if you have a chunk of money at stake, an overnight express mail service may be worth the cost and save you the time of going to a branch office.

✔ **Go to your local bank.** Establish your retirement account in a savings or money market type of account at the bank. Later, when the dust settles and you have breathing room, call your favorite fund company for its application and transfer forms to move the money.

Bank employees will more than likely try to talk you into a CD or one of the mutual funds that they sell. Skip the CD, because you're looking for a short-term and flexible parking place for your retirement contribution. Bank mutual funds tend to be commission-based (load) funds and aren't among the best choices.

✔ **File for a tax extension.** If you're opening a non-IRA retirement account, such as an SEP-IRA or a Keogh, consider buying yourself more time by filing for an extension. Although you must still pay any outstanding tax owed by the April 15 deadline, filing for an extension by using IRS Form 4868 gets you six more months (until October 15) to file your Form 1040 and establish and fund your retirement accounts. (**Note:** This extension doesn't apply to normal IRAs; for those, April 15 is the absolute deadline.)

If you're self-employed, be aware that you need to file the paperwork for a Keogh retirement account by December 31 — no extensions are allowed (although, as with other retirement accounts, you do have until the time you file your tax forms to fund the Keogh). You can use the strategies I discuss in this sidebar to get the job done by year's end.

Filling out transfer forms

Transferring retirement accounts generally isn't too difficult. In most cases, all you need to do is complete a transfer form. You can use a mutual fund transfer form to move money that's in a bank account, in another mutual fund, or in a brokerage account. You may only use this form to move investment money that you want liquidated and converted to cash prior to transfer.

You'll probably need to use one of these retirement account transfer forms for each investment company or bank you're transferring IRA money out of. If you're transferring individual securities (for example, stocks or bonds) or want brokerage account features, you need a brokerage account transfer form (and brokerage application forms). The following sections detail the unique features that you should know about when completing a transfer form.

Account ownership and address

Be sure to list your name and address as it appears on the account you're transferring (look at a recent statement for that account). A discrepancy between the two accounts often leads to an incomplete transfer.

If you're transferring an IRA, look at a statement for the account you're transferring and see which type of IRA you have. If you can't figure it out, either call that company and ask which of the three types you have or just leave it blank, send it to the mutual fund, and let it figure it out from the statement for the account that you're transferring!

Where the retirement account funds will be invested

On most applications, you simply list the funds that you want the transferred money invested in and the percentage of the money that is to go into each (the percentages must total 100 percent). If you want to divvy up the money into more funds than the form allows space for, list the additional funds on a separate piece of paper and attach that sheet to the form.

Account being transferred

In this section of the transfer form, you tell the fund company where the account you want to transfer is currently held. If it's in another fund, list the name of the fund (if you're transferring more than one fund from the same company, just squeeze those names into the space provided). If it's money in a CD that you're moving, try to send your transfer form several weeks before the CD is scheduled to mature.

If you don't get around to sending the form until right before your CD matures, buy yourself more time by directing your bank to place the CD proceeds into a money market or savings type account from which you then can do the transfer.

List the firm where your account is currently being held. You may see the term *custodian,* which is simply the term for the company holding your IRA — for example, First Low Interest Bank & Trust or Prune Your Assets Brokerage. Some transfer forms ask for a specific department or person who handles account transfers at your old firm. You probably won't have a clue as to which person or department has this responsibility. If you don't, you can call the company and try to find out. My advice: Don't bother. Most funds don't burden you with having to find this information out — the funds should already know from other transfers that they've done with that firm. If they don't, let them do the work to find out.

List the mailing address and phone number of the company where your account is currently held, and also list your account number there. Attach a copy of the statement for the account that you want to move. If you don't know the phone number, don't worry — it isn't critical.

Authorization to transfer your account

It's a pain, but some firms that you're transferring out of may require that you burn a chunk of your day to go get your signature guaranteed at your local bank (a notary doesn't do this). Fortunately, most companies don't require this effort — but the only way to know for certain is to call and ask.

Investing on Autopilot

You may have noticed if you were reading earlier in this chapter that I mention that some mutual fund applications include sections that allow you to establish an automatic investment program. This program allows the fund to electronically transfer money from your bank account at predetermined times. You'll probably need to complete a separate form to establish this service if your fund company doesn't have this option listed on its original application, you didn't fill out that part when you opened the account, or you're investing through a discount brokerage firm. (See the explanation in "Filling in the blanks: Application basics" earlier in this chapter.)

If you have a pile of money sitting in a money market fund and you want to ease it (dollar-cost averaging) into mutual funds, you can use the services most fund companies and discount brokers offer for this purpose. They may have separate forms to fill out or, even better, some companies allow you to establish this service by phone after your money fund account is open. (See Chapter 10 for a discussion of the pros and cons of dollar-cost averaging.)

If you're investing outside a retirement account into fund(s) at different points in time, here's a hint: For tax recordkeeping purposes, save your statements that detail all the purchases in your accounts. (Most mutual fund companies also provide year-end summary statements that show all the transactions you made throughout the year.)

If you don't save your statements, it won't be the end of the world — as long as you're investing through most of the larger and better fund companies, which are able to tell you your average cost per share when you need to sell. Average cost isn't the only or even necessarily the most advantageous method for you to use in determining your cost basis (see Chapter 18).

Finding Help for a Overwhelmed Brain

If you get stuck or can't deal with filling out forms — not even with the comfort and solace you get from this book — you have two safety nets:

✔ **Call the fund company or discount broker and ask for help.** (The number is usually listed at the top of the first page of the application.) Providing assistance is one of the many tasks those phone reps are paid to do. If you get someone who's impatient or incompetent, simply call back, and you'll get someone else. (Should this happen with the companies recommended in this book, please let me know!)

If you're dealing with a problem that can't be solved during the first phone call and you're working with a representative on it, jot down the person's name and extension number. And don't forget to ask which office location he's in. Some of the larger fund companies route their toll-free calls to various offices, so you may not know where your call has ended up unless you ask.

✔ **Visit a branch office.** Accessibility is one of the reasons that branch offices exist. Some companies have them; others don't (see Chapter 9).

Part V
Keeping Current and Informed

The 5th Wave   By Rich Tennant

"The first thing we should do is get you two into a good mutual fund. Let me get out the 'Magic 8 Ball,' and we'll run some options."

In this part . . .

*I*n this part, I explain how to evaluate the performance of your funds, how to decide when to sell, how to understand tax forms that your mutual fund companies send you, and how to fix the rare but downright aggravating technical glitches and problems that you may encounter. And, to help you keep current with the latest mutual funds news, I cover fund ratings systems and forecasters and how to use your computer to research and manage your mutual fund portfolio.

Chapter 17

Evaluating Your Funds and Adjusting Your Portfolio

. . . .

. . . .

*A*fter you've explored different funds, filled out the application forms, and mailed your money, the hard part is over. Congratulations! You've accomplished what millions of people are still thinking about but haven't gotten off their blessed behinds to do (probably because they haven't read this book yet).

Now that you've started investing in funds (or even if you've been doing so for years), of course, you want to know how your funds are doing — specifically, you want to know how much return your funds are generating. You may also be interested in evaluating funds you already owned before you and I met, wondering if your prior holdings are greyhounds or basset hounds.

In this chapter, I explain how to evaluate the performance of your funds and decide what to do with them over time. I also explain why most of the statements you get from fund companies make your head spin and leave you clueless as to how you're doing.

Deciphering Your Fund Statement

Every mutual fund company has its own statement design. But they all report the same types of information, usually in columns. The following sections present the type of entries you find on typical fund company statements, along with my short explanations of what they all mean.

Trade date or date of transaction

The *trade date* (or date of transaction) is the date that the mutual fund company processed your transaction. For example, if you mailed a check as an initial deposit with your account application, you can see which date the company actually received and processed your check. If the fund company receives your deposit by 4 p.m. EST, it will generally purchase shares that same day in the bond and/or stock funds that you intended the check for.

Money market funds work a little differently than bond and stock funds. Money market fund deposits don't start earning interest until the day after the company receives your money. The delay is due to the fact that the fund company must convert your money into federal funds.

Transaction description

In the *transaction description* column, you find a brief blurb about what was actually done or transacted. In this column, you're likely to see a few things:

- **Annual maintenance fee charge:** You may see this entry, although not necessarily. (Try to pay these fees outside the account so that more of your money continues compounding inside the retirement account.)

- **Asset transfer:** This term refers to a transfer of money into your retirement account from another investment company or bank.

- **Capital gains reinvest:** Funds may pay capital gains, and you can choose to reinvest those into purchasing more shares in the fund. In order to satisfy the IRS, capital gains are specified, for example, as short-term capital gains or long-term capital gains, for which different tax rates apply. (See Chapter 18 for the reasons the IRS cares, and the consequences for your tax return. And check out the "Capital gains distributions" section later in this chapter for more on the subject.)

- **Check-writing redemption:** On the statement for a money market fund, you may see such entries to show the deduction of a check that has cleared your account (should you use the option of writing checks that draw from the fund — like a checking account).

✔ **Contribution:** Often, new purchases for retirement accounts are referred to as a contribution (such as *2010 IRA contribution*).

✔ **Dividend reinvestment:** This term simply means that the fund paid a dividend that you reinvested by purchasing more shares of that same fund in your account. (See details in the section "Dividends" later in the chapter if you're not sure what a dividend is.)

✔ **Income dividend cash:** If you so desire, you may receive your dividends as cash — the fund company can send a check to you, or it can electronically deposit the money into your bank checking account.

✔ **Phone exchange from so-and-so fund:** For example, if you moved money into a fund from your U.S. Treasury money market fund by phone, this item may read *phone exchange from U.S.T. money fund.*

✔ **Purchase or purchase by check:** If you mailed a deposit, you may see this notation.

Dollar amount

The *dollar amount* column simply shows the actual dollar value of the transaction. If you sent a $5,000 deposit, look to make sure that the correct amount was credited to your account. Fund companies calculate and credit the appropriate amount of dividends and capital gains to your account. There's really no need to check these distributions. At any rate, I'm not aware of a fund company making a mistake with these, other than possibly a delay (a few days beyond the promised deadline) in crediting shareholder accounts.

Share price or price per share

The *share price* (or *price per share*) column shows the price per share that the transaction was conducted at. When you're dealing with a *no-load* (commission-free) fund, such as those that I recommend in this book, you get the same price that everyone else who bought or sold shares that day received. Money market funds maintain a level price of $1 per share.

If you're concerned that a load was charged, check with the company to see the buy (bid) price and sell (asked) price on the day you did a purchase transaction. If a load wasn't charged, these two prices should be identical. If a load was charged, the buy price is higher than the sell price, and the purchase on your statement was done at the buy price.

Share amount or shares transacted

The *share amount* (or *shares transacted*) column simply shows the number of shares purchased or sold in the particular transaction. The number of shares is arrived at by default: The fund company takes the dollar amount of the transaction and divides it by the price per share on the date of the transaction.

For example, a $5,000 investment in a bond fund at $20 per share gets you 250 shares. You detail-oriented types will be happy to know that fund companies usually go out to three decimal places in figuring shares.

Shares owned or share balance

If money was added to or subtracted from your account, the share balance changes by the amount of shares purchased or redeemed and listed in the prior section, "Share amount or shares transacted."

In one unusual instance, the number of shares in an account changes even though no transactions have occurred: when a fund *splits.* If it splits 2 for 1, for example, you receive two shares for every one that you own. This split doesn't increase the worth of the investments you own; the price per share in a 2-for-1 split is cut by 50 percent.

Why do funds split? It's a gimmick. In the world of individual securities, stock splits are often associated with successful, growing companies; likewise, mutual fund splits are usually trying to cash in on positive connotations. The fund company wants potential buyers to think that the fund has done *so* well that the company has split its shares in order to reduce the price; that way, new investors won't think that they're paying a high price. But the high price doesn't matter because fund minimum investment requirements, not the share price, determine whether you can afford to invest in a fund. (*Reverse splits* can be done as well to boost a laggard fund's price per share.)

Some exchange-traded funds (ETFs) have split, which may make some sense. The reason is that ETFs trade on a stock exchange, so if an ETF's share price has risen too high, it may actually keep buyers with small amounts to invest from being able to buy some shares. (See Chapter 5 for details on ETFs.)

Account value

Typically, on a different part of the account statement separate from the line-by-line listing of your transactions, fund companies show the total *account value* or market value of your fund shares as of a particular day — usually at the end of a given month. This value results from multiplying the price per share by the total number of shares that you own.

Four out of five fund investors care about total account value more than the other totals (at least, according to my scientific surveys of fund investors that I work with!). So you'd think that the fund companies would list on your statement how this value has changed over time. Well, many don't, and that's one of the reasons why examining your account statement is a lousy way to track your fund's performance over time.

Some fund companies show how your current account value compares to the value when your last statement was issued. This comparison sheds some useful light on your account's performance, but it still doesn't tell you how you've done over longer time periods (since you originally invested, for example). See the later section, "Assessing Your Funds' Returns," for how to determine your funds' performance.

Interpreting Discount Brokerage Firm Statements

Discount brokerage statements may look a bit different from those that mutual fund companies produce. In a discount brokerage statement, the *portfolio overview* (summary of the value of each fund holding) and the transaction details are usually listed in separate sections. This section breaks down a typical brokerage firm statement.

Portfolio overview

A *portfolio overview* section on a brokerage account statement lists funds from your various fund companies. As on a mutual fund statement, the *number of shares* (quantity), *price per share* (latest price), and *market value* of the funds held as of the statement date are listed.

Brokerage statements may use terms like *long,* which simply means that you bought shares and you're holding those shares. (You may — although I don't recommend it — actually *short* shares held in nonretirement brokerage accounts. Shorting shares simply means that you sell the shares first, hope that they decline in value, and then buy them back.) You may also see the term *cash* or the letter *C* associated with your fund holdings. These items mean that this fund is a cash holding (as opposed to one purchased with borrowed money).

Account transaction details

An *account transaction details* section, which summarizes any transactions occurring on your fund holdings since the last statement, often confuses people because transactions seem to be repeated. The apparent repetition occurs because of the silly accounting system of debits and credits that brokerage firms use.

For example, you might see a line item for one of your funds that shows that 5.953 shares of the fund were purchased at $9.80 per share for a total purchase of $58.34. Where did this odd amount of money come from for the purchase? The next line on the statement tells you the fund paid a dividend of $58.34. It'd be logical and more understandable if these two lines were reversed, wouldn't it? First the money comes in, and then it's reinvested into purchasing more shares!

Assessing Your Funds' Returns

Probably the single most important issue that fund investors care about — how much or little they're making on their investments — isn't easy to figure from those blasted statements that fund companies send you. That is, it isn't easy to figure unless you know the tricks regarding what to look for and what to ignore.

If you've just started investing in funds — or even if you've held funds a long time — you need to realize that what happens to the value of your stock and bond funds in the short term is largely a matter of luck. Don't get depressed if your fund or funds drop in value the day after you buy them or even over the first three or six months. When you invest in bond and stock funds, you should focus on returns produced over longer periods — periods of at least one year and preferably longer.

Getting a panoramic view: Total return

The *total return* of a fund is the percentage change in the overall value of your investment over a specified period. For example, a fund may tell you that its total return during the year that just ended December 31 was 15 percent. Therefore, if you invested $10,000 in the fund on the last day of December of the prior year, your investment is worth $11,500 after the year just ended.

This section explains the three components that make up the total return on a fund: dividends, capital gains distributions, and share price changes. These are the three ways you can make money in a mutual fund.

Dividends

Dividends are income paid by investments. Both bonds and stocks can pay dividends. As I explain in Chapter 12, bond fund dividends (which come from the interest paid by bonds) tend to be higher than stock fund dividends. When a dividend distribution is made, you can receive it as cash (which is good if you need money to live on) or reinvest it into more shares in the fund. In either case, the share price of the fund drops by an amount that exactly offsets the payout. So if you're hoping to strike it rich by buying into funds just before their dividends are paid, don't bother. All you may accomplish is increasing your income tax bill!

If you hold your mutual fund outside a retirement account, the dividend distributions are taxable income (unless they come from a tax-free municipal bond fund). When you're ready to buy into a fund outside a retirement account that pays a decent dividend, you may want to check to see when the fund is next scheduled to pay it out. For funds that pay quarterly taxable dividends (such as balanced or hybrid funds), you may want to avoid buying in the weeks just prior to a distribution (which is usually late in each calendar quarter).

Capital gains distributions

When a stock or bond mutual fund manager sells a security in the fund, any gain realized from that sale (the difference between the sale price and the purchase price) must be distributed to fund shareholders as a *capital gain*. (Gains offset by losses — so called *net gains* — are what actually get distributed.) Typically, funds make one annual capital gains distribution in December. Some funds make two per year, typically making the other one mid-year.

As with a dividend distribution, you can receive your capital gains distribution as cash or use it to buy more shares in the fund. In either case, the share price of the fund drops by an amount to exactly offset the distribution.

For funds held outside retirement accounts, all capital gains distributions are taxable. As with dividends, capital gains are taxable whether or not you reinvest them into additional shares in the fund.

Before you invest in bond and stock funds outside retirement accounts, determine when capital gains are distributed if you want to avoid investing in a fund that's about to make a capital gains distribution. (Stock funds that appreciated greatly during the year and that do significant trading are most likely to make larger capital gains distributions. Money funds don't ever make these distributions.) Investing in a fund that will make a distribution soon increases your current-year tax liability for investments made outside retirement accounts. About a month before the distribution, fund companies should be able to estimate the size of the distribution.

Share price changes

You also make money with a mutual fund when the share price increases. This occurrence is just like investing in a stock or piece of real estate. If your fund is worth more today than when you bought it, you have made a profit (on paper, at least). To realize — or lock in — this profit, you need to sell your shares in the fund. A fund's share price increases if the securities that the fund has invested in have appreciated in value.

Tallying the total return

After you've seen all the different components of total return, you're ready to add them all up. For each of the major types of funds that I discuss in this book, Table 17-1 presents a simple summary of where you can expect most of your returns to come from over the long term. The funds are ordered in the table from those with the lowest expected total returns and share price volatility to those with the highest.

Table 17-1		Components of a Fund's Returns		
Funds	*Dividends* +	*Capital Gains* +	*Share Price Changes* =	*Total Return*
Money market funds	All returns come from dividends	None	None	Lowest expected returns but principal risk is nil
Shorter term bond funds	Moderate	Low	Low	Expect better than money funds but more volatility
Longer term bond funds	High	Low to moderate	Low to moderate	Expect better than short-term bonds but with greater volatility

Funds	Dividends	+	Capital Gains	+	Share Price Changes	=	Total Return
Stock funds	None to moderate depending on stock types		Low to high depending on trading patterns of fund manager		Low to high		Highest expected returns but most volatile

Focusing on the misleading share price

You probably know someone who's always glued to his computer screen or favorite wireless mobile device to check on the share prices of individual stocks and how much they've gone up or down.

Unfortunately, mutual fund share prices are also reported on various financial Web sites and through other media outlets. I say "unfortunately" because all too many fund investors, perhaps taking a cue from individual-stock owners, look to daily or other short-term-oriented sources of fund pricing information.

If you follow the price changes in your fund(s) every day, week, month, or other time period, you won't know how your fund is doing. Referring to Table 17-1, you can see that share price is but one of the three components that make up your total return. And to make matters worse for the share-price hawks, another one of the three components — dividends — directly affects share price. When a fund makes a distribution to you, you get more shares of the fund. But distributions create an accounting problem because they reduce the share price of a fund by the exact amount of the distribution. Therefore, over time, following just the share price of your fund doesn't tell you how much money you've made or lost.

The only way to figure out exactly how much you've made or lost on your investment is to compare the *total value* of your fund holdings today to the total dollar amount you originally invested. If you've invested chunks of money at various points in time, this exercise becomes much more complicated. (Some of the investment software I recommend in Chapter 21 can help if you want your computer to crunch the numbers. Frankly, though, you have easier, less time-consuming ways to get a sense of how you're doing.)

How often should I check on my funds?

I recommend that you *don't* track the share prices of your funds every day. It's time consuming and nerve-racking and can make you lose sight of the long term. Worse, you'll be more likely to panic when times get tough. A weekly, monthly, or even quarterly check-in is more than frequent enough to follow your funds. I know many successful investors who check on their funds' performance twice or even just once a year.

If you do check your funds more often, one day, usually soon after you talk with a friend and mention how pleased you are with your fund's returns, you'll receive a rude awakening. "It dropped

$1.21 per share!" That's what one of my clients said to me after noticing the price of one of her international stock funds in December. Guess what? The fund made a distribution that reduced the price per share but increased the number of shares. So she wasn't losing money after all.

If you follow your funds through the daily newspaper and you see such a large price drop, look again to see if any special letters are printed after the fund's name, such as *x*, which indicates that a fund paid its dividend, and *e* for payment of a capital gains distribution.

Figuring total return

As I mention in the "Account value" section earlier in the chapter, fund companies make determining your total return in the fund from the information they provide on their statements almost impossible for you.

Regardless of the time period over which you're trying to determine your funds' total return, here are the simplest ways to figure total return without getting a headache:

✔ **Call the fund company's toll-free number or visit its Web site.** The telephone representatives can provide you with the total return for your funds for various lengths of time (such as for the last three months, the last six months, the last year, the last three years, and so on). Most fund companies post similar information on their Web sites as well.

✔ **Examine the fund's annual and semiannual reports.** These reports provide total return numbers.

✔ **Keep a file folder with your investment statements.** That way, you can look up the amount you originally invested in a fund and compare it to updated market values on new statements you receive. You can make a handwritten table or enter the figures in the software I describe in Chapter 21.

> ✔ **Check fund information services and periodicals.** Fund information services and financial magazines and newspapers carry total return data at particular times during the year. Some, such as *The Wall Street Journal,* carry this information daily. See my favorite Web sites in Chapter 21.

If you've made numerous purchases in a fund, you may want to know your effective rate of return when you also factor in the timing and size of each purchase. The only way to make this calculation is with software. However, you don't need to know the exact rate of return for your overall purchases in order to successfully evaluate your fund investments. Comparing your funds' performance over various time periods to relevant *performance benchmarks* is sufficient. (I explain how to do just that in the next section.)

Examining online charts of mutual fund prices over time on financial Web sites provides an inaccurate picture of a fund's total return. The reason is that most online charting services fail to correct for the effect of fund distributions (for example, capital gains and dividends). Take a simple example of a fund that begins the year at $20 per share and in late December is at $22 per share. Thus, it has increased 10 percent. However, further suppose it makes a distribution of $2 per share and thus ends the year at $20 per share. With an online chart, it would appear that the fund dropped sharply at year-end and provided no return for the year when in fact shareholders were rewarded with a 10 percent return. (Charts on fund company sites that show the change in value of an investment in a particular fund correct for this problem and do accurately show the returns of a fund over time.)

Which total return figures are best for the long term?

Fund companies typically report fund total returns in one of two ways. The *absolute return* measures the total percentage increase from the beginning to the end of the time period being looked at. The *annualized return* measures the average increase *per year* during the specified time period. Over a five-year period, for example, the absolute return of the Blue Chip Stock fund may be 98 percent, which translates to an annualized return of about 14.6 percent.

Don't be fooled by a more impressive-sounding absolute return. Remember, both numbers are measuring the same real return. Beware of fund companies that exploit the eye-catching qualities of absolute return numbers to make themselves look good in their marketing literature:

200 percent, 300 percent! Sounds spectacular, but it doesn't mean anything unless the time period and the performance of comparable funds and benchmarks are taken into account. If the time period is long enough, just about any fund's absolute return figure, especially if it's for a stock fund, is impressive looking, even if it's actually below average.

Annualized return numbers are much more useful for comparative purposes. Because a time factor — per year — is built in to the number, a glance at the annualized return gives you a much better idea of how a fund has performed and a much easier time comparing that performance to similar funds for similar time periods.

Assessing your funds' performance

Whenever you examine your funds' returns, compare those returns to appropriate *benchmark indexes*. Although many stock market investors may have been happy to earn about 10 percent a year with their investments during the 1980s and 1990s, they really shouldn't have been because the market averages or benchmark indexes were generating about 15 percent per year.

You should compare each mutual fund to the most appropriate benchmark given the types of securities that a fund invests in. For the bond and stock funds that I recommend in Chapters 12, 13, and 14, I provide descriptions of the types of securities that each fund invests in. The following sections offer a brief rundown of the benchmark indexes you'll find useful. (I present benchmarks for the types of funds most people use for longer term purposes, such as retirement account investing.)

Don't get too focused on performance comparisons. Indexes don't incur expenses that an actual mutual fund does although, as you may know, expenses among funds vary tremendously. Remember all the other criteria — such as the fees and expenses and the fund company's and manager's expertise — that you should evaluate when you consider a fund's chances for generating healthy returns in the years ahead (see Chapter 7).

Bond benchmarks

A number of bond indexes exist (see Table 17-2) that differ from one another mainly in the maturity of the bonds that they invest in; for example, short-term, intermediate-term, and long-term indexes.

Table 17-2		Bond Indexes			
Year	Barclays Short-Term Bond Index	Barclays Intermediate-Term Bond Index	Barclays Long-Term Bond Index	Barclays U.S. GNMA Index	Barclays High Yield (Junk Bond) Index
2000	8.9%	12.4%	16.2%	11.1%	−5.9%
2001	9.0%	8.8%	7.3%	8.2%	5.3%
2002	8.1%	13.0%	14.8%	8.7%	−1.4%
2003	3.4%	6.0%	5.9%	2.9%	29.0%
2004	1.9%	5.3%	8.6%	4.4%	11.1%
2005	1.4%	1.8%	5.3%	3.2%	2.7%
2006	4.2%	3.8%	2.7%	4.6%	11.9%
2007	6.1%	5.0%	3.6%	7.0%	1.9%

Year	Barclays Short-Term Bond Index	Barclays Intermediate-Term Bond Index	Barclays Long-Term Bond Index	Barclays U.S. GNMA Index	Barclays High Yield (Junk Bond) Index
2008	−1.1%	−4.7%	−3.9%	7.9%	−26.2%
2009	13.5%	19.0%	16.8%	5.4%	58.2%
5-year annualized average	4.8%	4.7%	4.5%	6.0%	7.8%
10-year annualized average	5.9%	7.0%	7.5%	6.3%	7.4%

Many more specialized indexes exist than those listed in Table 17-2; for example, indexes for municipal bonds, treasury bonds, and so on. So if you're looking at these different types of funds, take a look in the fund's annual report to see which index it compares the fund's performance to. But don't assume that it's using the most comparable index.

U.S. stock benchmarks

The major U.S. stock indexes (see Table 17-3) are distinguished by the size of the companies (large, small, all sizes, and so on) whose stock they're tracking. The Standard & Poor's 500 index tracks the stock prices of 500 large-company stocks on the U.S. stock exchanges. These 500 stocks account for more than 70 percent of the total market value of all stocks traded in the United States. The MSCI 1750 index tracks 1,750 smaller company U.S. stocks. The MSCI Broad Market index tracks all stocks of all sizes on the major U.S. stock exchanges.

Table 17-3	U.S. Stock Indexes		
Year	Standard & Poor's 500 Index	MSCI U.S. Small Cap 1750 Index	MSCI Broad Market Index
2000	−9.1%		
2001	−11.9%		
2002	−22.1%		

(continued)

Table 17-3 *(continued)*

Year	Standard & Poor's 500 Index	MSCI U.S. Small Cap 1750 Index	MSCI Broad Market Index
2003	28.7%		
2004	10.9%		
2005	4.9%	7.5%	6.4%
2006	15.8%	15.8%	15.7%
2007	5.5%	1.2%	5.6%
2008	−37.0%	−36.2%	−37.0%
2009	26.5%	36.1%	28.8%
5-year annual-ized average	0.4%	1.8%	1.0%
10-year annual-ized average	−0.9%	n/a	n/a

If you're evaluating the performance of a fund that invests solely in U.S. stocks, make sure to choose the index that comes closest to representing the types of stocks that the fund invests in. Also, remember to examine a stock fund's international holdings. Suppose, for example, that a particular stock fund typically invests 80 percent in U.S. stocks of all sizes and 20 percent in the larger, established countries overseas. You can create your own benchmark index by multiplying the returns of the MSCI Broad Market index by 80 percent and the Morgan Stanley EAFE international index (which I discuss in the next section) by 20 percent, and then adding them together.

International stock benchmarks

When you invest in funds that invest overseas, you should use a comparative index that tracks the performance of international stock markets. The *Morgan Stanley EAFE* (which stands for Europe, Australia, and Far East) index tracks the performance of the more established countries' stock markets. Morgan Stanley also has an index that tracks the performance of the emerging markets in Southeast Asia and Latin America (see Table 17-4).

Table 17-4	International Stock Indexes	
Year	Morgan Stanley EAFE	Emerging Markets
2000	−14.2%	−31.8%
2001	−21.4%	−4.9%
2002	−15.9%	−8.0%
2003	38.6%	51.6%
2004	20.3%	26.7%
2005	13.5%	32.8%
2006	26.3%	29.7%
2007	11.2%	39.4%
2008	−43.4%	−53.3%
2009	31.8%	78.5%
5-year average	4.0%	15.9%
10-year average	1.6%	10.1%

You should know that emerging markets are volatile and risky. As I discuss in Chapter 13, diversified international funds that invest in both established and emerging markets offer a smoother ride for investors who want some exposure to emerging markets. More-diversified funds also aren't as constraining on a fund manager who believes, for example, that emerging markets are overpriced.

If you do invest in the more diversified international funds that place some of their assets in emerging markets, remember that it's not fair to compare the performance of those funds solely to the EAFE index. So how do you fairly compare the performance of this type of fund? Well, if an international fund typically invests about 20 percent in emerging markets, then multiply the EAFE return in the table by 80 percent and add to that 20 percent of the *Emerging Markets* index return. For 2009, for example: 0.318(0.8) + 0.785(0.2) = 0.411, or 41.1 percent. With this computation formula, you can see how any international fund that invested in emerging markets in 2009 couldn't help but look good in comparison to the EAFE index. (The numbers in Table 17-4 also suggest why you shouldn't be too impressed with an emerging markets fund that boasted of a 60 percent return in 2009 — if it did, it was well below average!)

The hard part is finding out the percentage of assets a fund typically has invested in emerging markets. Some international funds don't report the total of their investments in emerging markets. For the international funds I recommend in Chapter 13, I provide some general idea of the portion they've invested in emerging markets. Also, you can peek at a fund's recent annual or semiannual report, in which the fund managers detail investments held for each country.

Deciding Whether to Sell, Hold, or Buy More

Investors often ask me, "How do I know when I should sell a fund?" The answer is relatively simple: *Sell only if a fund is no longer meeting the common-sense criteria* (which I outline in Chapter 7) *for picking a good fund in the first place.* Stick by your fund like a loyal friend as long as it is

✔ Generating decent returns relative to appropriate benchmarks and the competition

(Even one or two years of slight underperformance are okay if the fund's five- and ten-year numbers are still comparatively good.)

✔ Not raising the fees that it charges and not charging more than the best of the competition

✔ Still managed by a competent fund manager

The only other reason to sell a fund is if your circumstances change. For example, suppose that you're 50 years old, and you inherit a big pot of money. You hadn't been planning to retire early, but with oodles of money suddenly at your disposal, maybe now you're thinking that early retirement isn't such a bad idea after all. This change in circumstances may cause you to tweak your portfolio so that you have more income-producing investments and fewer growth investments.

This section deals with two special situations that require further thought and reflection: down markets and the acquisition of your funds by another company.

Handling bear markets

No one enjoys losing money. Most people find it unpleasant and at times stressful. If you follow my advice in the rest of this book, you know that I advocate building a diversified portfolio of funds and investing for the long term, not tomorrow. Eventually, you'll suffer a down period. Anyone who was investing in the early 2000s and late 2000s understands firsthand that stocks and stock mutual funds can drop significantly. So for handling such *bear* (down) markets in your funds, here is my advice:

✔ **Don't watch your funds too closely.** Tracking your fund's prices daily or even weekly is sure to make you a nervous wreck if you're doing so because you fear a market slide. Don't dwell on daily news reports of the latest stock market gyrations. Remember that you're investing for future years, not next week and next month.

✔ **See the glass as half full, not half empty.** When certain types of funds that you own decline in value, don't get depressed. If you're still feeding new money into purchases (or perhaps reinvesting distributions), remind yourself that your next purchases will be at lower prices. If you're retired and not making more purchases, you surely have the wisdom that good days and periods follow difficult ones. Be patient for improvement.

✔ **Look at your portfolio's performance, not individual funds.** The whole point of diversifying is so that some of your funds may go up while others are down. So, when some of your funds do decline, remember to assess the performance of your entire portfolio, and you may be pleasantly surprised that things aren't as bad as you may have thought.

✔ **Buy value (and different assets) if you dislike volatility.** Stock funds that focus on value-oriented stocks (please see Chapter 13) tend to be less volatile. You can also dampen the gyrations in your portfolio by investing in different types of assets (bonds, real estate, and so on).

Dealing with fund company consolidations

The fund industry is increasingly competitive, and some fund companies (usually those of the larger variety) swallow other (usually smaller) fund companies. Such mergers can lead to problems, but you can steer clear of them:

✔ Financial firms, including fund companies, have been known to put deposits into the wrong account or to lose track of certain accounts altogether. During the transition period, be vigilant about ensuring that your account information, including recent transactions and current balances, is correct.

✔ The new parent company in a merger may jack up fees or make other unfavorable changes to your fund. Use the straightforward criteria that I outline earlier in this section to determine what you should do post-merger.

Tweaking and Rebalancing Your Portfolio

Over longer periods of time, you may need to occasionally adjust your portfolio to keep your investment mix in line with your desires. Unless you experience a major change in your circumstances, I advocate adjusting your investment mix every three to five years (see Chapter 10). Suppose that at the age of 40, you invest about 80 percent of your retirement money in stock funds with the balance in bonds. By the age of 45, you find that the stock funds now comprise an even larger percentage (maybe 85 percent) of your investments because they've appreciated more than the bond funds have. *You* are also appreciating (in age, that is) and should in fact be reducing your stock allocation as you get older.

Using the asset allocation guidelines in Chapter 10, you decide that at the age of 45, you now want to have about 75 percent of your money in stock funds. The solution is simple: Sell enough of your stock funds to reduce your stock holdings to 75 percent of the total and invest the proceeds in the bond funds. Don't forget to factor in the tax consequences when you contemplate the sale of funds held outside retirement accounts (see Chapter 18).

Trying to time and trade the markets to buy at lows and sell at highs rarely works in the short term and never works in the long term. If you do a decent job *upfront* of picking good fund companies and funds to invest in, you should have fewer changes to make over the long haul.

If you have a good set of funds, keep feeding money into them as your savings allows. As your portfolio value grows, add a new fund or two to broaden your overall mix. Holding a couple (or several) of each different type of fund makes a lot of sense. (I cover the common sense of fund diversification in much depth in Chapter 10.) Don't end up with 50 funds though — you won't keep up with what they're doing and reviewing their reports.

Chapter 18

The Taxing Side of Mutual Funds

*Y*ou invest in mutual funds to make money. But guess who starts licking his chops when he hears about money being made? That's right: good ol' Uncle Sam. And state governments, too. (In Chapter 17, I explain the different ways that mutual funds can make you money: either through distributions (capital gains and dividends) or through appreciation. If the fund that made the money is being held outside a tax-sheltered retirement account, federal and state governments will demand a portion of your fund's distributions and of your profits when you sell shares in a fund for more than you paid for them.)

Once each year, the mutual fund companies or brokerage firms where you're holding funds send you one or more tax forms that tell you how much taxable money you made on your mutual funds held outside of retirement accounts. (Remember, you don't need to file anything with funds held inside retirement accounts.) Come April (or whenever you get around to completing your tax returns), you must transfer the information on these fund-provided tax forms to your income tax return, where you calculate how much tax you actually owe on the money you made from your mutual funds.

If you cringed when you read the words *tax forms,* you've obviously battled these ugly beasts. I sometimes wonder if the people who write tax forms come from another planet — that would perhaps explain their use of what appears to be a nonhuman form of communication. But don't despair. I devote this entire chapter to helping you interpret the hieroglyphics on these sometimes intimidating documents.

Just for toughing out this chapter, you get a few rewards. I show you how to use a fund's tax forms to help you discover whether your mutual fund money is being invested in the most tax-friendly way. I also give you some tips on reducing your tax bill if you have to sell some mutual funds.

Mutual Fund Distributions Form: 1099-DIV

If you're an employee of a company, you're probably familiar with IRS Form W-2, that little piece of paper that comes in late January or early February and sums up the amount of money your employer paid you over the previous year. You're required to report this income on your income tax return.

Form 1099-DIV is similar to a W-2, but instead of reporting income from an employer, it reports income from mutual funds that you hold outside of retirement accounts. By income, I mean capital gains and dividend distributions, which I explain in Chapter 17.

Like the W-2, Form 1099-DIV should arrive in your mailbox in late January or early February. You should get one for every nonretirement account you held money in during the tax year. Call the responsible company if you don't get one for an account that you think you should. (And if you're tired of receiving these forms from so many fund companies, visit Chapter 9, where I explain the paperwork-friendly benefits of consolidating your mutual fund holdings into a discount brokerage account.)

Also like the W-2, a copy of each of your 1099-DIVs is sent to the IRS and your state authorities, so don't get any ideas about fudging the information on your tax return.

Figure 18-1 is a sample Form 1099-DIV, which I use to walk you through the form. First, notice that the distributions are divided into various boxes. (Actually, most mutual fund companies display this information in columns, but they're still called boxes.) This division is done because different parts of your distributions are taxed at different rates, and the IRS wants to know what is what.

Jump in to these boxes and see what you find. In the following sections, I discuss the boxes that pertain to mutual funds.

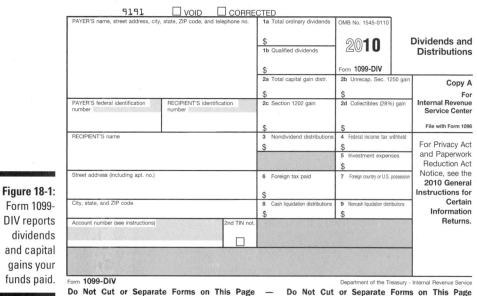

Box 1a: Total ordinary dividends

All types of mutual funds pay dividends, which account for all of a money market's return, most of a bond fund's return, and part of a stock fund's return. Thanks to tax laws passed in 2003, dividends paid by stocks are taxed at the same reduced tax rate that applies to long-term capital gains, which I discuss in just a bit. Stock dividends are termed *qualified dividends* and reported in Box 1b (discussed in the next section). Thus, Box 1a only includes dividends from taxable money market and bonds that are held by mutual funds.

Untrue to its name, however, ordinary dividends also include *short-term capital gains distributions* — profits from securities that the mutual fund bought and sold within a year. These short-term capital gains are lumped together with your dividend income because they're both taxed at your ordinary income tax rate.

The distributions reported as ordinary dividends are taxed at your highest possible rate: up to 35 percent on your federal income tax return depending on your annual income. If you're in a higher tax bracket, you don't want to see big ordinary dividends. You'd be better off with investments that don't produce so much taxable income. (Chapters 11 and 12 explain how to select tax-friendly money market and bond funds.) For stock mutual funds, if you're seeing big ordinary dividends, your fund must be making a lot of short-term trades. Outside of retirement accounts, regardless of your tax bracket, you have no reason to own mutual funds that generate a lot of short-term capital gains. Chapter 13 gives recommendations for tax-friendly stock funds.

Box 1b: Qualified dividends

Qualified dividends include dividends paid by corporations to their stockholders (stock dividends). If you're in the 10 or 15 percent federal income tax bracket, qualified (stock) dividends are tax-free — a 0 percent tax rate! For those in the higher federal tax brackets, the qualified dividend tax rate is 15 percent.

Box 2a: Total capital gains distributions

Because short-term capital gains are reported in Box 1a, this box would be more appropriately called "Long-term capital gains distributions," which are profits from securities sold more than 12 months after their purchase. Long-term capital gains are taxed at a lower rate than regular income, taxable money market and bond dividends, and short-term capital gains. The federal tax rate on long-term gains is 15 percent for those in an ordinary tax bracket of 25 percent or higher and long-term capital gains are tax-free for those in the 10 or 15 percent ordinary tax brackets.

You can count the lower tax rate on long-term capital gains as one more benefit of the buy-and-hold investing strategy (see Chapter 10). Not only does this strategy typically generate higher returns than short-term trading, but also for investments held outside of retirement accounts, it's gentler on your tax bill. The tax relief and the potential for higher returns are why mutual funds that tend to buy and hold their securities are preferable for nonretirement accounts.

Box 3: Nondividend distributions

You rarely see numbers in the *nondividend distributions* section of Form 1099-DIV. This box is where funds report if they made distributions during the year that repaid a shareholder's original investment. Like the principal returned to you if a bond or CD you've invested in matures, this chunk of money isn't taxable.

For shares held outside of retirement accounts, these nondividend distributions factor into your computation of the gain or loss when the shares are sold. For purposes of calculating any gain, if and when you sell these shares, you must subtract nondividend distributions from the amount you originally paid for these shares.

Box 4: Federal income tax withheld

 If your funds report that federal income tax was withheld, that can be bad news. It means that you're being subjected to the dreaded *backup withholding.* If you don't report all your mutual fund dividend income (or don't furnish the fund company with your Social Security number), your future mutual fund dividend income is subject to backup withholding of *28 percent!* To add insult to injury, in the not-too-distant future, you'll receive a nasty notice from the IRS listing the dividends you didn't report. You end up owing interest and penalties.

Find out right away what's going on here. Either you or the IRS could've made a mistake. Perhaps you didn't provide a correct Social Security number or you've been negligent in reporting your previously earned taxable income to the IRS. Fix this problem as soon as you can. Call the IRS at (800) 829-1040.

Don't despair about the tax that your fund withheld. The withholding wasn't for nothing — you'll receive credit for it when you complete your Form 1040 on the line "Federal income tax withheld."

Box 6: Foreign tax paid

If you invest in an international mutual fund, the fund may end up paying foreign taxes on some of its dividends. The foreign taxes paid by the fund are listed on Form 1099-DIV because the IRS allows you two ways to get some of this money back. You can choose one of the following:

- ✔ Deduct the foreign tax you paid on Schedule A (the "Other taxes" line), as long as you have enough deductions to itemize on Schedule A.
- ✔ Claim a credit on Form 1040 ("Foreign tax credit" line).

Because a credit is a dollar-for-dollar reduction in the tax that you owe, the latter move may save you more taxes — but it may also be more of a headache because you may need to complete *another* IRS form, Form 1116, which is a doozy. However, if the total foreign taxes you pay are $300 or less ($600 or less for a married couple filing jointly), you can claim the credit directly on Form 1040 without having to fill out Form 1116.

Get out last year's tax return

With all the fuss and muss over mutual fund distributions, you should note how the rest of your nonmutual-fund investments are positioned. Although taxes aren't everything, you may be paying much more than you need to.

Look at your Form 1040 to see how much taxable interest income you had to pay tax on. On Forms 1040 and 1040A, this figure goes on line

8a. If you filed 1040EZ (don't you just love that name?), the figure goes on line 2.

Now find out the rate of interest (percent yield) paid that generated this interest income. If it came from money in a bank account, odds are quite good that you could be earning more in a money market mutual fund (see Chapter 11).

When You Sell Your Mutual Fund Shares

Besides distributions, the other way to make money with a mutual fund is through appreciation. If the price of your shares moves higher than the price at which you bought them, your investment has appreciated. Your profit is the difference between the amount you paid for the investment and the amount the investment is currently worth. For investments held outside of retirement accounts, that profit is taxable.

However, you don't actually owe any tax on the appreciation until you sell the shares and lock up your profit. Then you must report that profit on that year's tax return and pay capital gains tax on it. Conversely, when you sell a fund investment at a loss, it's generally tax deductible. You should understand the tax consequences of selling your fund shares and always factor taxes into your selling decisions.

What's confusing to some people about this talk of capital gains and losses is that each year your fund(s) may have been paying you capital gains distributions (see the preceding section) which you also owed tax on. So you may rightfully be thinking, "Hey! I'm being taxed twice!"

It's true that you're being taxed twice but not on the same profits. You see, the profits the fund distributed, which resulted from the fund manager selling securities in his fund at a profit, are different from those profits that you realize by selling your shares.

You have no control over fund distributions. They happen at regular intervals — at least once a year — whether you like it or not, and you must pay taxes on them when they occur from nonretirement account holdings. Taxes on fund appreciation, on the other hand, can be indefinitely delayed if you choose. As long as you hold the investment and don't sell it, the federal and state governments can't get their hands on the profit — one more advantage of buy-and-hold investing. In fact, if you hold an appreciated asset outside of retirement accounts, that asset can be transferred at your death to your heirs, and the capital gain is eliminated for tax purposes. Of course, the other way to avoid taxes on mutual fund profits is to hold them inside retirement accounts; then you don't owe taxes at all (until, of course, you start taking retirement withdrawals).

Introducing the "basis" basics

Suppose that you sell a mutual fund. In order to compute the taxable capital gain or the deductible capital loss, you have to compute your fund's tax basis. *Basis* is the tax system's way of measuring the amount you originally paid for your investment(s) in a mutual fund. I say investments (plural) because you may not have made all your purchases in a fund at once; you may have reinvested your dividends or capital gains into buying more shares or simply bought shares at different times by sending the fund company additional money. For example, if you purchase 100 shares of the It's Gotta Rise mutual fund at $20 per share, your cost basis is $2,000, or $20 per share. Simple enough.

But now suppose that this fund pays a dividend of $1 per share (so that you get $100 in dividends for your 100 shares) and suppose further that you choose to reinvest this dividend into purchasing more shares of the mutual fund. The price of shares has gone up to $25 per share since your original purchase, so the reinvested $100 buys you four new shares. You now own 104 shares, which, at $25 per share, are worth $2,600.

But what's your basis now? Your basis is your original investment ($2,000) plus subsequent investments ($100) for a total of $2,100. Thus, if you sold all your shares at $25 per share, you'd have a taxable profit of $500 (current value of $2,600 less $2,100 — the total amount invested or basis).

For recordkeeping purposes, save your statements detailing the purchases in your accounts. Most mutual fund companies provide year-end summary statements that show all transactions throughout the year. Thanks to their computer systems, fund companies also should be able to tell you your average cost per share when you need to sell your shares. As I discuss in the following sections, using the average cost method isn't necessarily the optimal method to minimize your taxes.

Accounting for your basis

If you understand the concept of basis for your fund investments (see the preceding section), you can put that understanding to work. Here I introduce you to the different ways that taxpayers commonly use (and that the IRS approves) to calculate a basis when selling nonretirement account mutual fund investments.

If you sell all your shares of a particular mutual fund that you hold outside a retirement account at once, you can ignore this issue. (After reading through the accounting options that the IRS offers, you'll probably feel that you have more incentive to sell all your shares in a fund at once!)

 Be aware that after you elect one of the following tax accounting methods for selling shares in a particular fund, you can't change to another method for the sale of the remaining shares. Regardless of the method you choose, your mutual fund capital gains and capital losses are recorded on Schedule D of IRS Form 1040.

Regardless of which tax cost accounting method you choose for your fund sales, be careful not to overpay your capital gains tax when completing your annual tax return. Remember that the maximum tax rate for long-term capital gains (investments held more than 12 months) is 15 percent (tax-free if you're in the 10 or 15 percent federal tax bracket). Be sure to complete all the relevant portions of IRS Form 1040 Schedule D.

Specific identification method

The first fund basis option that the IRS allows you to use when you sell a portion of the shares of a fund is the *specific identification* method. Here's how it works. Suppose that you own 200 shares of Global Interactive Couch Potato fund (you laugh — but there really was a fund with a name similar to this!), and you want to sell 100 shares. Suppose further that you bought 100 of these shares ten years ago at $10 per share and then another 100 shares two years ago for $40 per share. (To keep this example simple, I'm assuming that you didn't make any other purchases from reinvestment of capital gains or dividends.) Today, the fund is worth $50 per share. (Being a couch potato has its rewards!)

Which 100 shares should you sell? The IRS gives you a choice. You can identify the *specific* shares that you sell. With your Global Interactive Couch Potato shares, you may opt to sell the last or most recent 100 shares you bought — or some combination of shares from each purchase that totals 100. (Selling the most recent shares will minimize your tax bill because you purchased these shares at a higher price.) If you sell this way, you must identify the specific shares you want the fund company (or broker holding the shares) to sell. To identify the 100 shares to be sold, use either or both of the following ways:

- ✔ Original date of purchase
- ✔ Cost when you bought the shares

You may wonder how the IRS knows whether you specified shares before you sold them. Get this: The IRS doesn't know. But if you're audited, the IRS will ask for proof that you identified the shares to be sold before you sold them. It's best to put your sales request to the fund company in writing and keep a copy for your tax files.

Although you can save taxes today if you specify selling the shares that you bought later at a higher price, don't forget (the IRS won't let you) that when you finally sell the other shares, you owe taxes on the larger profit. The longer you expect to hold these other shares, the greater your chances of earning more money when you sell (and thus owing more in taxes). Of course, you always run the risk that Congress raises tax rates in the future or that your particular tax rate rises.

The "first-in-first-out" method

Another method of accounting for which shares are sold is the method the IRS forces you to use if you don't specify before the sale which shares you want to sell: the *first-in-first-out* (FIFO) method. FIFO means that the first shares you sell are simply the first shares that you bought. Not surprisingly, because most stock funds appreciate over time, the FIFO method leads to paying more taxes sooner. In the case of the Global Interactive Couch Potato fund, FIFO considers that the 100 shares sold are the 100 that you bought ten years ago at the bargain-basement price of $10 per share.

The average cost method

Had enough of fund accounting? Well, unfortunately, we're not done yet. The IRS, believe it or not, allows you yet another fund accounting method: the *average cost method.* If you bought shares in chunks over time and/or reinvested the fund distributions (such as from dividends) into more shares of the fund, then tracking and figuring which shares you're selling could be a real headache. So the IRS allows you to take an average cost for all the shares you bought over time.

If you sell all your shares of a fund at once, you use the average cost basis method. You may also prefer this method when you sell a portion of a fund that you hold. Because many fund companies calculate this number for you, you can save time and possible fees paid to a tax preparer to crunch the numbers.

Deciding when to take your tax lumps or deductions

If funds held outside of retirement accounts increase in value, you won't want to sell them because of the tax bite. If, on the other hand, they decline in value, you may not know whether to sell them and, thus, lock in your losses. So how do you decide what to do and what role taxes should play in your decisions? As I discuss in Chapter 17, several issues can factor into your decision to sell a fund or hold on to it. Taxes are an important consideration. So, what do you need to know about them?

Cashing in long-term gains and keeping taxes low

You do need to realize that taxes are important, but don't let them keep you from doing something you really want to do. Suppose, for example, that you need money to buy a home or take a long-postponed vacation — and selling some mutual funds is your only source of money for this purpose. I say go for it. Even if you have to pay state as well as federal taxes totaling, say, 20 percent of the profit, you'll have a lot left over. Before you sell, however, do some rough figuring to make sure that you have enough money to accomplish your goal. Remember, you pay far lower tax rates when selling at a profit if you've held the fund for more than one year.

If you hold a number of funds, give preference to selling your largest holdings (that is, the ones with the largest total market value) with the smallest capital gains. If you have some funds that have profits and some with losses, you can sell some of each, subject to IRS rules, in order to offset the profits with the losses.

Selling for tax deductions and the famous wash sale rule

Some tax advisers advocate doing *year-end tax-loss selling.* The logic goes something like this: If you hold a mutual fund that has declined in value and you hold that fund outside a retirement account, you should sell it, take the tax write-off, and then buy the fund (or something similar) back. (In fact, you can employ this strategy at any point during the year, not just at year's end.)

I don't think that selling solely for taking a tax loss is worth the trouble, particularly if you plan on holding the repurchased shares for a long time. Remember that by selling and buying back the shares, you've lowered your basis, which increases the taxable profit after you sell the repurchased shares (assuming, of course, that they appreciate). To find out about your basis, see the section "Introducing the 'basis' basics," earlier in this chapter.

Plus, if you sell a fund for a tax loss and buy back shares in that same fund within 30 days of the sale, you can't deduct the loss because you violated the *wash sale rule*. The IRS won't allow deduction of a loss for a fund sale if you buy that same fund back within 30 days. As long as you wait 31 or more days, you won't violate the wash sale rule. If you're selling a mutual fund and want to reinvest that money soon, you can easily sidestep this rule simply by purchasing a fund similar to the one you're selling.

Try not to have *net losses* (losses plus gains) that exceed $3,000 in one year. You can't claim more than $3,000 in net short-term or long-term losses in any one year. If you sell funds with net losses that total more than $3,000 in a year, you must carry the excess losses over to future tax years. This situation not only creates more tax paperwork, but also it delays taking the tax deduction.

Looking at fund sales reports: Form 1099-B

When you sell shares in a mutual fund, you receive Form 1099-B early in the following year. This document is fairly useless because it doesn't calculate the cost basis of the shares that you sold. Its primary value to you is that it nicely summarizes all the transactions that you need to account for on your annual tax return. This form, which is also sent to the IRS, serves to notify the tax authorities of which investments you sold so that they can check your tax return to see if you report the transaction.

If some of the sales listed on your Form 1099-B are from check-writing redemptions, stop writing checks on those funds! Keep enough stashed in a money market fund and write checks only from that type of account. Money market fund sales aren't tax reportable because a money fund's share price doesn't change. Thus, you get fewer tax headaches!

Getting help: When you don't know how much you paid for a fund

When you sell a mutual fund that you've owned for a long time (or that someone gave you), you may have no idea of its original cost (also known as its *cost basis*).

If you can't find that original statement, start by calling the firm where you bought the investment. Whether it's a mutual fund company or brokerage firm, it should be able to send you copies of old account statements. You may have to pay a small fee for this service. Also, increasing numbers of investment firms (particularly mutual fund companies) automatically calculate and report cost-basis information on investments that you sell. Generally, the cost basis they calculate is the average cost for the shares that you purchased.

For a small fee, the research firm of Prudential American Securities may be able to help you figure out how much you originally paid for your funds. Contact the firm at (626) 795-5831 or online at www.securities-pricing.com.

Retirement Fund Withdrawals and Form 1099-R

Someday, hopefully not before you retire, you'll need or want to start enjoying all the money that you've socked away into great mutual funds inside your tax-sheltered retirement accounts. The following sections explain what you need to know and consider before taking money out of your mutual fund retirement accounts.

Minimizing taxes and avoiding penalties

Although many different types of retirement accounts exist (IRAs, SEP-IRAs, Keoghs, 401(k)s, 403(b)s, and so on), as well as many tax laws governing each, the IRS has declared one rule that makes understanding taxes on withdrawals a little easier. All retirement accounts allow you to begin withdrawing money, without penalty, after age 59½. (Why they didn't use a round number like 60 is beyond me.)

If you withdraw money from your retirement accounts prior to age 59½, in addition to paying current income tax on the distribution, you also must pay penalties — 10 percent of the amount of the taxable distribution at the federal level and whatever penalties your state charges. (You compute the penalty on Form 5329 — "Additional Taxes on Qualified Plans [Including IRAs] and Other Tax-Favored Accounts.")

Exceptions to the early withdrawal penalty do exist: You're allowed to make penalty-free withdrawals before the age of 59½ if any of the following conditions apply:

✔ You've stopped working after you reach age 55 (whether by retirement or termination).

✔ The withdrawal was mandated by a qualified domestic relations court order.

✔ You have deductible medical expenses in excess of 7.5 percent of your adjusted gross income.

Early retirement account distributions are also exempted from a penalty if they're paid because of death or disability, paid over your life expectancy, or rolled over to an IRA. Withdrawing money from an IRA for a first-time home purchase (up to $10,000) or higher education expenses is also permitted.

Issues to consider before making retirement account withdrawals

Generally speaking, most people are better off postponing withdrawals from retirement accounts until they need the money. But don't delay if waiting means that you must scrimp and cut corners — especially if you have the money to use and enjoy.

Suppose that you retire at age 60. In addition to money inside your retirement accounts, you have money available outside as well. If you can, you're generally better off using the money outside of retirement accounts *before* you start to tap the retirement account money.

If you're not wealthy, odds are good that you'll need (and want) to start drawing on your retirement account soon after you retire. By all means, do it. But have you figured out how long your nest egg will last and how much you can afford to withdraw? Most folks haven't. It's worth taking the time to figure how much of your money you can afford to draw on per year, even if you think that you have enough. Many good savers have a hard time spending and enjoying their money in retirement. Knowing how much you can safely use may help you loosen your purse strings.

One danger of leaving your money to compound inside your retirement accounts for a long time — after you're retired — is that the IRS *requires* you to start making withdrawals by April 1 of the year following the year you reach age 70½. If you don't, you pay a whopping 50 percent penalty on the amount that you should've taken out but didn't. (**Note:** This requirement doesn't apply to the new Roth IRAs.)

It's possible that because of your delay in taking the money out — and the fact that it'll have more time to compound and grow — you may need to withdraw a hefty chunk each year. Doing so could push you into higher tax brackets in those years that you're forced to make larger withdrawals.

If you want to plan how to withdraw money from your retirement accounts in order to meet your needs and minimize your taxes, some of the larger mutual fund companies that I recommend in this book have resources that can help you do the calculations. You can also hire a tax adviser to help. If you have a lot of money in retirement accounts, as well as the luxury of not needing the money until you're well into retirement, tax planning will likely be worth your time and money.

Of course, you pay current income taxes, both federal and state, when you withdraw money that hasn't previously been taxed from retirement accounts. The one exception is for withdrawing money early from the new Roth IRA accounts for a home purchase — in this case, you don't owe any income tax on the withdrawn investment earnings as long as you meet eligibility requirements.

Making sense of Form 1099-R for IRAs

If you receive a distribution from your mutual fund IRA, the mutual fund company or brokerage firm where you hold your funds will report the distribution on Form 1099-R (see Figure 18-2). These distributions are taxable unless you made nondeductible contributions to the IRA (a situation I cover momentarily).

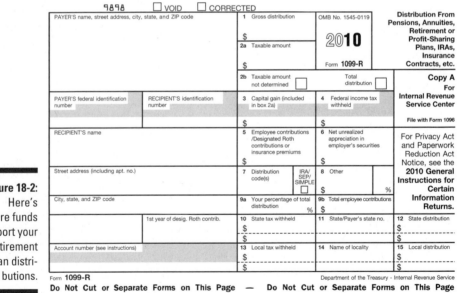

Figure 18-2: Here's where funds report your retirement plan distributions.

Here's a rundown of the relevant boxes on your 1099-R:

> ✔ **Box 1, Gross distribution:** The amount of money that you withdrew from your IRA. Make sure that this figure is correct: Check to see if it matches the amount withdrawn on your IRA account statement. This amount is fully taxable if you've never made a *nondeductible contribution* to an IRA — that's an IRA contribution in which you didn't take

a tax deduction and, therefore, filed Form 8606 ("Nondeductible IRA Contributions, Distributions and Basis").

✔ **Box 2a, Taxable amount:** The taxable amount of the IRA distribution. However, the payer of an IRA distribution doesn't have enough information to compute whether your entire IRA distribution is completely taxable or not. Therefore, if you simply enter this amount on your tax return as being fully taxable, you'll overpay on your taxes if you've made nondeductible contributions to your IRA. If you made nondeductible contributions, compute the nontaxable portion of your distribution on Form 8606, which you need to attach to your annual tax return.

Withdrawing from non-IRA accounts

Retirement account withdrawals from non-IRA accounts — such as 401(k), SEP-IRA, or Keogh plans — are taxed depending on whether you receive them in the form of an *annuity* (paid over your lifetime) or a lump sum. The amount you fill in on your 1040 tax return is reported on a 1099-R that you receive from your employer or another custodian of your plan, which may include an investment company, such as a mutual fund company or discount broker.

If you made nondeductible contributions to your retirement plan or contributions that were then added to your taxable income on your W-2, you aren't taxed when withdrawing these contributions because you've already paid tax on that money. The rest of the amount you receive is taxable.

Understanding form 1099-R for non-IRAs

You report non-IRA retirement account distributions on Form 1099-R, which is the same one you use to report IRA distributions. Sometimes people panic when they receive a 1099-R, and they intend to rollover their retirement account money into a fund from, say, their employer's retirement plan after they leave their job. Don't worry. You received this form because you *did* do a legal rollover and, therefore, won't be subjected to the tax normally levied on distributions.

The following list highlights how some of the other boxes on distributions for non-IRA retirement accounts come into play:

✔ **Box 3:** If the distribution is a lump sum and you were a participant in the plan before 1974, this amount qualifies for capital gain treatment.

✔ **Box 4:** This box indicates federal income tax withheld. (You get credit for this amount when you file your tax return.)

✔ **Box 5:** Your after-tax contribution is entered here.

✔ **Box 6:** Securities in your employer's company that you received are listed here. This amount isn't taxable until the securities are sold.

✔ **Box 7:** Your employer enters a code that explains the type of distribution you're receiving and why you're receiving it. (See the back side of your Form 1099-R for an explanation of the code.)

✔ **Box 8:** If you have an entry here, seek tax advice.

✔ **Box 9a:** This amount is your share of a distribution if there are several beneficiaries.

Chapter 19

Common Fund Problems and How to Fix Them

*E*stablished fund companies and discount brokerages have hundreds and, in some cases, thousands of telephone representatives who field phone calls and process stuff you send them in the mail. Most of the bigger and better companies recommended in this book do a good job of training their employees, so you should receive competent assistance. But keep in mind that these people are human — that is, not perfect. Some are more competent and service-oriented than others at getting the job done right the first time with the proper attitude. Although I can't guarantee that this chapter is a page turner, it can help bail you out and soothe your nerves when you just don't know how to get a problem fixed.

Playing the Telephone Game

When you call fund companies to ask a question or express a concern, you may end up speaking with someone who doesn't know how to fix your problem, gives you the runaround, or worse — gives you incorrect information. Here's what you can do to ensure that you get accurate solutions:

> ✔ **Know the representatives' limitations.** Fund company reps are there to provide assistance. Don't depend on them for tax advice. (Most of the larger fund companies have retirement account specialists who have more detailed knowledge about tax issues relating to those accounts.)

✔ **Talk to someone else.** If you don't get clear answers or answers that you're satisfied with, don't hesitate to ask for a supervisor. Or you can simply call back on the toll-free line, and you're sure to get another rep. This method is a proven way to get a second opinion to make sure that the first person knew what he was talking about.

✔ **Take names and notes for thorny problems.** If you're dealing with a problem that could cost you big bucks if not properly solved, take notes of your conversation. Write down the name of the representative you spoke to, the office she's located in, and her telephone extension. That way, you have some proof of your good efforts to fix things when you need to complain to or are summoned by a higher authority (for example, a supervisor, the IRS, and so on). E-mail or a written letter can be effective ways to document your problems and concerns, although some companies don't provide e-mail addresses.

✔ **Visit the fund company's Web site.** The larger fund companies have extensive Web sites that are equipped with good search capabilities. (See the Appendix for the addresses of the fund companies.)

Trouble-Shooting Bungled Transactions

With all the sound-alike fund names, you can mistakenly have your money deposited into the wrong fund at some firms. That's why it's a good idea to look at the statement that confirms your purchase to verify that the deposit amount and the fund into which the money was deposited are both correct.

If the fund company makes a mistake, it should cheerfully fix the problem. (It may need to do a bit of research first.) It should be willing to credit the correct amount to the fund you requested as of the date the money was originally received.

With increasing numbers of fund investors conducting transactions online, I'm hearing about more problems with such trades. Don't get me wrong — trading online is a fine thing to do, and the vast majority of transactions occur without a hitch. However, accidentally duplicating an online trade is a good example of a common mistake.

If you make a mistake trading online (or by phone), get on the phone and request help. Ask for a supervisor if frontline employees are unhelpful. Don't accept a response such as, "We can't correct online trades."

Specifying Funds to Buy at Discount Brokers

When you invest through most mutual fund companies, their account application and other forms allow you to indicate what fund(s) you want to make your deposit into. Not so at discount brokerage firms.

If you want your deposit to a discount brokerage to be immediately invested into a particular fund or funds, write your instructions and send them with your deposit. For example, if you mail $5,000 for an IRA deposit to a discount brokerage firm and you want the money divided between, say, the Fairholme Fund (FAIRX) and the Dodge & Cox International fund (DODFX), Figure 19-1 shows you how to word the letter.

Figure 19-1:
A sample
letter to
specify
funds with
discount
brokers.

Dear Sir or Madam:

Enclosed please find a check in the amount of $5,000 that I would like invested in my IRA account as a 2010 contribution (reference your account number or specify if new application is attached) as follows:

    $3,000 into Fairholme Fund (FAIRX)

    $2,000 into Dodge & Cox International (DODFX)

Please reinvest dividends and capital gains distributions.

Thanks a million,

Note the last sentence in the figure is a reference about what to do with dividends and capital gains distributions. Try to be as precise as possible with the fund names. The ultimate in precision for a broker is the fund's unique, five-letter trading symbol (three letters for exchange-traded funds).

Making Deposits in a Flash

Maybe you have an account open and just need to feed it in a hurry. Most often, this situation happens when you need to fund a retirement account, but it may also happen if you're on the verge of overdrawing a money market account due to outstanding checks and withdrawals.

If you need to make a deposit in a flash, you basically have the three following options:

✔ **Write a check.** You can stop by and deposit it at the company's local branch office if you're dealing with a company with a branch location near you.

✔ **Wire the money from your bank account.** If the fund company isn't in your neighborhood, don't despair. However, note that wiring usually costs money on both ends.

After you've set up the wiring feature on your fund account (see Chapter 16), call your fund company to see what information you need to provide to your bank in order for the wire to be correctly sent. This usually includes

- The name of the bank your fund uses for wires

- The bank's identification number (the nine-digit ABA number)

- The title and account number of the fund company's account at that bank

- Your name as it appears on your fund account

- The name of the fund account

- Your own account number

If you don't have the wiring feature set up on your account, establishing this feature takes some time because you must request, fill out, and mail a special form.

✔ **Electronically transfer the funds.** Electronic funds transfer, which is like a paperless check, usually takes a day longer than a wire, but it's free. Simply call your fund company and say how much money you want to move. As with wiring, if you don't have this feature set up, you can establish it by requesting and filling out a form from the fund company.

Verifying Receipt of Deposits

When you send money to a fund company, how do you know if the fund company received your money? Unlike when you use a bank ATM, you won't get a deposit slip with your transaction — at least, not right away. Fund companies mail you a statement (usually the day after they receive and process the deposit) that shows you the transaction. You can keep a log of deposits on paper or with a computer program and check them off when you receive the deposit statement, once a month, or quarterly.

If you can't wait for the mail, you can call the fund company's toll-free number and verify receipt over the phone. Many fund companies have secure Web sites and automated phone systems that allow you to check on stuff like this quickly, without waiting for a live person to talk to.

Transferring Money Quickly

For nonretirement accounts, if you have a money market fund with check-writing privileges, writing a check to get money is quick and simple and costs nothing. Another option, which you can use on all types of accounts, is to call the fund company and request a *telephone redemption*. The day after the next financial market close, a check should be cut and mailed to you. If you need the check faster than the mail service can get it to you, you can provide your express mail company (for example, FedEx, UPS, or DHL) account number. Some fund companies also allow you to pick up redemption checks at their headquarters. Call to see whether they provide this service.

Banks and other recipients of checks from your account may annoy you by placing a hold for a number of days on the funds from your checks. For checks that you write yourself, the hold is understandable because the check recipient has no way of knowing whether the money will be in the account when the check is ready to clear. But if the check was issued by the fund company, then the money has already been taken from your account, so the check is almost as good as cash to recipients — they just need to wait a couple of days for receipt of the funds.

Banks normally place up to a five-day hold on out-of-state checks. (Odds are that your fund company clears checks through an out-of-state bank.) If a bank doesn't make the money available to you quickly, ask to speak to the branch manager or some other higher-up. Gently remind him that you can move your bank accounts to a less bureaucratic bank.

Wiring and electronic funds transfers are other alternatives that you may prefer because you don't need to wait for a paper check to clear. If you just realized that you need money to close on a home purchase tomorrow, these are your best bets. See the section "Making Deposits in a Flash" earlier in this chapter for how these services work.

For retirement account withdrawals, you need to make requests in writing. Perhaps you need to withdraw money before the end of December to meet the IRS's mandatory withdrawal requirements after age 70½. The good news here is that you don't need to have received the funds before the end of the year. As long as the distribution is made by the end of December, the IRS will be satisfied.

Losing Checks in the Mail

Checks and other stuff can get lost in the mail. If you wrote a check and made it payable to the fund company, you don't need to stop payment. If you're depositing checks with your fund company that someone else wrote to you, the check's issuer may want to stop payment when you report to it that the check is lost and you want it reissued, if it's concerned that you might cash it.

A bigger pain is having to redo a bunch of account applications that you may have sent with the check(s). If you are completing a pile of applications and transfer forms, you may want to keep copies. Or, you investigate if the fund company allows you to complete forms through its Web site.

Registered mail and certified mail don't eliminate the problem of lost mail. They just indicate whether the mail was received. Don't waste the money or the time needed to go to the post office to use these extra mail services.

Changing Options after Opening Your Account

Perhaps now you wish you had check writing on your money market fund. Or you want to establish a regular monthly investment plan so that money is sent electronically from your bank account to some funds. How do you add these features after you've opened an account?

Although you can add some features over the phone, you can only set up most features, particularly the ones that require your signature — such as check writing — through short forms that you request by phone. (Some fund companies allow you to add these account features via their Web sites, as I discuss in Chapter 16.) You can change previously established options, such as reinvestment of dividends, over the phone or via the fund company's Web site.

Changing the registration of your accounts is more of a pain. A letter is generally required, for example, if you marry and change your name or want to add your spouse to the account. A *signature guarantee* may be required — these guarantees are provided by banks and brokerage firms. Don't confuse this requirement with getting something notarized, which is different.

Making Sense of Your Statements and Profits

Can't understand your fund statement? Don't know how much money your fund is making for you? Welcome to a large and nonexclusive club. See Chapter 17 for the full scoop.

If you want a tax, financial, or legal adviser — or a savvy relative — to help you keep an eye on your investments, you can ask that she be listed on your account as an *interested party* to receive duplicate statements. Simply write to the fund company and include the accounts you want the interested party to receive statements for and provide that person's name and mailing address.

Changing Addresses

Normally, fund companies require that you make a change of address in writing, but over time more fund companies are establishing security procedures that allow you to make a change of address by phone or via a Web site. The safeguards include a requirement that you prove that you're who you say you are on the phone (give your mother's maiden name and all that). The fund companies also mail confirmations of the changed address to both old and new addresses and don't allow money to be transferred out to the address for, say, 15 days to give the mail sufficient time to deliver confirmation of the address change to both the new and old addresses.

Finding Funds You Forgot to Move

Every year, people literally throw away hundreds of millions of dollars in investments, including investments in mutual funds. You may have done this if you've moved around a lot without systematically sending changes of address to fund companies and placing mail-forwarding orders with the post office. After fund companies try for a long time to send mail to your old address, they eventually throw in the towel, and your account becomes dormant. No more statements are sent for a number of years, after which time your account is considered abandoned!

By law, the mutual fund company must transfer your abandoned money to the treasurer's office (called *escheatment,* for you Trivial Pursuit or game show buffs) of the state in which the fund company does business or the state in which the last registered address appeared on your account. This transfer may happen from within a few years to more than a decade after the fund company loses contact with you. If you don't claim the money within a certain number of years after that, the state gets to keep it.

If you vaguely recall that you had funds with a particular fund company way back when, call the company. You don't need to remember the specific funds you invested in. By using your name, Social Security number, old mailing addresses, and personal stuff like that, the fund company's computer system can find your accounts and determine whether they were turned over to the state. You can also try contacting the state treasurer's office in the states in which you've lived to see whether they have any of your abandoned accounts. (You can do this as well for recently deceased relatives in the event you're concerned that you may have overlooked some of their accounts.) If you find your accounts, please write to me in care of the publisher and let me know — these successes make me happy!

Untangling Account Transfer Snags

Transferring accounts from one investment firm or bank to another can be a big pain. Even obtaining the correct transfer paperwork and completing it are challenges — that's why I detail how to do these steps in Chapter 16.

Problems happen most often with retirement accounts and with brokerage account transfers. Some firms are reluctant to give up your money, and so they drag their feet, doing everything they can to make your life and the lives of employees who transfer accounts at your new investment company a nightmare. The biggest culprits are the supposed "full-service" brokerage firms that employ commission-based brokers. They've lost a lot of money flowing out to no-load and discount brokers' mutual funds, and they do what they can to hang on. The unfortunate reality is that they'll cheerfully set up a new account to accept your money on a moment's notice, but they'll drag their feet, sometimes for months, when it comes time to relinquish your money.

Don't let this foot dragging on the part of brokerage firms deter you from moving your money to a better investment firm. Remember that the transfer should, under securities industry regulations, be done within 30 days. If it's not, hammer the villains! Should the transfer not be complete within a month, get in touch with your new investment firm to determine what the problem is. If your old company isn't cooperating, a call to a manager there may help get the ball rolling. To light a fire under his behind, tell the manager at the old firm that you'll be sending letters to the Financial Industry Regulatory Authority (FINRA) and the Securities and Exchange Commission (SEC) if he doesn't complete your transfer within the next week. Then do it.

In addition to uncooperative brokers, certain assets present problems with transfers. If you purchase any house-branded mutual funds at commission-based brokerage firms, in addition to buying into what's likely a relatively mediocre family of funds, you also can't transfer their funds as they are. You must first have them liquidated through the broker whose name is on them so that the cash proceeds can be transferred. Most annuities work the same way.

Transfer individual securities, such as stocks and bonds, to a discount broker. That way, if you later decide to sell them, you save on commission charges. Limited partnerships generally can't be liquidated, and everybody levies fees to hold them — another reason not to buy them in the first place. If you want less account clutter, transfer these to the discount broker you're otherwise going to be using.

Eliminating Marketing Solicitations

If you do business with many companies and their marketing folks are driving you batty, call your fund companies and ask them to code your account on their advanced computer systems so that you won't receive anything other than statements and reports on your funds. Fund companies are required under SEC regulations to honor such a request. Fund companies are happy to oblige — they don't want irritated customers.

As for all the other junk mail you get, send a request not to receive junk mail (including your name, complete home address) to the Direct Marketing Association, Mail Preference Service, P.O. Box 643, Carmel, NY 10512. You can also complete the form on the association's Web site at www.dma choice.org.

Some fund companies and brokers may call you at home soliciting your purchase of investments. They tend to focus on people with large cash balances sitting in their accounts. To stop any type of sellers from calling you in the future, you have the Do Not Call Registry on your side. Register for free either online at www.donotcall.gov or call (888) 382-1222 from the number you want to register.

Digging Out from under the Statements

If you're being buried in paperwork from statements and transaction confirmations from too many fund companies, consider consolidating your fund holdings through a discount broker. Trade-offs do exist — you pay more in fees for the convenience that these accounts offer (see Chapter 9). Some fund companies also have ways to consolidate statements, but you may have to specifically request this service for your statements.

If you truly abhor getting paper statements in the mail, increasing numbers of fund firms allow you to "turn off" receiving such clutter and view your statements online. Visit your favorite fund company Web sites for details.

Getting Older Account Statements

Perhaps, for reasons of nostalgia or taxes, you need copies of a statement that's more than a year old. Most companies should have no problem providing it (and some have Web sites allowing you to retrieve such history). Some smaller companies may, however, charge you something like $10 per fund per year requested. So be choosy. The main reason you'd request a statement is to research how much you originally invested in a mutual fund held outside of a retirement account. If you sold or are thinking about selling shares of the fund, you may have to figure out the fund's cost basis for tax reporting purposes (see Chapter 18). In the future, be sure to keep your statements so you don't need to ask for copies.

If you're going to sell _all_ the shares that you hold in a fund, check to see if your firm can report the average cost of the shares sold. If its accounting system can do this, you're golden, and you don't need to bother with getting the old statements.

Chapter 20

Fund Ratings and Forecasters

In This Chapter

▶ Steering clear of the lousy newsletters

▶ Getting investment information from the best sources

My father loves data and analyzing it. He likes figuring out how things work. Before he retired, he was a mechanical engineer. (Impressively, he worked his entire career in one field.) He loves making charts and graphs. During the months that I wrote the first edition of this book, he was poring over a veritable truckload of data and information on mutual funds and investing.

So I wrote this chapter for people like my dad. Even if you're not an engineer by training, there may be a bit of a data lover in you. The challenge as you navigate the landscape of mutual fund data, newsletters, references, and gurus is discerning the good from the merely mediocre — as well as the downright useless and dangerous information and advice. Unfortunately, more of the latter are out there waiting to trip you up.

Avoiding the Bad Stuff

I start with the bad stuff because so much bad investment advice is out there, and odds are good that you may currently be using some of it or thinking of using it, or it may be pitched to you in the future. Finding out the tricks of the trade enables you to better identify the good stuff. But if you're pressed for time and can't bear to see the ugly side of the investment newsletter business, skip ahead to the good sources that I recommend later in this chapter. (I cover software and Web sites in Chapter 21.)

Newsletters cost you time and money. Don't use newsletters for predictive advice. If these prognosticators were that smart about the future of financial markets, they'd be successful money managers making a lot more money. The only types of publications you should consider subscribing to are those that offer research and information rather than predictions. (I discuss those publications in the "Getting In on the Good Stuff" section in this chapter.)

Looking into market timing and crystal balls

Market timing — even in the form of slick, professional-looking packaging and claims — is a losing proposition. Many fund investors believe that they can increase their chances of success if they follow the predictions of certain gurus. Gurus often say (or imply) that they can tell you when you should be in or out of the markets or particular investments. Whenever a prognosticator near you treats you to such "wisdom," just repeat after me:

"No one can predict the future."

"No one can predict the future."

"No one can predict the future."

If you can remember this one simple fact — a fact supported by mountains of evidence and plenty of good, old-fashioned common sense — you'll dramatically increase your chances for successful investing in funds, and you will decrease the odds of making major mistakes. *And* you'll have a much clearer vision about which resources to use for further reading and research about funds. As I explain in Chapter 10, the strategy of market timing is doomed to failure in the long run.

Take a look at the performance track record of investment newsletters. According to *The Hulbert Financial Digest* (see the next section), which looks at risk as well as return, only a few newsletters have managed to keep ahead of the market averages over the past 15 years. And these newsletters only managed to do so by a small margin (and that doesn't take into account the cost of subscribing to a newsletter). The worst investment newsletters, on the other hand, have underperformed the market averages by dozens of percentage points: Some would've even caused you to lose money during time periods when the financial markets performed extraordinarily well.

Of course, you'd never know about newsletters' dismal performances if all you ever listened to were the claims made by newsletter writers themselves. Most claim that they told their loyal followers to sell everything just before the last dozen times that the stock market plunged. They also usually go on to proclaim that they advocated buying at every bottom in the market.

Newsletter writers don't know anything that isn't already reflected in the prices of securities. If newsletter writers did have a knack for unearthing information that no one else typically knew, they'd be too busy investing their own money and making millions off their predictions to waste their time publishing a newsletter.

Keeping them honest and providing new fodder: The Hulbert Financial Digest

Mark Hulbert started a useful business in the 1980s. Almost every investment newsletter was making outrageous claims about the success of its previous predictions. But how could you, the potential new subscriber, know whether a newsletter was telling the truth or blowing smoke? Answer: You couldn't.

Not until Mark Hulbert came along, that is. He tracks the actual performance of the newsletters' investment picks. He tracks each newsletter's recommendations. So, over time, Hulbert knows exactly how the newsletters' picks have done.

Has *The Hulbert Financial Digest* stopped the outrageous claims of the investment newsletters? No, but the claims seem to be slowly getting more accurate, thanks to Hulbert's influence. The problem is that people still believe the marketing hype of the newsletters and never bother to check with Hulbert's service.

Hulbert's service has created another problem, however. Many newsletters can claim to be number one by selecting short time periods when they actually were number one, even though they've underperformed the rest of the time. And some falsely lay claim to the number one status by simply comparing their performance to all those that are worse, while ignoring the ones that perform better!

Using bogus rankings, token awards, and mystery testimonials

Newsletters also cite rankings from other organizations (such as *Timer's Digest*) in their efforts to justify their claims of *numero uno* status. Given enough time periods and categories of newsletters, many newsletter writers can claim the coveted number one spot at some time or another.

Newsletters also refer to awards they've won from the Newsletter Publisher's Association (NPA). My advice: Ignore NPA awards. They're meaningless. They have nothing to do with the performance of a newsletter's advice. And because the NPA is an association made up of the newsletters themselves, they're just giving themselves a pat on the back! Not a very objective way to dole out awards, eh? (The association isn't very large and is always doling out awards, which doesn't hurt newsletter writers' chances of winning, either.)

And, of course, you have the inevitable customer testimonials. Curiously, though, testimonials almost always parrot the promotional material for the newsletter, and they never include the person's name. All they provide are the person's initials, such as B.S., and good old B.S.'s home, such as Brooklyn, N.Y. Some of these testimonials are made up — so they really are B.S.!

Pitching a product: Filler and ads in newsletter form

Many newsletter writers publish newsletters as a means of drawing people into their money management business. For some, that's the only reason they produce the newsletter. So they don't really want to teach you too much about investing; they want to convince you that your money is best off in their hands — which means that their articles are usually trying to tell you that investing is complicated and market timing is everything.

Some newsletters that are already short on content plug their money management service *right in the newsletter.* One monthly newsletter that sells for more than $100 per year publishes issues that are 80 percent filler; performance numbers for funds are an example of this filler. In the four pages of articles in the typical newsletter, readers often confront a plug for the editor's money management business because (according to him) a newsletter's advice can't substitute for the daily oversight of your portfolio.

Don't believe it. Of course, this claim isn't what they told you in their marketing materials to get you to subscribe to the newsletter. What the newsletter should've said (and what would've been accurate) is that the editor nets a lot less profit by selling a newsletter than he does by landing another client for his money management business.

Investing newsletter Hall of Shame

The following sections reveal some of the many examples of the really heavy stuff that gets shoveled by some of these folks to sell you on their investment newsletters. All the examples are drawn from real-world newsletters. However, I've modified the names to keep you focused on the types of misleading practices that marketing newsletters engage in instead of having you focus on the particular scoundrels behind each of these disreputable newsletters.

Dwayne Dweeb's Personal Finance

Dwayne Dweeb's newsletter marketing materials issue the following proclamation about Dweeb, a veteran newsletter writer: "A Millionaire Maker Outsmarts the Market. Again." In a glossy, multipage brochure, Dweeb is said to have "the highest IQ of them all . . . somewhere between Einstein, Mother Theresa, and an IBM mainframe." (I'm not making this up!)

His literature goes on to say: "The reason he can expand your money by 30 percent to 50 percent a year is sheer mental horsepower." You're also told that his newsletter is rated number one by "both of the major rating services." Dweeb's materials assert that he's developed a brilliant and totally awesome proprietary model, which he calls the "Numero Uno Indicator." His claim is that this model has predicted the last 28 (count 'em, 28) upturns in the market in a row without a single miss. The odds of doing this, according to Dweeb, are more than 268 million to 1!

But wait, it gets better. The ad goes on to claim that Dweeb's "Numero Uno Indicator" market timing system could've turned a $10,000 investment into $39.1 million in 12 years. That would be a return of 390,000 percent!

Does this claim sound too good to be true? You got it. This outrageous claim, if not purely fabricated, was based on *backtesting,* looking back over historical returns and creating "what if" scenarios. In other words, Dweeb didn't turn anyone's $10,000 into $39.1 million. Much too late after that ad appeared, the Securities and Exchange Commission (SEC) finally charged Dweeb with false advertising. Dweeb settled out of court, and a $60,000 fine was imposed.

Here's the real scoop on Dweeb's investing ability. In 1991, Dweeb established a mutual fund. Over the next decade, this fund was one of the worst growth stock funds around. His fund underperformed about 90 percent of its peers.

Harry Hacker's Mutual Fund Investing

Steer clear of anyone who claims to be "America's #1 Mutual Fund Adviser." I remember Hacker's name as if it were my own, because for a while, it seemed, once a month I'd receive a glossy color brochure more than 20 pages long from him in the mail. Like Dweeb (see the preceding section), Hacker claimed to have been rated number one by Hulbert. Hulbert responds, "It is a fabrication. *Mutual Fund Investing* is not now, nor has it ever been, rated number one by my digest." Hulbert was so incensed by Hacker's claim that he devoted an entire column, appropriately entitled "Lies and near lies" to setting the record straight in *Forbes* magazine.

Mutual confusion: Misuse of fund ratings

Rating mutual funds has become a national obsession. When you check out business and financial publications, be cautious about fund ratings. Whether they're letter grades (ranging from "A" for best to an "F" for worst or a number system, *fund ratings* purport to rank how good particular funds are. The most common mistake investors make in using even the better mutual fund publications is focusing too much on the ranking of specific funds.

Dan Wiener, editor of *The Independent Adviser for Vanguard Investors* newsletter (discussed in the next section of this chapter), did an interesting analysis of four major financial magazines lists of best funds. Amazingly, more than 80 percent of the chosen funds appeared on just one of the four lists and not even one fund made it on all four lists. Clearly, different publications have widely varying criteria.

The problem with many fund-rating systems is that they're based on history and overweight the most recent performance of funds. The mutual fund landscape is littered with plenty of funds that were yesterday's stars that have become today's losers and has-beens (see Chapter 7). A problematic fund rating system is one that

✔ Ignores the risk of a fund and its costs

✔ Gives costs little weighting to these two important factors

Soon after Hulbert's scathing column about Hacker appeared in *Forbes,* in Hacker's next mailing he changed his tune a bit. His newer marketing materials displayed a colorful chart showing that his stock and bond fund picks returned 1,517 percent over a 15-year period — for a nearly 20 percent annualized rate of return, which would've put him in an exclusive league with the like of investing legend Warren Buffett. This return would imply that his advice had beaten the average stock fund, which over the same time period returned just 14.7 percent per year, and the average bond fund, at 9.1 percent per year, by some distance significantly greater than a country mile.

Hulbert's tracking of Hacker's recommendations clearly shows that Hacker's portfolio returns fell *well below* the market averages.

Getting In on the Good Stuff

If you want to read more about investments, by all means read more. But read *useful* information. Most of the better financial magazines and newspapers, for example, cost a fraction of the newsletters' prices, and provide more useful information.

Many of the major financial publications — *Barron's, Business Week, Forbes, Fortune, Kiplinger's Personal Finance, SmartMoney,* and *The Wall Street Journal* — do annual mutual fund roundups. Most newspapers and many large news magazines provide fund coverage as well. Some good newsletters are available, too.

Morningstar Mutual Funds

If you want a snapshot summary of a lot of data, as well as some thoughtful analysis about a fund you're considering investing in or currently own, Morningstar can't be beat. Most of the information summarized on its pages comes from a fund's prospectus and semiannual reports. Some of the data it provides for funds may take you hours to calculate and may require a sophisticated computer software program.

Morningstar Mutual Funds covers load funds (funds that carry commissions) as well as no-load funds. As I explain in Chapter 7, loads are an additional cost to buy funds that brokers sell. If you have load funds that you want to evaluate, Morningstar Mutual Funds can help.

A one-year, Web-based subscription costs $179. (See Chapter 21 for details on the Morningstar Web site and software offerings.) In the sections that follow, I highlight the more pertinent information in an individual Morningstar bond fund and stock fund report.

Reading a Morningstar bond fund report

In this section, I highlight some of the more useful features to examine for bond funds that you may be considering.

- ✔ **Quote:** This section presents a data dump of all sorts of information for the fund over more than the past decade. Here you can see how the total return, performance versus benchmarks, dividend (income), capital gains, the fund's annual operating expenses, and trading (turnover rate) have varied over the years.

- ✔ **Management:** This section highlights the fund's managers and notes the date the manager(s) started managing the particular fund as well as their investment management experience.

- ✔ **Strategy:** This section provides a summary of the general investment objectives and limitations that a fund subjects itself to.

- ✔ **Performance:** The first section displays the total amount that investors made or lost (from dividends, capital gains, and share price changes) for each quarter over the past seven years. This section can give you a sense of the likely volatility of an investment in the fund. (Remember, though, that this is history, and the future will differ.) If you get queasy looking at these numbers, don't invest.

The second section — the trailing returns — shows annualized total return information over longer time periods. (Total return numbers don't account for loads, but you're not going to pay any anyway, are you?) The fund's returns are also compared to benchmark indexes, which in some cases aren't so comparable. (See Chapter 17 for more background on benchmarks.)

✔ **Portfolio:** This data is summarized from a fund's most recent reporting. Detailed are the total number of securities this fund holds and the listing of the top 25 holdings.

- The *Investment Style* box shows you which types of bonds the fund mainly holds at the moment (in this case, high-quality, intermediate-term bonds). Measures of interest rate sensitivity — average maturity and duration (both of which I explain in Chapter 12) — are provided here, as well as the average credit quality of the fund's bonds.

- *Sector Weightings* quantifies the fund's current holdings of the major types of bonds. *Asset Allocation* details the fund's recent holdings of cash, bonds, and other securities. This section is worth looking at to determine whether a fund really is what it says it is.

- The *Bond Quality* section highlights the fund's holdings by the credit rating of the bonds it is invested in (see Chapter 12).

✔ **Fund Analysis:** Each fund at Morningstar is assigned an analyst. Analysts use available information, as well as interviews with fund company managers (and others), to summarize the fund strategies. This section is usually well worth reading, especially if you're *not* a numbers kind of person.

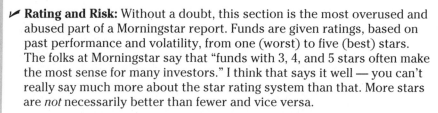

✔ **Rating and Risk:** Without a doubt, this section is the most overused and abused part of a Morningstar report. Funds are given ratings, based on past performance and volatility, from one (worst) to five (best) stars. The folks at Morningstar say that "funds with 3, 4, and 5 stars often make the most sense for many investors." I think that says it well — you can't really say much more about the star rating system than that. More stars are *not* necessarily better than fewer and vice versa.

Here you see more details for the determination of the ranking and the way the fund rates over different periods.

All sorts of other quantitative measurements of risk are presented here. One of the more useful is *beta,* which helps you calibrate the volatility of a fund compared to relevant benchmarks. The overall bond market benchmark is assigned a beta of 1.00. Thus, a fund with a beta of 1.2

implies that it's 20 percent more volatile on average (perhaps because it invests in longer term bonds or lower credit-quality bonds).

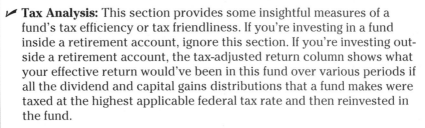

✔ **Tax Analysis:** This section provides some insightful measures of a fund's tax efficiency or tax friendliness. If you're investing in a fund inside a retirement account, ignore this section. If you're investing outside a retirement account, the tax-adjusted return column shows what your effective return would've been in this fund over various periods if all the dividend and capital gains distributions that a fund makes were taxed at the highest applicable federal tax rate and then reinvested in the fund.

Potential Capital Gains Exposure measures how much, if any, unrealized profit exists. The larger the number here, the greater the potential risk of larger distributions in the future, particularly for funds that trade a lot (that is, that have a high turnover), as this one does.

✔ **Purchase Information:** Here's where you see how to get in touch with the fund, how much is required as a minimum investment, and so on.

Reviewing a Morningstar stock fund report

Morningstar's stock fund reports carry much of the same types of information that its bond fund reports contain. I won't repeat my explanations of the same sections I cover for a bond fund report. (To see what I'd be repeating if I *did* talk about it here, skip back to the preceding section.) The sections of a stock fund report that significantly differ from a bond fund page include

✔ **Quote:** Stock funds, of course, have different benchmark indexes suitable for comparison purposes.

✔ **Portfolio:** The summary of a fund's holdings is the most important area of difference between a stock fund report and a bond fund report. That's no surprise, though, because stocks are quite different from bonds.

Similar to the bond fund report, the stock fund page notes the total number of securities that it holds. A list of the top 25 securities, along with what portion each stock comprises of the fund's assets and its recent return and price-earnings ratio, also shows up here.

- *Investment Style* classifies a fund's current stock holdings based on the size of the company, as well as on whether those stocks tend to be growth, value, or both. (I cover the difference among these various types of stocks in Chapter 13.) The page also presents a variety of statistical measures for the stocks that the fund holds. For example, you can see the average rate of growth in the earnings of the companies that this fund invests in and how that rate compares to that of other funds in its category.

- *Asset Allocation* is also useful because it indicates whether a fund is holding major cash positions and whether it invests in securities other than stocks. *Market Cap* shows how the fund is allocating its holdings among stocks of companies of varying sizes. *Sector Weightings* breaks down a fund's stock holdings by industry and compares the fund's holdings to those of a relevant index.

No-Load Fund Analyst

Those people who enjoy doing more reading about funds and the financial markets should consider the *No-Load Fund Analyst* newsletter, which tracks a much smaller universe of the better no-load funds than Morningstar does. This monthly publication provides commentary and analysis of trends in the economy, happenings in the fund industry, and fund manager interviews and profiles. In an industry in which many publications claim that they can double your money in a snap if you become a subscriber, the *No-Load Fund Analyst* is a breath of fresh air — it includes no hype or inflated marketing claims.

Personal interviews and the tracking of individual fund managers are unique and valuable aspects of this publication, which tries to identify talented fund managers at some of the smaller, lesser known funds. These funds, of course, are riskier to invest in. Also, because the *No-Load Fund Analyst* recommends funds in numerous fund families, as an investor you must be willing to deal with many fund companies or establish an account at a discount brokerage firm (see Chapter 9). The editors' primary business has been their investment management company. They manage money for institutions and wealthy individuals in mutual funds — their minimum account size for new clients is $3 million.

The *No-Load Fund Analyst* also follows and discusses closed-end mutual funds, which I cover in Chapter 2. An annual subscription to the *No-Load Fund Analyst* costs $600. For $50, you can obtain a sample issue by calling (800) 776-9555 or visiting its Web site at www.nlfa.com.

The Independent Adviser for Vanguard Investors

As you may have guessed from its name, the *Independent Adviser for Vanguard Investors* is a useful publication that focuses exclusively on Vanguard's extensive family of mutual funds (and now exchange-traded funds). Editor Dan Wiener, who's a former financial journalist, also operates a money management business.

What I really like is that Wiener does his research and homework. He's adept at sifting through the large number of Vanguard funds and highlighting those that do the best and are likely to continue performing well. That said, he isn't like many other newsletter writers who make predictions about the stock market and economy. He also shies away from making major shifts in his suggested holdings — he's much more of a buy-and-hold investor. This newsletter costs $99.95 for the first year, and you can order by calling (800) 211-7641 or going to the Web site at www.adviseronline.com.

EricTyson.com

Drop on by and visit my Web site — www.erictyson.com — where I digest and summarize what the best newsletters and other resources highlighted in this chapter are saying now. I also discuss current economic news, books worth reading, and prominent gurus, among other topics.

Chapter 21

Harnessing Your Computer's Power

In This Chapter

▶ Finding your way around mutual funds with software

▶ Locating the best mutual fund Web sites

*W*hen you invest your money, especially in mutual funds, having a computer at your disposal to make wise investing decisions and to manage your portfolio is *not* necessary nor is it advantageous. In fact, the use of a computer when investing may prove detrimental to your investing success. Why?

My experience with counseling clients, reading letters and e-mails from readers and visitors to my Web site, and instructing students in my courses is that heavy computer users tend to focus too much on daily price changes and the short-term news and, thus, they trade too much — losing sight of the important bigger-picture issues. So if you're not online yet or don't own a computer to play around with investing software or Internet sites, don't be sad. If you decide to spend money on a computer or you already own one but don't know how it can help you invest in funds, this chapter assists you with finding out how to put it to work.

I divide this chapter into two parts — software and Web sites. Some of the stuff I discuss does some of both categories. Those that do are generally placed in the category that they do more of.

Using Computer Software

Most software reviewers can agree that good software must be easy to use. Software that helps you make mutual fund and other investing decisions must also provide well-founded advice and information. Not all of it does.

Knowing which software is best for you depends on your goals and level of investment expertise. The financial software in the marketplace today can help you with a variety of activities that range from simply tabulating your mutual fund's values and getting current prices to researching investment choices. You can even execute fund trades on your computer.

As I discuss later in this chapter (see the section, "Entering Cyberspace: Internet Sites"), thanks to technological advances, Web sites are offering features that were once the exclusive domain of software programs. Before you rush out to purchase a specific software program to accomplish a certain task, check to see what the Internet has to offer in that area.

Getting-and-staying-organized software

Checkbook software programs, such as Quicken, help with checkbook accounting, expense tracking, and bill paying. But checkbook software is also useful for keeping track of your mutual fund investments. By remembering your original purchase price, as well as factoring in dividend and capital gains distributions, checkbook software automatically calculates your current rate of return, both annualized and cumulative, for each individual fund, as well as for your entire portfolio.

However — and this is a big however — in order for software to keep track of your returns, you must plug in *all* your transactions, distributions, and share price changes when you receive your account statements. If you have a lot of funds at different accounts, this process could be tedious, depending on how much you like detail work. Some (primarily) larger investment companies allow you to download your account statement details directly into your software program. But even this procedure usually requires you to work with the downloaded transactions and assign them to appropriate categories.

 Software can be useful if you have accounts at numerous investment firms and want to keep tabs on your various accounts and overall performance. But remember that consolidating your investments at a larger mutual fund company or through a discount brokerage account can accomplish the same goals for you — without your having to invest hours in studying software and entering data.

Also keep in mind that one of the most attractive features of checkbook software — its ability to track your cost basis — is irrelevant for funds held in retirement accounts. (See Chapter 18 for more information on cost basis as used for tax purposes.) Most mutual fund companies in this day and age track your cost basis for you, too.

Accessing investment research software

Investment research software packages usually separate investment beginners (and others who don't want to spend a lot of time managing their money) from those who enjoy wallowing in data and conducting primary research. The best reason to use research software is to access quality information in a way that may be more cost-effective than doing so through traditional channels. Research software may allow you to peruse more information more efficiently.

Although these packages can be cost-effective, they're still expensive. Don't jump in to one of these programs until you've done a careful comparison between the information it offers and the data you need. Most investment software packages offer more raw data than you can ever use.

Mutual fund data hounds delight in the software products that Morningstar offers. However, if you're an investing and mutual fund novice, don't expect an easy time working with these sometimes jargon-laden and costly packages. Also expect to invest several hours of your time to figure out how to work with a program. (Morningstar offers more affordable and scaled-down information through its Web site, which I discuss later in this chapter.) Here's my take on Morningstar's mutual fund software:

- ✔ **Principia Mutual Funds:** This software provides most of the data that's provided on Morningstar's fund reports, which I discuss in Chapter 20. You can search and screen for funds that meet the specific criteria that you enter into the program. The program also comes with a feature called the Portfolio Developer, which allows you to gather a portfolio of funds and then view a pie chart of that particular portfolio's asset allocation. A subscription is $675 a year. Call (877) 586-5405 for more info.

- ✔ **Principia Mutual Funds Advanced:** The ultimate for the mutual fund data junkie, its interface is similar to Principia Mutual Funds', but you get more historical data and features. All the data available on Morningstar's reports comes with this program, and then some. For example, each fund has an archive of all the analyst's reviews of that fund. The program also lets you print these reports on your own printer. The Portfolio Developer allows you to track the performance of your mutual fund portfolio over time. The price for Morningstar's first-class ticket is steep: An annual subscription is $1,220. Call (877) 586-5405 for more information.

Before plunging in to the data jungle, be honest about your reasons for doing research. Some investors fool themselves into believing that their research will help them beat the markets. As I say many times in this book, though, few of even the so-called professional investors ever beat the markets.

Entering Cyberspace: Internet Sites

The Internet is a vast network of computers all over the world that share information. Just about anyone can plug in to the Internet right from home — all you need is a personal computer and a connection. Fund investors online have some of the following possible benefits:

- ✔ **Quick access to info:** The Internet can give you faster access to important resources than traditional channels allow. Before the Internet, investors had only one way to get their hands on, say, a fund prospectus: Call the folks at the fund company, give them an address, and wait up to a week for the mailman to deliver the goods. With Internet access, you can log on to the fund company's Web site and view the prospectus immediately, and even print it, if you want to. The same goes for annual reports, account applications, research reports, account statements, and so on.

- ✔ **Interactive features:** The best Internet sites are similar to software programs in that they're interactive. The phenomenon of retirement-planning calculators is a good example. The best online calculators ask you questions, you plug in the answers, and on your computer screen you see your personalized plan calculated for you, complete with graphs and charts — sure beats slugging it out with a calculator and pencil over a fill-in-the-blank retirement-planning workbook.

- ✔ **Up-to-date info:** Information on the Internet can be kept up-to-date, even up-to-the-minute. Larger companies have entire staffs that are responsible for keeping their Web sites current. If a prospectus is revised or a new tax law affects a retirement-planning calculation, a well-maintained Web site can reflect these changes the next time you log on. This advantage is one over the traditional print medium and software programs.

Of course, every coin has a flip side. The Internet has introduced plenty of hazards for mutual fund investors to be concerned about, but here, to steer clear of the pitfalls, I give you a few tips:

✔ **Free information, at a price:** After you've paid your toll to get on the Information Superhighway, many things that you find there have the illusion of being free. Don't be fooled. Somebody has to pay to put that info on the Internet, and nine times out of ten it's a company that's trying to sell you stuff that you're better off not buying. Before you trust a Web site with information on mutual funds, find out who's paying the bucks for the site to be there. (See the sidebar, "Who's footing the bill?")

✔ **Minutia to fixate on:** An advantage of the Internet — its capability to keep information up-to-date — is also its Achilles' heel. Too many Internet sites get so focused on the short term that they lose sight of the big picture. For example, many Web sites center on up-to-the-minute investment price quotes and late-breaking financial news: This type of information doesn't serve a healthy, long-term investment strategy perspective. Don't let the Internet distract you from your focus on the investment horizon. Don't be as enamored with the Internet's up-to-the-minute update ability as most Web sites seem to be.

✔ **Too many "experts":** Message boards and chat rooms are a unique aspect of the Internet. The way that these mediums can facilitate communication between people in various towns, cities, and states is potentially exciting. But message boards and chat rooms are dangerous places to tread for the naive and too trustful. Remember, you don't have to take an entrance exam or have a license requirement for joining a chat room or posting a message on an electronic bulletin board. The anonymity makes pretending to be someone you're not easy. Therefore, *participate cautiously.* Never trust any advice you get from a chat room or message board without verifying it through a reliable independent source. And never share confidential personal or financial details online.

✔ **Information overload:** The possibilities on the Internet are so endless that they can be overwhelming, and the easiest way to find bad advice is to be unsure about what you're looking for in the first place. Knowing what information you want before you start searching pays. If you enter a vague term into an Internet search engine — say, "mutual funds" — you'll probably end up more lost than you were to begin with. If, on the other hand, you enter a specific term — such as *TIAA-CREF mutual funds* — you'll probably find the information you're looking for.

That said, let me speed up your search for good resources on the Internet by recommending what I think are the best mutual fund Web sites out there. You'll recognize some of the names behind these sites because they're companies I recommend throughout the book. Not surprisingly, the organizations that demonstrate excellence offline seem to be the ones that do best online as well.

Who's footing the bill?

You need to know that the Internet is primarily funded by companies' marketing departments. Of course, nothing is intrinsically wrong with this arrangement; magazine articles and television programs are also paid for with advertising dollars. What's problematic about the Internet, however, is that the line between advertising and content is much fuzzier and more blurred than in other mediums. In fact, some Web sites obscure the difference between content and advertising in a manner that could be called deliberate.

For example, consider a Web site that hypes itself as the "best independent mutual fund resource" and even goes on to boldly declare that "Content is what makes us different." However, this content, such as the text that appears in the site's "Expert's Corner," turns out to be nothing more than thinly veiled marketing fodder from financial newsletter writers who are intent on selling you a subscription to their wares.

So how can you tell whether the objective content you're reading on the Web is really just a paid advertisement? Begin by thoroughly checking out the fine print. In the preceding example, I found this little disclaimer in the corner: "These articles are sponsored by the featured experts. . . ." *Sponsored* means that the "experts" (newsletter writers) were paying to put their articles on the Web site.

If the Web page has a button that reads something like *About Us,* click it. Sometimes you can get information on who's sponsoring the site. Also click any buttons that say something such as *For Clients Only* or *How to Join Us.* You may discover that the site only mentions fund companies that pay a fee to be represented.

Keep an eye out for advertisements that spill over into the content when you read articles on independent sites. For example, if an article recommends a fund company whose advertisement appears at the top of the page, consider surfing elsewhere.

If you can't find out who's behind a particular site, don't trust it. A Web site that has nothing to hide has no reason to be evasive. To be safe, stick with sites that are totally upfront about who's paying for them. A site whose Web address is www.fundcompanyxyz.com is obviously not trying to fool anybody.

Investment Company Institute

The Investment Company Institute (ICI) is the investment companies' trade association; it includes mostly mutual funds but also closed-end funds, exchange-traded funds (ETFs), and unit investment trusts (UITs). This site has a wealth of industry data that's of greater use to financial professionals who enjoy wallowing around such numbers. Check it out online at www.ici.org.

Be forewarned, however, that the educational materials on this site won't show you to avoid load funds or other high-cost investments, such as most UITs — some ICI members sell them, so telling you to avoid these investments would be self-detrimental.

Morningstar.com

Morningstar's site (www.morningstar.com) is one of the better mutual fund Web resources. You find Morningstar's well-known research reports on individual funds, which feature long-term performance data and graphs, risk ratings, manager profiles, information on fees, and a list of discount brokers who sell the fund. Surprisingly, considering that Morningstar was built on the basis of research and no advertising, the mutual fund companies with their banner advertisements at the top of every page pay for this Web site.

The site also features articles on advanced concepts of fund investing and developments in the fund industry. For $179 per year, a premium membership gives you online access to more fund information and tools.

T. Rowe Price

On this site (www.troweprice.com), you can find some of the best retirement-planning tools available — for individuals saving for retirement, as well as for those already in or near retirement. Interactive worksheets can help you determine which type of IRA may be best for you to invest through.

This site also has a good selection of articles on various fund-investing topics as well as interviews with leading fund managers at the company. Should you invest in any of T. Rowe Price's solid mutual funds, the Web site provides convenient access to your account information.

Securities and Exchange Commission

Although the government's Securities and Exchange Commission (SEC) Web site is far from being the most user-friendly one, it contains a truckload of the required documents that all funds must file with this agency, whose purpose is to oversee the investment industry. The EDGAR database enables you to access documents that mutual funds have filed with the SEC at www.sec.gov/edgar/searchedgar/webusers.htm.

To look at a particular fund's documents on file with the SEC, simply choose the general-purpose search option for companies and other filers. The site then provides a few different ways to search, but the easiest is to enter as much of the fund's name as possible — don't use abbreviations or acronyms — in the company-name search box. If the fund name you provide is associated with more than one particular fund (for example, if you simply type Vanguard), a list of choices appears from which you can choose. After you narrow it down to the particular fund you're looking for, you get a laundry list of all the documents that the fund has filed with the SEC in recent years. (The most recent filings will be at the top of the screen.)

Vanguard.com

Among the fund company Web sites that I've examined, Vanguard's (www. vanguard.com) is unsurpassed. In addition to housing an extensive online library of brochures on important fund-investing topics, this site also boasts numerous planning tools. For example, you can calculate how much to save for retirement or determine whether to convert your regular IRA into a Roth IRA.

Vanguard's Web site also enables you, if you so desire, to track and manage your investments in one central location. You can buy and sell mutual funds from hundreds of fund companies, stocks, bonds, and many more investments all in one account.

Part VI
The Part of Tens

The 5th Wave — By Rich Tennant

Being Dracula's slave didn't pay much, but Renfield always found extra money to invest.

In this part . . .

Why include lists of ten-somethings? Why not? Life is all about priorities, and more than ten of anything is too many to remember. Fewer than ten leaves you with that empty feeling you have after eating a hearty plate of bean sprouts for lunch. So — ten it is. Like Goldilocks, here you get just the right amount of information about some important fund concepts and concerns.

Chapter 22

Ten Common Fund-Investing Mistakes and How to Avoid Them

In This Chapter

▶ Designing the right plan for you

▶ Keeping taxes and fund fees in mind

▶ Staying away from shady advisers and market predictors

*F*rom getting your finances in order to selecting funds to maintaining your portfolio over time, various potholes and dangers can get in your way. This chapter highlights the ten most common fund-investing mistakes you're likely to make and how you can sidestep them.

Lacking an Overall Plan

Just as you shouldn't build a house without an overall plan, you shouldn't start buying funds until you have your arms and mind wrapped around a sound financial plan. The plan doesn't have to be a fancy, professionally or computer-generated one, but it should include the basics:

✔ Proper insurance coverage, like health, disability, auto, home, excess liability if you hold sufficient assets, and life insurance if others depend on your income

✔ A plan for paying off consumer debt on credit cards and auto loans, if you have any

✔ Savings goals for retirement, buying a home, starting a business, putting your kids through college, and anything else your heart desires

✔ An overall *asset allocation* — what portion of your money should be invested in different assets, such as stocks (foreign versus domestic), bonds, and so on

Failing to Examine Sales Charges and Expenses

Would you ever buy a car without considering its sticker price? How about checking out the car's safety record and insurance costs? Mutual funds are like cars in one respect — you should check under the hood before you buy. But the good news is that fund fees are actually a lot easier to comprehend compared to the various car costs.

Before you consider buying any mutual fund, be sure you understand precisely any sales charges as well as the fund's ongoing operating expense ratio. Over the long term, a fund's fees are one of the biggest (and most predictable) determinants of the fund's likely future returns. This point is especially true with boring old money market and conservative bond and stock funds. Please see Chapter 7 for more on fees.

Chasing Past Performance

Before anyone hires a job applicant, he likes to know that person's track record. Ditto for professional sports teams seeking new players. Of course, when hiring a money manager, which is what you're doing when you invest in a mutual fund, you should examine that manager's prior experience. However, many investors simply throw money at funds currently posting high returns without thoroughly examining a fund manager's experience.

More often than not, current hot funds cool off (especially as small funds get larger and market conditions change), and many underperform in the future. The reason is quite simple: The market forces that lead to the relatively brief period of high performance inevitably change. Peruse Chapter 7 for how to avoid tomorrow's losers and maximize your chances of picking a consistent winner.

Ignoring Tax Issues

Do you know your current federal and state income tax brackets? When a particular type of stock or bond fund makes a dividend or capital gains distribution, do you know what rate of tax you'll pay on that?

Many fund investors aren't well informed when it comes to the tax consequences of their fund purchases and sales. Although you don't want the tax tail to wag the fund selection dog, you should know how taxes work on your funds and which funds fit best for your tax situation. See Chapter 10.

Getting Duped by "Advisers"

Some people want to hire a financial adviser to help them navigate financial choices. But many so-called financial consultants or advisers have serious conflicts of interest. Their recommendations and objectivity are tainted by commissions earned from products that they sell or from their money-management services.

If you seek to hire a financial planner/adviser, it's a good rule of thumb to hire someone who's selling his time and nothing else. If what you're really looking for is someone to manage your money, seek out a money manager. See Chapter 24.

Falling Prey to the Collection Syndrome

Some people buy mutual funds the way they build a clothing collection. Visits to different stores and articles recommending specific items lead to purchases. Before you know it, you may own numerous funds that don't really go together well.

This mismatching is another reason you should develop your overall plan first. For example, after you decide that you're going to invest, say, 20 percent of your retirement plan money into international stock funds, then you can set out to identify and then invest that amount of money into your chosen foreign funds. Check out Chapter 10, which provides a guide to putting together a sound portfolio that matches your needs.

Trying to Time the Market's Movements

Just as no one enjoys losing a game, who wants to invest in a fund only to see it fall in value? Sometimes, though, that may happen even though you've done your homework and selected a good fund.

Stock and bond funds fluctuate in value, and you must accept that inevitability when you invest. Some people like examining pricing charts online to guess when a fund is about to turn around and increase in value. Don't waste your time on such unproductive and time-consuming endeavors. Identify good funds, buy into them over time, and don't jump in and out.

Following Prognosticators' Predictions

Don't make the mistake of believing that some supposed expert bold enough to make financial market forecasts on television, on radio, or in print actually has any proven talent to do so. Such blustery babblings are merely for the publicity of a given firm or individual.

Your long-term goals and desire or lack thereof to accept risk and volatility in your investments should drive your fund selection. Please read Chapter 20 to discover how to use information, not predictions, in building a winning fund portfolio.

Being Swayed by Major News Events

You're human and have emotions. September 11, 2001, was a horrible day for Americans (and many other people around the world) that caused some people to panic and sell investments when the financial markets reopened. Similar emotions and reactions happened during the 2008 financial crisis/panic. Wars, oil price spikes, large corporate layoffs, the latest retail sales and consumer confidence reports, and Federal Reserve meetings and interest rate changes are but a few of the news reports that can move the markets.

Don't make your investing decisions based on the news of the day. The only action you should consider taking if doom and gloom are in the air is to consider using some of your spare cash and buying when a sale is going on.

Comparing Your Funds Unfairly

While teaching adult courses and working with clients as a counselor, I've witnessed many people who were disenchanted with otherwise good funds. Often this effect was the result of their knowledge that other funds, often seeming similar on the surface, were doing better. Perceptions changed when these people found out that the other funds weren't holding the same types of securities and that their funds were actually doing fine compared with a relevant market index (see Chapter 17).

Don't be quick to assume that your funds aren't doing well simply because they've gone down recently or are producing lower returns than some other funds. Compare them fairly over a long enough period (years, not months or weeks) and then decide.

Chapter 23

Ten Fund-Investing
Fears to Conquer

. . . .

In This Chapter

▶ Avoiding the tendency to predict (and the anxiety that comes with it)

▶ Learning to relax and watch your investments grow over time

. . . .

*E*xperiencing the worries that I identify in this chapter is a sign that you're a normal person. But these concerns are also something I want you to overcome. When you do, you're well on your way to avoiding common painful and costly fund-investing blunders and oversights.

Investing with Little Money

You have to start somewhere. People with less to invest actually benefit more from mutual funds than investors with heftier balances (although those investors benefit a lot as well). With just several hundred or a few thousand dollars to invest, you can't diversify well or avoid commissions that gobble a significant percentage of what you have to invest when you buy individual securities. By investing in mutual funds, you can invest efficiently.

If you invest money for the longer term, especially inside retirement accounts, start with a hybrid fund or a fund of funds. Some of these funds have low minimum initial investment requirements of $1,000, and they'll go even lower — $50 — if you sign up for an automatic investment plan that regularly makes electronic withdrawals from your bank account. (See the examples in Chapter 15.) Invest just $1,000 today in good mutual funds and add just $50 per month. With funds that average a 10 percent annual return, in 20 years you'll have about $44,000! Invest over 40 years, and you'll have about $336,000. If you can manage $100 per month rather than $50, you'll have about $82,000 in 20 years and $628,000 in 40 years!

Investing in Uninsured Funds

Lack of insurance (think FDIC on bank accounts) isn't what makes funds risky. Mutual fund risks are driven by the price changes of the securities, such as bonds and stocks, that they invest in. Unlike banks and insurance companies, mutual funds can't go bankrupt (see Chapter 2). Funds that invest in municipal bonds may have insurance against the default of the bonds. Otherwise, insurance isn't necessary or available for funds.

Don't overlook other not-so-obvious types of risk. Bank accounts don't carry the price risk, or volatility that bond and stock mutual funds do. However, bank accounts are exposed to the risk that the value of your money may not grow fast enough to keep ahead of inflation and taxes.

 If you don't like significant volatility, even with money you've earmarked for long-term purposes, invest more of your money in balanced or hybrid funds. These funds tend to mask the volatility of their individual stock and bond components because they're all mixed together (see Chapter 13).

Rising Interest Rates

After a lengthy period of declining and stable interest rates, speculation inevitably surfaces about when interest rates will rise. This spooks not only some bond investors but also stock investors. Rates rarely rise when they're widely expected to and even when they do rise, it's nearly impossible to know how significantly rates will increase and what, if any, impact that will have on the bond and stock markets.

 The financial markets tend to lead these sorts of economic changes. The stock market, for example, often peaks six months to a year before the economy does. Conversely, stock prices usually head back up in advance and in anticipation of an actual economic recovery. Interest rates and bond prices typically have the same kind of interaction. For example, by the time everyone's talking about the damage to the bond market from rising interest rates, the bond market has usually hit bottom.

Missing High Returns from Stocks

Perhaps you've read about how investment legends like Peter Lynch and Warren Buffett make wise stock picks, so you figure that if you do what they do, you can, too. (After all, numerous books out there say that you can.)

Nothing personal, but it isn't going to happen. You're probably a part-time amateur, at best. If you enjoy playing pickup basketball games, it'd be fun, if somewhat humbling, to play against greats like Kobe Bryant and Lebron James. But I assume that you'd play these stars for the fun of it instead of in an expectation or vain hope of beating them. Buying individual stocks is the same — don't do it thinking that you'll beat the better mutual fund managers.

Don't fool yourself into thinking that you're an expert just because you know more than most people about a particular industry or company. Many others have this knowledge, and if you have truly inside information that a company is about to be acquired, for example, and you invest your money based on this insider knowledge, you can end up with a large fine or jail sentence or both. (See Chapter 4 for a thorough discussion about investing in stocks of your own choosing.)

Waiting to Get a Handle on the Economy

Although I don't advocate sticking your head in the sand, the big-picture economic issues such as interest rates, employment, corporate profits, trade agreements, and tax and budget reform are well beyond your (or, really, anyone else's) ability to accurately forecast. Besides, investors' expectations are already generally reflected in the prices of securities in the financial markets.

Read about, listen to, and absorb what's going on in the world. But don't use this noise of the day to help make your investing decisions. You should determine your investment portfolio by considering your financial situation, your personal goals, and your plans for the future (see Chapter 10).

Buying the Best-Performing Funds

Most people want to jump on board the winning bandwagon. But the best performers all too often turn into tomorrow's mediocre or loser funds (see Chapter 7). Look at what happened in the early 2000s to the high-flying funds that focused on technology and Internet stocks during the late 1990s. The same thing happened with the seemingly unstoppable financial companies in the late 2000s.

The types of securities that do best inevitably change course. You may actually increase your chances of fund-investing success by minimizing exposure to recent hot performers and investing more into fund types that are currently depressed but otherwise fundamentally sound.

Waiting for an Ideal Buying Opportunity

Some stock market investors like the idea of waiting for a big drop before they start investing. This strategy seems logical, especially coming on the heels of years of advancing prices or if a major decline happened in the recent past. It also fits the philosophy of buying when prices are discounted. The problem is, how do you know when the decline is over? A 10 percent drop? How about after 20 or 30 percent? If you're waiting for a 20 percent drop and the market only drops 15 percent before it then rises 100 percent over the coming years, you'll miss out. If you're waiting for a 40 percent decline, will you really have the courage to invest if that happens?

Especially if you're just starting to save and invest money, invest regularly so that, if prices drop, you'll buy some at lower prices. That way, if prices don't decline, you won't miss out on the advance. If you have a large amount of money awaiting investment, move it gradually (dollar-cost averaging) — a portion every month or quarter over a year or two into different types of funds (see Chapter 10).

Obsessing Over Your Funds

There's a big difference between monitoring and obsessing. You don't need to follow the daily price changes of your mutual funds, which is an incomplete and often misleading way to discern the amount of return from your fund. In addition to share price changes, you must take into account dividend and capital gains distributions when you calculate a fund's performance (see Chapter 17).

Tracking and hovering over your funds increases your chances of panicking and making emotionally based decisions. The investors I know who bail out when prices are down almost always are the ones who follow prices too closely. Keep your sights on the big picture — why you bought the fund in the first place and what financial goal you're trying to fulfill. To reduce your risk and sleep soundly at night, diversify.

Thinking You've Made a Bad Decision

Don't be so hard on yourself. Invest in the funds that I recommend in this book and use good selection criteria in picking funds on your own. Then, if one of your funds goes down, the decline is — 99 times out of 100 — because the types of securities it focuses on (for example, bonds, United States stocks, or international stocks) are down.

If, for example, your fund is down about 5 percent over the past year, find out how similar funds have done over the same time period. If the average comparable fund is down more than 5 percent, you have cause to be happy; if comparable funds are up an average of 20 percent, you have reason to worry. See Chapter 17 for some ground rules for deciding whether to dump or hold a laggard fund.

Lacking in Performance

Stop looking at fund performance top-ten lists. Most of these lists completely ignore risk. Many of these lists rank funds based on short time periods. The funds on top are constantly changing. And no one knows which ones will be on next year's top-ten list.

If a fund is taking so much risk that it's in the top-ten list, then such a status also means that it's risky enough to end up in the bottom-ten list someday. (See the examples in Chapter 7.) The categories that are used in these types of lists are also flawed, because many of the funds aren't really comparable. Read Chapter 17 to find out appropriate ways to evaluate and track the performance of your funds.

Chapter 24

Ten Tips for Hiring a Financial Adviser

Hundreds of millions of people worldwide have successfully invested in mutual funds on their own. Investing in mutual funds isn't difficult; common sense and an ounce of financial sense are all you need.

You have no compelling reason to hire a financial adviser in order to invest in mutual funds. So if you jumped to this chapter first, *stop!* I recommend that you march back to the earlier chapters. You'll be better able to understand this chapter after you've read the ones that come before it, not to mention the fact that you'll be improving your ability to save yourself possibly thousands of dollars in financial advisory fees. But if you've arrived here because you just don't want to deal with handling fund-investing or financial-planning decisions on your own, keep on keepin' on.

Communicator or Obfuscator?

In your preliminary meetings with a financial adviser, develop a sense and opinion about the person's ability to clearly communicate with you. Take your time and speak with prospective advisers before deciding whom to hire. Don't rush yourself or allow an adviser to pressure you into making a decision before you're ready and comfortable.

Consider these questions: Does he clearly and patiently explain things or use a lot of jargon and talk down to you? Is he forthright and candid or evasive?

Financial Planner or Money Manager?

As you search for help, you'll confront a variety of people who call themselves "advisers" and who're eager to assist you with investing and other financial matters. People who claim to be advisers but who derive commissions from the products that they sell are salespeople (Chapter 9). Keep this warning in mind as you consider the different types of people you could hire:

- ✔ **Financial planner:** True financial planners generally provide objective help with issues, such as retirement planning, using and paying off debt, investing, insurance, and even real estate. The charge for these services should be a fee based on the time involved. A good planner should help restructure your financial situation before your money gets invested in funds. If a planner provides specific fund recommendations, implement them on your own and save yourself ongoing advisory fees.

- ✔ **Money managers:** Money managers or financial advisers who perform money management invest your money and charge you a fee — usually expressed as a percentage of assets under management (that's the money you turn over to them to manage). Some advisers only do money management, but increasing numbers of financial planners offer money-management services as well. Using money managers can make sense for people who've finished their planning and need someone to help manage their money. Money managers argue that, because they devote themselves full time to investing, they're more adept at it.

Planner/money managers may be reluctant to recommend — and, in fact, have an incentive to ignore — strategies that deplete the money you have to invest. The more you have to invest with them, the greater the fees they earn. All the following financial moves result in less money that you can invest, so planners/money managers may not recommend these often-advisable paths:

- ✔ Paying down debt of all types, such as credit cards, auto loans, mortgages, business loans, and the like

- ✔ Maximizing saving through your employer's retirement savings plan(s)

- ✔ Purchasing real estate — either through buying a primary home or investing in rental property

- ✔ Buying and investing in your own business or someone else's privately held business

Another problem with planners who also manage money is that they may be short on specific advice in the planning process. Sadly, I've seen cases in which people paid planners thousands of dollars for a largely boilerplate, computer-generated financial plan and received little, if any, specific financial planning and investment advice. If you want to invest in no-load funds, the planner should willingly and happily provide specific fund recommendations and help you build a portfolio for the fee that you pay her.

Market Timing and Active Management?

Much of what you're paying a planner for is the time spent reviewing your financial situation and matching your needs and goals to a suitable portfolio of funds. If your needs and situation are relatively stable and you do your homework right the first time and select good mutual funds, you shouldn't need to make frequent changes to your portfolio.

If anything, constant tinkering with a portfolio tends to lower returns. In Chapter 20, I cover this same issue on the perils of blindly following some newsletters' and gurus' timing advice to switch into this fund and out of that one. Trading in nonretirement accounts also increases your tax burden.

Who's in Control?

If you hire a money manager, you should consider if the manager requires that you turn control of the account over to him. Specifically, you'll sign or initial a form, as shown in Figure 24-1. Here's the outline of the form:

- **Line 1:** Grants the adviser authority to execute trades in your account — otherwise known as granting a *limited power of attorney*.

- **Line 2:** Gives your adviser power to move money out of your account. I recommend against giving your adviser this power unless you need to withdraw money from your account frequently and find it more necessary to have your adviser do it for you.

- **Line 3:** Allows your adviser to deduct his ongoing fees from the account. Definitely do *not* allow this deduction to be taken from retirement accounts because it diminishes the amount of money that you have compounding tax deferred. (But, unless you're already well into retirement and taking plan distributions, paying fees from your retirement account may be okay — you're paying with before-tax dollars that would otherwise be withdrawn and taxed.) For nonretirement accounts, it's up to you, although many advisers insist on this feature to make collecting their fees easier.

- **Line 4:** Requests the brokerage firm to send duplicate copies of your account statements and trade confirmations to your adviser. That's acceptable and to be expected.

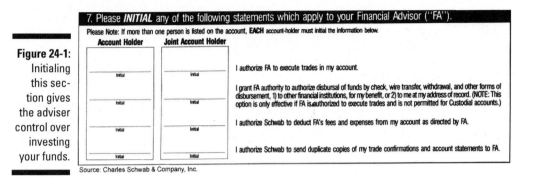

7. Please **INITIAL** any of the following statements which apply to your Financial Advisor ("FA").

Please Note: If more than one person is listed on the account, **EACH** account-holder must initial the information below.

Account Holder   **Joint Account Holder**

I authorize FA to execute trades in my account.

I grant FA authority to authorize disbursal of funds by check, wire transfer, withdrawal, and other forms of disbursement, 1) to other financial institutions, for my benefit, or 2) to me at my address of record. (NOTE: This option is only effective if FA is authorized to execute trades and is not permitted for Custodial accounts.)

I authorize Schwab to deduct FA's fees and expenses from my account as directed by FA.

I authorize Schwab to send duplicate copies of my trade confirmations and account statements to FA.

Source: Charles Schwab & Company, Inc.

Figure 24-1:
Initialing this section gives the adviser control over investing your funds.

Almost all money managers manage money on what's called a *discretionary basis* — they make decisions to buy and sell funds without your prior approval. In other words, you're turning control over to them. You find out about transactions *after* they've occurred, usually when you receive the trade confirmations in the mail and through your monthly or quarterly statement.

At a minimum, before you turn control over to the money manager, make sure that you discuss your investment objectives with him. These overall goals should drive the way he manages your money.

Fees: What's Your Advice Going to Cost?

If you hire a planner on an hourly basis, expect to pay at least $100 per hour — you can easily pay more; planners with the $300+ per-hour billing rates tend to work exclusively with affluent clients.

Fee-based money managers work on an entirely different basis. See this fee schedule example:

Amount You Invest	Fee Percentage	Annual Fee
$1,000,000	1.10%	$11,000
$2,000,000	1.00%	$20,000
$5,000,000	0.90%	$45,000

What's amazing to me about this type of fee schedule is that, although the percentage charge declines slightly as the amount you invest increases, look at how the total charges increase. This firm sends the same quarterly reports out to the client with $5 million invested, who pays $45,000 per year, as it does to the client with $1,000,000 invested, who pays $11,000 per year for the same service. Advisers' fees are often negotiable. The more you have to invest, the greater your ability should be to negotiate lower fees.

Also, ask what sort of transaction and other fees you have to pay in addition to the advisory fee paid to the money manager. Most money managers ask that you establish an account at one of the discount brokerage firms, such as Schwab, Fidelity, TD Ameritrade, or with a mutual fund company. Ask who they use and why. If you're going to consider hiring a mutual fund money manager, add up all the costs. Table 24-1 helps you do the job.

Table 24-1	Adding Up All the Costs
Cost	**Annual Percentage of Your Assets**
Money manager's fee	For example, 1.0%
Operating fees on mutual funds invested in (Don't let the adviser say that she can't figure this amount because the funds she uses vary over time — she can base the calculation on her current portfolio or the amount she used over the past year.)	For example, 1.0%
Transaction and other fees (Your adviser can convert these dollar expenses to a percentage.)	For example, 0.2%
Total	For example, 2.2%

Over the long haul, a diversified portfolio that's primarily invested in stocks has usually returned around 9 to 10 percent annually. If you're paying a total of 2.5 percent to have your money managed, you're giving away 25 to 28 percent of your expected return. And don't forget, because the IRS sure won't, that you'll owe taxes on your nonretirement account profits, so you're giving away an even greater percentage of your after-tax returns.

How Do You Make Investing Decisions?

Throughout this book, I discuss the good and bad ways people can and have invested in mutual funds over the years (Chapter 7, in particular). The process isn't rocket science — it can be as simple as picking any other product or service. You want value — where can you invest in funds that meet your needs and that are managed by a fund company and fund managers that have good track records and that charge competitive fees. Most advisers try to factor their economic expectations and prognostications into their investment strategies. But this is much easier said than done.

The fundamental problem with some money managers is they try to convince you that they have a crystal ball. Specifically, some claim (explicitly or implicitly) that they can time the markets, that they'll get you out of the market before it falls and put your money back in time for the next rise. Over long time periods, beating the markets is virtually impossible, even for acknowledged experts (see Chapter 20). Great investors, such as Warren Buffett and Peter Lynch, say you can't time the markets. Believe 'em!

What's Your Track Record?

Mutual fund companies must have their performance records audited and reviewed by the United States (U.S.) Securities and Exchange Commission (SEC). Most also provide an independent auditor's report. Private money managers face no such SEC requirement. Few provide independent audits. Of course, you really want to know the performance facts about the money manager who you're considering for ongoing management of your funds. What rate of return has he earned year by year? How has he done in up and down markets? How much risk has he taken, and how have his funds performed versus comparable benchmarks (see Chapter 17)? These are important questions. Getting objective and meaningful answers from most investment advisers who manage money on an ongoing basis is difficult.

Money managers play a number of marketing games to pump themselves up. If all the money managers are telling the truth, 99 percent of them have beaten the market averages, avoided major market plunges over the years, and just happened to be in the best-performing funds last year. Money managers pump up their supposed past performance to seduce you into turning your money over to them through common marketing ploys:

- ✔ **Select accounts:** If you can get the money manager to give you performance numbers and charts, too often an asterisk refers you to some microscopic footnote somewhere. If you have a magnifying glass handy, you can see that the asterisk states something like *select* or *sample accounts*. What this term means, and what they should've said instead is "We picked the accounts where we did best, used the performance numbers from those, and ignored the rest." (Interestingly, using smaller type in this way is a violation of SEC regulations.) Advisory firms also may select the time periods when they look best. Finally, and most flagrantly, some firms simply make up the numbers (such as Bernie Madoff did).

- ✔ **Free services:** Some money managers will produce performance numbers that imply that they're giving their services away. Remember, money managers charge a fee (a percentage of assets) for their services — they are required to show your returns net of fees [or after fees have been deducted] to clearly show the amount that, as an investor using their services, would've made. Because most money managers place their fund trades through discount brokers who charge transaction fees, they must deduct these fees from returns as well.

✔ **Bogus benchmarks:** Some money managers make their performance numbers higher than they really are; some also try to make themselves look good in relation to the overall market by comparing their performance numbers to inappropriate benchmarks. For example, money managers who invest worldwide (including in international stocks) may compare their investment performance only to the lowest-returning U.S.-based indexes.

✔ **Switching into (yesterday's) stars:** Money managers don't want to send out updates that show that they're sitting on yesterday's losers and missed out on yesterday's winners. So guess what? They may sell the losers and buy into yesterday's winners, creating the illusion that they're more on top of the market than they are. (Some newsletters also engage in this practice.) This strategy, known as *window dressing,* is potentially dangerous because they may be making a bad situation worse by selling funds that have already declined and buying into others after they've soared (not to mention possibly increasing transaction and tax costs).

What Are Your Qualifications and Training?

An adviser should have experience in the investing or financial services field — generally, the more the better. But also look for someone with intelligence and ethics who has good communication skills.

Check out credentials but don't be overly impressed by some, such as the CFP (Certified Financial Planning) degree. Too many planners with this "credential," which you can largely earn by taking a self-study course at home and then an exam, sell financial products. Other common credentials include

✔ **CFA (Chartered Financial Analyst):** This credential means that the adviser knows how to analyze securities and investments and the fundamentals of portfolio management.

✔ **MBA (Master of Business Administration):** An adviser with an MBA should've had coursework dealing with investments and finance. Find out where he earned the MBA and check out the school's reputation.

- ✔ **PFS (Personal Financial Specialist):** A PFS is a credential conferred on accountants who pass an exam similar to the CFP.

- ✔ **CLU (Chartered Life Underwriter) and ChFC (Chartered Financial Consultant):** These credentials are for insurance and carry little, if any, value in advising on mutual funds. These credentials may be a red flag that you're dealing with a salesperson or with someone who knows more about insurance than investments.

The term *Registered Investment Adviser* denotes that the adviser is registered with the SEC; it means nothing as a professional credential. (Smaller advisory firms with assets under management of less than $25 million generally register with state regulatory agencies.) The SEC doesn't require a test; however, it does require that the adviser file *Form ADV,* also known as the Uniform Application for Investment Adviser Registration. This document asks for specific information from investment advisers, such as a breakdown of the sources of their income, relationships and affiliations with other companies, each adviser's educational and employment history, the types of securities the firm recommends, and the firm's fee schedule. (Many states require passing a securities exam, such as a Series 2, 63, or 65.)

In a pitch over the phone or in marketing materials sent by mail, an adviser may gloss over or avoid certain issues. Although it's possible for an adviser to lie on Form ADV, it's likely that an adviser will be more truthful on this form than in marketing materials. Ask the adviser to send you a copy of his Form ADV, or visit the SEC Web site at www.sec.gov. You can also call them at (202) 551-8090 or fax your request to (202) 777-1027.

What Are Your References?

Ask other people about how the adviser benefited them. This process is one way to verify the rates of return the adviser may claim (although you're smart enough to recognize that the adviser will refer you to the clients who've done the best with her). Also ask about the adviser's strengths and weaknesses.

Virtually all money managers offer a free introductory consultation if you meet their minimum investment requirements. Planners who work on commission also tend to offer free sessions. So the "free" consultation ends up being a sales pitch to convince you to buy certain products or services.

Busy advisers who charge by the hour usually can't afford to burn their time for a free in-person session, especially a lengthy one. Don't let this deter you; this fee is probably a good sign. These advisers should be willing, however, to spend a modest amount of time in person or on the phone answering background questions free of charge. They should also send background materials and provide references if you ask.

Do You Carry Liability Insurance?

Some advisers may be surprised by the question of liability insurance or may think that you're a problem customer looking for a lawsuit. On the other hand, if your adviser gets you into some disasters, you'll be happy you have the insurance coverage. Financial planners and money managers should carry *liability insurance* (sometimes called *errors and omission insurance*). This coverage provides you (and the adviser) with protection in case a major mistake is made for which the adviser is liable.

Appendix

Recommended Fund Companies and Discount Brokers

Artisan Funds
☎ 800-344-1770
www.artisanfunds.com

Cohen & Steers Capital Management Inc.
☎ 800-330-7348
www.cohenandsteers.com

Dodge & Cox Funds
☎ 800-621-3979
www.dodgeandcox.com

The Fairholme Fund
☎ 866-202-2263
www.fairholmefunds.com

Fidelity Brokerage
☎ 800-544-6666
www.fidelity.com

Fidelity Funds
☎ 800-343-3548
www.fidelity.com

Harbor Funds
☎ 800-422-1050
www.harborfunds.com

Masters' Select Funds
☎ 800-960-0188
www.mastersselect.com

The Oakmark Funds
☎ 800-625-6275
www.oakmark.com

Sequoia Fund
☎ 800-686-6884
http://www.sequoiafund.com

T. Rowe Price Brokerage
☎ 800-225-7720
www.troweprice.com

T. Rowe Price Funds
☎ 800-638-5660
www.troweprice.com

TD Ameritrade
☎ 800-454-9272
www.tdameritrade.com

TIAA-CREF
☎ 800-223-1200
www.tiaa-cref.org

Tweedy, Browne Funds
☎ 800-432-4789
www.tweedybrowne.com

USAA Funds
☎ 800-382-8722
www.usaa.com

Value Line Funds
☎ 800-223-0818
www.vlfunds.com

Vanguard Brokerage
☎ 800-992-8327
www.vanguard.com

The Vanguard Group
☎ 800-662-7447
www.vanguard.com

Index

Business/Accounting & Bookkeeping
Bookkeeping For Dummies
978-0-7645-9848-7

eBay Business
All-in-One For Dummies,
2nd Edition
978-0-470-38536-4

Job Interviews
For Dummies,
3rd Edition
978-0-470-17748-8

Resumes For Dummies,
5th Edition
978-0-470-08037-5

Stock Investing
For Dummies,
3rd Edition
978-0-470-40114-9

Successful Time
Management
For Dummies
978-0-470-29034-7

Computer Hardware
BlackBerry For Dummies,
3rd Edition
978-0-470-45762-7

Computers For Seniors
For Dummies
978-0-470-24055-7

iPhone For Dummies,
2nd Edition
978-0-470-42342-4

Laptops For Dummies,
3rd Edition
978-0-470-27759-1

Macs For Dummies,
10th Edition
978-0-470-27817-8

Cooking & Entertaining
Cooking Basics
For Dummies,
3rd Edition
978-0-7645-7206-7

Wine For Dummies,
4th Edition
978-0-470-04579-4

Diet & Nutrition
Dieting For Dummies,
2nd Edition
978-0-7645-4149-0

Nutrition For Dummies,
4th Edition
978-0-471-79868-2

Weight Training
For Dummies,
3rd Edition
978-0-471-76845-6

Digital Photography
Digital Photography
For Dummies,
6th Edition
978-0-470-25074-7

Photoshop Elements 7
For Dummies
978-0-470-39700-8

Gardening
Gardening Basics
For Dummies
978-0-470-03749-2

Organic Gardening
For Dummies,
2nd Edition
978-0-470-43067-5

Green/Sustainable
Green Building
& Remodeling
For Dummies
978-0-470-17559-0

Green Cleaning
For Dummies
978-0-470-39106-8

Green IT For Dummies
978-0-470-38688-0

Health
Diabetes For Dummies,
3rd Edition
978-0-470-27086-8

Food Allergies
For Dummies
978-0-470-09584-3

Living Gluten-Free
For Dummies
978-0-471-77383-2

Hobbies/General
Chess For Dummies,
2nd Edition
978-0-7645-8404-6

Drawing For Dummies
978-0-7645-5476-6

Knitting For Dummies,
2nd Edition
978-0-470-28747-7

Organizing For Dummies
978-0-7645-5300-4

SuDoku For Dummies
978-0-470-01892-7

Home Improvement
Energy Efficient Homes
For Dummies
978-0-470-37602-7

Home Theater
For Dummies,
3rd Edition
978-0-470-41189-6

Living the Country Lifestyle
All-in-One For Dummies
978-0-470-43061-3

Solar Power Your Home
For Dummies
978-0-470-17569-9

Internet

Blogging For Dummies,
2nd Edition
978-0-470-23017-6

eBay For Dummies,
6th Edition
978-0-470-49741-8

Facebook For Dummies
978-0-470-26273-3

Google Blogger
For Dummies
978-0-470-40742-4

Web Marketing
For Dummies,
2nd Edition
978-0-470-37181-7

WordPress For Dummies,
2nd Edition
978-0-470-40296-2

Language & Foreign Language

French For Dummies
978-0-7645-5193-2

Italian Phrases
For Dummies
978-0-7645-7203-6

Spanish For Dummies
978-0-7645-5194-9

Spanish For Dummies,
Audio Set
978-0-470-09585-0

Macintosh

Mac OS X Snow Leopard
For Dummies
978-0-470-43543-4

Math & Science

Algebra I For Dummies,
2nd Edition
978-0-470-55964-2

Biology For Dummies
978-0-7645-5326-4

Calculus For Dummies
978-0-7645-2498-1

Chemistry For Dummies
978-0-7645-5430-8

Microsoft Office

Excel 2007 For Dummies
978-0-470-03737-9

Office 2007 All-in-One
Desk Reference
For Dummies
978-0-471-78279-7

Music

Guitar For Dummies,
2nd Edition
978-0-7645-9904-0

iPod & iTunes
For Dummies,
6th Edition
978-0-470-39062-7

Piano Exercises
For Dummies
978-0-470-38765-8

Parenting & Education

Parenting For Dummies,
2nd Edition
978-0-7645-5418-6

Type 1 Diabetes
For Dummies
978-0-470-17811-9

Pets

Cats For Dummies,
2nd Edition
978-0-7645-5275-5

Dog Training For Dummies,
2nd Edition
978-0-7645-8418-3

Puppies For Dummies,
2nd Edition
978-0-470-03717-1

Religion & Inspiration

The Bible For Dummies
978-0-7645-5296-0

Catholicism For Dummies
978-0-7645-5391-2

Women in the Bible
For Dummies
978-0-7645-8475-6

Self-Help & Relationship

Anger Management
For Dummies
978-0-470-03715-7

Overcoming Anxiety
For Dummies
978-0-7645-5447-6

Sports

Baseball For Dummies,
3rd Edition
978-0-7645-7537-2

Basketball For Dummies,
2nd Edition
978-0-7645-5248-9

Golf For Dummies,
3rd Edition
978-0-471-76871-5

Web Development

Web Design All-in-One
For Dummies
978-0-470-41796-6

Windows Vista

Windows Vista
For Dummies
978-0-471-75421-3